Thomas Jefferson
A Biographical Companion

Gilbert Stuart painting of Thomas Jefferson.

Thomas Jefferson
A Biographical Companion

David S. Brown

ABC-CLIO
BIOGRAPHICAL
COMPANION

Library of Congress Cataloging-in-Publication Data

Brown, David S. (David Scott), 1966–
   Thomas Jefferson—a biographical companion / David S. Brown.
     p. cm.—(ABC-CLIO biographical companion)
   Includes bibliographical references and index.
   1. Jefferson, Thomas, 1743–1826—Encyclopedias, Juvenile. 2. Presidents—
United States—Biography—Encyclopedias, Juvenile. [1. Jefferson, Thomas,
1743–1826—Encyclopedias. 2. Presidents—Encyclopedias.] I. Title. II. Series.
E332.79.B76   1998   973.4'6'092—dc21   98-7991

ISBN 0-87436-949-5

04 03 02 01 00 99 98   10 9 8 7 6 5 4 3 2 1 (cloth)

Photo research: Corinne Szabo

ABC-CLIO, Inc.
130 Cremona Drive, P.O. Box 1911
Santa Barbara, California 93116-1911

This book is printed on acid-free paper ∞.
Manufactured in the United States of America

For Shoko
Ai o komete

ABC-CLIO BIOGRAPHICAL COMPANIONS

Benjamin Franklin, by Jennifer L. Durham
Susan B. Anthony, by Judith E. Harper
Thomas Jefferson, by David S. Brown

CONTENTS

Preface   *ix*

Introduction   *xi*

Thomas Jefferson   *3*

Primary Source Documents   *221*

Chronology   *243*

Bibliography   *249*

Illustration Credits   *257*

Index   *259*

PREFACE

Thomas Jefferson casts a long shadow upon American history. Books are written about him, films speculate on his private life, and his name is invoked by aspirants to public office. The attention and interest given to Jefferson within America and around the world are unique. We may admire the other members of America's founding generation, but only Jefferson truly intrigues us, only to him do we return when we seek to answer the most difficult challenge presented by our heritage: what does it mean to be a republican citizen?

On a more personal level, most Americans "like" Jefferson. In truth there was much to like. He was an intellectual who spoke of the dignity of the farming class, an aristocrat who championed democracy. His tastes in music, books, and wines were legendary, and largely admired. To a group of Nobel laureates in the Americas, John F. Kennedy described his guests as "the most extraordinary collection of talents . . . that has ever been gathered together at the White House, with the possible exception of when Thomas Jefferson dined alone." And yet we cannot forget that Jefferson not only held slaves but believed in the innate inferiority of blacks. We understand that Jefferson lived at a time when slavery was practiced, and yet the issue still lingers in our minds and we are hesitant to give it up. We want Jefferson not so much to represent his times as to transcend them.

These contradictions in Jefferson's life attract Americans, challenge them, and force them to reevaluate perpetually the meaning and progress of the country's democratic experiment.

Interest in Jefferson has naturally corresponded to a wealth of historical and fictional treatments of the nation's third president. Today we know more about Jefferson than we do about any other member of the founding generation, and perhaps about any public figure in our nation's history. With quantity, however, one can lose perspective and insight. It is for this reason that an encyclopedia on Thomas Jefferson is appropriate. *Thomas Jefferson: A Biographical Companion* assembles in one volume the most pertinent aspects of Jefferson's life and Jeffersonian thought.

The key issues, events, and personalities that shaped Jefferson are analyzed in a style designed to provide the specialist as well as nonspecialist with concise references. The encyclopedia entries are arranged in alphabetical order with cross-references to connect related terms and entries. A chronology of key events in Jefferson's life provides an overview of his experiences, and a bibliography is included for those who wish to read more deeply in the life of Thomas Jefferson or the Jeffersonian era.

I owe a special thanks to Kay Blalock, who introduced me to this project but was a friend long before that. Regan Lutz has provided judicious counsel and warm friendship ever since we met in graduate school. Harvey Wachtell made Thomas Jefferson real to me many years ago in a summer history course while Jerome Mushkat, Alfred Cave, and William Longton encouraged my interest in the Early Republic.

INTRODUCTION

In 1874 the historian James Parton wrote, "If Jefferson was wrong America is wrong. If America is right, Jefferson was right." Parton's simple axiom reflects a tendency on the part of Americans to associate their experiment in republican government with the figure of Thomas Jefferson. If Jefferson is the poet laureate of American democracy, they reason, so too must his personal values perpetually shape and inform the nation's soul. In the search for a high priest of democracy, Americans have rightly looked to Jefferson as their secular leader. More than any member of the founding generation, Jefferson advocated a society based on talent and virtue rather than hereditary station. His belief in the innate goodness of mankind coupled with his faith in science made him the beau ideal of a gentleman-aristocrat-statesman. To his champions—that is, those who believe Jefferson was "right"—the Sage of Monticello embodies the best liberal-democratic ideals that Western humanism has to offer. To this camp, Jefferson's faith in self-government, natural laws, and reason enshrines him for all posterity as a proponent of human rights. This is the Jefferson who wrote in 1790, "it rests now with ourselves . . . to enjoy in peace and concord the blessings of self-government, so long denied to mankind: to show by example the sufficiency of human reason for the care of human affairs and that the will of the majority, the Natural law of every society, is the only sure guardian of the rights of man."

There is, however, another Jefferson, one far more parochial than his eclectic tastes in art, wines, and books would betray. This Jefferson was the spokesman for southern nationalism, and his concern was for the perpetuation of Virginia's agrarian economy across the western frontier. Jefferson's sectional bias led him to combat those northern interests that encouraged the expansion of industry. Certainly the agrarian ethos had much going for it in Jefferson's time. Most Americans were engaged in farming and could take pride in Jefferson's claim that "those who labour in the earth are the chosen people of God, if he ever had a chosen people. . . ." Even more forceful was the Virginian's claim that "the mobs of great cities add just so much to the support of pure government as sores do to the strength of the human body." Yet even as these words were being written, Jefferson's America was quickly changing into a nation of diverse social, cultural, and economic interests. Try as he might, the Great Virginian could neither restrain nor steer the pace and course of national development. In his efforts to promote the rapidly fading agrarian values of the "old republic," Jefferson spent the latter part of his public career defending southern interests by advocating states' rights over the prerogatives of the central government. This meant that the author of the Declaration of Independence, which defined and celebrated the natural rights of "all men," was also the

Portrait of Thomas Jefferson painted by Thomas Sully in the collection of the Architect of the Capitol.

away by the deaths of his wife and four of his six children prior to Jefferson's fortieth birthday. Was he a scientist by distinction of inventing a lap desk and moldboard plow? Was he an intellectual by virtue of his speculative essays on the natural history of Virginia and his collection of some 6,400 books? In a broader context, some prefer to interpret Jefferson as the apostle of liberty, designating his work in the American Revolution as his most lasting contribution. Others, however, see Jefferson as a political realist who became the first president to lead a party into power. Finally, some see Jefferson as the architect of southern domination of the federal government. They interpret his support for slavery, states' rights, and southern particularism as the intellectual capital that southerners would later use to justify secession from the Union.

In sum, Jefferson was all of these things, and we look to him, as previous generations have, as a reflection of our highest ideals and our most common realities. Removed from the shackles of ideology, the contours of Jefferson's public life become evident. He loved liberty yet feared the loss of that liberty to an intrusive national government ruled by the interests of northern industrialists. To Jefferson, protection of slavery, which was tantamount to the protection of peculiar state folkways, meant the preservation of southern liberty.

Perhaps Parton should have rephrased his "right" or "wrong" analysis of Jefferson by stating that the Virginian operated within the cultural framework of a nation politically devoted to democracy yet economically tied to slavery. At times this great contradiction promoted liberty and gave currency to America's republican experiment; simultaneously, however, it fostered the seeds of tyranny. Jefferson and his generation were unable to resolve this contradiction.

wary defender of slavery, the engine that made southern agrarianism potent. Critics of Jefferson, who declare him and by extension the American experiment to be "wrong," cite the Virginian's racism as the Achilles' heel in an otherwise impressive edifice. This is the Jefferson who wrote in reference to the institution of slavery, "we have the wolf by the ears and we can neither hold him, nor safely let him go. Justice is in one scale, and self-preservation in the other."

Jefferson's legacy, though secure, lends itself to continual reinterpretation. Historians still debate the question of who Thomas Jefferson really was. Was he the best architect in the Old Dominion? Certainly his designs for the Virginia capitol, his home at Monticello, and the University of Virginia are lasting monuments to his skills as a draftsman. Was he America's leading student of agricultural philosophy? His accounts of farming practices in *Notes on the State of Virginia*, the only book he wrote, reflect a serious interest and command of knowledge in this area. Was he a devoted family patriarch? Letters to his eldest daughter reveal an inner life of joy and contentment that was taken

ADOLESCENCE TO ADULTHOOD

Thomas Jefferson was born on April 13, 1743, at Shadwell, the family farm in Albemarle

County, Virginia. Jefferson's father, Peter, enjoyed a reputation as a distinguished surveyor and served in the House of Burgesses. Jefferson's mother, Jane Randolph Jefferson, was a product of one of Virginia's oldest and most distinguished families. When Jefferson was 14, his father died and Thomas, as eldest son, became head of the family. From his father's legacy Jefferson inherited both land and slaves, which were managed by a guardian until the boy reached the age of 21.

Jefferson began his education under a tutor and later moved in with a Scottish clergyman who taught languages. At 16, Jefferson entered the College of William and Mary at Williamsburg, where he was introduced by George Wythe to the study of law. During his two years at the college, Jefferson gradually lost his belief in the Anglican faith and developed a distrust of organized religion that would last throughout his life. Following his formal education Jefferson was admitted to the bar and built up a successful practice.

Following in the footsteps of his father, Jefferson was elected to the House of Burgesses in 1769 and demonstrated an ability to write laws in brilliant prose. It was during this introduction to the world of Chesapeake politics that Jefferson married Martha Wayles Skelton, a widow and the daughter of a prominent Williamsburg lawyer. Over the course of their ten-year marriage Martha bore six children, only two of which lived to maturity. Martha's death in 1782 left Jefferson, in the words of his daughter, in a state of "desolation."

REVOLUTIONARY

While serving in the Burgesses, Jefferson became a leader in moving the Old Dominion toward a position of nonimportation of British goods. Great Britain's efforts to tax its colonies in North America in order to defray the cost of maintaining a global empire were roundly criticized in Virginia. Jefferson hoped that economic coercion would induce Britain to rescind the Townshend Acts, which placed duties on goods colonials purchased and then used the money to enforce British laws prohibiting colonial autonomy. Following the Boston Tea Party in 1773, Jefferson led another nonimportation agreement in Virginia and represented Albemarle County at the Virginia convention that elected delegates to the first Continental Congress.

More importantly, in 1774, Jefferson wrote *A Summary View of the Rights of British America,* which effectively articulated the colonial perspective on the emerging conflict with Britain. Jefferson argued that Britain's Parliament could not pass laws affecting the colonies because the original European settlers in North America had used their natural or free rights to emigrate. Jefferson compared settlement in America to that in England, arguing that while the original Saxons who came to England beginning in the fifth century originated from the Germanic states, they owed no current allegiance to their former home or its leaders. The same held true for the Anglo colonists, Jefferson noted, for "America was conquered, and her settlements made and firmly established, at the expense of individuals, and not of the British public. Their own blood was spilt in acquiring lands for their settlement, their own fortunes expended in making that settlement effectual. For themselves they fought, for themselves they conquered, and for themselves alone they have right to hold."

In 1775, Jefferson was chosen as a delegate to the second Continental Congress in Philadelphia. The following year, after armed conflict with Britain commenced, he was asked to draft a statement describing to the world America's break with its former mother country. Jefferson's Declaration of Independence affirmed the natural rights of humanity to protect itself from arbitrary and autocratic forms of government. Though the Declaration is Jefferson's most renowned work, he made no pretense of originality. Rather, he skillfully wove together various strands of liberal and Enlightenment thought in an elegant and readable way. Intending the

An ink sketch by Jefferson of his first plan for Monticello. In spite of his presidential duties, Jefferson found time to continue the development of Monticello.

Declaration to "be an expression of the American mind," Jefferson wrote that his task was "to place before mankind the common sense of the subject in terms so plain and firm as to command their assent."

Returning to Virginia's House of Delegates, Jefferson was instrumental in removing some of the weakened remnants of aristocracy from the Old Dominion. He sponsored bills that commenced a more equal distribution of land, which had the effect of expanding the electorate in Virginia, as suffrage was based on property qualifications. Equally important was Jefferson's bill to abolish the special privileges that the Anglican Church enjoyed in the Old Dominion. Jefferson's Statute of Religious Freedom, which guaranteed religious liberty, was passed into law a few years after it was proposed. Jefferson spent the rest of the American Revolution serving without great distinction as governor of Virginia. A British invasion of the state in 1781 forced Jefferson to flee the capital. To some observers it appeared that the governor was more interested in completing

Notes on the State of Virginia than in preparing the militia to defend the state. Jefferson was greatly relieved when his term ended.

Angered by public criticism during his tenure as governor, Jefferson vowed never to reenter national affairs. The death of his wife in 1782, however, left him bereft and in search of distraction, and in 1784 he agreed to replace Benjamin Franklin as America's minister to France. Jefferson enjoyed the five years he spent in Paris. An avid accumulator of luxury items, Jefferson traveled extensively in Europe, adding to his collections. More importantly, he witnessed the beginning of the French Revolution and offered advice to the French reformers. But his sympathies for the movement in France, which he saw as an extension of the American Revolution, could not keep him from sailing back to America. In 1789, Jefferson left France intending to return after taking care of affairs at home. When he returned to Virginia, however, he found waiting for him a letter from President George Washington asking him to serve as the nation's first secretary of state.

REPUBLICAN STATESMAN

When Jefferson joined Washington's cabinet in 1790, the Constitution was only recently completed and its powers were ill defined. Jefferson preferred a weak Constitution that would give the preponderance of power to the states. This way, he reasoned, the southern states would never lose control over the institution of slavery. However, Secretary of the Treasury Alexander Hamilton had a different interpretation. Hamilton lived in New York City and experienced democracy in a more authentic and at times frightening way than Jefferson, who wrote his treatises on liberty from the security and isolation of his home in the mountains of Virginia. Hamilton preferred a strong Constitution that would tip the balance of power in favor of the federal government, underwrite the process of industrialization, and thus weaken the states.

The rivalry between Jefferson and Hamilton soon developed into a contest for the soul of the young republic. In Jefferson's view, either his agrarian vision for America would win out and liberty would reign supreme or Hamilton's autocratic-industrial vision would produce tyranny. In truth, Hamilton's promotion of manufactures was as sectional in its orientation as Jefferson's states' rights proclivities, for Hamilton's programs proposed to centralize capital and power in the Northeast. As Hamilton's bills succeeded in the Congress, James Madison encouraged Jefferson to use his influence to oppose the treasury secretary in public. Toward this end Jefferson accepted the leadership of a broad coalition of southern agrarians and small independent farmers in the North who feared the growth of federal power. These "Democratic-Republicans," or "Jeffersonians," constituted the first opposition party in the nation's history and were instrumental in electing Jefferson vice president in 1796.

Jefferson's tenure as vice president was spent solidifying the Republican party for the next national election, when he planned to oppose the Federalist candidate and cur-rent president, John Adams. The Republicans were aided in their quest for power by an unofficial Quasi War between the United States and France. Hamilton's financial bills required access to British credit and markets. In 1795, Jay's Treaty codified American reliance on Britain and signaled an end to America's hitherto friendly relations with France, Britain's mortal enemy. Though the Quasi War was limited to naval engagements, the Federalist party dramatically expanded the size of the army to ward off a feared French invasion. To pay for this new military the Federalists were forced to institute direct taxes on land, houses, and slaves.

More ominous was the Sedition Act, which declared in part that as the nation was in a time of crisis, criticism of the national government or its Federalist stewards would not be tolerated. To the Republicans, the purpose of the increased military appeared to be intimidating Americans into compliance with the government, while the Sedition Act prohibited loyal opposition or even questioning the operations or values of the federal government. Republicans, in other words, charged that Federalists were trying to outlaw their opposition and remain in power indefinitely. In defiance Jefferson authored the Kentucky Resolutions, which argued that ultimate sovereignty belonged to the states, and that states maintained an obligation to their constituents to repel illegal federal encroachments upon private actions.

A division within the Federalist party between supporters of Adams and Hamilton combined with lingering animosity over the Sedition Act to doom the Federalists in the presidential election of 1800. Through error, Jefferson and his running mate, Aaron Burr of New York, received the same number of electoral votes. The House supported Jefferson, who won the presidency on the thirty-sixth ballot a little more than two weeks prior to inauguration. Despite the narrowness of his election, Jefferson called his victory "as real a revolution in the principles of our government as that of 1776 was in its form." In sum, he saw his victory as a continuation of the principles articulated during the American Revolution.

THE FIRST TERM

Jefferson believed the central government should play a limited role in national life. Under his direction as president, the budgets of the army and navy were slashed and most American diplomatic missions were withdrawn. The government repealed taxes while simultaneously making payments toward reducing the national debt. Though Jefferson's inaugural address was conciliatory toward the Federalists, he tended to appoint Republicans to vacated government positions. This strengthened the Jeffersonian party by dramatically expanding its powers of patronage and made Jefferson the first sitting president to operate primarily from party motives. The philosopher-king was in fact a political boss.

Jefferson's first term was marked by great successes in foreign policy. The purchase of the Louisiana Territory from France provided Jefferson with his much coveted "Empire of Liberty." Unlike European empires that spread autocracy through colonial rule, the American West, Jefferson believed, would become the repository of independent white farmers. He did not question the commitment by some to use this same territory as a vast cotton empire peopled largely by African-American slaves. In North Africa the American navy successfully fought a war with Tripoli over the right not to pay tribute to the Barbary pirate states of North Africa. Though the conflict would continue, the war brought a measure of prestige to the infant U.S. navy.

At home, Jefferson faced stiffer problems. The federal court system was still in the hands of the Federalist party. To make matters worse, John Adams spent the final days of his presidency appointing Federalists to new judicial positions. Jefferson believed that the Federalists were opposing the will of the people, who had voted the Republicans into power.

If the judicial positions were to be filled, Jefferson reasoned, they should go to the victorious Republicans. Jefferson thus gave his consent to a strategy to impeach Federalist judges and appoint Republicans to replace them. During the trial of Supreme Court Justice Samuel Chase, however, some congressional Republicans began to break ranks, fearing that the "Revolution of 1800" was going too far. To Jefferson's disappointment, the Republican assault on the judiciary stalled. Despite this setback and Jefferson's questionable tactics, the Virginian was overwhelmingly reelected in 1804. The second term would be much more difficult than the first.

THE SECOND TERM

Early in Jefferson's final term, former Republican vice president Aaron Burr devised a plot to sever the western territories from the Union. Burr was a brilliant man confined within the limits of a structured political system. However, after challenging Jefferson for the presidency in 1800 and killing Hamilton in a duel in 1804, he could no longer hope to achieve power through party politics. In 1806, Burr and his followers set off down the Ohio River to New Orleans, where they apparently planned to raid Spanish Mexico and the Louisiana Territory. Before Burr's plot could reach fruition, however, it was discovered. Brought to Richmond, Virginia, for trial, Burr managed to elude prosecution, much to Jefferson's disgust.

Even more problematic for the president was the effect of the Anglo-Franco war on American shipping. Early in Jefferson's presidency the United States served as a neutral shipping carrier for both nations and made a fortune carrying colonial goods to Europe. By 1806, however, the warring parties began to confiscate American ships trading with the enemy. In 1807 the British frigate *Leopard* attacked the American ship *Chesapeake* in the course of searching for sailors who had deserted. The incident nearly provoked a war, but Jefferson realized the United States was too weak to fight. Republican frugality had made the country fiscally sound but militarily unprepared to force its will upon other nations. Jefferson responded with an embargo that he called an effort of "peaceable coercion." The United States closed American markets to the world in the hopes that a necessity for New World foodstuffs would force compliance with America's version of neutrality. Not only did the embargo fail, to Jefferson's great disappointment, but it also caused much damage. The American economy suffered greatly from its effects, and Federalists in New England openly talked of secession. Not wishing to saddle his successor, James Madison, with a doomed policy, Jefferson consented to the removal of the embargo in the final days of his presidency. Though still widely popular in many parts of the country, Jefferson left the presidency under the cloud of a foreign policy failure that would soon explode into the War of 1812.

RETIREMENT

When he retired in 1809, Jefferson was 65. Anticipating living out his remaining years as a country gentleman, Jefferson wrote, "never did a prisoner, released from his chains, feel such relief as I shall on shaking off the shackles of power." And yet Jefferson's final years were filled with much activity and influence. In 1812 he reconciled with John Adams, and the two men commenced an exchange of notes on a variety of topics that has left American letters immeasurably enriched. Jefferson came to the aid of the Library of Congress after that institution lost its valuable collection of books when the British burned the capital during the War of 1812. By selling his personal library of over 6,000 volumes to the government, Jefferson both enriched the intellectual life of the country and helped momentarily repair his personal finances.

His most important service, however, was founding the University of Virginia. Jefferson wanted the university to be "based on the illimitable freedom of the human mind to explore and to expose every subject susceptible of its contemplation." He also wanted the university to attract young men throughout the South who might otherwise attend the more established universities and colleges in the North. Jefferson feared that a northern education might turn the sons of the South into abolitionists. The university opened to the instruction of 40 students in the spring of 1825.

Jefferson died on July 4, 1826, the fiftieth anniversary of the adoption of the Declaration of Independence. His epitaph was prepared in advance and describes the accomplishments he wished to be remembered for. It reads: "Here was buried Thomas Jefferson, Author of the Declaration of Independence, of the Statute of Virginia for religious freedom, and Father of the University of Virginia."

Thomas Jefferson
A Biographical Companion

Adams, John (1735–1826)

*O*ne of the most intelligent and coura-
geous statesmen of his generation, John
Adams devoted his life to the construction
and development of the American republic.
If Adams is not remembered with the same
affection or esteem as his friend Jefferson, it
is largely because his pessimistic temperament
and general contempt for the failings and
frailties of humanity made him, apart from
his brilliant work in the cause of independence, an unsympathetic figure. In discuss-
ing Adams's character, a recent work
concludes that

> Adams always thirsted for fame, but it
> had to be on his terms, and his terms
> seldom fitted anyone else's. He could
> never put himself out to flatter others
> or to court popularity, these things in
> any case a matter of instinct, and
> Adams had no such instinct. He talked
> too much, was too opinionated and
> too censorious, too often he said what
> he thought (though he often fretted
> about it afterward); he was too irri-
> table and irritated too many others.
> He rather expected to be unpopular;
> indeed, he was all but determined to
> be so, and in large part he was.

Unlike Jefferson, Adams lived close to the
surface of life. There were no deep recesses
where half-submerged truths lurked. Rather,
all thoughts, impressions, and emotions rose
to the surface, usually resulting in Adams
expressing his triumphs and resentments with
a candor that his colleagues respected but did
not always appreciate.

Adams was born in Braintree, Massachusetts, in 1735. Educated at Harvard College,
he rejected his parents' wishes that he join
the clergy and accepted a teaching position
while he considered his future. In time,
Adams decided to pursue a career in law, and
he returned to Braintree with hopes of becoming a member of the prestigious Boston
bar. A growing legal practice did bring Adams
into close contact with Boston, where he
made contacts with future revolutionaries, including distant cousin Samuel Adams. The
young lawyer opposed the Stamp Act of 1765
and wrote anonymous articles for the Boston *Gazette* articulating his view that the legal rights of the English in America had been
violated by both King and Parliament.

As the years went by, Adams became increasingly involved in the emerging patriot
cause. He championed the Boston Tea Party
of 1773, and when Britain retaliated by closing down Boston Port, Adams immediately
threw all of his considerable support and talent to the American cause. From 1774 to
1777, he worked as a delegate to the Continental Congress in Philadelphia and was instrumental in pushing this body into
recognizing America's independence from

An E. Savage painting of John Adams, the
second president of the United States, circa 1800.

England. The labor Adams performed for the republic was among the most important he would ever do. He lobbied unceasingly to see that George Washington won appointment to command the Continental army. He also took the lead in encouraging the newly independent states to craft republican constitutions and, as a member of the committee commissioned to express America's break with Britain, he encouraged Jefferson to write the Declaration of Independence.

Adams spent part of the Revolution in diplomatic service. In 1778 he sailed to Paris to secure a commercial and military alliance with France before returning to Massachusetts, where he served as a delegate to that state's constitutional convention. Adams then returned to Paris as minister plenipotentiary to negotiate the peace treaty with Britain that ended the Revolution. While there, he managed to antagonize the French delegates, whom he correctly believed were meddling in American affairs, as well as his colleague Benjamin Franklin, whose charm and facility with the social graces incurred Adams's jealousy. Withdrawing to the Netherlands, Adams secured Dutch recognition of American independence and negotiated a loan for the young republic. Returning to Paris, Adams joined Franklin and John Jay in concluding a peace treaty with Great Britain, thus officially ending the military phase of the American Revolution.

Adams was appointed American minister to Britain in 1785 and remained in that capacity for three difficult years. Due largely to British intransigence, no friendly relations could be worked out between England and its former colonies. Nevertheless, the time was productive for Adams who, among other accomplishments, became more intimately acquainted with Jefferson, then serving across the Channel as America's minister to France. Though foreign service barred his attendance at the Constitutional Convention, Adams approved of the work concluded by the delegates. He believed that the Confederation government was too weak and feared that anarchy within the individual states would destroy the republican experiment. He declared the new Constitution "admirabley calculated to preserve the Union" and returned home to take his place within the new government as the nation's first vice president.

During Washington's two terms in the executive office, Adams attempted to stay aloof from party politics. Very early in Washington's tenure the president's secretary of the treasury, Alexander Hamilton, proposed a grand vision of American development predicated upon the expansion of central government powers at the expense of states' rights. Opposed to Hamilton was Secretary of State Jefferson, and the two men formalized their positions by creating rival parties, the Hamiltonian Federalists and the Jeffersonian Republicans. Though Adams respected Jefferson more than Hamilton, whom he thoroughly detested, the vice president nonetheless was more sympathetic to the Federalist persuasion. Federalism, after all, championed deference to authority over democracy, industry over agrarianism, and order over liberty. Culturally and temperamentally, Adams understood that the tenets of Federalism promised the expansion of New England values across the republic.

Upon Washington's retirement in 1796, both Hamilton and Jefferson were opposed to Adams's bid to replace the general as president. Jefferson's challenge was the greatest, since he stood for the office himself through the support of the Republican party. Adams defeated Jefferson in a narrow contest by a mere three electoral votes (71–68) and took office in March 1797. Adams's lack of political acumen took its toll over the next four years. With no precedent to act upon, Adams kept Washington's cabinet on as his own, though it consisted of men who openly aligned themselves with Hamilton.

The most pressing issue during Adams's tenure concerned the "quasi" naval war with France. Opposed to America's close relationship with Britain, France confiscated American ships in the Atlantic and sold their stores for profit. The United States retaliated in kind, but the Hamiltonian Federalists wanted the country to formally declare war on France in order to enlarge the military and thus demonstrate the republic's power. The Jeffersonians believed, however, that the Federalists intended to use American military might to destroy states' rights and operate the country through a military dictatorship. Adams tried to walk a middle line. Rather than give in to the war impulse, he sent two missions to negotiate a settlement with France.

At the same time, however, he signed into legislation Federalist bills that dramatically increased the size of the military. More damaging was the president's support for the Alien and Sedition Acts of 1798, which curbed civil liberties by imposing penalties for criticizing the government. Ultimately, Adams's policy toward France worked, and in 1800 a peace settlement was concluded. The price Adams had to pay, however, was the presidency. Most Federalists opposed Adams's overtures to France and wanted war. Jeffersonians, on the other hand, concentrated their attack on the expansion of the central government's powers and blamed Adams. The result was that in the election of 1800, Adams lost the presidency to Jefferson and the Federalists lost Congress to the Republicans.

Retiring to Massachusetts, Adams became president of various art, science, and agricultural societies in his home state. Though his enmity with Hamilton proved lasting, he was more forgiving toward Jefferson, with whom he resumed a correspondence in 1812. Adams died on July 4, 1826, on the fiftieth anniversary of the Declaration of Independence. He outlived Jefferson by five hours.

See also:
Declaration of Independence
Election of 1800
Federalist Party

Reference:
Brown, Ralph. 1975. *The Presidency of John Adams.* Lawrence: University Press of Kansas.

Adams, John Quincy (1767–1848)

The only son of a president to be a president, John Quincy Adams was one of the most respected men of his generation. Born in Braintree, Massachusetts, in 1767 to John and Abigail Adams, the "Second Adams" was educated principally at home. At the age of ten he accompanied his father on various diplomatic missions to Europe and studied at private schools in Paris and at the University of Leiden. Adams returned to the United States in 1785 where, within two years, he completed a degree at Harvard College. Tutored in the study of law, Adams soon settled into a successful practice in Boston.

Due to family connections as well as his substantial skills, Adams was selected by President George Washington to assume the post of U.S. minister to the Netherlands in 1794. He left this position in 1797 to take up similar duties in Berlin, where he stayed for four years. Adams returned to Boston in 1801 and was elected to the U.S. Senate in 1803 as a Federalist. He proved to be independent of his party, however, and often voted in favor of Jeffersonian bills. One such example is Adams's affirmative vote for Jefferson's embargo bill in 1807, which sought to punish British and French intrusions on America's neutral rights by refusing to export agricultural and manufactured goods to Europe. Knowing that such an embargo would hurt New England's economy but believing that the country must stand up to European aggression, Adams broke with his party and his region to back Jefferson's proposal. In this and in other actions, he demonstrated that he was an agent not of a faction but rather of a nation.

Adams's independent course was appreciated by the Republican party, and in 1809, Jefferson's successor to the presidency, James Madison, made Adams American minister to Russia, a post he filled until 1814. While at the court of Alexander I, Adams oversaw American interests in the War of 1812. He also witnessed Napoleon's invasion of Russia and the defeat of French forces in Europe, which spelled the end of the French Revolution. In recognition of his capable service, Adams was called on to conduct peace negotiations at Ghent, which ended the American war with Great Britain.

Returning to America in 1817, Adams was made head of the State Department by James Monroe. Thus, this former Federalist and son of John Adams, the only Federalist to become president, was again proving himself to be a most capable servant in Republican foreign policy. Simply put, Adams was perhaps this nation's greatest secretary of state. In the eight years he held the office, he helped design the contours of an American foreign policy that would last throughout the nineteenth century. He made the Monroe Doctrine a unilateral policy by insisting that protection of the Western Hemisphere be the sole responsibility of the United States. He also procured a transcontinental treaty with Spain in 1821 that bequeathed to the nation millions of acres of new lands. This Adams-Onis Treaty gave to America East and West Florida and settled the country's western boundary dis-

pute in favor of U.S. claims. More importantly, the treaty gave the nation lands in the Oregon territory and thus, for the first time in its history, the United States reached the Pacific Ocean. Also during Adams's tenure in the State Department, nearly all of the Central and South American republics were recognized by the United States, a treaty with Russia was successfully concluded, and America's northeastern land claims were held firm against British entreaties.

Though Jefferson was wary of any non-slaveholder becoming president, he was not afraid of the prospect of an Adams presidency. With Monroe's retirement in 1824 spelling the end of the "Virginia Dynasty," Adams and several other men offered the nation their services as president. The election was inconclusive, since no candidate was able to garner a majority of electoral votes and, just as in 1800 when Jefferson won the presidency from Aaron Burr, the election was held in the House of Representatives. Though the names of three men were sent to the House, only two were significant candidates: Adams and Andrew Jackson, a Tennessee military hero who had won more popular and electoral votes than any other candidate. Though Jackson believed he had a moral claim on the office, others, including Jefferson, disagreed. The House elected Adams and he became the nation's first minority president.

The emerging Jacksonian party claimed that Adams had stolen the election from the general and attacked the president throughout his tenure in office. Adams made this task easy by opposing the democratic trend of his day and proposing to exert national power through a strong central government that would influence banking, tariff, and land policies in a way that would bring about a more centralized society. While some have argued that his programs anticipated Theodore Roosevelt's "New Nationalism" and Franklin D. Roosevelt's "New Deal," Adams's form of government paternalism found little sympathy in a nation increasingly worried about the demise of democracy and individual freedom in the emerging industrial age. Adams served a largely unproductive four years in the presidency before his defeat to Jackson in 1828.

Almost any other man would have welcomed retirement, but Adams was no ordinary man. After being repudiated by the American people, Adams returned to the House as the representative of the Plymouth District of Massachusetts. In his new capacity, Adams played the role not of a party man but rather of an ex-president bestowing his considerable wisdom and character upon the nation. Throughout the 1830s and 1840s he spoke passionately against the division of the nation along sectional lines. Not quite an abolitionist, he nevertheless understood slavery to be an evil and worked against its extension. To this degree, he almost single-handedly kept Texas out of the Union until its annexation by a joint resolution of Congress in 1845. He also opposed the "gag rule" that prevented discussion in Congress of issues relating to slavery. Viewing this rule as a challenge to free speech, Adams's consistent attack against all attempts to quiet northern opinion against slavery earned him the nickname "Old Man Eloquent." Well loved in Massachusetts for his independence, Adams was returned to the House in every election from 1830 until his death in 1848.

See also:
Adams-Onis Treaty
Election of 1824
War of 1812

Reference:
Bemis, Samuel Flagg. 1949. *John Quincy Adams and the Foundations of American Foreign Policy.* New York: Alfred A. Knopf.

Adams-Jefferson Correspondence

Though only seven years older than Jefferson, John Adams recalled in his advanced years that the Virginian had been as a son to him. Hyperbole aside, Adams's fondness for Jefferson was sincere, and the two revolutionaries were close associates throughout the early years of the republic. But huge differences in character existed. Adams was egocentric, vain, and pompous. His temperament was that of a pessimist, and he never believed that life had been fair to him. The descendant of New England Puritans, Adams was short, balding, and vaguely porcine. Nothing seemed to come easily for him; his brilliance came from sheer exertion. For Jefferson, however, brilliance came naturally. He enjoyed the aristocratic pleasure of achievement without appearing to tax his faculties. He was tall, good-looking, and believed in democracy to a degree that Adams thought naive. Moreover—and this bothered Adams to no end—Jefferson's reputation exceeded his own.

A wedge was driven between the two Founders when they chose to align themselves with different political parties and thus different visions of American development. Adams reflected the cultural prejudices of his section by advocating a strong central government and became a Federalist. Jefferson was true to Virginia in forming the Republican party, which attempted to offset the Federalist initiative by locating the preponderance of power in the hands of the states. In 1796 the two men opposed each other for the presidency, and Adams eked out a narrow victory. The scenario was played out again in 1800, but this time it was Jefferson who captured a close election. Prior to leaving office, however, Adams assigned a host of judicial positions to Federalist partisans in order to keep that party alive in government. Interpreting this blatant partisanship as an affront to his own victorious election, Jefferson ceased communication with Adams.

For several years no correspondence between the two Founders existed, and mutual enmity over the issue of party politics mixed with the silence of time to ensure a seemingly complete break. In 1811, however, Dr. Benjamin Rush, a friend of both men, gently pushed Adams for a rapprochement with Jefferson. "I consider you and [Jefferson] as the North and South Poles of the American Revolution," he explained. "Some talked, some wrote, and some fought to promote and establish it, but you and Mr. Jefferson thought for us all." Fortunately Adams's passions had cooled somewhat through the years, and he acknowledged to Rush an interest in renewing his contact with Jefferson whom, he noted, "I always loved . . . and still love him." Upon learning of his former colleague's warm sentiments, Jefferson wrote to Rush that Adams's

> statement of love is enough for me. I only needed this knowledge to revive towards him all the affections of the most cordial moment of our lives . . . I knew him to be always an honest man, often a great one, but sometimes incorrect and precipitate in his judgments. . . . I have ever done him justice myself, and defended him when assailed by others, with the single exception as to political opinions. But with a man possessing so

many other estimable qualities, why should we be dissocialized by mere differences of opinion in politics, in religion, in philosophy, or anything else? His opinions are as honestly formed as my own. Our different views of the same subject are the result of a difference in our organization and experience. I never withdrew from the society of any man on this account, . . . much less should I do it from one with whom I had gone through, with hand and heart, so many trying scenes.

Jefferson's comments were relayed to Adams who, on New Year's Day of 1812, at the age of 77, reopened the most fruitful political dialogue in the nation's history.

The Adams-Jefferson correspondence extended for over a decade, encompassing 158 letters, of which Adams wrote 109. The Master of Monticello, it would seem, was putting the bulk of his energies into founding the University of Virginia as well as trying

One of Jefferson's ingenious inventions, by which he could copy any letter without any extra effort. Some 18,000 letters in his own hand survive.

to stay financially solvent. Adams proved to be the most earnest in his letters, explaining to Jefferson, "You and I ought not to die, before We have explained ourselves to each other." Nevertheless, the correspondence tended to shy away from the political battles that had once driven the two men apart. More consistent in the correspondence were reflections on the classics, the Revolution, and aging, a subject of mutual interest for the two octogenarians. This tender friendship, rooted in the past, renewed itself in the twilight of Jefferson's life, adding to the richness of his retirement and certainly to the richness of American letters.

See also:
Adams, John
Retirement

Reference:
Peterson, Merrill. 1976. *Adams and Jefferson: A Revolutionary Dialogue*. Athens: University of Georgia Press.

Adams-Onis Treaty

*I*n 1819 the United States and Spain signed the Adams-Onis Treaty, which extended the nation's western boundary to the Pacific coast and ceded all of Florida to the United States in return for American assumption of private claims against Spain up to $5 million. Though Jefferson was then retired and living a quiet life at Monticello, the treaty aptly reflected his vision of American expansion. As president, Jefferson had tried desperately on several occasions to purchase Florida, all to no avail. The region served as a refuge for runaway slaves and Seminole Indians, and thus was a point of contention among southerners. Jefferson did purchase the Louisiana Territory, but Bourbon interests in Spain contended that France, which had received the territory from the Spanish government, had no right to sell it to the United States. Moreover, the western boundary of the purchase was ill-defined and thus cause for concern.

The Adams-Onis Treaty, concluded under the auspices of James Monroe, the third and final member of the "Virginia Dynasty," legitimized Jefferson's actions in Louisiana by extending the boundary of the United States to the Pacific Northwest. This was the region where the Sage of Monticello had sent Lewis and Clark nearly a generation before. Jefferson's "Empire of Liberty" now reached the Pacific as well as the eastern coast of the Gulf of Mexico.

See also:
Adams, John Quincy
Empire of Liberty
Monroe, James

Reference:
Bemis, Samuel Flagg. 1949. *John Quincy Adams and the Foundations of American Foreign Policy*. New York: Alfred A. Knopf.

Alien and Sedition Acts

*I*n the field of foreign policy, Jefferson preferred a closer alliance with the French republic than with the British monarchy. The Federalist party, however, sought to ally the United States with English merchants and markets and thus carried forth a pro-British diplomacy that antagonized the French. By 1798, war between the United States and France seemed likely, and Federalists began to prepare for this possibility. As part of their agenda, Federalists in Congress moved to dilute the power of their political enemies, the Jeffersonian Republicans. Federalists believed that Jefferson's pro-French stance weakened the country, and they wanted to keep both Jefferson and his supporters out of power. They realized, however, that Jefferson's political philosophy, which proposed increasing the personal liberty of white males, appealed to foreigners who entered the country and thus strengthened the Jeffersonian coalition. In an attempt to secure the nation from French influence, strengthen the power of the Federalist party, and weaken

Contemporary cartoon portraying a scuffle between congressmen Matthew Lyon and Roger Griswold. Briefly imprisoned under the Alien and Sedition Act, Lyon was later reelected by an overwhelming majority.

its Republican opposition, the Federalists passed the Alien and Sedition Acts, which limited freedom of speech and press while curtailing the liberty of recent immigrants.

The Enemies Alien Act empowered the president to imprison or deport foreigners in time of war. It would also have the effect of removing a large number of Republican supporters from the country. The Naturalization Act revised the number of years a foreigner needed to wait to become a U.S. citizen from five to fourteen. Thus, the Jeffersonian party would have to wait an additional nine years before recent European immigrants could vote for the Republicans. The most disturbing part of the legislation, however, was the Sedition Act, which forbade the writing, publishing, or speaking of anything of "a false, scandalous, and malicious" nature against the federal government or its officials. Under this law, the editors of Republican party newspapers who criticized Federalist programs were liable to prosecu-

tion. In fact, three editors from among the largest circulating pro-Jefferson papers were convicted by pro-Federalist courts in an attempt to muzzle political opposition.

To Jefferson, the real aim of the Alien and Sedition Acts was not to prepare the nation for war against the French, but rather to prop up the Federalist party and make it impossible for its power to be challenged. At stake, Jefferson further noted, was the right of Americans to express themselves and show dissent against existing forms of power. If political opposition could not exist, he contended, then the republic would cease to function. At bottom, Jefferson concluded, the Federalists were attempting "an experiment on the American mind, to see how far it will bear an avowed violation of the Constitution." Thus, in Jefferson's mind, the Alien and Sedition Acts were merely the first step in the Federalist party's attempt to take power away from the people and centralize it in the federal government.

As vice president, Jefferson initiated the Republican party's response to the acts. He proposed that the state legislatures assert their right to protect their own citizens from an overzealous federal government. While serving in the federal government as vice president, Jefferson authored the Kentucky Resolutions, which repudiated the Alien and Sedition Acts and championed state sovereignty. As president, Jefferson pardoned those convicted of violating the Sedition Act and watched contentedly as a Republican-dominated Congress refused to renew the acts.

See also:
Anglo-French Wars
Kentucky Resolutions

Reference:
Smith, James Morton. 1956. *Freedom's Fetters: The Alien and Sedition Laws and American Civil Liberties*. Ithaca, NY: Cornell University Press.

American Philosophical Society

By nature a curious soul, Jefferson turned increasingly toward political and scientific enterprises in the second half of his life, following the death of his wife and most of his children. The American Philosophical Society provided Jefferson an outlet for his intellectual pursuits and put him into contact with some of the greatest minds of his time. In an artistically, scientifically, and intellectually underdeveloped nation, American astronomers, botanists, anthropologists, physicians, and theologians all spoke the same language and pushed for the same goal: the rapid development of a cultured society.

The intellectual energies of this group were organized by Benjamin Franklin in 1743, the year Jefferson was born. Franklin announced in a circular letter that "the first drudgery of settling new colonies, which confines the attention of people to mere necessaries, is now pretty well over and there are many in every province in circumstances that set them at ease, and afford leisure to cultivate the finer arts, and improve the common stock of knowledge." This American declaration of intellectual independence from Europe came to fruition in 1769 with the organization of the American Philosophical Society in Philadelphia, the cultural capital of the colonies. The society advocated speculation into both the material and moral worlds and promoted as its purpose "all philosophical experiments that let light into the nature of things, tend to increase the power of man over matter, and multiply the conveniences and pleasures of life." Consciously modeled on the Royal Society of London, the society invited its members to join one or more of its six committees: Geography, Mathematics, Natural Philosophy and Astronomy; Medicine and Anatomy; Natural History and Chemistry; Trade and Commerce; Mechanics and Architecture; Husbandry and American Improvements.

The society attracted the intellectual elites of British North America. Jefferson joined in 1780 and was appointed to a councilor position the following year. From Jefferson the society received an original design for a moldboard plough, observations on weights and measures, and communications on a variety of subjects ranging from meteorology to fossils. In 1796, Jefferson became president of the society and served in that capacity for nearly twenty years.

See also:
Enlightenment
Franklin, Benjamin

Reference:
Boorstin, Daniel J. 1948. *The Lost World of Thomas Jefferson*. Chicago, IL: University of Chicago Press.

American Revolution

The American Revolution was the defining experience of Jefferson's life. For this child of the Enlightenment, the movement of the American colonies away from Old World influence and toward a more liberal social order appeared to be part of the natural course of history. Just as in the physical world great storms beget destruction and rebirth, so too, Jefferson surmised, would revolutions.

The movement toward independence began in 1763 with the conclusion of the French and Indian War. Britain's acquisition of Canada not only enlarged the size of the British Empire but dramatically increased the cost of colonial upkeep as well. Britain was compelled to use new methods to collect revenue, such as the Sugar and Stamp Acts of 1764 and 1765. The latter tax was particularly offensive to the colonials because it was a direct form of revenue collection. Hitherto, colonials had generally paid duties on "luxury" items such as wines and sugars. The Stamp Act tax, though, fell on nearly all. The resulting riots and protests ensured that the acts would not be adhered to, and England's financial troubles persisted. By 1767, Jefferson was involved in the colonial protest against British taxation through his work in Virginia's House of Burgesses. Like most colonials, he did not want to sever the relationship between the Crown and its colonies; he only wanted to preserve the traditional ties that had existed prior to the French and Indian War. "My first wish is restoration of our just rights," he contended, "my second, a return of the happy period when, consistently with duty, I may withdraw myself totally from the public stage and pass the rest of my days in domestic ease and tranquillity . . . looking with fondness towards a reconciliation with Great Britain."

Jefferson's wishes were not to be fulfilled, however. The Boston Tea Party in 1773 brought about a draconian response from England that compelled the colonials to put in motion the forces that would ultimately bring about independence. Jefferson proved to be in the forefront of this movement when in 1774 he authored *A Summary View of the Rights of British America*. His writing talents were noted by his peers, and when the break with Britain came, Jefferson was one of five men appointed to a committee to draft the colonies' statement of independence. Jefferson's work on the committee, captured in the Declaration of Independence, expressed the Anglo-American tradition of protection of human rights as well as property rights.

The period 1776–1779 was perhaps the most prolific of Jefferson's life. Aside from his work on the Declaration, Jefferson helped brush aside some of the last vestiges of titled aristocracy in Virginia. Though he encountered much opposition, Jefferson was in the forefront of the movement that successfully abolished entail and primogeniture in the Old Dominion. These practices had legally bound fathers to provide estates only for eldest sons and contributed to an undemocratic tone in Virginia society. Jefferson also took the lead in severing Virginia's relationship with the Anglican church, which had been the official denomination of the colony since its inception. This bill on religious freedom ensured that the state would give no sanction, money, or privilege to any form of organized religion. Efforts at organizing a public school system and gradually emancipating slaves, both pet projects of Jefferson's, were less successful.

During the final phase of the Revolution, 1779–1781, Jefferson was a largely ineffective governor of Virginia. Head of an invaded, war-exhausted state, the governor demonstrated a surprising lack of interest in the details of basic defense. Rather than make provisions against British attacks, Jefferson left the capital and returned to his home—an action that nearly cost him his reputation. The successful conclusion of the Revolution following the Battle of Yorktown in 1781 and the Peace of Paris in 1783, however, lifted Jefferson's spirits immeasurably. To the Virginian, the American Revolution represented the first phase in a worldwide movement toward increased personal liberty. "A just and solid republican government maintained here," he concluded, "will be a standing monument and example for the aim and imitation of the people of other countries; and I join . . . in the hope and belief that the . . . inquiry which has been excited among the mass of mankind by our Revolution and its consequences will ameliorate the condition of man over a great portion of the globe."

See also:
Declaration of Independence
A Summary View of the Rights of British America
Virginia Statute of Religious Freedoms

Reference:
Countryman, Edward. 1985. *The American Revolution*. New York: Hill and Wang.

Anglo-French Wars

During the period 1689–1815, Great Britain and France fought a series of wars for commercial and dynastic supremacy in Europe. These conflicts necessarily spilled over into Europe's colonial outposts, turning what began as continental contests into world wars. Jefferson's birth in 1743 overlapped with King George's War, the third of the four major confrontations prior to the American Revolution. Jefferson was 20 when the French and Indian War eliminated French power in Canada and precipitated the American Revolution by enlarging the debt of the British Empire to the degree that it was forced to directly tax its colonies. Resistance by the colonials brought independence in 1776.

The American Revolution benefited from the ancient animosity between the British and the French. France, looking to even the score for its loss of Canada, provided military, financial, and diplomatic aid to the fledgling republic. U.S. hopes of steering a neutral course between Britain and France were overturned, however, when the French Revolution began in 1789. To many Americans, the French Revolution represented an excessively democratic movement that needed to be contained. To these individuals it was in the best interest of the United States to maintain good relations with Britain since the country needed access to Anglo credit and markets. To statesmen like Jefferson, however, the French Revolution seemed intent on replicating the American model of republican government. Thus, every effort to further the Revolution needed to be made, including a severing of relations with the British. As secretary of state and head of the Republican party in the 1790s, Jefferson battled the pro-British Federalist party over the U.S. response to the Anglo-French Wars of that period. Jefferson believed that the United States operated more as a satellite of the British Empire than as a free and sovereign nation. Nevertheless, American "neutrality," at the expense of caving in to British trade demands and fighting a Quasi War with the French navy, was secured.

The emergence of Napoleon as first consul and then emperor of France initiated the final phase of the Anglo-French Wars. The United States could no longer afford to be neutral in a world dominated by hostile European camps. Throughout Jefferson's presidency, American commercial ships were in perpetual danger of being picked up by the two major powers. Though Jefferson tried to steer a middle course, it ultimately proved impossible.

In 1812 the United States went to war with Britain over neutrality violations. The conclusion of the war in late 1814 came about not because of any major battles in North America, but rather because Napoleon had been defeated and exiled from Europe. The conclusion of the Anglo-French conflict or, what some historians refer to as the Second Hundred Years War, also brought an end to the worst aspects of Anglo-American enmity. The protracted affair between the European powers had defined the terms by which England would operate its empire, had precipitated the American Revolution, and dictated Europe's stance toward American neutrality in the postindependence period. In other words, the Anglo-French Wars defined the course of early American history and shaped Jefferson's world.

See also:
American Revolution
French and Indian War
Great Britain

Reference:
Brewer, John. 1988. *The Sinews of Power: War, Money, and the English State, 1688–1783*. New York: Alfred A. Knopf.

Anglophobia

For the first 33 years of his life, Jefferson was an English subject. Like most Americans, he accepted independence from the mother country reluctantly and maintained that the Revolution was fought not to break with the past but rather to preserve traditional English rights. But Jefferson's reputation as an Anglophobe, that is, one who detests Great Britain, was well earned.

The Virginian believed that England's rapid financial, industrial, and military rise in the eighteenth century corrupted its traditional agrarian culture. He worried that American reliance on England for credit and protection would bring the fledgling republic into the British orbit and make it once again a satellite in the empire. Personal animosity also figured into Jefferson's disdain for the British after the Revolution. Following a visit to London in 1786 in which he tried to facilitate a trade agreement, Jefferson remarked:

> That nation hates us, their ministers hate us, and their King more than all other men. They have the impudence to avow this. . . . Our overtures of commercial arrangements have been treated with a derision which shows their firm persuasion that we shall never unite to suppress their commerce, or even to impede it. I think their hostility towards us is much more deeply rooted at present than during the war.

Though such animosity was certainly unfortunate, Jefferson believed that time was on the side of the United States. "We are young," he contended to a colleague in France, "and can survive them; but their rotten machine must crush under the trial. . . . Peace and friendship with all mankind is our wisest policy; and I wish we may be permitted to pursue it. But the temper and folly of our enemies may not leave this in our choice."

Jefferson was particularly antagonistic toward the British in the period between 1793 and 1815, when the King's Royal Navy refused to accept American neutrality in the Anglo-French Wars. Instead, Britain picked up American ships sailing to its enemy's harbors and sold them and their cargoes in English ports. Though France did much the same to American ships trading in the British Empire, English affronts seemed more ominous. The British navy often kidnapped American sailors and used them on their ships, a practice the French rarely engaged in. Moreover, Britain's occupation of Canada ensured an English foothold on the North American continent from which Britain could secure relations with the Native American tribes in the Northwest. In short, Americans were convinced that England threatened U.S. interests on the Atlantic as well as on the western frontier.

To demonstrate that the federal government could protect the property rights of its citizens, Jefferson's Republican party declared war on Britain in 1812. The fighting in North America was generally inconclusive, and the war ended not because victory was attained in the New World, but rather because England's true enemy, Napoleon, was defeated in Europe. With the demise of French power the British had no reason to violate American neutrality and ceased such actions. A treaty between the two nations was quickly signed, and Anglo-American relations, after a half century of mutual animosity, began to heal. Jefferson looked forward to the prospects of a communion between the two

English-speaking nations, understanding clearly the benefits of friendship with Britain and its empire. In the final years of his life, he wished for a rapprochement that would link the Anglo world in the common pursuit of freedom and equality. "There is not a nation on the globe with whome I have more earnestly wished a friendly intercourse on equal conditions," he concluded.

On no other would I hold out the hand of friendship to any. Were they once under a government which should treat us with justice and equity, I should myself feel with great strength the ties which bind us together, of origin, language, laws and manners; and I am persuaded the two peoples would become in future as it was with the ancient Greeks. . . . Instead of endeavoring to make us their natural enemies, will see in us what we really are, their natural friends and brethren, and more interested in a fraternal connection with them than with any other nation on earth. No one feels more indignation than myself when reflecting on the insults and injuries of that country to this. But the interests of both require that these should be left to history, and in the meantime be smothered in the living mind. I have indeed little personal concern in it. Time is drawing her curtain on me. But I should make my bow with more satisfaction if I had more hope of seeing our countries shake hands together cordially.

See also:
Anglo-French Wars
Francophilia

Reference:
Boyd, Julian, ed. 1964. *Number 7: Alexander Hamilton's Secret Attempts to Control American Foreign Policy, with Supporting Documents.* Princeton, NJ: Princeton University Press.

Anti-Federalists

As American minister to France, Jefferson was unable to participate in the Constitutional Convention of 1787. He did, however, give qualified approval to the document produced in Philadelphia, insisting only that a bill of rights be attached. In supporting the Constitution, Jefferson sided with the Federalists, a group of progressive-minded nationalists who championed an assertive federal government. In opposition were the Anti-Federalists, who feared the loss of local power and the potential corruption of a centralized government. At one time, the Anti-Federalists, led by such respected figures as Patrick Henry and Edmund Randolph, held a majority in Virginia. Jefferson, like these men, did not want to see the power of the Old Dominion eclipsed, yet he believed that a strengthened central government was necessary to preserve the republic. Insurrections and tax rebellions within the states in the period immediately prior to the convention warned Jefferson that local power could lead to corruption and anarchy.

Following the ratification of the Constitution, Jefferson returned home to take part in George Washington's cabinet as secretary of state. Upon occupying his new office, Jefferson learned that the head of the Treasury Department, Alexander Hamilton, had introduced into Congress a series of bills that dramatically increased the powers of the central government and bound affluent interests closer to that government by means of state-sponsored speculation. To Jefferson, such actions violated the spirit if not the letter of the Constitution, and he quickly took up opposition to "Hamiltonianism." Since the Anti-Federalist label was associated with the opponents of the Constitution, the Jeffersonians called themselves Republicans, to insinuate that Federalism was really the ideology of monarchists who wished to locate power in the hands of the executive, cabinet, and a few congressional seats. Many who would flock to the Republican party were former Anti-Federalists, delighted that Jefferson had taken up their cause. For Jefferson, however, being a Republican was different from being an Anti-Federalist. The former approved of the Constitution as it was written; the latter did not and preferred a nation based on radical state sovereignty.

See also:
Confederation Period
Constitution
Federalist Party

Reference:
Ketcham, Ralph, ed. 1986. *The Anti-Federalist Papers and the Constitutional Convention Debates.* New York: Mentor.

Articles of Confederation

The Articles of Confederation were adopted by the Continental Congress in 1777 to allow the states to prosecute the American Revolution more effectively. Jefferson was not a member of the Congress that drafted this important document; rather he served in the Virginia Assembly. Like other men of his station, however, he approved of the Articles as a wartime necessity. Each state entered the conflict with Great Britain as a sovereign entity.

Very quickly, however, the states learned that only a more concerted effort would secure independence. They were worried, however, that the creation of a powerful central government might one day be a source of corruption and take the place of the "odious" British Empire. With this in mind, the confederation or compact that emerged from Congress in the winter of 1777 recognized the concerns of the states by creating a very weak central power. The new body of government, the Congress of the Confederation, would not have the power to tax. Rather, it merely had the right to request money from the states. It could make treaties with foreign nations but had no power to enforce them. Finally, the Congress could borrow money

to prosecute the war, but it had no way to ensure repayment of loans.

Though the American Revolution was brought to a successful conclusion, the weaknesses of the Articles of Confederation paralyzed the country in the 1780s as debt, class antagonisms, and public insurrection threatened to destroy the infant republic. It was from evidence of these weaknesses that a group of "nationalists" emerged who promoted the formation of a more powerful federal government under a new compact. The result of their labors was the United States Constitution written in Philadelphia in 1787. Though Jefferson was in Paris at the time and could not attend the convention, he would play a vital role over the next two decades defining how it would be interpreted.

See also:
American Revolution
Confederation Period
Constitution

Reference:
Bowen, Catherine Drinker. 1966. *Miracle at Philadelphia: The Story of the Constitutional Convention, May to September 1787.* Boston, MA: Little, Brown.

Assumption

Jefferson's opposition to the Federalist party began to crystallize in 1790 when Secretary of the Treasury Alexander Hamilton produced *A Report on the Public Credit*. The report projected a vision of a strong central government guiding national development. A vital element of Hamilton's report was the stipulation that debts owed by the states to investors, citizens, and foreign nations be "assumed" by the federal government. The bulk of state debts was incurred during the American Revolution and the period immediately following the war, when the national economy was in a state of decline. On the surface, it appeared that Hamilton's plan offered a helping hand to the states by financing them back to solvency.

Behind the secretary's plan, however, lurked a deeper issue, namely, how much sovereignty states were to be permitted in the new federal republic. Hamilton wanted to bring the states within the orbit of the federal government and feared that if local governments paid back their citizens, these Americans would continue to confer their allegiance to the states rather than to the nation. If, however, financial obligations were met by the federal government, in paper money printed and backed by that government, then the repaid investors would understand two important things: first, that it was the national legislature rather than local governments who paid them back; second, that the money they had received would be worthless if the central government fell. Thus, these individuals, some of the most affluent and influential citizens of the country, would work very hard to ensure that the federal government maintained solvency and was successful. In other words, Hamilton tied the fate of the nation to the fate of a prosperous elite and in turn created an aristocracy of wealth and talent that would watch over the security of the federal government.

Jefferson did not openly oppose the assumption plan, but his Virginia colleague, James Madison, did. Madison correctly argued that states with low indebtedness would be obliged to help pay off the debts of more heavily indebted states. Additionally, Madison realized that the bulk of debt was in the North, since most southern states, including Virginia, were financially stable. In broad terms, assumption would pump southern money into the northern economy without an equal recompense. For this reason it could not be supported by southern members of Congress. Between April and July 1790, the House defeated several assumption bills, and tensions ran high as both sections talked openly of secession. With the Union endangered by a congressional roadblock, a bill proposing the permanent placement of the national capital appeared to offer room for a compromise. Jefferson wrote:

Going to the President's one day I met Hamilton as I approached the door. His look was sombre, haggard, and dejected beyond description. Even his dress uncouth and neglected. He asked to speak with me. We stood in the street near the door. He opened the subject of the assumption of the state debts. . . . On considering the situation of things I thought the first step towards some conciliation of views would be to bring Mr. Madison and Colo. Hamilton to a friendly discussion of the subject. I immediately wrote to each to come and dine with me the next day, mentioning that we should be alone. . . . they came. I opened the subject to them, acknoleged that my situation had not permitted me to understand it sufficiently but encouraged them to consider the thing together. They did so. It ended in Mr. Madison's acquiescence in a proposition that the question should be again brought before the house by way of amendment from the Senate, that he would not vote for it, nor entirely withdraw his opposition, yet he should not be strenuous, but leave it to its fate. It was observed, I forget by which of them, that as the pill would be a bitter one to the Southern states, something should be done to soothe them; that the removal of the seat of government to the Patowmac was a just measure, and would probably be a popular one with them, and would be a proper one to follow the assumption.

The deal secured, the South supported assumption and the capital was removed from New York City to Philadelphia and finally, in 1800, to the newly created District of Columbia along the banks of the "Patowmac." Though Jefferson was pleased with the compromise at the time, he quickly grew disenchanted with the growth of the federal government and commented to President Washington that he had been "duped . . . by the Secretary of the Treasury, and made a tool for forwarding his schemes, not then sufficiently understood by me; and of all the errors of my political life, this has occasioned in me the deepest regret."

See also:
Hamilton, Alexander
Madison, James

Reference:
McDonald, Forrest. 1979. *Alexander Hamilton: A Biography*. New York: W.W. Norton.

Atlantic Economy

Jefferson's vision of a self-sufficient economy for the United States was based on the assumption that the Atlantic Ocean trade encompassing the markets of North America, Europe, and the Caribbean would be opened to American goods. The Atlantic economy was constructed in the colonial period as English capital and credit flowed into the colonies. This flow stimulated the North American economy directly as investments in the region brought in much needed currency while indirect investments were procured through the extension of credit. Colonists responded by putting more land into cultivation, increasing their production of agricultural goods, and purchasing large quantities of labor in the form of indentured servants and African slaves.

It was Jefferson's hope that following the American Revolution and the drafting of the Constitution, the Atlantic economy could be used as a tool not to enrich the coffers of Europeans or wealthy Americans, but rather to unite a nation fragmented by economic, religious, sectional, and social differences. Jefferson realized that a diverse people needed to find common interests or the security of the Union would be imperiled. He sought to promote the expansion of the Atlantic economy into the American interior in order that western farmers, and not simply eastern merchants, could participate in the transatlantic trade of Anglo-American goods. Thus Jefferson rejected the principle of mercantilism, which was based on selective governmental aid to a few major interests in the economy. Instead, Jefferson saw the Atlantic commercial economy as a free-trade zone where the proliferation of American agricultural and, to a much lesser degree, manufacturing goods would create new markets for American products around the world while unifying a diverse population around the promise of expanding economic opportunities for all.

Moreover, Jefferson envisioned the Atlantic economy as playing a vital role in the foreign affairs of the United States. Following the Revolution, Great Britain shut the United States out of its trading empire. The biggest blow was the inability of American ships to buy and sell produce in the British West Indies, traditionally America's largest foreign market in the Western Hemisphere. As Jefferson saw it, British discrimination against American shipping was a threat to the infant American economy and thus to the nation as a whole. He believed that in order to combat Britain's restrictive trade policy, the United States should enhance its commercial relations with other European nations, most notably the French and Dutch. If such a rapprochement took place, Jefferson concluded, the Atlantic economy would provide for self-sufficiency at home and rising prosperity among trade partners in both the United States and Europe. It would also serve to punish Great Britain while strengthening relations between the United States and Continental Europe.

See also:
Anglophobia
Smith, Adam
West Indies

Reference:
Appleby, Joyce O. 1984. *Capitalism and a New Social Order: The Republican Vision of the 1790s.* Princeton, NJ: Princeton University Press.

Attack on the Judiciary

Following the election of 1800, the Jeffersonian rout of Federalism was nearly complete. Both houses of Congress as well as the presidency were controlled by Republicans. Unfortunately for Jefferson and his followers, the judiciary, the most aristocratic branch of the federal system, was still under the control of the opposition party. Even more depressing to Republicans was the fact that many of the judicial positions were lifetime appointments. To make matters worse, the Judiciary Act of 1801, sponsored by the outgoing Federalist party, created several new judicial positions that were distributed solely to Federalist partisans. The act also reduced the Supreme Court by one following its next vacancy, an obvious attempt to stall President Jefferson's appointment to the Court of Republican partisans. Though the act was quickly overturned by the Jeffersonians upon reaching office, the federal judiciary appeared to many Republicans to be little more than the last outpost of Federalism.

Early in his presidency, Jefferson began to attack Federalist elements in the judiciary. He instructed Secretary of State James Madison not to deliver commissions to Federalist judges newly appointed under the Judiciary Act. Yet Republicans wanted more: they wanted to remove Federalists who were already sitting on the bench. The only way to do this was through impeachment. In 1804, the Republican party, with Jefferson's support, began to arraign Federalist judges with the intent of removing them from their positions. The first impeachment concerned Federal District Judge John Pickering of New Hampshire. The alcoholic and mentally disturbed Pickering was an easy mark, and his removal was secured with little difficulty. The Republicans' success encouraged them to go after bigger game, and the party set its sights on Samuel Chase, associate justice of the Supreme Court. Chase was a narrow-minded arch-Federalist who had vigorously prosecuted Republicans under the Sedition Act, and while sitting on the bench, had been highly critical of the Jefferson administration.

In January 1805, the House moved for articles of impeachment against Chase on the grounds that he had attempted to influence the people against the government. Chase's defense counsel insisted that a judge could only be removed for a criminal act, but the real issue was how democratic the young nation would be. The Jeffersonians operated from the premise that impeachments were the only way to make the judiciary responsive to the public will. Many observers argued, however, that the judiciary was intended to be beyond the will of the people.

Eventually articles of impeachment were drawn up, and the Senate conducted a trial. Chase was charged with eight violations and threatened with conviction if two-thirds of the members of the Senate agreed on any of the charges. Much to Jefferson's dismay, no such consensus was reached on any of the eight charges. It seems that some Republicans backed away from convicting Chase because, in truth, the justice had not committed an impeachable offense. He may have demonstrated partisanship, but he had not broken the law. Furthermore, the more conservative Republicans feared that the Jeffersonian movement was in danger of becoming too democratic. If Supreme Court justices could be removed for questionable offenses, then no public position was safe. Jefferson backed away from the impeachment strategy following Chase's acquittal and quietly made his peace with the judiciary. If Jefferson lost the battle, though, he won the war: he got to appoint three Republicans to the Supreme Court during his tenure in office.

See also:
Judiciary Act of 1801
Midnight Appointments

Reference:
Ellis, Richard. 1971. *The Jeffersonian Crisis: Courts and Politics in the Young Republic.* New York: Oxford University Press.

Barbary War

One of Jefferson's most difficult tasks in foreign policy was coming to terms with the Barbary pirates of North Africa. American trade in the Mediterranean was endangered following the Revolution as U.S. merchants lost the protection of the British Royal Navy. The states of Morocco, Algiers, Tripoli, and Tunis began to prey upon U.S. shipping, hoping to push the American government into signing treaties that would ensure peace at the price of tribute. From Paris, Jefferson observed the actions of the Pirates at close range and was determined that they should be given nothing. Rather than pay a bribe, he contended, "would it not be better to offer them an equal treaty; if they refuse, why not go to war with them? . . .We ought to begin a naval power if we mean to carry on our own commerce. Can we begin it on a more honorable occasion, or with a weaker foe?"

The hawkish Jefferson did more than suggest an enlarged American navy, he also proposed a general European front against the pirates. He later recalled: "I . . . endeavored to form an association of the powers subject to habitual depredations from them. I accordingly prepared, and proposed . . . articles . . . for concerted operation among the powers at war with the piratical states of Barbary. . . . It was expected [that our American Confederation] would contribute a frigate,

and its expenses, to be in constant cruise." Unfortunately for Jefferson, however, a lack of participation killed his diplomatic efforts. "Contributions were so openly neglected by the several states," he noted, "that they declined an engagement . . . and so it fell through."

In spite of Jefferson's aggressive plans to repudiate the tributary process, the American government acquiesced to the demands of the pirates and signed a treaty with Algiers in 1795, with Tripoli in 1796, and with Tunis in 1797 that codified the demands of the North African states. The treaty with Algiers, for example, cost approximately $650,000 in bribes, ransoms, and commissions, and the United States agreed to pay an annual tribute of naval stores at a value of over $20,000. Eventually relations between the United States and the pirate states broke down over demands for increasingly larger bribes. When Jefferson became president in 1801, he placed frigates in the Mediterranean in hopes of protecting American shipping. The ensuing Barbary War was inconclusive; both sides claimed minor success as well as defeats.

Jefferson did declare a moral victory of sorts for the United States, which had finally exerted itself to protect the trade of its countrymen. "The bravery exhibited by our citizens [in the naval war]," he noted, ". . . will . . . be a testimony to the world that it is not the want of that virtue which makes us seek their peace." During his second term,

Jefferson was unable to provide a large naval presence in the Mediterranean due to the emerging naval conflict with the British. Following the War of 1812, however, two American squadrons under the command of Commodore William Bainbridge and Commodore Stephen Decatur forced the dey of Algiers and the beys of Tunis and Tripoli into treaties that effectively ended North Africa's war on American shipping.

See also:
Foreign Policy
Navy

Reference:
Field, James. 1969. *America and the Mediterranean World: 1776–1882*. Princeton, NJ: Princeton University Press.

Battle of New Orleans

*T*he Battle of New Orleans was the culminating military episode in the War of 1812. The American victory over the British, which actually occurred weeks after the peace treaty of Ghent officially ended the war, infused the country with a new sense of nationalism. Briefly, a motley American army of Creoles, frontier militia, free blacks, and pirates under General Andrew Jackson repulsed a frontal assault in the early morning hours on January 8, 1815. The British endured just over 2,000 casualties, the Americans less than 40. This victory appeared to many to be providential, a signal that republican purity was ordained to eclipse the power of the Old World monarchies. From his retirement in Monticello, Jefferson could not help but be pleased at the good fortune that had been bestowed upon the country. Perhaps even more than a military victory, the American conquest at New Orleans represented to Jefferson the continuation of Republican party rule.

Throughout his presidency, Jefferson had searched for a way to address U.S. grievances against violations of its neutral rights.

Jefferson's failure to secure such rights propelled the country toward the War of 1812 under his successor, James Madison. More than a national calamity, however, Jeffersonians feared that the Republican party was on trial. If the war ended in anything less than victory, then the party would suffer the scorn of the people and be removed from office. The Battle of New Orleans appeared to be a vindication not merely of republican ideology but also of the Republican party. Suddenly, the disastrous American foreign policy of Jefferson and Madison was forgotten and Republican rule had been rejuvenated in the wake of martial triumph. Jefferson himself believed the war created a new spirit and confidence in the country that promised much benefit in the future. "Throughout the whole period of the war," he contended,

> we have beaten [Britain] single-handed at sea, and so thoroughly established our superiority over them with equal force that they retire from that kind of contest, and never suffer their frigates to cruise singly. . . . The disclosure to the world of the fatal secret that they can be beaten at sea with an equal force, the evidence furnished by the military operations of the last year that experience is rearing us officers who, when our means shall be fully under way, will plant our standard on the walls of Quebec and Halifax, their recent and signal disaster at New Orleans . . . will probably raise a clamor in the British nation which will force their ministry into peace.

Such belligerence was rare for Jefferson, but the monumental American victory at New Orleans under General Jackson engendered much faith in the Republican party's fortunes and in the nation's future.

See also:
Jackson, Andrew
War of 1812

Engraving after a painting of the Battle of New Orleans by D. M. Carter, circa 1858.

Reference:
Remini, Robert. 1977. *Andrew Jackson and the Course of American Empire, 1767–1821.* New York: Harper & Row.

Battle of Tippecanoe

Jefferson's work on the Land Ordinance of 1784 influenced the development of American settlement in the Northwest Territories. Jefferson's plans for the region, however, did not take into account the reality that Native American communities already existed there. Throughout the 1790s, destructive wars between the native peoples and the U.S. army secured most of what is now Ohio for the expanding Anglo-Americans. Members of the Shawnee Nation realized that if they were to maintain their viability as an autonomous people, they would have to offer a more aggressive resistance. With this in mind the Shawnee leader Tecumseh

began to ally his people with tribes in the Mississippi Valley, particularly the Creeks, Cherokees, Choctaws, and Chickasaws. Tecumseh's brother, Tenskwatawa, remained in the Northwest and initiated a revitalization movement aimed at maintaining the beliefs and practices of Shawnee culture.

Americans did not believe that the native peoples could organize such a spirited resistance on their own and blamed the British, who kept a visible presence in the region thanks to their possession of Canada. At this time the United States was preparing to go to war with Britain over violations of neutrality incurred in the Atlantic trade. Foremost in the eyes of some expansionists, however, was the realization that a war would present the U.S. army in the West with a justification to remove native communities from the area that Jefferson fondly called an "Empire of Liberty." With war appearing imminent, an American army under the leadership of General William Henry Harrison gathered its forces near Tecumseh's capital on the Tippecanoe River in present-day Indiana. Fearing for their safety, the Shawnees attacked Harrison's encampment, though without the aid of Tecumseh, who was not present. After a bloody battle, Harrison's victorious army burned the Shawnee town and destroyed their supplies. The Battle of Tippecanoe ended any hopes by the British or the native peoples of limiting American expansion into the Old Northwest.

See also:
Empire of Liberty
Tecumseh
War of 1812

Reference:
Coles, Harry. 1965. *The War of 1812*. Chicago, IL: University of Chicago Press.

Botanizing Tour

*I*n 1791, Secretary of State Jefferson and his Virginia neighbor, Congressman James Madison, traveled to upstate New York visiting various historical sites and collecting samples of the local flora and fauna. In a letter to a relative, Jefferson related how

> Mr. Madison and myself . . . have visited . . . the principle scenes of General Burgoyne's misfortunes [the British defeat at Saratoga] . . . We have also visited Forts William Henry and George, Ticonderoga, Crown Point, etc., which have been scenes of blood from a very early part of our history. We were more pleased, however, with the botanical objects which continually presented themselves: . . . the sugar maple in vast abundance; the silver fir, white pine, pitch pine, spruce pine, a shrub with decumbent stems which they call juniper, an azalea very different from the nudiflora, with very large clusters of flowers, more thickly set on the branches, of a deeper red, and high pink-fragrance.

What Jefferson did not relate in his letter was the true intent of the excursion. Though he dearly loved visiting the natural wonders of the Empire State, the Virginian and his compatriot traveled to the North to solidify a political axis between Republicans in New York and Republicans in the Old Dominion. Large elements in each state feared that the federal government was assuming powers beyond its constitutional limitations, thus diluting the authority of the states. New York and Virginia were the two largest and most powerful states within the republic, and representatives from both provinces feared the loss of traditional rights and prerogatives to a distant central government. Seeking to redress this, Jefferson and Madison conceived of a large Republican coalition that would purify the government by consigning its duties to what they deemed to be the original intent of the Constitution. In support of this goal, they successfully petitioned for aid from New York under the pretense of a botanizing tour.

See also:
Madison, James
Republican Party

Reference:
Malone, Dumas. 1948–1981. *Jefferson and the Rights of Man,* vol. 2 of *Jefferson and His Time*. Boston: Little, Brown.

Burr, Aaron (1756–1836)

*A*side from Alexander Hamilton, Aaron Burr was Jefferson's most powerful political enemy. Though in many ways he enjoyed a distinguished career enumerated by military service, leadership in the Republican party, and one term served as vice president, Burr is most noted for his duel with Alexander Hamilton and his attempt to carve out an empire in the American West.

Burr was born in Newark, New Jersey, in 1756. The son of the cofounder of the College of New Jersey (Princeton University) and the grandson of the remarkable theologian Jonathan Edwards, Burr could point with pride to a distinguished ancestry. As an adolescent, Burr enjoyed the opportunity to receive a formal education, and he graduated with honors from Princeton in 1772, where he studied theology. During the Revolution he served on Benedict Arnold's staff and, briefly, George Washington's. He participated in several major skirmishes, including the Battle of Monmouth, and resigned from the service in 1779 due to bad health.

Taking up residence in New York, Burr gravitated toward the practice of law. His natural brilliance, a measure of personality and a quick mind rather than sheer intelligence, brought him to the attention of the state's political elite. At the time, the New Yorker was divided between followers of Hamilton's father-in-law, Philip Schuyler, and loyalists to George Clinton. Burr joined the latter camp and was rewarded in 1789 with appointment as the state's attorney general. Two years later, Burr defeated Schuyler for a U.S. Senate seat.

Though he failed to win reelection, Burr held significant power in the New York legislature due to the fact that he was part of a coalition that controlled the state's presidential electoral votes. This was particularly important because in the upcoming election of 1800, the Republican party understood that if it did not win New York, which it had lost in 1796, it could not make Jefferson president. To ensure Burr's support, Republicans placed the New Yorker on the party ticket. Although there was no way to distinguish between presidential and vice presidential candidates on ballots, it was understood that Jefferson occupied the top spot on the ballot. With Burr's aid, the Jeffersonians did win the election, yet by miscalculation both Republican candidates garnered the same number of electoral votes. In such circumstances the Constitution dictates that the election go to the House of Representatives, where each state casts a single ballot. Because the outgoing Federalist party still controlled Congress and was not pleased with the prospect

of either a Burr or a Jefferson presidency, it took 36 ballots before a decision could be rendered. In the end it was a Federalist Congress rather than the American people who made Jefferson president. With good reason Jefferson believed that Burr had vigorously contested for the position in an attempt to steal the presidency from the Virginian. In return, Jefferson froze Burr out of the Republican party, ensuring that his political career within the Jeffersonian coalition was over.

Casting about for opportunities to rehabilitate his career, the lame-duck vice president found succor in the arms of a group of New England Federalists who opposed the onset of Jeffersonian democracy. These disgruntled Federalists, known as the Essex Junto, proposed to sever New England and New York from the Union and form a northern confederation. To do so they needed control of New York and successfully proposed to Burr that he submit himself as a Junto-backed candidate in the upcoming gubernatorial race. Apparently, if Burr won the election, he would have removed New York from the Union and joined the New England states. In the course of the campaign, however, Hamilton made public comments criticizing Burr's character, which may have played a part in the latter's defeat. In response, Burr killed Hamilton in a duel in July 1804.

At this point Burr was completely divorced from the traditional avenues of power. He had incurred the wrath of Republicans by challenging Jefferson for the presidency and then killed Hamilton, the most brilliant Federalist. Still, Burr was filled with ambition, and his energies naturally flowed toward any promising outlet. Eventually he conceived of a scheme to lead a volunteer army to the West to carve out an empire. Details are sketchy, but it is clear that Burr envisioned the conquest of northern Mexico and perhaps the trans-Appalachian states of the Union. He proposed, in other words, treason. Burr traveled through parts of the West in the spring of 1805 making contacts and accumulating men, materials, money, and promises.

By the summer of the following year, the New Yorker was ready to put his plans into action. Setting out from Blennerhasset Island on the Ohio River, Burr and some 60 followers traveled down the Mississippi to join General James Wilkinson. Wilkinson commanded the American army in the West, enjoyed a salary as a Spanish spy, and now appeared willing to promote Burr's plans for a western empire. Burr's extensive preparations made his exploit too visible, however, and the cautious Wilkinson feared that he would be implicated in a failed plot to wrestle the nation's western territories from the government in Washington. He thus betrayed Burr by informing Jefferson of his colleague's movements. With orders to make an arrest, Wilkinson moved in quickly and captured Burr.

Taken to Richmond to stand trial for treason, Burr was acquitted because government prosecutors were unable to find an adequate number of witnesses who could testify that Burr's actions constituted treason. Burr lived in Europe for a few years, avoiding creditors and fruitlessly pursuing Napoleon's support for further adventures in the American West. Returning to the United States in 1812, Burr quietly practiced law in New York City until his death in 1836.

See also:
Burr Conspiracy
Election of 1800
Essex Junto

Reference:
Vail, Philip. 1973. *The Great American Rascal: The Turbulent Life of Aaron Burr.* New York: Hawthorn Books.

Burr Conspiracy

*I*n 1800, Republicans nominated Jefferson for the presidency with the understanding that Aaron Burr would be the party's choice for vice president. Burr was attached to the ticket because of his ability to bring his home state of New York into the Republican fold. Due to a mix-up, however, Jefferson and Burr received the same number of electoral votes and the election went to the House of Representatives. Most Republicans expected Burr to step aside in deference to Jefferson, the party's obvious choice. Instead, the ambitious Burr campaigned for the presidency, but to no avail. The election went to Jefferson, and Burr was left with the lasting enmity of the Virginian.

The lame-duck vice president understood that he had no future in the Republican party and made himself available to opportunities that promised access to greater power. In 1804 he joined forces with the Essex Junto in hopes of winning the gubernatorial election in New York and then perhaps severing the Empire State and New England from the rest of the Union and leading a great northern confederation. These plans, too, came to naught as Burr's rival, Alexander Hamilton, worked for his defeat. Incensed, Burr challenged Hamilton to a duel and killed the former secretary of the treasury. By 1805, Aaron Burr could not hope to gratify his considerable personal ambitions through traditional avenues of power. Denounced as both a usurper and a murderer, he was a political outcast. Opportunity lay elsewhere, however, and Burr set his sights on a great empire in the West.

Burr hoped to use America's antipathy toward Spain to his advantage. An ongoing boundary dispute between U.S. and Spanish claims in West Florida encouraged Burr to believe that he could rally support from westerners to invade Spanish-held areas. In March 1805 the former vice president left the capital and traveled throughout the Southwest, familiarizing himself with the landscape and enlisting associates to his cause. He visited several prominent westerners, including Andrew Jackson, described his mission to wrestle part of Mexico away from the Spanish, and claimed his proposed adventure was backed by the government in Washington. Though his plans were never finalized, Burr appeared to be rallying support from private citizens to carry out simultaneous attacks on Mexico from St. Louis and New Orleans. More devious, however, was Burr's relationship with General James Wilkinson, the commander of U.S. forces in the West and a Spanish agent. Wilkinson's task was to provide transportation to Burr and foment dissent against Jefferson's government by telling the people of the western territories that their land titles were jeopardized by incorporation into the United States. From this evidence, some Americans began to perceive that Burr not merely wanted to take territory from the Spanish but also wished to assume U.S. lands in Louisiana.

Burr put his plans into action in the summer of 1806, moving with a small flotilla from Blennerhasset Island on the Ohio River toward the Mississippi. By this time, however, Jefferson had received several notices concerning Burr's actions and was growing increasingly suspicious. In October the president ordered marines to New Orleans and sent the Orleans territorial secretary, John Graham, to sniff along Burr's path. Sensing that Burr's game could not work, Wilkinson decided to save his own neck. He wrote to Jefferson warning of Burr's movements south, then proceeded to New Orleans to, as he informed Jefferson, "save the country." Jefferson issued a proclamation prejudging Burr guilty of treason and ordering his arrest.

When Burr reached Natchez he learned of Wilkinson's betrayal. The former vice president took off through the swamps of the lower Mississippi attempting to reach Spanish-held Pensacola, from where he probably would have sailed to Europe. Before he could reach Florida, however, Burr was captured and taken to Richmond for trial. Burr was arraigned in March 1807 on charges of organizing an anti-Spanish filibuster in the Court of Chief Justice John Marshall. Though distantly related to Jefferson, Marshall and the president were political enemies. Marshall

was particularly incensed over the Republican party's attempts to impeach federal justices. In Jefferson's opinion, Marshall's Federalist sympathies reduced him. Ultimately, Marshall's insistence that the Constitution's treason clause be narrowly interpreted made the court favorable to Burr's case. This clause, which states that at least two witnesses must testify to the same treasonable action in order to secure conviction, saved Burr, who kept his plans shrouded in mystery. Though many westerners thought they understood Burr's intentions, the New Yorker actually communicated very little. To Jefferson, however, there could be no doubt of Burr's intentions. He wrote, "Burr's enterprise is the most extraordinary since the days of Don Quixote. It is so extravagant that those who know his understanding would not believe it if the proofs admitted doubt. He has meant to place himself on the throne of Montezuma and extend his empire to the Allegheny, seizing on New Orleans as the instrument of compulsion for our Western States."

Though Jefferson was incensed over Burr's acquittal, he might have blamed himself for enticing such intrigues. As president, Jefferson attempted to erase the nation's debt by minimizing the federal government's presence. This included the evacuation of foreign posts by American ministers and the reduction of the army and navy. While such austerity could be safely endured in the more established regions of the country, the West appeared to be ripe to fall into the hands of the first strong force that appeared on the horizon. In other words, by negating the federal presence in the West, Jefferson left that section vulnerable to would-be empire builders like Burr.

See also:
Burr, Aaron
Essex Junto

Reference:
Abernathy, Thomas. 1954. *The Burr Conspiracy*. New York: Oxford University Press.

C

Callender, James T. (1758–1803)

James Callender was a disgruntled office seeker who printed the first allegation that Jefferson sired mulatto children with his slave, Sally Hemings. Forced to leave the British Isles after printing scandalous remarks about the British government, the pamphleteer-journalist came to America and found employment at the *Philadelphia Gazette*, a Republican party organ that attacked Federalist policies while lauding the efforts of the Jeffersonians. In 1797, Vice President Jefferson visited Callender at his printing office to discuss a project that would further weaken the Federalist party. Though no account exists of the topic of their conversation, shortly after Jefferson's visit Callender published "History of the Year 1796," which charged the Federalists in general and Alexander Hamilton in particular with unethical activities. Callender's charges were unsubstantiated by evidence, but nevertheless the manuscript was a success. Jefferson continued to send Callender work and, on at least one occasion, gave him money.

By 1799, Callender was working at the *Richmond Examiner*, which produced a steady stream of Anti-Federalist material. Jefferson encouraged the partisan journalist, telling him that "such papers cannot fail to produce the best effects." One of Callender's articles, however, was deemed so offensive that he was prosecuted for attacking in print President John Adams. This violation of the nation's Sedition Act landed Callender in jail for several months. Fortunately for the imprisoned journalist, Jefferson defeated Adams for the presidency in 1800, and upon taking office the new executive pardoned Callender and others who had violated the sedition law.

Callender believed that his efforts played a significant part in the Republican party's victory and now sought his reward. He informed Jefferson that he expected to be appointed to the Richmond postmastership, which carried a lucrative remuneration of $1,500 per year. Jefferson was cool to the notion of giving Callender such a plum position and ceased communication with him. Callender threatened to unleash information that would prove damaging to Jefferson, but his best efforts could not gain him the position. In a fit of anger Callender commenced writing anti-Jefferson pieces for a Federalist paper in Virginia. While there, he heard rumors that Jefferson had fathered several children with one of his slaves. Without any conclusive evidence Callender began to print stories in 1802 that Jefferson kept a "Congo Harem" at Monticello and his favorite mistress was "Dusky Sally" Hemings. Federalist papers from around the country picked up the story and disseminated it among their readers. Callender did not have long to enjoy his handiwork. In 1803, his body was found in the James River, a consequence of excessive drinking.

See also:
Hemings, Sally
Slavery

Reference:
Dabney, Virginius. 1981. *The Jefferson Scandals.*
  New York: Madison Books.

Classical Republicanism

Classical republicanism refers to the emergence in antiquity of a body of thought that promoted republican rather than absolute rule. As America turned toward a liberal form of government during the Revolution, Jefferson and the Founders searched for ideological precursors to demonstrate that republics, that is, nations ruled by the people, could survive in a world of monarchies. Their search ultimately led them to the classics. From the writings of Plato and Aristotle they learned of the virtues of Athenian democracy while Cicero and Tacitus provided an understanding of how the Roman Republic developed and declined. From reading Cicero in particular, Jefferson came to believe that republics could work properly only if they were not corrupted through the attainment of an empire or a bureaucratic leisure class.

The Founders also detected the seeds of republicanism in English thought. In the seventeenth century, writers such as Algernon Sidney and James Harrington opposed Crown intrusions on civil liberties and promoted the concept of a "mixed" republic. In Harrington's *The Commonwealth of Oceana*, the author followed the great republican theorists of antiquity by arguing that a mixture of each social class could be incorporated into the corpus of government in order that all interests of society be accounted for. In Harrington's analysis, three sociopolitical elements existed: the monarchy, the aristocracy, and the people. The virtue of the monarchy was force; in a time of crisis it could act quickly. To its detriment, however, a monarchy was prone to despotism because

there was no power to check it. The virtue of the aristocracy was intelligence. This leisure class enjoyed time to pursue education and thus could provide excellent counsel to its ruler. The aristocracy was prone to corruption, however, because it controlled the bureaucratic functions of the state. The virtue of the people was its love for liberty. More than the other classes, this third estate gravitated to individual freedom. To their discredit, however, the people's thirst for democracy could easily turn into anarchy. Individually, Harrington concluded, each class was incapable of securing the long-term health of a nation, but collectively, or "mixed," the best qualities of each would be exemplified while their worst excesses would be checked.

In Jefferson's opinion the English writers represented the true heirs of Anglo-American liberties borrowed from the classical age. To justify America's break with Great Britain during the Revolution, therefore, Jefferson had to explain how England deviated from the republican model and posed a threat to traditional colonial freedoms. In a series of provocative essays, the Founders contended that the British were corrupted by a thirst for empire. Beginning in 1689 and extending into the early nineteenth century, England had fought a series of costly wars that extended its empire throughout the world. To cover the cost, it underwent a financial revolution that transformed the traditional agrarian economy into an increasingly commercial and speculative one. By introducing a stock market and national bank, England also increased opportunities for corruption within its borders. With the military and the financiers calling for increased expansion to keep this great machine going, some Americans argued that it was only a matter of time before England infringed upon the ancient liberties of the colonists. In explaining what the Declaration of Independence represented to Americans, Jefferson recalled the convictions of classical republicanism, remarking that the document was neither aiming at originality of principle or sentiment, nor yet copied from any particular and previous writing, it was intended to be an expression of the American mind and to give to that expression the proper tone and spirit called for by the occasion. All its authority rests then on the harmonizing sentiments of the day, whether expressed in conversation, in letters, printed essays, or in the elementary books of public right, as Aristotle, Cicero, Locke, Sidney, etc.

See also:
American Revolution
Locke, John

Reference:
Banning, Lance. 1978. *The Jeffersonian Persuasion: Evolution of a Party Ideology*. Ithaca, NY: Cornell University Press.

Clinton, DeWitt (1769–1828)

As the leader of the Republican faction in New York, DeWitt Clinton was for most of his professional life a key political lieutenant in the Jeffersonian party system. His interests in banking, manufacturing, and internal improvements, however, forced him to break with the more agrarian wing of the Jeffersonian party and thus endanger his political career.

Clinton was born in Little Britain, New York, in 1769. He was educated privately before attending Kingston Academy and then Columbia College. He studied law and served as secretary to his uncle, George Clinton, long-term governor of New York. In 1797 the younger Clinton was elected to the New York Assembly as a Republican, and from there his political career took off. He held various offices, including state senator, U.S. senator, and mayor of New York City, but his most important work was done as governor.

Although he championed the Jeffersonian principles that had furthered his uncle's political career, Clinton opposed American participation in the War of 1812 because he believed its effect on New York's economy would be disastrous. Breaking with the Jeffersonian party, Clinton opposed Madison for the presidency on the Federalist ticket and was defeated. Among his most cherished achievements was sponsorship of the Erie Canal, which was completed in 1825 and proved a catalyst for a transportation revolution that defined the latter years of the early republic.

See also:
Transportation Revolution
War of 1812

Reference:
Shaw, Ronald. 1966. *Erie Water West*. Lexington: University Press of Kentucky.

Clinton, George (1739–1812)

This New York politician was instrumental in forming the Democratic-Republican party in the 1790s. Clinton was born in Little Britain, New York, in 1739 and served in the French and Indian War prior to studying law. Clinton became known as a radical Whig during the crisis leading up to the American Revolution and was elected to the Second Continental Congress. He proved an ineffectual officer in the New York militia and returned to politics in 1777, becoming the state's first governor.

Following the Revolution, Clinton opposed the Constitution because he feared it would take power from the states and centralize authority in the national government. He acquiesced in the document's ratification in New York only after the requisite nine states had approved it and the Constitution was the law of the land. His fear of a powerful central government was heightened in the early 1790s when Secretary of the Treasury

Alexander Hamilton proposed a series of bills that shifted the financial leverage of the republic toward the federal government. Approached by Jefferson and Madison to form an "axis" of republicanism between New York and Virginia, Clinton agreed and worked for the overthrow of the Federalist party in the Empire State as well as around the nation. A disappointed candidate for his party's nomination to the presidency, Clinton served nearly two complete terms as vice president under Jefferson and Madison before his death in 1812.

See also:
Botanizing Tour
Hamilton, Alexander
Republican Party

Reference:
Young, Alfred. 1967. *The Democratic Republicans of New York: The Origins, 1763–1797.* Chapel Hill: University of North Carolina Press.

College of William and Mary

Jefferson came to Williamsburg, Virginia, in 1760 at the age of 17 and stayed for two years of study at the College of William and Mary. At this time many of Virginia's elite sons did not attend the local college, preferring instead an education in England or perhaps New England. But William and Mary held certain charms for Jefferson. The college was located in the provincial colonial capital of Williamsburg, seat of Britain's New World Empire and center of Virginia politics, society, and culture. Its 1,500 inhabitants enjoyed a genteel lifestyle that was the admiration of the Chesapeake region. During his stay in the capital, Jefferson was surrounded by Tidewater aristocrats, many of whom attended college with him. He was known to frequent the Raleigh Tavern, where he danced on occasion, and attended Sabbath worship services at Bruton Church.

William and Mary was chartered in 1693 with a slightly clerical mission. The acquisi-

tive environment of Williamsburg, however, along with the reluctance of planters' sons to choose the church as a profession, secularized the culture of the college. During Jefferson's preparation at William and Mary, the college, attended by about 100 students, consisted of various schools: a preparatory or grammar school, an Indian School intended to Christianize the natives, a philosophy school, and a divinity school. Jefferson enrolled in the school of philosophy, the equivalent of a present-day liberal arts college. In his autobiography Jefferson related that

> it was my great good fortune, and what probably fixed the destinies of my life that Dr. William Small of Scotland, was then Professor of Mathematics, a man profound in most of the useful branches of science, with a happy talent of communication, correct and gentlemanly manners, and an enlarged and liberal mind. He, most happily for me, became engaged in the school; and from his conversation I got my first views of the expansion of science, and of the system of things in which we are placed.

"Happily" for Jefferson, Small, the sole nonclergyman on the faculty, was a talented and effective scholar who taught from a rational and scientific rather than religious perspective. Small was the first true scientist Jefferson encountered, and he left a powerful impact on the young man's mind. Jefferson made himself a fixture in Small's courses in mathematics, natural philosophy, natural history, logic, ethics, rhetoric, and belles lettres. Though he would drift into the study of law for professional reasons, Jefferson's love of science and rationalism, first evidenced in his work at William and Mary, would last throughout his life.

See also:
Deism
Enlightenment

Reference:

Adams, Herbert B. 1887. *The College of William and Mary.* Washington, DC: Government Print Office.

Confederation Period

The Confederation period commences with the conclusion of the American Revolution in 1783 and culminates in the ratification of the Constitution in 1788. During this brief period the nation operated under the Articles of Confederation, a loose compact that bound the states together under a weak central government. The Articles were written in 1777 to help the United States prosecute its war for independence against Great Britain. However, fear of centralized power and the erosion of customary prerogatives influenced the states to make the national government subservient in most instances to local rule. Jefferson and others favored this type of relationship between federal and state governments because it seemed to minimize the opportunity for corruption while preserving Virginia's dominant role in the Union.

As the Confederation period wore on, however, it became evident to some Americans that a weak central government made for a weak nation. Financially, for example, the country was in terrible straits. Under the Articles of Confederation the federal government was authorized to conduct the military phase of the Revolution. It did this through the procurement of loans from private citizens and foreign nations, particularly France. These debts had to be paid off to secure the nation's credit, but the power to raise revenues through taxation belonged not to the federal government but to the states, which were reluctant to tax their citizens to pay off what they considered to be a federal debt. Moreover, soldiers in the Continental army had not been paid for some time, and there was a real concern that the military might overthrow the national government in order to secure payment.

In terms of foreign diplomacy, the inability of the federal government to speak with force also hampered American interests. Great Britain and Spain, for example, illegally kept military posts on U.S. soil in order to maintain an influence in the region. These nations also kept a hand in the lucrative fur trade and cultivated relations with native peoples in an attempt to limit further American expansion west. Moreover, the British shut the United States out of its trading empire following the Revolution, and the American economy was suffering for it. Britain could punish the United States in this manner because under the Articles of Confederation, the federal government had no power to levy retaliatory tariffs against foreign nations; only the states could do that.

Finally, the Confederation government proved inadequate because it did not have the ability to put down internal insurrections within the country. In 1786, for example, a group of Massachusetts farmers under the leadership of Daniel Shays took up arms to prevent the state government from taking their property as a result of unpaid taxes. Shays' Rebellion threatened to topple the ruling coalition of Massachusetts, and the federal government had no legal way to prevent it. Though the rebellion was quickly put down, fear of future insurrections convinced some Americans that a more vigorous federal government was needed. These men called themselves "Nationalists," and they were the architects of the Constitution.

Throughout most of this period, Jefferson was out of the country. As America's minister to France, he did not experience the effect that the proposed military conspiracy or Shays' Rebellion had on Americans. Had Jefferson spent the 1780s in America and witnessed firsthand the dangers of a weak central government, he might have been more forgiving of the Nationalists' attempt in the 1790s to dramatically increase federal power at the expense of state prerogatives.

See also:
Constitution
Minister to France
Shays' Rebellion

Reference:
Morris, Richard. 1987. *The Forging of the Union: 1781–1789.* New York: Harper & Row.

Constitution

Following the American Revolution, the states were largely in control of their own affairs. The lesson of the Revolution seemed to be that centralized power, as personified by the British Empire, led to tyranny rather than liberty. The states thus kept authority localized and created a federal republic. Throughout the 1780s, however, the nation experienced difficulties meeting its financial obligations because the federal government had no power to collect taxes—only the states could do so. Within the states, small groups of Nationalists emerged, demanding that more power be given to the central government to ensure that it could meet its financial and military obligations. Interstate commerce conventions at Mount Vernon and Annapolis in 1785 and 1786 led to the Constitutional Convention in Philadelphia in the summer of 1787. The states gave their representatives the authority to recommend changes to the existing confederation system. The representatives did more than that. They devised an entirely new form of government centered around a more powerful central government.

Jefferson had no part in the proceedings in Philadelphia. He was not even in the country when the Constitution was drafted. Rather, Jefferson spent the summer of 1787 traveling through southern France and northern Italy collecting plant specimens while taking time off from his duties as foreign minister to France. Jefferson was apprised of the business in Philadelphia by his friend and neighbor, James Madison, the primary architect of the Constitution. Though wary of any attempt to centralize power, Jefferson cautiously recommended the work being done in America. "I approved, from the first moment," he wrote Francis Hopkins, "of the great mass of what is in the new Constitution: the consolidation of the government; the organization into executive, legislative, and judiciary; the subdivision of the legislative; the happy compromise of interests between the great and little states, by the different manner of voting in the different Houses; the voting by persons instead of states; the qualified negative on laws given to the executive."

Despite such praise, Jefferson did not believe the document to be an unqualified success. He expressed disenchantment, for example, that a Bill of Rights, "to guard liberty against the legislative as well as the executive branches of the government," was not included. Without this, he lamented, "freedom in religion, freedom of the press, freedom from monopolies, freedom from unlawful imprisonment, freedom from a permanent military, were not secured. Moreover, Jefferson "disapproved also, the perpetual re-eligibility of the President." But in spite of these caveats the Virginian concluded that "we can surely boast of having set the world a beautiful example of a government reformed by reason alone, without bloodshed." And to be sure, bloodshed would not follow during Jefferson's lifetime.

As part of a compromise to ensure the states' acceptance of the Constitution, a Bill of Rights was added following ratification. Moreover, the issue of the "re-eligibility of the President" was not a practical concern during Jefferson's lifetime. The nation's first president, George Washington, left office after two terms, setting a precedent that Jefferson and his Virginia successors would follow. When Franklin D. Roosevelt won four terms during the 1930s and 1940s, Congress demonstrated the currency of Jefferson's concerns by adding an amendment to the Bill of Rights that stated in part that "no person shall be elected to the office of the

President more than twice, and no person who has held the office of President, or acted as President, for more than two years of a term to which some other person was elected President shall be elected to the office of the President more than once."

See also:
Confederation Period
Minister to France

Reference:
Bowen, Catherine Drinker. 1966. *Miracle at Philadelphia: The Story of the Constitutional Convention, May to September 1787.* Boston, MA: Little, Brown.

Cosway, Maria (1759–1838)

Half-tone reproduction of a rare mezzotint by Valentine Green after a self-portrait by Maria Cosway.

While serving as American minister to France, Jefferson met the English artist Maria Cosway. Maria was by all accounts a charming and intelligent woman with blue eyes and golden hair. In her twenties when she met the 43-year-old Jefferson, Maria presented an image of vibrant youth and genteel manners that the Virginian found irresistible. Jefferson's wife, Martha, had died in 1782, and Maria proved to be Jefferson's first significant attachment to a woman since that time.

Though Maria's life appeared to be one of contentment, in reality she was unhappily married to Richard Cosway, a London artist and miniaturist. Because of her Catholic background, however, as well as societal expectations, Maria could not think of divorcing her husband for Jefferson or any man. Jefferson undoubtedly understood this, and his natural attraction to Maria might have been enhanced by the understanding that any relationship with her would be strictly platonic. This sort of relationship would have been in keeping with the fact, recollected by a slave, that Jefferson had promised his wife he would never remarry. Moreover, Jefferson's emotional withdrawal after this painful episode and his subsequent behavior with women make it doubtful that he would have consummated another love relationship.

Maria was thus ultimately attainable to Jefferson only as a close friend. Their brief two-month association, from August to early October 1786, was nevertheless among the happiest of Jefferson's life. The two attended concerts and galleries, traveled the countryside, and flirted, secure in the knowledge that both had safely established lives waiting for them elsewhere. In a fit of boyish playfulness, Jefferson tried to impress Maria by leaping over a fence. He fell in the attempt and dislocated his right wrist, a lasting, painful memento of his relationship with the beautiful artist. At their parting, Jefferson left Maria a long letter in which he related the conflict between "my Head and my Heart." The letter is moving yet reserved in the formal style that Jefferson was careful to keep. Speaking from his "Heart," Jefferson proclaimed to Maria:

Let the gloomy Monk, sequestered from the world, seek unsocial pleasures in the bottom of his cell! Let the sublimated philosopher grasp visionary happiness while pursuing phantoms dressed in the garb of truth! Their supreme wisdom is supreme folly: and they mistake for happiness the mere absence of pain. Had they ever felt the solid pleasure of one generous spasm of the heart, they would exchange for it all the frigid speculations of their lives.

Jefferson's "Head," though, counseled caution:

Do not bite at the bait of pleasure till you know there is no hook beneath it. The art of life is the avoiding of pain. . . . The most effectual means of being secure against pain is to retire within ourselves.

Following Maria's departure, she and Jefferson maintained a correspondence for many years but never tried to recapture the feelings they aroused in one another during their summer in Paris.

See also:
Minister to France

Reference:
Bullock, Helen Claire Duprey. 1945. *My Head and My Heart: A Little History of Thomas Jefferson and Maria Cosway.* New York: G.P. Putnam's Sons.

Cotton Gin

As secretary of state in George Washington's cabinet, Jefferson was in charge of issuing patents. To a self-taught mechanic-architect like Jefferson, this task was immensely rewarding, and he spent many pleasant hours examining drawings of inventions and attempting to ascertain their value. In this capacity, Jefferson was presented with a request by Eli Whitney asking that his invention, a cotton gin, be granted a patent.

Jefferson was intrigued with the designs and wrote back to the Connecticut inventor:

Your drawing of the cotton gin was received. . . . As the State of Virginia, of which I am, carries on household manufactures of cotton to a great extent, as I also do myself, and one of our great embarrassments is the clearing the cotton of the seed, I feel a considerable interest in the success of your invention for family use. Permit me therefore to ask information from you on these points. Has the machine been thoroughly tried in the ginning of cotton, or is it yet but a machine of theory? What quantity of cotton has it cleaned on an average of several days, and worked by hand, and how many hands? What will be the cost of one of them made to be worked by hand? Favorable answers to these questions would induce me to engage one of them.

More than merely engaging one of them for his own benefit, Jefferson forwarded a patent to Whitney, and the gin subsequently revolutionized the production of cotton in America.

Jefferson's association with the cotton gin is a great historical irony. As a younger man, Jefferson proposed ending slavery or at least preserving the West for free labor. Toward this goal he successfully worked to keep the northwest territory, encompassing Ohio, Indiana, Illinois, Michigan, and Wisconsin, closed to slavery. Yet in the 1790s, the cotton gin revitalized what had hitherto been a stagnant southern agricultural market and enhanced the profitability of slavery through the establishment of a new staple crop. Cotton became even more important to the southern economy in the nineteenth century than tobacco and rice had been during the colonial era. Jefferson's purchase of the Louisiana Territory in 1803 recognized the profitability of cotton by opening up a new frontier to slavery. Thus the man who created free territory in the 1780s was in the 1790s bestowing his blessing on an invention that would push slavery into the American West.

See also:
Secretary of State
Slavery

Reference:
North, Douglass. 1961. *The Economic Growth of the United States, 1790–1860.* New York: Prentice Hall.

Cuba

Jefferson was a strong advocate of Cuban statehood within the American republic. He believed it to be strategically dangerous for European possessions to lie so close to the United States and sought as well an end to colonialism in the Western Hemisphere. Moreover, in Jefferson's mind, Cuba was the only offshore territory that could be occupied by the United States without a heavy financial burden or a large navy. Thus America would be able to expand without incurring a crushing debt or enlarging the federal government. Finally, Cuban statehood appealed to Jefferson because it fit into his vision of an "Empire of Liberty." He had long promoted the rapid expansion of American institutions across the frontier as a way to spread republican values in the New World. The acquisition of Cuba promised to take Jefferson's vision into the Caribbean.

As president, Jefferson nearly went to war with Great Britain over that nation's confiscation of American ships trading with the French empire. Though the question of preserving American sovereignty was primary in his mind, Jefferson also considered going to war with Britain and its ally Spain for territorial aggrandizement. "I had rather have war against Spain than not, if we should go to war against England," he told James Madison. "Our southern defensive force can take the Floridas, volunteers for a Mexican army will flock to our standard, and rich pabulum will be offered to our privateers in the plunder of their commerce and coasts. Probably Cuba would add itself to our confederation." Though the eventual war with Great Britain, fought after Jefferson retired from the presidency, did not bring Cuba into the American fold, the Sage of Monticello never gave up on acquiring the island. When President James Monroe sought Jefferson's advice in 1823 on whether the United States should declare the Western Hemisphere off-limits to future European colonization, the latter quickly concurred. Moreover, while encouraging the president to warn Europe away from the Americas, he also put in a bid for Caribbean expansion, remarking to Monroe that he had "ever looked on Cuba as the most interesting addition which could ever be made to our system of states."

At the time of Jefferson's death in 1826, the issue of slavery made the acquisition of Cuba a political impossibility. Northerners feared that if Cuba were acquired, then the entire Caribbean would soon be turned into a great southern slave empire. Though various "filibusters" or invasions of Cuba by private proslavery American armies took place in the antebellum period, the island remained attached to the Spanish empire until the Spanish-American War of 1898. At the conclusion of the war, the United States acquired the Philippines and Puerto Rico from its enemy. However, as if to prove it did not enter the war merely to acquire an empire, it did not assume control over Cuba but allowed it to become an independent nation.

See also:
Empire of Liberty
Monroe Doctrine

Reference:
McCoy, Drew. 1980. *The Elusive Republic: Political Economy in Jeffersonian America.* Chapel Hill: University of North Carolina Press.

Death of Jefferson

On June 24, 1826, Jefferson wrote two letters. The first was to decline, due to failing health, an invitation from the citizens of Washington to attend a celebration of the fiftieth anniversary of the Declaration of Independence. The second letter summoned Jefferson's physician, Dr. Robley Dunglison, a professor of history at the University of Virginia, to Jefferson's bedside at Monticello. Upon examining him, Dr. Dunglison announced that there was no hope of recovery for the ailing 83-year-old and remained at Jefferson's home for the next several days. Preparations were made for Jefferson's death, and family members scattered abroad were called home. Jefferson's daughter Martha could be found at her father's bedside throughout the days, and Jefferson's male nephews kept watch during the evenings.

Jefferson remained lucid until the first of July, when he lapsed into unconsciousness. On the second of July he awakened only a few times and, on at least one occasion, inquired if it were yet the fourth. Whether or not it was Jefferson's will that kept him alive till the national birthday or merely coincidence, he did not perish until 50 minutes past noon on the fourth. That afternoon the celebratory atmosphere in Charlottesville was dampened by the news of Jefferson's demise. Bells tolled throughout the community and business was suspended. Ironically, Jefferson's friend and former political nemesis, John Adams, also died on the fourth. His final words were "Thomas Jefferson still survives." Jefferson was buried at Monticello the day following his death. His epitaph, celebrating his authorship of the Declaration of Independence and the Statute of Virginia, which provided for religious freedom, and his founding of the University of Virginia, reflects what he believed were his most endearing contributions to Virginia, the United States, and personal freedom.

See also:
Adams, John
Declaration of Independence
University of Virginia

Reference:
Malone, Dumas. 1948–1981. *The Sage of Monticello,* vol. 6 of *Jefferson and His Time.* Boston: Little, Brown.

Declaration of Independence

Though he served in a variety of official capacities including governor of Virginia, minister to France, and president of the United States, Thomas Jefferson is best remembered for his authorship of the Declaration of Independence. More than a mere document of principles, the Declaration sought to explain to the American people why they were breaking the bonds of unity

Engraving by Ormsby after a painting by Trumbull. The artist painted Jefferson's portrait from life during the winter of 1787–1788, but did not finish the painting until 1820.

with Great Britain. In declaring independence the Founders asked their countrymen to endure great sacrifices until that autonomy was secured. Jefferson's statement of Americans' resolve to assert their natural rights succinctly defined the parameters of the revolutionary movement and placed the motives of those championing independence upon a higher plane. The Declaration made clear that the break with Britain was not for monetary gain but rather intended to preserve ancient liberties that were in danger of being lost.

The movement toward independence began in the 1760s following Britain's victory over France in the French and Indian War. Taking Canada as a sinecure and thus enlarging its colonial domains, Britain was compelled to find new ways to finance its empire. In a series of revenue acts, including the Stamp Act of 1765 and the Townshend Duties of 1767, Parliament tried to directly tax its North American colonies, something it had never done before. Peaceful resistance forced Britain to back down in each instance, but in 1773 the British attempt to coerce Americans to pay a minor duty on tea resulted in the Boston Tea Party. Parliament retaliated by closing the Port of Boston and leveling other punitive measures at the colony of Massachusetts.

In order to develop a common response, twelve of the colonies sent delegates to the Frst Continental Congress, which met in Philadelphia in the autumn of 1774. This body did not seek independence but rather adopted resolutions declaring Britain's actions against Massachusetts null and void, urged the Bay State to arm for defense, and called for economic sanctions against British commerce. Momentum for independence increased dramatically in the spring of 1775, when American militia engaged British forces at Lexington and Concord. Further, Britain's continued military buildup in North America as well as new restrictions against American trade compelled colonists to reconsider their place in the empire. In April 1776, North Carolina authorized its representatives in the

Continental Congress to seek independence, and one month later the Rhode Island legislature declared the colony independent of Britain.

On the national level, Richard Henry Lee, a member of the Virginia delegation to Congress, introduced a series of resolutions on June 7 that declared that "these United Colonies are, and of right ought to be, free and independent States, that they are absolved from all allegiance to the British Crown, and that all political connections between them and the State of Great Britain is, and ought to be, totally dissolved." Though much support for the resolution existed in New England and Virginia, other colonies hesitated, hoping for reconciliation with the mother country. Though consideration of Lee's resolution was put off until July 1, a committee of five was appointed to draft a document outlining American grievances and declaring independence. The committee was made up of John Adams of Massachusetts, Benjamin Franklin of Pennsylvania, Roger Sherman of Connecticut, Robert Livingston of New York, and Thomas Jefferson of Virginia, just 33 years old. Jefferson later recalled:

> The committee of five met; no such thing as a subcommittee was proposed, but they unanimously pressed on myself alone to undertake the draught. I consented; I drew it, but before I reported it to the committee, I communicated it separately to Dr. Franklin and Mr. Adams, requesting their corrections, because they were the two members of whose judgments and amendments I wished most to have the benefit before presenting it to the committee. . . . Their alterations were two or three only, and merely verbal. I then wrote a fair copy, reported it to the committee, and from them unaltered, to Congress.

Jefferson's draft was reported to Congress on June 28, and four days later the colonies voted

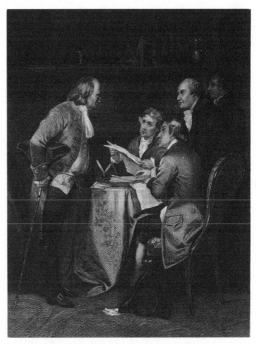

A committee of five was formed to draft the Declaration of Independence; it consisted of Franklin, Jefferson, Adams, Livingston, and Sherman. Engraving after a Chappel painting, 1867.

in the affirmative for independence. The Congress then turned its attention to Jefferson's draft of the Declaration of Independence and, after deleting several passages and phrases, formally adopted it on July 4. A few days later, the Declaration was publicly proclaimed in Philadelphia and New York, and George Washington had it read to the Continental army. During the month of August, 56 members of Congress affixed their signatures to the document.

The Declaration of Independence is divided into several sections. The preamble is the most famous portion of the document, echoing Jefferson's profound belief in the moral correctness of natural rights. "When, in the course of human events," he wrote, "it becomes necessary for one people to dissolve the political bands which have connected them with another, and to assume, among the powers of the earth, the separate and equal station to which the laws of nature and of nature's God entitle them, a decent respect to the opinions of mankind requires that they

A Declaration by the Representatives of the UNITED STATES
OF AMERICA, in General Congress assembled.

When in the course of human events it becomes necessary for one people to
dissolve the political bands which have connected them with another, and to as
-sume among the powers of the earth the separate and equal station to
which the laws of nature & of nature's god entitle them, a decent respect
to the opinions of mankind requires that they should declare the causes
which impel them to the separation.

We hold these truths to be self-evident; that all men are
created equal, that they are endowed by their creator with
inherent & inalienable rights; that among these are
life, & liberty, & the pursuit of happiness; that to secure these rights, go
-vernments are instituted among men, deriving their just powers from
the consent of the governed; that whenever any form of government
becomes destructive of these ends, it is the right of the people to alter
or to abolish it, & to institute new government, laying it's foundation on
such principles & organising it's powers in such form, a to them shall
seem most likely to effect their safety & happiness. prudence indeed
will dictate that governments long established should not be changed for
light & transient causes: and accordingly all experience hath shewn that
mankind are more disposed to suffer while evils are sufferable than to
right themselves by abolishing the forms to which they are accustomed. but
when a long train of abuses & usurpations [begun at a distinguished period
&] pursuing invariably the same object, evinces a design to reduce
them under absolute Despotism, it is their right, it is their duty, to throw off such
government & to provide new guards for their future security. such has
been the patient sufferance of these colonies; & such is now the necessity
which constrains them to expunge their former systems of government.
the history of the present king of Great Britain is a history of [unremitting] injuries and
usurpations, [among which appears no solitary fact to contra-
dict the uniform tenor of the rest [but all have] in direct object the
establishment of an absolute tyranny over these states. to prove this, let facts be
submitted to a candid world, for the truth of which we pledge a faith
yet unsullied by falsehood.]

should declare the causes which impel them to the separation." Jefferson next discussed a long list of charges against King George III concerning the monarch's attempts to subvert the liberty of his subjects in North America. Then follows a summation of the colonies' unsuccessful attempts to secure redress of their grievances and the document concludes with an assertion of independence.

In terms of political principles, Jefferson's Declaration adhered closely to the natural rights perspective that had emerged from the Enlightenment. One of the most powerful advocates of this school was John Locke, a British philosopher who declared that the concept of divine right monarchy was antiquated and inappropriate to the needs of the present day. Only governments that protected property rights and acted in responsible ways toward their citizens, he contended, were legitimate. Influenced by Locke, as well as representatives of the Scottish Enlightenment and republican theorists of classical Rome and Greece, Jefferson wrote from a humanistic perspective rooted in the political culture of the Athenian city-states and western Europe. Thus, Jefferson's Declaration was not original, nor did it contain unique ideas. Rather the document is best viewed as an Anglo-American expression of the progress of liberalism in the late eighteenth century. Jefferson later noted that

> all American Whigs thought alike on these subjects. When forced, therefore, to resort to arms for redress, an appeal to the tribunal of the world was deemed proper for our justification. This was the object of the Declaration of Independence. Not to find out new principles or new arguments never before thought of, not merely to say things which had never been said before; but to place before mankind the common sense of the subject, in terms so plain and firm as to command their assent, and to justify ourselves in the independent stand we

are compelled to take. Neither aiming at originality of principle or sentiment, nor yet copied from any particular and previous writing, it was intended to be an expression of the American mind and to give to that expression the proper tone and spirit called for by the occasion.

See also:
American Revolution
Locke, John
A Summary View of the Rights of British
   America

Reference:
Ellis, Joseph. 1997. *American Sphinx: The Character of Thomas Jefferson.* New York: Oxford University Press.

Deism

*D*eism, or the "cult of reason," was a religious movement that enjoyed a modicum of popularity in the revolutionary era. Rational religion, as practiced by Jefferson as well as other prominent American and French thinkers, was a product of the Enlightenment. This body of thought posited that reason and scientific knowledge, rather than revelation, could serve as a guide to morality and religion. The wellsprings of deism can be found in the cosmology of Newtonian physics as well as the philosophy of John Locke. Both men argued in their work that the universe was a "natural" and therefore understandable entity that operated in an orderly and rational way. They sought to remove the veil of superstition and mysticism that had marred previous attempts to explain man's role in the world. By meshing Christian morality with rational skepticism, members of the revolutionary generation created a worldview that worked for them. As John Adams put it:

> One great advantage of the Christian Religion is that it brings the great

principle of the law of nature and nations, love your neighbor as yourself, and do to others as you would that others should do to you, to the knowledge, belief and veneration of the whole people. Children, servants, women and men are all professors in the science of public as well as private morality. No other institution for education, no kind of political discipline, could diffuse this kind of necessary information, so universally among all ranks and descriptions of citizens. The duties and rights of the man and the citizen are thus taught from early infancy to every creature.

Other Anglo-American thinkers, such as Ethan Allen, Joel Barlow, and Thomas Paine, were more critical of Christianity, attacking the Bible as mere "priestcraft" and calling into question its usefulness in a nation influenced by French liberalism and anticlericalism.

Jefferson was not so radical in his Deism as the brilliantly precocious Paine. His antipathy toward the "formal" church came more from reflection than experience. Jefferson was a rationalist in principle because he was an optimist. He demonstrated throughout his life an appealing faith in the betterment of mankind, a sort of flowering of the human condition brought about by a rational approach to the world. In a perfect society, he reasoned, men would understand that kings were not divine rulers, that God was not judgmental, and that humans could restructure the natural world around them to create a more realistic and vibrant existence.

See also:
Nature
Religion

Reference:
Ahlstrom, Sydney. 1972. *A Religious History of the American People.* New Haven, CT: Yale University Press.

Democratic Societies

*T*he Democratic Societies in America supported the French Revolution, the Republican party, and Thomas Jefferson. Though never a member of any of the 35 societies that were formed in the United States throughout the 1790s, Jefferson sympathized with their efforts to champion liberty and democracy in American life. The first Democratic Society formed in 1793 in Philadelphia, where Jefferson was serving as secretary of state. Its origins were linked to both domestic and foreign concerns, reflecting the influence of the Sons of Liberty, who had opposed colonial rule during the American Revolution, and the Jacobin Clubs of contemporary France, which battled monarchy at home and abroad. With the French Revolution in danger of being destroyed by the other European powers, many Americans believed that republican government was on trial. To serve the cause of liberty, broadly understood as rule by and for the people rather than a monarch, some U.S. citizens joined the pro-French Democratic Societies.

Though the societies professed to be "unbiased by any party views, and actuated solely by patriotic motives," their anti–British stance and democratic ideology attracted very few Federalists. Consequently, the clubs became not simply the promoters of republican values in America, but they also attacked the narrowly elitist Federalist party for its role in raising taxes, sending a federal army to put down a farmers' Whiskey Rebellion in Pennsylvania, and attempting through Alexander Hamilton's financial plans to locate power in the central government. As president, George Washington took these criticisms of his administration personally and chastised the "self-created societies" as clubs "fomented by combinations of men, who, careless of consequences . . . have disseminated . . . suspicions, jealousies, and accusations, of the whole government."

Jefferson, however, believed the societies served a useful purpose and was critical of

Washington's condemnation, calling it regrettable that the president should have permitted himself to be the organ of such an attack on the "freedom of discussion, the freedom of writing and publishing." In sum, Jefferson interpreted criticism of the societies as but one of a series of attacks on freedom that originated from the federal government. To this end he proclaimed that "the denunciation of the Democratic Societies is one of the extraordinary acts of boldness of which we have seen so many from the faction of monocrats." Moreover, he praised the democratic workings of the societies and compared them favorably against the Society of Cincinnati, an organization made up primarily of Federalist military officers and their firstborn sons. To Jefferson, the Democratic Societies represented "the nourishment of the republican principles of our Constitution."

See also:
French Revolution
Whiskey Rebellion

Reference:
Elkins, Stanley, and Erick McKitrick. 1993. *The Age of Federalism: The Early American Republic, 1788–1800.* New York: Oxford University Press.

Diffusion

*P*roponents of the diffusion theory argued that by enlarging the area of slavery, the condition of bondsmen would be uplifted because their labor would be dispersed and thus made more expensive and less efficient. Where slavery was concentrated, on the other hand, labor, and thus life, remained cheap and the condition of slaves would be of little consideration to owners of large plantations. Southerners first voiced the principles of diffusion in 1798 when debating the issue of slavery expansion in the Mississippi Territory. In 1804, President Jefferson appropriated this line of reasoning in his efforts to extend slavery into the recently acquired Louisiana Territory. Jefferson argued that by allowing slavery to push west, a safety valve would be opened for the South that would release surplus concentrations of slaves into the American interior.

Early in his public career, Jefferson sought an end to slavery in Virginia. In later years, he latched on to the principle of diffusion as a possible, though slow, form of emancipation. He reasoned that slavery would be weakened and thus ultimately extinguished if allowed to expand across American territory. If slaves were dispersed, the number of small slaveholders would increase, the number of large slaveholders would decline, large concentrations of slaves would disappear, and slaves' conditions would improve. Over time, he concluded, the institution of slavery would merge with the dominant free-labor system around it. If Jefferson's belief that slavery would be weakened by expansion seems paradoxical, consider the case of Virginia. In the Old Dominion, Jefferson was witness to the process by which the abolition of primogeniture and entail, that is, the practice of leaving property to eldest sons, broke up and dispersed large slaveholdings among several dependents.

Yet in practical terms, diffusion held little hope for the amelioration of slavery. Moreover, there is no evidence that small slaveholders would emancipate their "property" any more willingly than plantation owners. And even if diffusion did serve to lessen the plight of slaves and eventually bring about their freedom, it could not compel whites to accept blacks on an equal social, economic, or political basis. That is, diffusion did not and perhaps could not address the issue of racism. Finally, Jefferson accepted diffusionism probably because of his faith in the inherent goodness of mankind. Just as he believed that independent small-scale farmers made the best republicans, he believed that this same class would ultimately recognize that for moral, economic, and patriotic reasons, the institution of slavery must end. Broadly speaking, the opening of the national domain to slavery throughout the antebellum period did not serve to extend slavery since few plantations actually uprooted and traveled west. But it did leave the South in control of the national government, from which it promoted a pro-southern agenda that antagonized the North and helped precipitate war in 1861.

See also:
Slave Trade
Slavery

Reference:
Miller, John. 1977. *The Wolf by the Ears: Thomas Jefferson and Slavery.* Charlottesville: University Press of Virginia.

District of Columbia

*L*ike many Americans, Jefferson envisioned the United States as the ideological heir to Athenian democracy. In support of this vision, the Founders sought to create a democratic culture that would link the sister republics together. Foremost in this line of thinking was the need to establish a federal city that would represent, through its architectural design, the simplicity and nobility that characterized republican life. Jefferson's interest in the development of the national capital was understandable. In 1777 the Virginian sponsored a removal bill to have

Pierre L'Enfant's map of the city of Washington, District of Columbia, engraved by Ellicott in 1792.

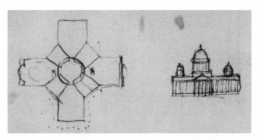

Ink drawing of the design of the Capitol by Jefferson, 1792. The architectural suggestion is taken from the Pantheon in Paris, subdivided in plan to give rooms to the Senate, House, and Conference, as well as a monumental rotunda and vestibule.

the state capital at Williamsburg transferred to Richmond. The classical motif used in the Old Dominion's new capital was based on the Roman Maison Carrée at Nimes and built from a design that Jefferson had prepared.

The nation's capital could not be built, however, until a permanent site was located. The original capital, New York City, was a choice of compromise and convenience, but it engendered hostility among southerners who wished to see the nation's seat of power located in their own region. A deal of sorts was worked out in 1790 when, in return for southern support on a financial bill that aided northern interests, the nation's capital was to be removed to Philadelphia for ten years, and from there to a permanent southern location. Jefferson recorded that "it was observed . . . that as the pill [financial legislation] would be a bitter one to the Southern states, something should be done to soothe them; that the removal of the seat of government to the Patowmac was a just measure, and would probably be a popular one with them."

With the compromise in tow, Jefferson and others began to submit designs for the new capital. The plans chosen were not Jefferson's, however, but those of Major Pierre Charles L'Enfant, a French engineer. Despite the Founders' desire for democratic simplicity, L'Enfant's design resembled the French palace at Versailles, where he spent his early years. Due to various difficulties, L'Enfant's plans were not completed until the twentieth century. Nevertheless, the capital city did bring Jefferson much joy. He was the first chief executive to spend his entire presidency in Washington, D.C., and he believed that the capital's southern location would serve to enhance Virginia's interests. He also held lofty hopes that the nation's capital would become the center of art, culture, and education in the United States. He hoped, for example, that a national university might be constructed and that the faculty of the University of Geneva might be induced to come to the banks of the Potomac and offer instruction. Though nothing came of such plans, the capital did assume many of the features that Jefferson appreciated. Classical designs exemplified the nation's republican heritage, while debate of public questions in a region dominated by the institution of slavery could not help but make members of Congress aware of the sensitive issues that literally surrounded them.

See also:
Assumption

Reference:
Lewis, David. 1976. *District of Columbia: A Bicentennial History*. New York: W. W. Norton.

E

Economic Nationalism

During the period 1815–1824, America began to move rapidly beyond the Jeffersonian ideal of a localist agrarian republic toward a more centralized and industrial vision. Jefferson was in retirement during these years and gave his cautious approval to this unremitting process because the Republican party, which he and James Madison organized in the 1790s, was the dominant political entity in the nation. Jefferson seemed to believe that as long as "Jeffersonians" were in power, the changing economic and social landscape could be fitted to Republican ends. In this faith, he could not have been more in error.

The push toward economic nationalism, that is, using the federal government to enhance the productive powers of the economy, came about following the United States' near-disastrous military effort in the War of 1812. Though the country was not defeated, and indeed in many quarters claimed victory, it was apparent to the national government in Washington, a city put to the torch by the British, that a small, decentralized nation could not effectively protect itself against the emerging industrial powers of Europe. Rather, for America to compete on the world stage as a nation that commanded respect, the country's defenses, economy, and productivity would have to be increased. Toward this goal Jeffersonian Republicans such as Madi-

son and James Monroe began to champion the kinds of governmental activism that they had repudiated in the 1790s.

Principally, Republicans were interested in shoring up the nation's economy. In 1816 the government enacted the country's first protective tariff. Though the Constitution gave Congress no direct power to do so, the war scare was enough to induce the Jeffersonians into taking nationalistic measures. The tariff promoted northern industry by raising the prices of manufactured items coming from Europe and the British Isles. The effect of the tariff was to make American products cheaper and thus more attractive to the home market. That same year, Congress created the Second National Bank of the United States, which served to provide capital and credit to states, corporations, or individuals for purposes of internal improvements, that is, the construction of roads, bridges, canals, and so on. Again, the Constitution did not specifically give Congress the power to create such an institution, and when the Federalists organized the "first" National Bank in the 1790s, Republicans denounced it as unconstitutional and presided over its demise in 1811. The experience of war, however, demonstrated to Republicans, including Jefferson, that the nation required a centralized banking structure. Without it, the country's infrastructure would remain primitive.

Economic nationalism was also evident in the federal judiciary in various court cases that allowed for an increase of national power over local prerogatives. In *McCullogh v. Maryland* (1819), for example, the Supreme Court confirmed the implied powers of Congress by concluding that the national banking system, a product of the "necessary and proper" clause, was constitutional and that states could not ban or tax federal banks within their borders, even when these banks competed against them. In the case of *Gibbons v. Ogden* (1824), the Court declared that the power of Congress to regulate interstate commerce superseded any claims that states might have to do the same. Such decisions not only established the primacy of the federal government over the states in promoting or regulating economic development, but they also protected corporations from local interference.

Finally, economic nationalism in the postwar period affected foreign policy. With Jefferson's blessing, both Madison and Monroe pushed hard to induce Spain to sell the Floridas to the United States. The Adams-Onis Treaty of 1824 accomplished this goal and also gave to America a vast empire in the Pacific Northwest. It seemed to many Republican purists, however, that the party had succumbed to the temptations of power and empire building. Perhaps, to a degree, it had. More to the point, however, Jefferson and his followers were generally comfortable with economic and territorial expansion as long as it was conducted by their party rather than the Federalist opposition. In the wake of the War of 1812, Federalism was extinguished as a political force and the Jeffersonians held the field. Moreover, if the Jeffersonians used the nationalistic impulses engendered by the war to further their own political goals, it should also be remembered that they, too, were caught up in the moment, and many of their accomplishments, including the tariff and the National Bank, would be repudiated by a second generation of "Jeffersonians" in the 1830s.

See also:
National Bank
War of 1812

Reference:
Dangerfield, George. 1952. *The Era of Good Feelings.* New York: Harcourt, Brace & World.

Election of 1792

Near the end of his first term as president, George Washington strongly considered retiring from public service. By 1792 the 60-year-old general was tired of the acrimony that existed in his cabinet between Jefferson, who favored a weak federal government, and Alexander Hamilton, who wanted a powerful national government. Moreover, after a distinguished career spent largely apart from loved ones, Washington longed to retreat to his home and family at Mount Vernon. He went so far as to have James Madison draft a farewell message that he expected to be his final public pronouncement. As the year wore on, however, Washington was increasingly besieged by pleas that he serve another term.

No one was more supportive of this proposition than Jefferson, who believed that little stood between the Federalist party's accession to power besides Washington. Indeed, many in the Republican fold wanted Washington to serve as a check on Hamilton who, they believed, sought to destroy constitutional limitations and alter the existing republican form of government into a monarchy. Hamilton also wanted the president to stand for a second term, reasoning that Washington's support for the National Bank predisposed him to a nationalist rather than localist perspective. In sum, both Hamilton and Jefferson believed that Washington was above party politics and thought his successful candidacy was necessary to calm the inflamed passions of Federalists and Republicans alike.

Deciding that the needs of the country outweighed any personal considerations, Washington announced a month prior to the contest that he would be a candidate for reelection. Washington's popularity ensured that he would be unopposed for the executive

George Washington and his cabinet. From left to right: Washington; General Henry Knox, secretary of war; Alexander Hamilton, secretary of the treasury; Thomas Jefferson, secretary of state; and Edmund Randolph, attorney general.

office. There was significant maneuvering, however, over the position of vice president. Factions in New York and Virginia believed that the incumbent, John Adams, was a monarchist and wanted to make Jefferson a candidate. Jefferson was not interested in the position, however, and was still performing valuable service in Washington's cabinet as secretary of state. The Republican party then turned to New York governor George Clinton, who accepted the coalition's invitation to challenge Adams. Throughout the fall and early winter, election returns trickled in to the capital at Philadelphia. For the office of chief executive there was never a doubt: Washington, as he had in 1788, captured every available electoral vote and is to this day the only president to do so.

The contest for the vice presidency was much more interesting. Clinton won 50 electoral votes in the Republican-controlled states of New York, North Carolina, Geor-

gia, and Jefferson's Virginia. Though Adams was reelected by winning 77 electoral votes, the close contest underlined the fact that the infant Republican coalition was emerging as a real political power. As if to accentuate this point, Republicans also did well in the congressional races that year. Pleased with the outcome, Jefferson believed that the results were "generally in favor of republican and against aristocratical candidates." The election of 1792 was the first to be contested along party lines and demonstrated the ability of the Jeffersonians to win votes on a national scale. Such positive results went a long way in convincing Jefferson to make his first of three presidential bids just four years later.

See also:
Election of 1796
Washington, George

Reference:
John C. Miller. 1960. *The Federalist Era*. New York: Harper & Row.

Election of 1796

On December 31, 1793, Jefferson quit his post at the State Department and returned home to Virginia. At the time he believed his political career was over and looked forward to retirement at Monticello. Over the next three years, however, the behavior of the Federalist party convinced Jefferson that republicanism was in danger and forced him to reevaluate his decision to leave public life. In 1794, Federalists sent an army to Pennsylvania to put down a small tax revolt by local farmers. In 1795, that same party concluded a treaty with Great Britain that many Americans believed infringed upon the nation's sovereignty. In retaliation, Democratic-Republican Societies around the country began to coalesce, supporting the Jeffersonians as the party of liberty while denouncing the Federalists as the party of tyranny. These societies wanted Jefferson to run for president in 1796 and formed a strong, if infant, party coalition. Early that same year, George Washington made it known to associates that he would not run for a third term, and the way was now clear for Jefferson to become a candidate.

Jefferson was not the only man who coveted the office, however. Vice President John Adams desired the position as well. The antagonism between the Jeffersonian Republicans, who wanted to limit the power of the central government, and the Federalists, who wanted to expand that power, ensured that the election would be the first party contest for the presidency. Acceding to the acceptable tenets of early American campaigning, both Jefferson and Adams were largely inactive, deeming it improper to seek office. Newspapers largely carried the attack against the opposition. Nevertheless, the campaign was hard-fought, and the only real issue was the candidates themselves. The Republicans called Jefferson a "steadfast friend for the rights of the people" while charging that Adams was an "advocate of hereditary power." For their part, the Federalists claimed that while Jefferson "possessed much knowledge," it was "chiefly . . . of the scientific kind, the least useful for a statesman; whose business it is to judge an act, not to write books." In other words, the Federalists saw Jefferson as a visionary and a theorist. Perhaps he would make a good professor, but certainly not a good president.

Election procedures in the states were not uniform in 1796, and it was not until December that the candidates could get a clear idea of how the contest was shaping up. One thing was certain: the election would be close. There was even talk of a tie. Jefferson wrote to Madison that in such a scenario, Adams should get the prize since, as he put it, "he has always been my senior." When the final results were tabulated, however, Adams won outright, taking 71 electoral votes to Jefferson's 68, with other ballots scattered among several candidates. Adams won his home province of New England as well as New York, New Jersey, Delaware, and a majority of the districts of Maryland. Jefferson swept most of the South and captured a majority of electoral votes in Pennsylvania. The Constitution did not provide for separate balloting for the presidency and vice presidency at this time, and thus Jefferson, by virtue of his second-place finish, became the vice president. Though he was now serving a Federalist, Jefferson vowed to work with Adams, noting that "Mr. Adams speaks of me with great friendship, and with satisfaction in the prospect of administering the government in concurrence with me." In March 1797, after a retirement of three years, Jefferson returned to Philadelphia as both vice president of the nation and leader of the Republican party.

See also:
Adams, John
Democratic Societies
Hamilton, Alexander

Reference:
Malone, Dumas. 1948–1981. *Jefferson and the Ordeal of Liberty,* vol. 3, *The Sage of Monticello.* 6 vols. Boston: Little, Brown.

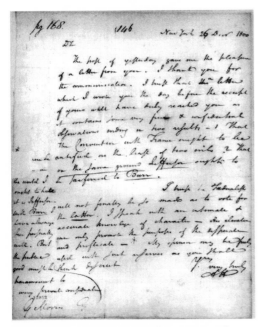

Print of a letter in which Hamilton recommends Jefferson over Burr in the presidential election tie.

Election of 1800

Jefferson and Aaron Burr tied for the presidency in 1800 by defeating their Federalist opponent, President John Adams. Through error, the two Republican candidates both received 73 electoral votes. Though all Republicans understood that Jefferson was the true party choice for the presidency, Burr campaigned behind the scenes for Federalist support in the House of Representatives in the hope that he could leapfrog over Jefferson and become president. This strategy failed, and for his efforts Burr earned the lasting enmity of the Republican party. Jefferson called the election the "Revolution of 1800," because the Federalist party, which had dominated national politics since the early 1790s, was now removed from power, their place taken by "Jeffersonian-Republicans." Incidentally, though Jefferson saw the election as a repudiation of Federalism, had it not been for the three-fifths compromise of the Constitution, which awarded the South extra representation and thus electoral votes

for slaves, Jefferson would never have been elected president.

See also:
Adams, John
Revolution of 1800

Reference:
Peterson, Merrill. 1970. *Thomas Jefferson and the New Nation.* New York: Oxford University Press.

Election of 1804

It had been Jefferson's hope to retire from the presidency after one term in office. However, he cited public attacks by the Federalists upon his conduct as the reason he sought reelection. "The unbounded calumnies of the federal party," he contended, "have obliged me to throw myself on the verdict of my country for trial." It should also be noted, however, that Jefferson was deeply in debt and in need of the salary he would draw as chief executive.

Republicans were delighted with their leader's decision, knowing that he was an unbeatable candidate. One hundred and eight Republican members of Congress met in a nominating caucus in 1804 and unanimously renominated Jefferson. The only drama was the caucus's decision to drop Aaron Burr, the incumbent vice president, from the ticket. Burr's behavior in the election of 1800, when he challenged Jefferson for the presidency, had not been forgotten by his party, and political banishment was his reward. In his place, the Republicans nominated George Clinton for the party's second slot. Clinton was the ideal choice; he was from New York, which sectionally balanced the ticket, and at age 67, was not likely to challenge James Madison for the Republican nomination in 1808.

For reelection, Jefferson had little more to do than stand on his record. By cutting taxes, shrinking government, and purchasing the Louisiana Territory, the Virginian had made himself an invincible candidate. Early in the year, Jefferson predicted he would win every state in the Union but four. The actual results eclipsed even his most optimistic hopes. Jefferson carried all but two states and defeated his Federalist opponent, Charles Cotesworth Pinckney, in the electoral college, 162 votes to 14 votes. The Federalists managed to win only Connecticut and Delaware and a minority of Maryland's electoral votes. Jefferson won 17 states and cracked wide open for the Republicans the hitherto solidly Federalist states of New England. On the defection of Massachusetts from the ranks of Federalism, Jefferson remarked that "this is truly the case wherein we may say, 'this our brother was dead, and is alive again: and was lost, and is found.'"

See also:
Burr, Aaron
Election of 1800
Election of 1808

Reference:
Malone, Dumas. 1948–1981. *Jefferson the President, First Term, 1801–1805,* vol. 4 of *Jefferson and His Time.* Boston: Little, Brown.

Bust of Thomas Jefferson by Houden, probably during his presidency.

Election of 1808

*T*he election of 1808 effectively ended Jefferson's 40 years of public service. Like Washington, Jefferson chose not to seek a third presidential term, even though it was easily within his grasp. Instead, he promoted the candidacy of his neighbor and political ally, James Madison. Due to Madison's impeccable ties to the Republican party, as well as his friendship with Jefferson, he easily carried the election, defeating his Federalist opponent, Charles Cotesworth Pinckney, by the imposing tally of 122 electoral votes to 47.

Jefferson's only regret was that he did not leave his successor in a more stable position. The election of 1808 took place amidst American complaints that Great Britain and France were illegally confiscating American ships and cargoes in the Atlantic. Jefferson responded by prohibiting American goods from leaving the country, in hopes that by starving the European economy of American products, the major Continental powers would accept the U.S. definition of neutral trade. Unfortunately for Jefferson and the Republican party, the resulting "embargo" was a miserable failure. As Madison took power in March 1809, he was forced to wrestle with an international problem that threatened to wreck the nation and its economy. Though disappointed at leaving this legacy, Jefferson nevertheless exulted at his own freedom:

> Never did a prisoner released from his chains feel such relief as I shall on shaking off the shackles of power. Nature intended me for the tranquil pursuits of science, by rendering them my supreme delight. But the enormities of the times in which I have lived have forced me to take a part in resisting them, and to commit myself on the boisterous ocean of political passions. I thank God for the opportunity of retiring from them without censure, and carrying with me the most consoling proofs of public

approbation. I leave everything in the hands of men so able to take care of them that if we are destined to meet misfortunes it will be because no human wisdom could avert them.

Thanks to the Republican victory in 1808, Jefferson did enter into a pleasing retirement, though it would not be as uneventful, nor would he be as disinterested in public affairs, as he anticipated.

See also:
Embargo of 1807
Madison, James
Retirement

Reference:
Rutland, Robert. 1990. *The Presidency of James Madison.* Lawrence: University Press of Kansas.

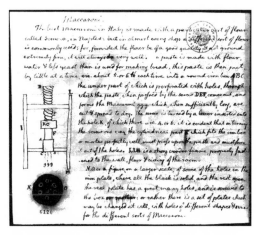

After choosing not to run again, Jefferson was left to develop more of his inventions, including this design for a macaroni machine accompanied by a recipe.

Election of 1812

The election of 1812 was the most closely contest campaign for the presidency since 1800, when Jefferson and Aaron Burr tied in the electoral college.

During his own presidency, Jefferson firmly established Republican party rule as a fixture in American politics. The importance of Jefferson's legacy became evident in 1808 when his successor, James Madison, easily captured the presidency. By 1812, however, the nation had drifted to war with Great Britain, largely because of the failings of Republican foreign policy as practiced by both Jefferson and Madison. For a period of time in 1812, it seemed possible that the Federalist party, which had not won a presidential election since 1796, might come back into power and challenge the tenets of "Jeffersonianism," that is, rule by southerners who wanted to promote agrarianism over industrialism. The Jeffersonians, however, were able to rally around Madison in 1812, and the president managed to defeat his Federalist foe, DeWitt Clinton, by 128 electoral votes to his opponent's 89. Clinton's tally,

however, was the highest ever achieved by a Federalist and demonstrated cracks in the Republican machine. Even so, Madison's victory ensured that Republican control of the national government would last for at least four more years, providing the party with time to solidify its control over national affairs and pursue a war against Great Britain.

See also:
Madison, James
War of 1812

Reference:
Brown, Roger. 1964. *The Republic in Peril: 1812.* New York: Columbia University Press.

Election of 1816

The presidential election of 1816 found Jefferson in a mood of contentment. The War of 1812 had been recently concluded, with Napoleon banished from Europe. The removal of the French general from power signified the end of the wars of the French Revolution, which meant a return to peaceful commercial relations among the United States, western Europe, and the British Isles. Moreover, James Monroe, the Republican candidate for the executive office in 1816, was a staunch Jeffersonian. The Master of Monticello could count on him to ably succeed James Madison and continue the "Virginia Dynasty." Monroe's opponent in the election, Rufus King, was a New York Federalist who hoped to appeal to northern voters wary of continued presidential rule by southerners. King's hopes were not to be realized, however. Monroe won an overwhelming victory in the electoral college, taking 183 of the possible 217 ballots cast.

The election of 1816 also signified the end of the Federalist party in American politics. Throughout the 1790s, Federalism had dominated the national government, but the party became increasingly unpopular due to its efforts to centralize power to a degree that most Americans could not abide. Jefferson's victory in 1800 took the presidency away from the Federalists, but the party lingered on, recouping some of its lost popularity during the War of 1812. By 1816, however, Federalism had run out of political capital and would never again contend for national office. Jefferson praised Monroe's victory, describing it as an efficient "circumstance in our felicities," and further noted that "four and twenty years, which [Monroe] will accomplish, of administration in Republican forms and principles will so consecrate them in the eyes of the people as to secure them against the danger of change. The evanition of party dissensions has harmonized intercourse and sweetened society beyond imagination."

See also:
Era of Good Feelings
Monroe, James
Virginia Dynasty

Reference:
George Dangerfield. 1965. *The Awakening of American Nationalism, 1815–1828*. New York: Harper & Row.

Election of 1820

The presidential election of 1820 was one of the quietest in the nation's history. From his retirement in Monticello, Jef-

ferson must have been pleased that James Monroe, the current Republican president and candidate, was running unopposed for reelection. The War of 1812 had culminated in the demise of the Federalist party and ushered in what some contemporaries called the "Era of Good Feelings." Moreover, Jefferson's support for Monroe was based on a shared ideological perspective. The two men were both thoroughgoing Republicans who championed agrarianism and kept a wary eye on government involvement in the economy. Both Jefferson and Monroe promoted a states' rights philosophy that culminated in increased power for the southern half of the nation. Finally, both statesmen were Virginians and slaveholders, which meant, to Jefferson and many other southerners, that Monroe was "safe" on the issue of slavery. Without opposition, Monroe swept the electoral college, taking 231 out of a possible 232 votes cast. One elector, deciding that only the great George Washington should enjoy a unanimous victory, cast a ballot for John Quincy Adams. Monroe's election signaled the continued leadership of the Virginia Dynasty along good Jeffersonian—that is, southern—principles.

See also:
Monroe, James
Virginia Dynasty

Reference:
Ammon, Harry. 1972. *James Monroe: The Quest for National Identity*. New York: McGraw-Hill.

Election of 1824

The election of 1824 was the last election Jefferson would live to see and one of the most vital in the nation's history. For 24 years, from 1800 to 1824, the Virginia Dynasty of Jefferson, James Madison, and James Monroe had led the nation along the principles of agrarian republicanism. In 1824, however, there was no obvious successor to the Virginians. Without a dominant candidate, regionalism had taken over, and each quarter of the nation offered up its favorite native son. The most serious candidates were John Quincy Adams from Massachusetts, William Crawford from Georgia, Henry Clay from Kentucky, and Andrew Jackson from Tennessee. Jefferson's preference was for Crawford who, of all the candidates, seemed to represent most closely a continuation of the Virginia presidents. Crawford promoted states' rights and a strict interpretation of the Constitution. Moreover, he was a slaveholder who understood the anxiety and fears of southerners on this touchy subject. Jefferson's second choice was Quincy Adams, who had been effective in Monroe's cabinet as secretary of state.

The large number of candidates, combined with their various sectional strengths and weaknesses, ensured that no one would receive a majority in the electoral college. When the final votes were tabulated, Jackson emerged as the leader with 99 electoral votes. Adams was next with 84 votes, followed by Crawford with 41 and Clay with 37. The Constitution stipulates that when there is no majority in the popular election, the president is chosen by the House of Representatives, with each state receiving one vote. Only the top three candidates would be considered; thus Clay was no longer in contention. Because Crawford had suffered a stroke and was partially paralyzed, the real contest came down to Jackson and Adams. On the surface, it appeared that Jefferson might prefer a Jackson presidency because the two men shared a few similarities. Both were southern slaveholders and had an abiding faith in agrarian democracy over a more industrial state. Adams, on the other hand, promoted national strength through a centralized government predicated on the expansion of federal power. Yet Jefferson opposed Jackson's candidacy. To colleagues who visited him at Monticello, Jefferson stated that

I feel much alarmed at the prospect of seeing General Jackson President, he is one of the most unfit men, I know of for such a place. He has had very little respect for laws or constitutions,—& is in fact merely an able military chief. His passions are terrible. When I was President of the Senate, he was a Senator, & he could never speak from the rashness of his feelings. I have seen him attempt it repeatedly, & as often choke with rage. His passions are no doubt cooler now;—he has been much tried since I knew him—but he is a dangerous man.

Jefferson preferred Adams over Jackson because he believed the former to be more representative of the kind of cultural values he felt aligned with. Jefferson and Adams lived their lives like eighteenth-century court aristocrats. Jackson, on the other hand, represented the rising democratic ethos of the nineteenth century. Adams, like Jefferson, was a representative of the East Coast ruling class, while Jackson represented a new western democratic movement that was more aggressive than Jefferson was comfortable with. Adams, however, represented the kind of educated leadership he thought essential in a republic.

To Jefferson, Jackson was little more than a "military chief" who had little use for the higher values of reflection and patience. In the House, many Republicans seemed to agree with Jefferson's view of Jackson: they chose Adams as the nation's sixth president. Jackson would, of course, eventually serve two terms as president, calling himself a follower of Jefferson. However, the Virginian would not live long enough to see the tenets of "Jeffersonian democracy" linked to "Jacksonian democracy."

See also:
Adams, John Quincy
Jackson, Andrew

Reference:
Malone, Dumas. 1981. *Jefferson and His Times: The Sage of Monticello*. Boston, MA: Little, Brown.

Embargo of 1807

Jefferson's most difficult task as president was finding a suitable reply to the violations of American neutral rights by Great Britain and France. With the Napoleonic wars diverting Europe's attention, the United States made tremendous profits serving as a neutral shipping carrier for the combatants. By 1805, however, both France and England began to confiscate American ships that were headed to the ports of their enemies. These actions were a clear violation of the rights of a neutral nation to transport commerce around the globe, contradicting the tradition that "free ships" made "free goods." After various diplomatic efforts failed, Jefferson proposed to his cabinet in December 1807 that an embargo be employed against Europe. That is, American goods would not be sent abroad, and the resulting deprivation would cause the people of Europe to force their leaders to pursue a more peaceful relationship with the United States.

In the days that followed, Jefferson's proposal was accepted, though not without opposition in both houses of Congress. The Senate passed a bill for a general embargo by a vote of 22 to 6, while the House passed the measure by a vote of 82 to 44. By his own count, Jefferson estimated that half the opposition came from the Federalist party, one-fourth from dissident Republicans, and only one-fourth from "true" Republicans. In private correspondence, Jefferson described the justification for the embargo as self-preservation as well as self-defense.

> The embargo keeping at home our vessels, cargoes, and seamen saves us the necessity of making their capture the cause of immediate war; for, if going to England, France had determined to take them, if to any other place, England was to take them. Till they return to some sense of moral duty, therefore, we keep within

ourselves. This gives time. Time may produce peace in Europe; peace in Europe removes all causes of difference, till another European war; and by that time our debt may be paid, our revenues clear, and our strength increased.

Thus, the embargo represented to Jefferson not merely an attempt to coerce the Old World into abiding by the principles of the New World through economic means, but, in more practical terms, it seemed to offer the infant United States a very precious commodity: time. America needed breathing space, following the tumult of the Revolution and the formation of a constitutional republic, to develop into a respectable power. In many ways, Jefferson believed that the embargo of 1807 promised the nation a season of peace during which its power would grow and eventually make it impervious to European aggression.

Though the embargo began with favorable public support, it quickly became unpopular once Americans realized that the consequence was a significant downturn in the economy. Smuggling along the borders of Canada and Florida, along with coastal trading, badly damaged Jefferson's embargo as well as the Virginian's belief that the public would place duty over self-interest. In April 1808 the Enforcement Act proclaimed the Canada–New York border in insurrection and invoked civil officers to eradicate illegal trade. Rivers, estuaries, and other outlets were likewise patrolled more vigorously by the government, but without positive effect. The nation was simply too large and the coercive powers of the federal government too weak to force Americans to abide by an unpopular government edict.

Smuggling was particularly aggressive in New England, which had enjoyed close economic relations with England for two centuries. Moreover, New England was the stronghold of the Federalist party, Jefferson's chief opposition, and the Virginian believed that pro-British Federalists sought to undermine the embargo and thus destroy his presidency. "They are now playing a game of the most mischievous tendency, without perhaps being themselves aware of it," he complained. "They are endeavoring to convince England that we suffer more by the embargo than they do, and if they will but hold out awhile, we must abandon it. It is true that time will come when we must abandon it. But if this is before the repeal of the orders of council [British laws that violate American neutrality], we must abandon it only for a state of war. . . . If we have war with England, it will be solely produced by their maneuvers." The infractions of the embargo from Maine to Massachusetts by the Tory party caused Jefferson much discomfort, but aside from largely private condemnations, there was little he could do.

The failure of the embargo was fully evident to Jefferson toward the end of his presidency. Not wishing to impose a botched policy on his handpicked successor, James Madison, Jefferson ended the embargo in March 1809, just days prior to his retirement from office. Fourteen months of embargo had produced little more than discord throughout the country and brought the nation no closer to peace with Europe than it had been in 1807.

Viewed from a broader perspective, Jefferson's embargo reflected the Republican party's disdain for both war and cooperative negotiations. The problem was not simply that the Jeffersonians pursued peace, but they did so with the understanding that the terms of peace would suit them fully. In the 1790s, the Federalist party had concluded a treaty with Great Britain that was pro-British but ensured a generation of peace between the two nations. Republicans, on the other hand, liked to contend that they operated from higher principles and believed that America's moral superiority would ensure its success in foreign relations. The result of such thinking was not merely a disastrous embargo but

ultimately the War of 1812, fought under a Jeffersonian government. In sum, the embargo was a reflection of Jefferson's foreign policy: it was predicated on an optimistic and abstract faith in public virtue rather than on the realities of position and power.

See also:
Macon's Bill Number Two
Non-Intercourse Act
War of 1812

Reference:
Smelser, Marshall. 1968. *The Democratic Republic, 1801–1815.* New York: Harper & Row.

Empire of Liberty

Jefferson firmly believed that the United States was destined to lead the world toward a more democratic age, a rehabilitation, in a sense, of the virtues of antiquity, embellished in the New World. America would thus become the chief medium from which an "empire of liberty" would expand throughout the Western Hemisphere. The implications were staggering, if not revolutionary.

Traditionally, the concept of "empire" denoted a mother country exercising power and

Jefferson's stamp bears the inscription "Rebellion to tyrants is obedience to God."

coercion over colonies. By its nature, this system promoted inequality between rulers and ruled in social, economic, and cultural relations. To Jefferson, it invariably led, be it in months, years, or centuries, to dissension and revolution. Jefferson needed to look no further than his own life for proof of this scenario, for he was a leader of one of the greatest colonial rebellions in history.

In contrast to empires built on coercion, Jefferson believed that freedom could be the guiding principle for territorial expansion in the Americas. As president, his most successful political action was the purchase of the Louisiana Territory. Though Jefferson was obviously pleased with the addition of more acreage to the Union, he was more impressed with what the land symbolized: the opportunity for America's republican institutions to spread across the continent. In service to this goal, Jefferson could be quite belligerent in his foreign policy. He pushed very hard, for example, to acquire the Floridas and Cuba. During the War of 1812 he urged the American government to wrest Canada from the British Crown and give it a tutorial in democratic principles. Toward the end of his life, Jefferson advised President James Monroe to declare the Americas free from future European colonization, remarking that "America, North and South, has a set of interests distinct from those of Europe. . . . While the last is laboring to become the domicile of despotism, our endeavor should surely be, to make our hemisphere that of freedom."

In sum, Jefferson was a missionary for republicanism. The French Revolution taught him that America's democratic germ was capable of crossing oceans, and he was eager that the impetus toward liberal change not be checked by reactionary powers. As one of Jefferson's contemporaries noted: "All the doors and windows of the temple of nature have been thrown open, by the convulsions of the late American Revolution. This is the time, therefore, to press upon her altars." And

press Jefferson did, promoting a new kind of empire based upon expansionist tendencies. The irony is that much of Jefferson's empire of liberty became an empire of slavery. The southern portion of the Louisiana Purchase and Texas laid the foundations for a new cotton frontier in which not free whites but enslaved African-Americans were spread across the landscape. Moreover, the western territories Jefferson hoped would nurture peaceful republican institutions were already peopled by thousands of Native Americans who were at various times displaced or dispatched in order to get their land.

See also:
Monroe Doctrine

Reference:
Tucker, Robert, and David Hendrickson. 1990. *Empire of Liberty: The Statecraft of Thomas Jefferson*. New York: Oxford University Press.

Enlightenment

Jefferson and Benjamin Franklin were the preeminent American spokesmen for the European-based intellectual movement known as the Enlightenment. In brief, Enlightenment or Age of Reason thinking posited that at their best, humans are reasonable organisms who, through observation and experimentation, can understand the world. Proof was evident in the seemingly mechanical and orderly nature of the physical environment as reflected in the mathematics of René Descartes and in the physics of Sir Isaac Newton. In sum, the intellectual leaders of eighteenth-century Europe advocated a more rational and less mystical approach to understanding the world. To Jefferson, Enlightenment thinking promised a world free of the more debilitating influence of the clergy and the monarchy.

Though Jefferson was introduced to his own holy trinity of Isaac Newton, John

Locke, and Francis Bacon while studying at the College of William and Mary, it was not until he traveled to Paris in the 1780s that he became fully steeped in the tenets of Enlightenment thought. From his readings of Linnaeus and Buffon, Jefferson gravitated to the principle that man is in harmony with the natural world and, through dispassionate, empirical study, can understand the inner workings of his environment. This sort of "playing God" appealed to Jefferson, who appreciated the secularism inherent in the Enlightenment. Jefferson's own experiments, which included such activities as taking the measurements of grass, testify to his optimistic faith that the world could literally be taken apart, put under a magnifying glass, analyzed, and understood.

Politically, the Enlightenment promoted liberalism with its roots firmly embedded in English law and government. During the Revolution, Jefferson had no further to go to justify America's break with the mother country than the writings of England's great political theorists, John Locke and Viscount Bolingbroke. From these men Jefferson understood that the divine rule of kings was a superstition implemented to overawe an unsophisticated peasantry.

With the proliferation of literacy and education, however, thinking people understood that monarchy was in place to serve citizens rather than to overwhelm them. Locke, and later Jefferson, argued that if a king forgot this, overstepped his bounds, and behaved tyrannically toward his people, then the people were justified in overthrowing him. Thus Enlightenment thinking served Jefferson in rationalizing America's break with Great Britain.

See also:
Locke, John
Nature

Reference:
Gay, Peter. 1966–1969. *The Enlightenment, an Interpretation.* 2 vols. New York: Alfred A. Knopf.

Environmental Degeneracy

*J*efferson believed that the American environment produced a beneficial climate that would foster human equality through agricultural surpluses and territorial expansion. He promoted a kind of environmental nationalism that countered European perceptions that the New World was inferior to the Old.

The French philosopher Montesquieu wrote that the environment imposed a hierarchy upon mankind that favored Europe: "People are . . . more vigorous in cold climates. This superiority of strength must produce various effects [such as] a greater boldness . . . more courage . . . more frankness, less suspicion, policy, and cunning." Montesquieu's logic implied that since the Creator had made the warm as well as the cold regions of the earth, inequality was intentional and had existed from the beginning of time. Similarly, the French naturalist Count de Buffon argued that animals in the Americas were generally smaller and weaker than their European counterparts and thus inferior. The environment in America, he explained, was too warm to allow for the kinds of vigorous species that existed throughout Europe. Thus the Creator had designed Europe to be superior to the Americas, and those Europeans who migrated to the New World, as Jefferson's family had, were unwittingly conditioning themselves to a lower standard.

The final indignity to American sensibilities was when the Abbé Raynal predicted that Europeans who transplanted themselves to the inferior climate of America would eventually lack genius as well as vigor. One reply came from Benjamin Franklin in an amusing story related by Jefferson.

The Doctor [Franklin] . . . had a party to dine . . . one day at Passy, of whome one half were Americans, the other half French, and among the last was the Abbé [Raynal]. During the dinner he got on his favorite theory of the degeneracy of animals, and even of man, in America, and urged it with his usual eloquence. The Doctor at length noticing the accidental stature and position of his guest, at table, "Come," says he, "M. l'Abbé, let us try this question by the fact before us. We are here one half Americans, and one half French, and it happens that the Americans have placed themselves on one side of the table, and our French friends are on the other. Let both parties rise, and we will see on which side nature has degenerated." It happened that his American guests were . . . of the finest stature and form; while those of the other side were remarkably diminutive, and the Abbé himself particularly, was a mere shrimp.

For his part, Jefferson acknowledged that though America had yet to produce great artistic works, this fact could not be explained by the theory of environmental degeneracy. The nation was quite young, he contended, and its art should not be compared to the best fruits of Greek, Roman, or European civilization. As for the flora and fauna of the Americas, Jefferson's love of science induced him to collect various plant and animal specimens from his native land, which, he observed, proved that the Western Hemisphere produced abundant and vigorous life. Jefferson was careful, however, not to promote the environmental superiority of the Americas, which would serve little purpose other than to undermine his claim that equality was the province of biology rather than environment.

See also:
Montesquieu, Baron de
Nature

Reference:
Boorstin, Daniel. 1948. *The Lost World of Thomas Jefferson*. Chicago, IL: University of Chicago Press.

Era of Good Feelings

The term "era of good feelings" appeared in a Boston newspaper to describe the mood of the country following the War of 1812. With Federalism extinguished as a political force and the Jeffersonian-Republicans uncontested for public office, it seemed that party warfare in America was over.

This period, 1816–1824, also marked the final years of Jefferson's life. Though he was no longer serving in an official capacity, the Sage of Monticello kept abreast of national affairs through an extensive correspondence with the leading figures of his day.

Early in the period, Jefferson had much to be pleased with. The South's hold on the executive office continued as James Monroe became the nation's fourth Virginia president in 1816. In 1818 the United States concluded a successful trade treaty with Great Britain and the following year signed a treaty with Spain that brought Florida and the Oregon country within the nation's boundaries. Personally, Jefferson was putting the finishing touches on his academic village, the newly created University of Virginia.

In 1819, however, two events shook Jefferson's confidence in the strength of the Union. A major financial panic weakened the national economy, and the Missouri crisis induced a national debate on the wisdom of allowing more slave states to enter the Union.

The Panic of 1819 was caused by the rapid expansion of the economy following the War of 1812. With banks offering excessive credit, it was only a matter of time before speculators, farmers, and businessmen were unable to pay back loans. Jefferson found himself a victim of the nation's economic collapse and saw his own fortune, built substantially upon credit, decline. In dire financial straits, he remarked that "never were such times seen as we have now here. . . . Not a dollar is passing from one to another. Everyone had been pressing and so pressed that finding it useless they from necessity give it up and bear and forbear with one another." Predictably, Jefferson blamed the banks and the memory of Alexander Hamilton for letting in "this torrent of swindling institutions, which have spread ruin and wretchedness over the face of our country."

The Missouri crisis concerned the feasibility of making a new slave state in the upper South. The desire by northern Republicans to exclude slavery in all new states struck Jefferson with fear, and he claimed that the news came to him as "a firebell in the night. . . . I never had any apprehensions equal to what I feel from this source." A compromise managed to alleviate the sectional issue by making Missouri a slave state and bringing in a free Maine, but the disruption of the American economy and the infusion of sectionalism marked Jefferson's final years with apprehension and worry.

See also:
Missouri Compromise
Panic of 1819

Reference:
Dangerfield, George. 1965. *The Awakening of American Nationalism, 1815–1828.* New York: Harper & Row.

Essex Junto

*I*n 1801, Jefferson became president and his Republican coalition took control of Congress. The hitherto ruling party, the Federalists, were then politically moribund with little hope of resurrection. To compound the misery of the Federalists, Jefferson's first term proved to be a success. The Louisiana Purchase, for example, brought in millions of acres of arable land soon to be populated by yeoman farmers and plantation owners who would become Jeffersonian partisans. Federalism's strength lay in the commercial Northeast, and that party understood very clearly that territorial expansion beyond the Mississippi would serve to link Republicans

in the South with Republicans in the West, isolating the North politically as well as economically.

Moreover, the Jeffersonian assault on the largely Federalist-influenced court system suggested to Jefferson's political opponents that non-Republican partisans would be systematically eradicated from all avenues of influence and power. Jefferson's policy of patronage—that is, awarding government positions to his own political followers—increased the Federalists' sense of impotence. For New England Federalists in particular, the loss of power was a bitter pill to swallow. Descendants of the Puritans, these proud men had participated in the American Revolution, helped write the Constitution, and been among the country's staunchest nationalists. When they suddenly found themselves out of power and out of opportunities, these men began to lose faith, not merely in the government but in a country that repudiated their leadership.

This feeling was particularly strong in Massachusetts, where a group of disgruntled Federalists, nominally led by Timothy Pickering, a former secretary of state, began to meet to commiserate about their condition. Called the "Essex Junto" in reference to the location of their meetings, these men gradually formulated a plan to split the Union, with New England, New York, and perhaps Pennsylvania joining in a grand "Northern Confederacy" that would link Yankee cultural and commercial values and shake off the twin threats of slavery and excessive democracy. Vital to their plan was the assent of New York, which the Confederation needed for both commercial as well as defensive purposes. Toward this end, the Junto approached Aaron Burr, the country's vice president but a man no longer in Jefferson's favor. It appears that a bargain was reached whereby the Junto promised to get Burr elected governor of New York. Once that was accomplished, Burr would bring that state into the New England confederation.

When Burr lost the gubernatorial election, the door all but closed on the Junto's plans. Though Federalism's disenchantment with the Jeffersonian party would continue for several more years, particularly during the War of 1812, the Essex Junto represented the first and last real attempt by a northern constituency to secede from the Union.

See also:
Burr, Aaron
Federalist Party
Louisiana Purchase

Reference:
Miller, John. 1960. *The Federalist Era.* New York: Harper & Row.

Federalist Party

*I*n Jefferson's opinion, the Federalist party, which dominated American politics in the 1790s, represented a monarchical spirit that threatened to destroy the republican institutions that emerged from the Revolution. Federalism was much more than a political party, however; it was a persuasion, a culture rooted in the old Puritan colonies of the Northeast. Federalism personified the interests of the commercial class of New England, a constituency that pushed hard for a more industrial vision of America. Federalists were not antiagrarian, but they did believe that the future of the country lay in the mechanical rather than the farming arts.

In the promotion of manufactures, Federalists found a champion in Alexander Hamilton, the nation's first secretary of the treasury and a member, along with Jefferson, of George Washington's first cabinet. Hamilton created, Congress assented to, and Washington signed into law various financial programs that solidified the nation's credit through the expansion of governmental powers and the championing of speculation, commerce, and industry. To Jefferson, these were unfortunate consequences that threatened the future of his beloved Virginia. An economy based increasingly on capital worked against southerners, who measured wealth in terms of land and slaves, while the enlargement of the central government threatened to overawe the states' rights proclivities of the South, which aimed primarily at preventing a northern majority from touching the institution of slavery.

Nor could Jefferson accept Federalism's foreign policy. Because the economy of the North was still closely attached to that of Great Britain, Federalists promoted close ties to that nation. This strategy is best exemplified in Jay's Treaty of 1795, which allowed the United States limited access to trade with the British Empire in return for a U.S. agreement to aid Britain in its war against France. Jefferson, however, believed that America should have closer ties with the French who were undergoing a republican revolution. To make common cause with the British would enhance the quickening pace of industrialism in the North while simultaneously aiding in the destruction of a sister republic.

Federalism's mistrust of democracy also struck Jefferson as dangerous to the country's livelihood. Yet most Federalists understood democracy better than Jefferson, for they tended to live in heterogeneous northern cities and experienced both the happy and unhappy effects of democracy on a daily basis. Unlike the Master of Monticello, who pontificated about democracy from the relative seclusion and security of his "little mountain" in Virginia, Federalists in Boston, New York, and Philadelphia encountered mobs that could be manipulated for a variety of purposes. Certainly the Federalists were pessimistic in their view of human nature, but just as certainly they had more practical experience with democracy than most southerners.

The Federalist party's strength was as a nation builder. In the first decade of life under the Constitution, it secured the public credit, it signed a host of treaties with European nations and Native American tribes that codified economic relations and geographic boundaries, and it provided, as some historians have noted, a sense of legitimacy to the workings of a republican government. Its distrust of the people, however, led it to become increasingly unpopular, and in 1800, Jefferson and his Republican party swept the Federalists out of power. Federalism existed as a political entity until 1815, when its failure to support the War of 1812 finally doomed it.

See also:
Hamilton, Alexander
Hartford Convention
War of 1812

Reference:
Elkins, Stanley, and Eric McKitrick. 1993. *The Age of Federalism: The Early American Republic, 1788–1800*. New York: Oxford University Press.

Ferguson, Adam (1723–1816)

Adam Ferguson was part of a small cadre of eighteenth-century European intellectuals known as the "Physiocrats." His work on economic theory influenced Jefferson and helped shape the Virginian's free-trade inclinations. Ferguson's understanding of socioeconomic development contributed to the rise of "classical" economics, which posited that mercantilism, or government management of the economy, was an outdated form of commercial activity, soon to be replaced by the more natural appetites of the market. In other words, government should stop regulating the economy because it hinders the honest flow of goods and services.

Ferguson was not a blind champion of the marketplace, however. Anticipating Jefferson, the Scottish physiocrat warned that the materialistic impulses released in a "natural," that is, unregulated, economy could have a deadening effect on society. Ferguson's 1767 masterpiece, "Essay on the History of Civil Society," warned that instead of want, men would have to wrestle with a new social problem: luxury. He conceded that luxury introduced a certain "ease and convenience of life" in the form of clothing, buildings, and furniture, but pointed out that luxury was also a "source of corruption, and the presage of national declension and ruin." Luxury benefited society to the degree that it contributed to the arts, the advancement of the economy, and national greatness. However, it was debilitating when it lent itself to vice, corruption, and speculation.

In 1769, the same year he entered the House of Burgesses, Jefferson ordered a shipment of books from Britain that included Ferguson's work on society. In Jefferson's later writings on luxury, vice, and criticism of the British mercantilist system, it is not difficult to spot Ferguson's influence. Both men were writing in the context of the commercialization of their societies in Scotland and America, and both shared a generally positive view of the social and commercial development of the Atlantic world. Moreover, both men believed that the biggest threats to civil society were inequalities of wealth, status, and power fostered by the mercantilist policies of Great Britain.

See also:
Atlantic Economy
Physiocrats
Smith, Adam

Reference:
Ferguson, Adam. 1783. *The History of the Progress and Termination of the Roman Republic*. Dublin, Ireland: Printed for Price.

First Administration

Jefferson's first presidential administration, March 1801–March 1805, is considered by most historians to have been a success. During his term of office, the Virginian wanted to guide the nation through geographical expansion, to remain at peace with the European nations, and to quiet political opposition at home. To a remarkable degree Jefferson was able to accomplish all of these goals. In terms of expansion, the Louisiana Purchase, a most unexpected acquisition from France, solidified Jefferson's popularity in the West and provided the land that the president believed necessary for the United States to maintain an agrarian economy and culture. The admission of Ohio as a new western state in 1803 seemed to foreshadow the expansion of American civilization across the continent.

Jefferson's first term also witnessed the resumption of warfare between Great Britain and France, but this time, unlike the American experience of the 1790s, the United States was not drawn into a quasi naval war with either combatant. Rather, in the early years of this conflict, Jefferson's America became the primary neutral carrier for both nations and enjoyed tremendous profits for its troubles. Even more pleasing to Jefferson, who desired a frugal government with little allocation for military defense, the war in Europe was inadvertently financing an American navy, since the rapidly expanding commercial fleets of New England could be outfitted for military purposes if necessary. The only real points of conflict were the Barbary states of North Africa—Morocco, Algiers, Tunis, and Tripoli. These "pirate" states were accustomed to extracting bribes from the European nations engaging in the Mediterranean trade. American resistance to such demands provoked the Barbary War, which ultimately ended with the United States asserting its right not to pay tribute yet paying a substantial sum of money for the release of American sailors taken prior to and during the conflict.

Probably most important to Jefferson was the realization that his first term solidified the Republican party's claim to be the legitimate ruler of the nation. Though often portrayed as a fuzzy-headed philosopher, Jefferson was in reality a pragmatic thinker. One of his primary goals as president was to replace Federalist partisans in government with his own supporters. In the process he built a political machine that would run beyond the lifetime of his own presidency. Through the use of appointment and patronage powers, Jefferson was able to construct a Republican party that was beholden to the executive office. Though he liked to think of himself as something akin to Aristotle's philosopher-king, he was in fact a political boss with the instincts of a political animal.

To be sure, contention arose during Jefferson's first term. His efforts to replace Federalists in the nation's courts with Republican partisans through the impeachment process, for example, was repudiated by the more moderate members of his own party. Moreover, attempts to purchase the Floridas through congressional bribes were similarly unsuccessful and called into question the character of the president. Nevertheless, by expanding the nation's boundaries in a very popular treaty with France and laying the groundwork for a political system dominated by his partisans, Jefferson's first term brought him all the fruits he could have hoped for.

See also:
Barbary War
Louisiana Purchase
Midnight Appointments

Reference:
Malone, Dumas. 1948–1981. *Jefferson the President, First Term, 1801–1805,* vol. 4 of *Jefferson and His Time.* Boston: Little, Brown.

First Party System

The term "party system" is a tool historians often use to conceptualize particular periods in the American past. Several party systems have been designated, including those dominated by the Jacksonian Democrats in the 1830s and the modern

Democratic party of the New Deal and Great Society era of the period 1933–1968. The first party system institutionalized the differences between Jeffersonian Republicans and Federalists from 1790 to 1815.

The Constitution made no mention or provision for political parties, assuming them to be corrosive to the spirit of the nation. The rise of federalism under the leadership of Alexander Hamilton in the early 1790s, however, and the implementation of his financial programs, which sought to bring about a less agrarian and more industrial vision of America, forced self-proclaimed Republicans like Jefferson to oppose such measures.

Differences between Federalist and Republican partisans went beyond issues of political economy, however. Culturally, Federalists tended to come from New England and maintain close ties with benefactors, creditors, merchants, and other contacts in Great Britain. Republicans, on the other hand, were often from the South; many of them were deeply in debt to British merchants. In foreign policy, Republicans believed the United States should have a closer relationship with republican France than with monarchical England. Federalists responded, however, that such a foreign policy would be driven by abstract claims of ideology rather than by realistic issues of finance and power.

Throughout the 1790s, while the Federalists were in power, Jefferson and his supporters were forced to act as an opposition party. Jefferson's victory over John Adams in 1800, however, ushered in what the Virginian called the "Revolution of 1800" because of its symbolic overthrow of Federalism. More importantly, the election ushered in a 24-year reign by Jefferson and fellow Virginians James Madison and James Monroe. All three men pursued Republican policies of agrarian expansion, a wary stance toward Great Britain, and a rhetorical embrace of democracy that Federalists found appalling. Federalism was vanquished as a political force over its lack of support for the War of 1812, and with it perished the first party system, marked, as few periods in American history have been, with a sincere and passionate debate over the development of the nation's foreign and domestic policies.

See also:
Hamilton, Alexander
Election of 1800

Reference:
Chambers, William, and Walter Burnham, eds. 1967. *The American Party Systems: Stages of Development.* New York: Oxford University Press.

Foreign Policy

Jefferson firmly believed that democratic values, codified in legal constitutions and promoted by a representative government, were destined to spread throughout the world. In this assumption Jefferson was certainly not alone. Other presidents, particularly those belonging to the Democratic party, have envisioned the United States as a leader in a world increasingly receptive to liberal values. In the twentieth century, both Woodrow Wilson and Franklin Roosevelt sought to usher in an era of "liberal internationalism," an American view of social, political, and economic development that received its intellectual currency from the revolutionary movements of the seventeenth and eighteenth centuries.

The promoters of such visions tend to be optimists, and Jefferson certainly was. He presumed that the American and French Revolutions initiated an age of democracy that would soon spread from the New World to the Old. Jefferson believed that mankind was becoming increasingly receptive to rule by the people and less patient with the rule of autocrats. More importantly, Jefferson assumed that the United States could take the lead in this worldwide movement by creating a free and democratic nation. Certainly a successful model of republican government in America would convince other peoples of the feasibility of creating republics elsewhere. With this idea in mind, Jefferson sought to make the United States a bulwark for republicanism, staunchly independent of the political machinations of other nations yet pushing hard to open foreign markets to America's agricultural surpluses. Jefferson referred to such themes in his first inaugural address when he called for "peace, commerce, & honest friendship with all nations, . . . entangling alliances with none."

Jefferson was also concerned with securing U.S. borders. As president the Virginian removed the French presence from North America through the Louisiana Purchase and moved vigorously to replace Spain in Florida, which would happen in 1819 during James Monroe's presidency. Acquiring this territory as well as securing navigation rights for American commerce on the Mississippi River were vital to Jefferson's conception of a vibrant, growing agrarian republic. Toward the end of his presidency, however, it appeared that the United States would be drawn into the war between Great Britain and France. At this juncture, Jefferson's foreign policy floundered. The president presumed, inaccurately, that a commercial shutdown of American goods to Europe would induce the warring parties to seek peace. Not only did the embargo fail to produce the desired results, it also damaged New England's economy and divided the nation between commercial and agrarian interests. In sum, Jefferson's dealings with other nations resulted in both great achievement as well as great disappointment. Westward expansion at the expense of Europe benefited the nation while the Jeffersonian policies that brought the country into the War of 1812 nearly wrecked the republic's economy.

See also:
Louisiana Purchase
War of 1812

Reference:
Onuf, Peter, ed. 1993. *Jeffersonian Legacies.*
    Charlottesville: University of Virginia Press.

Thomas Jefferson's passport signed by Louis XVI of France, dated September 18, 1789.

Francophilia

Throughout his political life, Jefferson was justly accused of exhibiting "Francophilia," that is, a love for all things French. Like that of his beloved Virginia, the French economy was driven by the fruits of agricultural labor, and Jefferson believed the two states shared a certain cultural and economic understanding born of common agrarian principles. Such values, he presumed, were conducive to liberty and democracy.

Thus, it was not difficult for Jefferson to surmise that the American and French Revolutions were inextricably intertwined, the former enjoying the role as libertarian vanguard for the rights of man and the latter bringing the republican experiment to the Old World. Jefferson believed in the redemptive power of mankind, and he saw in the French Revolution both a vindication of America's own independence and an example of a progressive trend in history in which tyranny would give way to liberty.

Jefferson's love for the French, however, was based not merely on abstract principles. During a five-year stay in Paris as American ambassador to France, Jefferson was enchanted with the intellectual and artistic treasures offered by the city. A great collector of luxury items, Jefferson's home at Monticello was well stocked with French books, wines, and paintings. Though a democrat and a republican in a political sense, Jefferson's domestic life was lovingly filled with the pretensions and paraphernalia of European court life, with particular fondness for French tastes and cuisines.

See also:
French Revolution
Minister to France
Physiocrats

Reference:
Horsman, Reginald. 1985. *The Diplomacy of the New Republic, 1776–1815.* Arlington Heights, IL: Harlan Davidson.

Franklin, Benjamin (1706–1790)

Printer, inventor, scientist, author, and diplomat, Benjamin Franklin was the only man who could rival, if not surpass, Jefferson's eclectic talents. At least as much as Jefferson, Franklin is remembered as the quintessential American. Franklin was reared in poverty; accumulated a fortune through thrift, effort, and foresight; and then retired to a long career of public service.

Franklin was born into a pious Puritan household in Boston in 1706. At a young age Franklin rejected his native religion and looked to French deism and English rationalism for a faith in science that he could subscribe to. Poverty barred any hope of a formal education, and at the age of 12, Franklin became an apprentice to his brother on a Boston newspaper, the *New England Courant.* Though Franklin proved a capable worker and even managed the paper for a

short period, a stormy fraternal relationship induced Franklin, at 17, to run away to Philadelphia. There he found a position as a printer. Franklin then trained as a master printer in England for a year and a half. He returned to Philadelphia in 1726, and soon afterward he owned his own press, the *Pennsylvania Gazette.* With contracts to do most of the public printing in the colony, Franklin became a wealthy man, and in 1748, at the age of 42, he retired from the printing business.

Turning his attention to education and science, Franklin took the lead in establishing a circulating library (1731), the American Philosophical Society (1743), and the University of Pennsylvania (1749). He invented the "Pennsylvania fireplace/stove" and the lightning rod, and proved that lightning was a form of electricity. For his efforts, the American inventor was elected to England's Royal Society in 1756 as well as the French Academy of Sciences in 1772. Much like Jefferson, Franklin demonstrated in his scientific endeavors a practicality as well as an optimistic belief in the capacity of humans to understand their role in the natural world.

In 1751, Franklin was elected to the Pennsylvania Assembly and thus began a new phase in his life. Over the next 40 years, he served as a public official in various capacities and garnered the affections and respect of his countrymen in return. Early in his new career, Franklin worked as a lobbyist for Pennsylvania, advocating his colony's interests in the British Parliament. He viewed the British Empire as a beneficial and necessary entity and supported the mother country during the French and Indian War. He even persuaded a Quaker-dominated assembly in Pennsylvania to allocate funds for defense.

Following the successful conclusion of the war, Franklin worked to lessen British proprietary control of Pennsylvania. Instead of suffering an intrusive central power meddling in the colonies' affairs, Franklin envisioned a loosely united empire in which each colony or group of united colonies would have the freedom to make their own laws. Throughout the 1760s he expanded his role by opposing British attempts to collect revenue from the colonies. His skills as a negotiator were quickly recognized, and the colonies of Georgia, New Jersey, and Massachusetts employed him as their spokesman in London, thus making him the single most important American in England prior to the Revolution. Much of Franklin's political clout was lost, however, when private letters written by Massachusetts governor Thomas Hutchinson and obtained by Franklin were published. The letters purported to show that the governor was a dishonest man and thus lent credence to the American claim that British tax policies were part of a broader plan to infringe upon colonial liberties. In England, however, Franklin was roundly criticized for his part in making the letters public. Under attack, Franklin left England in 1775.

Upon his return to Philadelphia, Franklin served in the Second Continental Congress, was elected postmaster general, and drafted the Articles of Confederation for the United Colonies. He also helped draft a new constitution for Pennsylvania and traveled to Canada in a futile attempt to entice that colony to join America's protest against Britain. Perhaps his most famous effort at this time was his membership on the committee to draft the Declaration of Independence.

In October 1776, Franklin accepted appointment as chief American commissioner to France. In Paris, the literary and scientific community extended him a hero's greeting, viewing Franklin as the embodiment of the virtuous *philosophe*. Turgot explained the French admiration for the American, proclaiming that "he seized the lightning from Heaven and the scepter from tyrants." Franklin worked diligently to secure French aid for America's independence movement and was rewarded in February 1778, when the American victory at Saratoga produced a French alliance. Franklin remained in Paris as first American minister to the court of Versailles, where he served as chief American negotiator for diplomacy, purchases, recruiting, and the procurement of loans. In this role, Franklin secured his reputation as America's most able diplomat. Following the British defeat at Yorktown, he led the American peace commission and secured a treaty favorable to the new United States.

Franklin returned to America in 1785 as a national hero. A final act of public service occurred in the summer of 1787, when Franklin attended the Constitutional Convention in Philadelphia. Though he did not participate in the floor debates, Franklin lent the proceedings dignity and authority merely by his presence. Franklin died in Philadelphia, his adopted city, in April 1790.

Perhaps no one admired the American philosopher more than Jefferson. Upon taking over for Franklin as American minister to France, Jefferson wrote that

there appeared to me more respect
and veneration attached to the
character of Dr. Franklin in France
than to that of any other person in the
same country, foreign or native. I had
opportunities of knowing particularly
how far these sentiments were felt by
the foreign ambassadors and ministers
at the court of Versailles. . . . When he
left Passy it seemed as if the village
had lost its patriarch. On taking leave
of the court, which he did by letter,
the King ordered him to be hand-
somely complimented, and furnished
him with a litter and mules of his
own, the only kind of conveyance
the state of his health could bear. . . .
The succession to Dr. Franklin at the
court of France was an excellent
school of humility. On being presented to anyone as the minister of
America, the commonplace question
used in such cases was "C'est vous,
Monsieur, qui remplace le Docteur
Franklin?"—"It is you, sir, who
replace Dr. Franklin?" I generally
answered, "No one can replace him,
sir; I am only his successor."

See also:
American Philosophical Society
American Revolution
Constitution

Reference:
Wright, Esmond. 1986. *Franklin of Philadelphia*.
    Cambridge, MA: Harvard University Press.

See also:
Peace of Paris (1763)
Peace of Paris (1783)
Virginia House of Burgesses

Reference:
Russell, Francis. 1962. *The French and Indian Wars*.
    New York: American Heritage.

French and Indian War

The conflict between imperial powers Great Britain and France on the North American continent in 1756–1763 is known by Americans as the French and Indian War, by Europeans as the Seven Years War, and by some historians as the Great War for Empire. Even though he was not involved, either as combatant or plenipotentiary, Jefferson would see his world changed dramatically and irrevocably as a result of this conflict.

The point of contention was the Ohio Valley, an area coveted by both Britain and France, and later by Jefferson, who envisioned the territory as an "Empire of Liberty" for American farmers. Britain's ultimate triumph in the conflict (which was really a world war, since combat took place in North America, the Caribbean, Europe, and India) made Britain unquestionably the most powerful nation on earth. At the same time, it sowed the seeds of the British overthrow in the Anglo-American colonies. By defeating the French and taking over Canada as well as various other French possessions, the British not only increased the territory of the empire but enlarged the imperial debt, and Britain did not have the funds to meet its obligations around the world. But by levying new taxes on its empire in North America, Britain precipitated the American Revolution, which transformed Jefferson from a moderate gentleman in the Virginia House of Burgesses to a revolutionary. Though the consequences were unforeseen at the time, the destruction of French power in North America made Britain susceptible to colonial demands for more autonomy and, ultimately, for independence.

French Revolution

Jefferson believed that the French Revolution (1789–1815) had the potential to redirect European life along the same liberal, democratic path enjoyed by Americans. Moreover, it was difficult for Jefferson, who served as ambassador to France during the five years immediately preceding the revolution, not to view French actions as inspired by America's own successful revolution. "The American war," he contended, "seems first to have awakened the thinking of this nation [France] in general from the sleep of despotism which they were sunk." In Paris during the initial days of the revolution, Jefferson became something of a celebrity among those seeking change. "I was much acquainted with the leading patriots," he reflected happily, ". . . being from a country which had successfully passed through a similar reformation, they were disposed to my acquaintance, and had some confidence in me."

In the early stages of the revolution, Jefferson was pleased with the pace and tone of genteel reform. He declared the opening of the Assembly of Notables, an aristocratic movement against absolutism, "a vast mass of improvement in the condition of the nation." As the revolution proceeded, the "Third Estate," or nonaristocratic and nonclerical portion of the country—approximately 96 percent of the population—gradually took over the revolution and replaced rule by divine right with a constitutional monarchy. Jefferson heralded the rise of the Third Estate as the catalyst to liberty in Europe. "I look with great anxiety for the firm establishment of the new government in France," he noted, "being perfectly convinced that if it takes place there it will spread sooner or later all over Europe. On the contrary, a check there would retard the revival of liberty in other countries."

Shortly thereafter, the revolution took a violent turn when King Louis XVI was beheaded for attempting to use foreign armies to put down the revolution. That event became a dramatic turning point in the revolution. For the French, it indicated that there could be no return to monarchy. For Americans such as John Adams and George Washington, who had supported the revolution in its early phase, the killing of a king was a brutal reminder of how excessive democracy could stain a people and a nation. Thus many Americans living in the East who had closer ties to Great Britain and favored a more subservient, less democratic society turned their backs on the French Revolution.

Jefferson, however, never lost faith during these dark years. While aristocrats and innocents alike were executed during the "Terror" of 1794, the Virginian continued to support the French cause. The king's death was justified, he proclaimed, since "it would be unfortunate were it in the power of any one man to defeat the issue of so beautiful a revolution." Moreover, he continued, the blow would "at least soften the monarchical governments by rendering monarchs amenable to punishment like other criminals, and doing away that . . . insolence and oppression, the inviolability of the king's person." Toward the innocents who perished, Jefferson's manner was cold. "The liberty of the whole earth was depending on the issue of the contest," he wrote to James Monroe, "and was ever such a prize won with so little innocent blood?" From the sanctuary of Monticello he contended that "my own affections have been deeply wounded by some of the martyrs to this cause, but rather than it should have failed, I would have seen half the earth desolated."

Jefferson was, however, as much a pragmatist as an optimist. With the ascension of Napoleon Bonaparte, first as consul for life and then as emperor of France, the Virginian

presumed that the revolution, at least as he understood it, was dead. "The events which have taken place in France," he wrote, "have lessened in the American mind the motives of interest which it felt in that revolution, and its amity towards that country now rests on its love of peace and commerce." In Jefferson's mind, Britain was still America's chief rival, but an aggressive French nation was a danger that could not be tolerated either. Thus, prior to the Louisiana Purchase, Jefferson proclaimed that the United States would be forced to "marry" itself to the "British fleet" before it would allow a French army in North America. Throughout his presidency and early years of retirement, Jefferson assumed an aggressive posture toward the French government, not trusting "the Attila of the age," as he referred to Napoleon, or the martial spirit he personified.

See also:
Anglo-French Wars

Reference:
O'Brien, Conor Cruise. 1996. *The Long Affair: Thomas Jefferson and the French Revolution.* Chicago, IL: University of Chicago Press.

Freneau, Philip (1752–1832)

In 1791, Jefferson and James Madison persuaded Philip Freneau to edit a newspaper critical of the Federalist party. The choice of Freneau was not a random one, since he had acquired a reputation as one of America's preeminent poets and literary men. His most renowned work, "The Rising Glory of America," championed political liberty and personal freedom and made him one of Jefferson's favorite men of letters. Access to Freneau was provided by Madison, who had attended Princeton College with the poet.

With the Federalist party using Alexander Hamilton's financial programs to dramatically increase the power of the central government, the newly established Republican coalition needed a mouthpiece from which to disseminate their views promoting local control. Freneau's *National Gazette*, which began publication in October 1791, attacked Hamilton's policies as well as his character, denouncing the leader of Federalism as a monarchist.

At the time of Freneau's assault against the Federalists, Jefferson was serving as secretary of state in George Washington's cabinet, which included Hamilton as head of the Treasury Department. Thus, Jefferson encouraged the demise of Hamiltonianism while serving in an administration that was supposed to be united and above partisan bickering. In fact, Jefferson did more then encourage Freneau. He paid him, finding the poet a position as a translating clerk in the State Department that left him ample time to devote to his editorial duties. Further, Jefferson rounded up subscriptions for the paper and promised Freneau that he would allow the editor "the perusal of all my letters of foreign intelligence and all foreign newspapers; the publication of all proclamations and other public notices within my department, and the printing of the laws."

Throughout the rest of the year and well into 1792, the *National Gazette* was involved in a bitterly partisan paper war with Federalist newspapers, most notably Hamilton's mouthpiece, the *Gazette of the United States*. His cabinet divided, Washington urged Jefferson and Hamilton to make "mutual yieldings." When none were forthcoming and his term was near its end, Washington seriously contemplated retirement. Both Jefferson and Hamilton, however, encouraged him to stand for a second term, which he reluctantly did. In the end, the two combatants agreed to end their newspaper war, though not their animosity toward one another. Freneau's paper, bereft of subscriptions and forced out of Philadelphia by the yellow fever, ceased publication in 1793.

Reference:
Ellis, Joseph. 1979. *After the Revolution: Profiles of Early American Culture*. New York: W. W. Norton.

Gabriel's Conspiracy

*I*n 1800, the year Jefferson won the presidency, a potentially large-scale slave insurrection in Virginia was narrowly averted. The rebellion was organized by Gabriel Prosser and a cadre of skilled artisan urban slaves who might have been influenced by the rhetoric of the American and French revolutions. The leaders met at black religious gatherings in and around Richmond, where Gabriel's brother, a preacher, told his slave audiences of "the days of old when the Israelites were in service to King Pharaoh," and how Moses broke their bonds of servitude and led his people to freedom.

Gabriel, a physically imposing blacksmith, told his followers that "we have as much right to fight for our liberty as any men." The uprising he planned was not to be a war against whites, however, but against the slave system. Certain religious orders that opposed slavery, the Quakers and Methodists, for example, would not be attacked. Though details are sketchy, it seems that Gabriel and his followers intended to burn Richmond and take Governor James Monroe hostage, along with other prominent Virginians. This action, Gabriel hoped, would inspire slaves from outlying plantations to join the insurrection. Presumably Gabriel expected that some sort of negotiations would follow that would allow those involved in the rebellion to secure their freedom.

The rebellion never occurred, however. Black informers warned of the plot. The state militia was mobilized, and Gabriel and his lieutenants were arrested, tried, and executed. Jefferson remarked to Monroe that rather than a mass killing, the slaves involved should be sold out of the state. Nevertheless, 34 blacks were hanged. To Jefferson's political enemies, the Federalist party, Gabriel's conspiracy proved the defects of democracy in a republic. The Virginians, one Federalist sarcastically remarked, were merely feeling "the happy effects of liberty and equality." Jefferson's impression, of course, was much different.

To him the conspiracy revealed the dangers of living in a state that had had slavery foisted upon it during the first decades of the colonial period. Jefferson believed that white Virginians, taking care of their "people" by offering them food, shelter, and religion, were the true victims in this affair. With no apparent understanding of the irony in his statement, Jefferson wrote to Benjamin Rush, "We are truly to be pitied."

See also:
Slave Insurrections
Slave Trade
Slavery

Reference:
Egerton, Douglas. 1993. *Gabriel's Rebellion: The Virginia Slave Conspiracies of 1800 and 1802.* Chapel Hill: University of North Carolina Press.

Gallatin, Albert (1761–1849)

Albert Gallatin was President Jefferson's secretary of the treasury and a key leader of the Republican party. Born in Geneva, Switzerland, to a noble family, Gallatin was educated at the Geneva Academy and came to America at the age of 19 to participate in the Revolution. Gallatin settled in Pennsylvania and began his political career as an anti-Federalist by opposing the Constitution, which he believed gave too much power to the central government. Elected to the U.S. Senate in 1793, Gallatin was expelled on the grounds that he had not been a U.S. citizen for the required nine-year period. His district sent him to the House of Representatives instead, where he vigorously opposed the Federalist party. Gallatin's strengths were in matters of finance, and the Jeffersonian party was pleased to count within their numbers someone who could challenge the Federalist secretary of the treasury, Alexander Hamilton, on his own terms.

When Jefferson assumed the presidency and Gallatin was elevated to head of the Treasury Department, the Republican party instituted a political economy of frugality that, Jefferson believed, would contribute to the health of the republic. Toward this end, budgets were cut, and Gallatin's department went a long way in reducing the federal debt. Gallatin was not shy of economic development, however, and proposed that the nation undertake a grand internal improvements campaign that would improve communications and link the country together. Gallatin later served on the U.S. peace commission that helped end the War of 1812, and from 1816 to 1823 he was American minister to France. In his final years, the Swiss emigré opposed the banking policies of the Jacksonians and criticized the annexation of Mexico. After a long and eventful life, Gallatin died in Astoria, New York, in 1849.

See also:
Hamilton, Alexander
Republican Party

Reference:
McCoy, Drew. 1980. *The Elusive Republic: Political Economy in Jeffersonian America*. Chapel Hill: University of North Carolina Press.

Genet, Edmond Charles (1763–1834)

French diplomat Edmond "Citizen" Genet came to America in 1793 in an effort to bind the United States to the French Revolution. Born in Versailles in 1763, Genet was the son of a prominent foreign officer and entered diplomatic service at an early age. In 1787 he headed the French legation in Russia, and in 1792 his close connections with the Girondin faction secured him an appointment to the United States.

Genet's instructions were to win over the United States to the French cause and arrange for the use of U.S. resources in France's war against Great Britain. Landing in Charleston, South Carolina, Genet immediately began to outfit privateers (American ships and citizens paid in French money to fight against Britain). By the time he reached the capital in Philadelphia, he was certain that his warm reception in the South was indicative of Americans' friendly attitude toward France. He was dismayed, therefore, when President George Washington introduced a proclamation of neutrality declaring that the United States would not become involved in the European war. Because the emerging Jeffersonian faction wanted closer ties with republican France, however, Genet presumed that there was enough support around the country to circumvent Washington's decree. Misjudging the climate of opinion in the country and abusing Jefferson's friendship in the bargain, Genet attempted to appeal directly to the people for their support. Though many Americans detested Great Britain and hoped France would win the war, they were nevertheless unwilling to allow France to dictate American foreign policy. Genet's mission ended in failure and he was recalled to France, where he surely would have been executed by the new Jacobin faction. Thus he remained in the United States, where he married the daughter of New York governor George Clinton, became an American citizen, and led a quiet life as a country gentleman until his death in 1834.

See also:
Anglo–French Wars
French Revolution

Reference:
Elkins, Stanley, and Eric McKitrick. 1993. *The Age of Federalism: The Early American Republic, 1788–1800.* New York: Oxford University Press.

Governor of Virginia

In June 1779, Jefferson was elected by both houses of the state assembly to succeed Patrick Henry as governor of Virginia. Jefferson's selection was anticipated but by no means unanimous. Two ballots were required before Jefferson acquired the necessary majority, defeating John Page by a score of 67 votes to 61. In victory, however, Jefferson had little cause for celebration. With the United States at war with Great Britain, the new governor could expect Virginia to play a demanding military role in the independence movement. To Richard Henry Lee, Jefferson wrote that "in a virtuous government, and more especially in times like these, public offices are, what they should be, burthens to those appointed to them which it would be wrong to decline, though foreseen to bring them intense labor and great private loss." Such sentiments were prophetic. Jefferson's two-year tenure as governor of the Old Dominion proved extremely trying and nearly wrecked his reputation.

In Virginia, the governor enjoyed very little in the way of real authority. The post was completely dependent upon the legislature, to which the state constitution of 1776 assigned supreme power. As governor, Jefferson was without veto power and, unlike royal governors, could not dissolve the assembly. Moreover, Jefferson exercised executive authority with the advice of a council of state that was made up of eight members elected by the assembly. His relationship with the council, which included James Madison, was warm, and there was little disagreement between the bodies as they crafted various bills in the spring of 1779 that were designed to put Virginia on a wartime footing.

As governor, Jefferson was referred to as "His Excellency" and was the last state executive to reside in the ancient capital of Williamsburg. The exposure of the city to capture, combined with the desire to find a more central location for the seat of government, encouraged the assembly to remove the capital to Richmond in May 1780. Jefferson's role as executive of Virginia was deemed by contemporaries to be vital to the patriot initiative.

A powerful state like Virginia, administered properly in the military defense of colonial rights, could do much to further the cause of independence. The British government sensed this and shifted its primary military efforts to the South in the spring of 1780. However, the defenses that Jefferson and the assembly erected were woefully inadequate to combat the British invasion. General Nathanael Greene, the commander of an American army in North Carolina, chastised the governor, remarking that "your troops may literally be said to be naked. . . . It will answer no good purpose to send men here in such a condition, for they are nothing but added weight upon the army and altogether incapable of aiding in its operations."

To make matters worse, the war was rapidly moving to Jefferson's front door. In January 1781, a British fleeted sailed up the James River and unloaded Benedict Arnold's invading army for an attack on Richmond. Jefferson had no available militia at the ready and was forced to vacate the capital, taking refuge across the James River. Arnold's forces destroyed several public and private buildings and carried off arms, munitions, and various types of military stores that Virginia could ill afford to lose. In May, a war-weary Jefferson was back home at Monticello awaiting the expiration of his tenure, satisfied that a successor would soon be in charge of state affairs. Since a large British force was operating in the region, Jefferson had chosen a most inopportune time, to say the least, to desert the capital and leave the state without an active executive officer. Almost as embarrassing, Jefferson was nearly captured when British cavalry were dispatched to Charlottesville hoping to catch the governor and members of the assembly. Jefferson barely escaped this snare and retreated to a farm inherited by his wife at Poplar Forest.

By this time a new governor was in office, but Jefferson's troubles were not over. George Nicholas requested a motion in the Virginia Assembly that an inquiry be made into the conduct of the late governor, who appeared to have left the capital and indeed the entire state woefully unprepared to meet the British threat. Fortunately, by the date of the inquiry, December 1781, Lord Cornwallis's forces had been defeated at Yorktown and the Revolution was brought to a successful conclusion. In such an atmosphere, a more charitable tone prevailed toward Jefferson and his services as executive of Virginia. Moreover, Jefferson vigorously and successfully deflected the charges against him through a public defense in which he answered his critics. For his efforts, Jefferson was given a special grant of appreciation by the assembly, which resolved that

> the sincere thanks of the General
> Assembly be given to our former
> Governor Thomas Jefferson Esquire
> for his impartial, upright, and attentive
> administration whilst in office. The
> Assembly wish in the strongest
> manner to declare the high opinion
> which they entertain of Mr. Jefferson's
> ability, rectitude, and integrity as chief
> magistrate of this Commonwealth,
> and mean by thus publicly avowing

their opinion, to obviate and to remove all unmerited censure.

Despite the clearing of his name, Jefferson's experience as wartime governor of Virginia was among the least rewarding of his entire life.

See also:
American Revolution
Henry, Patrick

Reference:
Malone, Dumas. 1948. *Jefferson the Virginian.* Boston, MA: Little, Brown.

Great Britain

Jefferson's opinion of Great Britain was generally negative, yet he was reconciled to the understanding that America was linked to the British Isles by unbreakable commercial and cultural ties. As a youth Jefferson was, of course, a British subject. He lived in the British Empire and enjoyed the rights of a free Englishman. During the American Revolution, the Virginian, like most of his compatriots, sought independence only with great reluctance. Jefferson's true displeasure with Britain probably occurred in the 1780s. In this decade Virginia was invaded by a British army, and Jefferson, the state's governor at the time, narrowly escaped censure for allowing the Anglos to run roughshod over the Old Dominion. Further, Jefferson spent several of these years in France and witnessed the coming of the French Revolution, which, at the time, appeared to be a celebration of republicanism over monarchy. Finally, as a member of George Washington's cabinet, Jefferson battled the "Anglophile," Alexander Hamilton, whose financial vision for the United States appeared to make the nation a vassal of the British state, complete with that nation's reliance on speculation, credit, and corruption. In sum, the Revolution and the founding of the new American nation represented, in Jefferson's view, a battle for the soul of the country, and Jefferson anticipated a future that was more agrarian, that is, less British. While he was personally attracted to various aspects of British life, particularly the customs of leisure, social deference, and civility, Jefferson's southern background did not favorably dispose him to accept the backbone of the British system, an expanding industrial state.

Nevertheless, Jefferson was a more practical man than is generally recorded, and he conceded, particularly later in his life, the need for relations between the United States and Britain. Several factors account for this practical concession, none more important than Jefferson's disillusionment with the French Revolution, which took a decidedly bloody turn in the 1790s. Instead of serving as a bulwark for republicanism in Europe, the French Revolution had given way to the despotism of Napoleon. Moreover, the bulk of America's trade and finances were tied to Great Britain, and though he did not like to admit it, Jefferson understood that Anglo-Americans enjoyed a natural commercial relationship built on common desires, customs, and practices. Finally, at the conclusion of the Napoleonic wars, the United States and Britain were united in promoting a common foreign policy: the opening of Central and South American markets to world trade. Though he always retained a sense of animosity toward the British, Jefferson nevertheless was a pragmatist who understood that America's greatest rival and greatest partner in the years of the early republic was the British Empire.

See also:
Anglo-French Wars
Hamilton, Alexander

Reference:
Morgan, Kenneth, ed. 1984. *The Oxford History of Britain*. Oxford, England: Oxford University Press.

H

Hamilton, Alexander (1757–1804)

Throughout his brief but brilliant public career, Alexander Hamilton was Jefferson's chief ideological enemy. Though the two men often worked closely together, particularly as members of Washington's cabinet, Hamilton had little sympathy for Jefferson's optimistic view of human nature, believing instead that the public was prone to corruption and thus required the leadership of elites. Hamilton's pessimistic interpretation of humanity was undoubtedly shaped by his environment. Unlike Jefferson, who was first and foremost a son of Virginia, Hamilton's allegiances were not confined to a particular state. In fact, he was born not in the North American colonies but rather on the British West Indies island of Nevis. While Jefferson grew up in a secure and affluent condition, Hamilton was orphaned at the age of 11 and labored at a retail firm on the island, determined to overcome his meager condition through self-discipline and education. Moreover, while Jefferson belonged by birth to the upper class of his society, Hamilton struggled to become successful, believing that effort and talent rather than name alone delineated the higher and lower orders.

Hamilton's life changed in 1772 when a benefactor, impressed with the young man's industrious habits, organized plans for his education in America. His passage and tuition paid for, Hamilton sailed to New York where he attended King's College, the present-day Columbia University. Hamilton set aside his studies to publish essays promoting the American Revolution, and in 1775 he was commissioned captain of an artillery company. Two years later he became George Washington's aide, a post he would hold for four years. In the final months of the revolution, Hamilton secured his standing among the nation's gentry by marrying Elizabeth Schuyler, who belonged to one of New York's most powerful families.

When the war ended in 1781, Hamilton turned to the study of law, convinced that the new nation required men trained in the legal arts. He worked diligently throughout the Confederation period to promote a stronger federal system. His efforts paid off in 1787, when the states allowed representatives to meet at a convention in Philadelphia to revise the Articles of Confederation. Once there, Hamilton and the other delegates exceeded their orders and created a new and more powerful Constitution. From Paris, Jefferson wrote to James Madison that aside from preferring a Bill of Rights, the document met his approval.

Following the ratification of the Constitution, Washington was elected to serve as the nation's first president. His administration included both Hamilton and Jefferson, who headed, respectively, the departments of Treasury and State. Hamilton's initial task was to devise a way to get the federal government out of debt. His plan, which he set forth in the "First Report on the Public Credit," consisted of three components: funding, assumption, and the creation of a national bank. Funding simply meant that the federal government would fund its debt by paying back what it owed to the patriots who had purchased bonds during the Revolution. Once these debts were paid, Hamilton argued, the government's reputation would be enhanced and it could then secure loans in the future. To Hamilton's surprise, Madison agreed with Jefferson on the matter and opposed the plan, arguing that since the Revolution, speculators from the North had purchased southern bonds at a pittance of their value. In sum, Madison contended that if the government funded the federal debt, then the money would go into the pockets of northern speculators rather than southern patriots. Madison's proposal to track down the original bonds holders was deemed impossible, however, and the funding bill passed.

Assumption, the second component in Hamilton's program, proposed that the federal government assume the debts incurred by the states since independence. Hamilton did not want the states to pay off their own debts because they would then remain independent of the federal government. Madison again opposed Hamilton's proposal, pointing out that the majority of southern states had already paid off their debts and it would be unfair to tax the entire nation to pay off what was primarily a northern debt. His financial plans in jeopardy, Hamilton went to Jefferson, who helped secure a bargain between the treasury secretary and Madison. Assumption would pass through Congress, and in ten years the federal government would move from Philadelphia to a location on the Chesapeake. Thus Hamilton increased the power of the central government while Jefferson and Madison removed the capital to the South.

Alexander Hamilton, from a mural painting by Constantino Brumidi of that still hangs in the United States Capitol.

The final component of Hamilton's report, the national bank, met with the greatest opposition. The bank was to be chartered by the government but primarily financed and run by private investors. To Jefferson this arrangement was a government-created monopoly and one the Constitution did not provide for. The fundamental question was how much authority central government possessed. If a national bank, which the Constitution said nothing about, could be created by Congress, then the "implied" powers of the federal government might continue to grow and perhaps one day, Jefferson feared, claim the authority to end slavery in the South. Thus Jefferson opposed Hamilton's financial plans because they gave too much power to the federal government and threatened state sovereignty in the South. The national bank passed through Congress, however, and despite Jefferson's protests Hamilton not only secured the public credit but dramatically increased the power of the central government.

In an effort to institutionalize and thus strengthen their opposition to "Hamiltonianism," Jefferson and Madison organized the Republican party. With Jefferson serving as party leader, the Democratic-Republicans were strongest in the agrarian South and weakest in the commercial Northeast, which became the stronghold of the rival Federalist party. With the nation's credit secure, attention turned to foreign policy and the European wars unleashed in the wake of the French Revolution. The Jeffersonians sided with the French, who they believed were modeling their Republican form of government on the American experiment. Hamilton and the Federalists, however, supported the British because they believed that in order for the United States to prosper economically, it needed the protection of the British navy to carry its goods across the Atlantic. Hamilton was accused by the Jeffersonians of supporting monarchism over republicanism, but to Hamilton the issue was pragmatic rather than ideological. America needed access to the British market more than to the French. The United States managed to stay neutral throughout Washington's second term. But as the European conflict continued, U.S. ships heading for Great Britain or ports within the British Empire were routinely confiscated by French naval forces. Hamilton, though now a private citizen, pressed strongly for war against the French. When the newly elected Federalist president, John Adams, resisted what he believed would be a disastrous war against a stronger European power, the party split between "High Federalists" who supported Hamilton and "Adams Federalists" who championed the president. With the party fatally weakened, Adams's bid for reelection foundered and Jefferson was elected president in 1800.

When a Federalist wrote to Hamilton expressing dismay over Jefferson's victory, Hamilton wrote a remarkable letter that provided a shrewd estimation of his old enemy's character and temperament. He admitted that Jefferson's views were "tinctured with fanaticism; that he is too much in earnest with his democracy." But it was not true, Hamilton concluded, "that Jefferson is zealot enough to do anything in pursuance of his principles which will contravene his popularity or his interest. He is as likely as any man I know to temporize—to calculate what will be likely to promote his own reputation and advantage."

Though out of power, Hamilton still had one more service to render to the Union that he had labored so hard to help create. In 1804 a group of New England Federalists proposed secession from the Union on the grounds that Jeffersonian rule worked to the advantage of the South and to the detriment of the North. To put their plan in motion they enlisted Aaron Burr to run for governor of New York. With a New England–New York axis, this "Northern Confederacy" would be a powerful nation. When Hamilton learned of the plot, he denounced Burr in print and was a chief cause of his electoral defeat. His reputation impugned, Burr challenged Hamilton to a duel. Despite having lost a son to dueling, Hamilton felt compelled to accept. The combatants met at a secluded spot in Weehawken, New Jersey, on July 11, 1804. Burr's shot struck Hamilton in the right side and passed through his liver. Within 36 hours, Alexander Hamilton, the architect of commercial capitalism in the United States, was dead.

See also:
Anglo-French Wars
Atlantic Economy
Federalist Party

Reference:
McDonald, Forrest. 1979. *Alexander Hamilton: A Biography.* New York: W. W. Norton.

Hartford Convention

*I*n December 1814, a group of disgruntled Federalists met in Hartford, Connecticut, to discuss the difficulties of living under the rule of the Jeffersonian-

Republican party. The immediate cause of their dissatisfaction was the War of 1812, which damaged the New England economy. But beneath this surface discontent ran a deep and abiding hostility toward the liberal, democratic leanings of Jeffersonianism. State legislatures in Massachusetts, Connecticut, and Rhode Island sent delegations to the convention, and counties in New Hampshire and Vermont were also represented. Though a radical element at the convention wanted New England to secede, moderate elements took command of the gathering and drew up a series of resolutions aimed at weakening the power of the Republican party and protecting the rights of New England.

The Federalist party controlled the national government during the Washington and Adams presidencies. But Federalism was not merely a political faction; it was, more importantly, a cultural party in that it represented an updated version of the social aspects of Puritanism. Generally speaking, Federalism was strongest in New England and promoted a pro-eastern agenda. This included beneficial relations with Great Britain abroad and social deference rather than democracy at home. These tenets of Federalism were overturned in 1800 when Jefferson won the presidency and ushered in a generation of Republican party rule. While Federalism had been amenable to the interests of New England, the new Jeffersonian coalition was oriented toward the South. More damaging to Federalists was the great popularity that the Republicans enjoyed in the emerging western states. It seemed to New Englanders that they would find themselves yoked to an agrarian rather than industrial vision of the nation. With the War of 1812 proving unpopular at home, Federalists sensed that this was their opportunity to address their grievances with the Jeffersonians.

The attendees to the Hartford Convention passed several resolutions that they hoped would protect and strengthen the interests of New England. They advocated, for example, the abolition of the three-fifths com-promise in the Constitution, which recognized ten slaves as the equal of six whites for purposes of taxation and representation. Federalists claimed that this clause gave the South, which held the preponderance of the nation's slaves, an unfair advantage in representation and made the North, which held the preponderance of the nation's free population, beholden to southern interests. The members of the convention also sought to prohibit embargoes of more than 60 days and require a two-thirds vote of Congress to declare war. They pointed out that Jefferson's embargo, which lasted 14 months, nearly destroyed New England's economy while the vote to go to war with Britain, which Federalists opposed, passed through Congress with nothing close to a consensus. Further, the convention sought to limit the presidency to one term and prohibit presidents from the same state from holding office consecutively. This measure was aimed at the "Virginia Dynasty," that is, national rule by Washington, Jefferson, Madison, and later Monroe, all Virginians, all slaveholders, and all two-term executives. Up to the Hartford Convention, the only northern president was John Adams, who had been turned out of office after a single term.

The timing of the Hartford Convention could not have been worse for the Federalists. Just weeks after their meeting, Andrew Jackson's forces in New Orleans won an incredible battle against the British following the Treaty of Ghent, which ended the war. With peace achieved and the country reverberating with nationalist pride, the demands of the Hartford Federalists appeared petty at best and treasonous at worst. With Jeffersonian diplomacy seemingly vindicated by America's surviving the war, Federalism was forever discredited as a political party and would never again seriously challenge for national rule.

See also:
Embargo of 1807
Virginia Dynasty
War of 1812

Reference:
Banner, James. 1969. *To the Hartford Convention: The Federalists and the Origins of Party Politics in Massachusetts, 1789–1815*. New York: Alfred A. Knopf.

Hemings, Sally (1772–1835?)

For nearly 200 years, rumors have circulated that Sally Hemings, a slave at Monticello, was Jefferson's mistress. Hemings was the daughter of John Wayles, an Englishman who emigrated to Virginia, and Elizabeth Hemings, a mulatto slave. Since John was the father of Martha Wayles, Jefferson's wife, Martha and Sally were half-sisters. Thus Sally was Jefferson's half-sister-in-law, a fact that Jefferson was probably aware of. Sally was described by a relative as "mighty near white . . . very handsome: long straight hair down her back." Jefferson's grandson remarked that she was "light colored and decidedly good looking."

Those who believe that a Jefferson-Hemings affair occurred contend the relationship commenced in Paris where Jefferson was serving as American minister and Sally, who was in her early teens at the time, accompanied Jefferson's daughter Polly. Word of a possible relationship did not leak out, however, until 1802, when a disgruntled office seeker published an account of the supposed sexual practices of the Master of Monticello.

What is certain is that Sally was not freed during Jefferson's lifetime, though she probably was released from her duties by Jefferson's daughter. Sally's history after she left Monticello is very sketchy, but it is believed that she died in Ohio in 1835.

See also:
Callender, James T.
Minister to France

Reference:
Gordon-Reed, Annette. 1997. *Thomas Jefferson and Sally Hemings: An American Controversy*. Charlottesville: University Press of Virginia.

Henry, Patrick (1736–1799)

This revolutionary leader proved to be one of Jefferson's most annoying political opponents. Born in Hanover County, Virginia, in 1736, Henry's education was limited to the rudiments of Latin and Greek, which were introduced to him by his father. After he had failed at business, Henry and his wife were given a small farm with a few slaves by both sets of parents, which they soon sold after the responsibilities of stewardship proved too much.

Again a failure at business, Henry pursued a law career, probably with as much desperation as hope. In 1760 he passed the Virginia bar and within three years was handling more than 1,000 cases. Henry's career reached its apex in 1765, when his opposition to the British Stamp Act (during which he supposedly said, "If this be treason, make the most of it") put him in the vanguard of the budding revolutionary movement.

Henry continued to advocate colonial rights in the early 1770s and pushed Virginia toward the path of independence. In recognition for his service, he was elected the first governor of the Commonwealth of Virginia in 1776. Following the Revolution, Henry feared that the power of Virginia would be diluted in a more centralized union and therefore opposed the ratification of the Constitution. James Madison, the primary architect of the document, was criticized by Henry for his efforts to displace liberty with power. On these personal grounds, Henry became an opponent of the emerging Jeffersonian movement, which, he mistakenly believed, championed nationalism over states' rights.

See also:
American Revolution
Madison, James
Virginia House of Burgesses

Reference:
McCants, David. 1990. *Patrick Henry: The Orator*. New York: Greenwood Press.

I

Impressment

Jefferson's presidency was complicated by Great Britain's impressment policy: the practice of taking American seamen from U.S. ships by force for service in the Royal Navy. To Great Britain, the interests of its navy were paramount in considerations of foreign policy. As a small island nation with limited national resources, Britain relied on its navy for protection and to ensure its independence. For several generations it held to a strategic policy that its navy must be twice the size of the next two largest navies combined. This policy proved difficult to manage, particularly considering the low pay and harsh discipline meted out to British sailors. Moreover, it was quite tempting and very easy for men sailing for the Royal Navy to jump ship at American ports and sign up on U.S. merchant or marine vessels—a practice that had been recognized if not well accepted in many American ports for years. With the renewal of war between Britain and France in 1803, however, and reports that in the last confrontation between the two nations just two years earlier some 42,000 British sailors had deserted the navy for American shipping, the British government pushed for a more aggressive policy of obtaining and keeping sailors in its service.

Impressment was not a novel policy, however. It had been practiced since the time of Richard II in the fourteenth century. Yet during Jefferson's presidency, the British were not merely taking American soldiers (approximately 9,000 prior to the War of 1812); they were also confiscating American ships heading toward France or the ports of French allies. This injury put impressment in another light, moving from a mere inconvenience to a seemingly well-organized attempt to subvert American neutrality to serve British foreign policy. In June 1807 the issue of impressment came to a head when the British ship *Leopard* assaulted the American frigate *Chesapeake* off the coast of Norfolk, taking several American and British seamen from the U.S. vessel. Jefferson's actions were swift. "I immediately interdicted our harbors and waters to all British armed vessels," he later recalled, and "forbade intercourse with them." This "embargo," Jefferson hoped, would teach the British a lesson by injuring their economy at home. If the impressment policy of the British had any positive result for Jefferson, it served to rally the nation together. To a French colleague, he remarked that

> Never since the battle of Lexington
> have I seen this country in such a state
> of exasperation as at present, and even
> that did not produce such unanimity.
> The Federalists themselves coalesce
> with us as to the object, though they
> will return to their trade of censuring

every measure taken to obtain it. "Reparation for the past, and security for the future," is our motto; but whether they will yield it freely or will require resort to non-intercourse, or to war, is yet to be seen. We prepare for the last.

Ultimately, Jefferson's embargo did not end British assaults on American neutrality, and continued impressment put the United States on the road to war with Great Britain. Yet for Jefferson, the war being thrust upon the country was for a noble cause: "We are to have war, then? I believe so, and that it is necessary. Every hope from time, patience, and the love of peace is exhausted, and war or abject submission are the only alternative left us. I am forced from my hobby, peace."

See also:
Embargo of 1807
Non-Intercourse Act
War of 1812

Reference:
Horsman, Reginald. 1962. *The Causes of War of 1812.* Philadelphia: University of Pennsylvania Press.

Inaugural Address (First)

*I*n 1801, shortly before noon on the first Wednesday in March, Jefferson walked from his lodgings to the only part of the new Capitol building that had been erected, the Senate wing of the Congress. There the tall and plainly dressed Jefferson, one month shy of his fifty-eighth birthday, took the oath of office from his distant cousin, John C. Marshall, and became the nation's third president. Aside from the presence of a company of Washington artillery and a company of Alexandria riflemen, Jefferson's first inaugural was a low-key affair. No parades or cavalcades followed the president-elect to the Capitol. He was accompanied only by a few friends. However, when he arose to speak following the swearing-in ceremony, he faced hundreds of citizens in the crowded Senate chamber. His predecessor, the defeated Federalist candidate John Adams, was not among the crowd, having left for Massachusetts at four o'clock that morning.

Jefferson was aware that the prospect of his presidency caused much anxiety for the Federalists, and his address was designed to be conciliatory and reassuring. Few heard Jefferson's speech—his voice was barely audible—but copies of the message were quickly printed and distributed around Washington and in American newspapers. The address resembled Washington's farewell valedictory of 1796 in that it condemned the spirit of party warfare that existed in the United States. In the most famous passage, Jefferson concluded that Federalists and Republicans had more in common than not and that

> every difference of opinion is not a difference of principle. We have called by different names brethren of the same principle. We are all republicans—we are all federalists. If there be any among us who would wish to dissolve this union or change its republican form, let them stand undisturbed as monuments of the safety with which error of opinion may be tolerated where reason is left free to combat it.

Jefferson further proclaimed that all Americans shared a belief in the same fundamental principles of freedom of religion, press, and person that have been passed down from generation to generation and enshrined as national rather than party values. The short speech concluded with an admonishment to Americans that they continue to enjoy "peace, commerce, and honest friendship with all nations" in their foreign policy but avoid "entangling alliances." Thus Jefferson marked out in his address the basic principles and policies he would pursue during his presidency: the destruction of the party system in American politics and a rejection of European alliances in the wake of continued warfare between mercantilist Great Britain and Napoleonic France.

See also:
Election of 1800
First Administration

Reference:
Cunningham, Noble E., ed. *The Early Republic, 1789–1828.* Columbia: University of South Carolina Press.

J

Jackson, Andrew (1767–1845)

The nation's seventh president, Andrew Jackson believed himself to be the ideological heir to Thomas Jefferson. Jackson's role in American history is significant, because he was a key figure in the second generation of American statesmen—those who came of age after the Revolution. Born in the Waxhaw region of South Carolina in 1767 to parents of Scotch-Irish descent, Jackson was orphaned in his early teens. Without parental guidance, Jackson developed into something of a bully, a trait that would both distinguish and mar his reputation. He displayed no temperament for scholarship, preferring action over contemplation; he was a great hater and inspired great hatred in others, yet was exceedingly loyal to friends.

Reading law in North Carolina prepared Jackson for a career as a lawyer. Since opportunities were limited in the East, he migrated west to seek his fortune, settling in the territory of Tennessee in 1787 at the age of 20. Jackson ingratiated himself with the state's ruling elite and won several key appointments, including a seat in the U.S. House of Representatives. Upon reaching Philadelphia, the young congressman was described as "a tall, lank, uncouth-looking personage, with long locks of hair hanging over his face, and a queue down his back tied in an eel skin; his dress singular, his manners and deportment those of rough back woodsman." Demon-strating little facility or interest in his relatively settled job in Congress, Jackson won a more coveted office in 1802 as major general of the Tennessee state militia. Further enhancing his reputation were several successful land deals, which quickly put him on par with other frontier aristocrats in the new West.

It was during the War of 1812 that Jackson emerged as a figure of national distinction. Moving against the Native American tribes in the present-day state of Alabama, Jackson secured the region, Jefferson's proposed Empire of Liberty, for future white migration. More importantly, the Jackson-led American victory over British forces at the Battle of New Orleans ushered in the era of the common man as well as an acute sense of national pride. Jackson, the nation's greatest military hero since George Washington, was in a position to lay claim to the highest public office a grateful nation could bestow: the presidency.

In 1824, Jackson and three other men, including John Quincy Adams, were candidates for the executive office. Though Jackson was a southern slaveholder, Jefferson, from his retirement at Monticello, let it be known that he was no champion of the general. Jefferson saw Jackson as little more than a military chieftain who owed his popularity to the whim of public opinion rather than to the virtues of sustained accomplishment and reflective decision making. At a more fundamental level, however, Jefferson was uncomfortable with Jackson because the two men differed socially and temperamentally. Jefferson belonged to a generation that cherished the ideals of the Enlightenment and sought insight into the "natural laws" of government, the economy, and the universe. He was, moreover, an educated and elegant man who believed in a limited kind of public suffrage. Jackson, on the other hand, operated from instinct and was at times crude and prone to settle disputes with duels. He was insecure where Jefferson was sure, in search of conflict where Jefferson sought peace, and in favor of mass democracy for white males, while Jefferson preferred a more limited type of suffrage. When the contest came down to Jackson and Adams, Jefferson made note of his preference for the latter and was pleased when Jackson lost.

Despite Jefferson's reservations, Jackson believed that he was the true heir to a Jeffersonian movement that had lost its focus. During the period 1815–1850, a tremendous expansion of the capitalist market took place, dislocating traditional patterns of agrarian society. For men like Jackson, this seemed a betrayal of the American Revolution and the Jeffersonian movement that had come to power in 1800. Though the acceleration of the market went far beyond the control of politics, the federal government had become involved in providing subsidies and protection for major players in the economy. To Jackson, this involvement implied favoritism on the part of the federal government. Jacksonians remembered that the Jeffersonians rode into power by promising a return to agrarian principles. In 1828, Jackson ran for the presidency again and this time won on the premise that he could stop government from playing favorites in the market and thus bring back the old republic.

Though the differences between Jackson and Jefferson were large, real similarities existed as well. Fundamentally, Jeffersonian democracy and Jacksonian democracy both personified southern rule. They promoted agrarian policies, championed national expansion, and gave prestige to the argument for states' rights. Where Jackson dramatically deviated from Jefferson was in his interpretation of the presidency. To Jackson, the ex-

Aquatint of Andrew Jackson's first inaugural reception in 1828 by Robert Cruikshank.

ecutive was the direct representative of the people and thus operated on their behalf. Eschewing the traditional belief that Congress was the chief voice of the people, Jackson elevated the power of the presidency through his use of the veto, killing bills that, though constitutional, did not, in his opinion, aid the people. The contradiction inherent in a strong executive who promoted states' rights was not lost on southerners, who feared that Jackson was setting an ominous precedent for the future. Jackson served two terms as president and left office in 1837 with his popularity very much intact. His final act as executive was to recognize the republic of Texas, an area first claimed by the United States in Jefferson's purchase of the Louisiana Territory. Jackson retired to his Nashville plantation, where he died in 1845.

See also:
Election of 1824
Jacksonian Democracy

Reference:
Remini, Robert. 1966. *Andrew Jackson.* New York: Harper & Row.

Jacksonian Democracy

As president, Andrew Jackson believed that he was the heir of Thomas Jefferson and the Jeffersonian values of states' rights, agrarianism, and frugal government. Loosely defined, Jacksonian democracy, which politically encompassed the period from 1828 to 1848, championed southern interests by diminishing the power of the federal government to centralize economic power in the North. Thus there were real similarities between Jefferson and Jackson. Both men harbored deep suspicions concerning the pace of the industrial process in America. Jefferson dissented from Alexander Hamilton's urban-industrial vision of the nation by repudiating the National Bank of the United States and denouncing Hamilton's "Report on Manufactures," which spelled out

in detail the prospects for the factory system in America. Jackson, too, wrestled with the issue of a centralized financial institution, and his veto in 1832 of the recharter of the Second National Bank of the United States ensured that throughout the antebellum period, the forces of large-scale capital would not dominate the Union. Moreover, Jackson attacked the industrial vision of his opponents, the Whig party, as vigorously as Jefferson had attacked the Federalists of his day. The Whig call for an "American System of Manufactures" with federal aid for internal improvement projects within the states sounded to Jackson like an attempt to re-create Hamilton's report two generations after it was first authored.

A deeper parallel is at work here, however. Both Jeffersonian democracy and Jacksonian democracy were born in times of crisis. In Jefferson's own day, southerners consented to the drawing up of a federal Constitution because they believed that such a document would have limited powers clearly spelled out. During the 1790s, however, the rise of Hamilton and the Federalist party demonstrated to the Jeffersonians that a limited Constitution was not enough to protect southern, or rather, slaveholder interests. A dominant party or faction was needed, one that could maintain power and stamp its interpretation on the Constitution as the Federalists had done. Hamilton's financial vision, with its promotion of industrial values over agrarian culture, threatened the Union by imperiling southern interests. Jeffersonians codified their opposition by forming the Democratic-Republican party. They made Jefferson their leader, got him elected president in 1800, and ruled uncontested for a generation.

The rise of Andrew Jackson followed a similar path. By 1815 the Federalist party was vanquished as a potent political force, and all contenders for office now claimed to be Jeffersonians. In other words, the Republican party was no longer responsive to the needs of a section, the South, but was instead nationalized, responding strictly to majority will. This development worked against southern interests, because the North contained a preponderance of the population and thus appeared to be on the verge of dominating the nation. In 1824, for example, John Quincy Adams was elected president by the House of Representatives when no candidate received a majority of the electoral votes. Not only did this election end 24 years of uncontested domination of the executive office by Virginia presidents (Jefferson, Madison, and Monroe), but it also indicated to southerners that a northern agenda was now being implemented. Adams was from Massachusetts, after all, and a former Federalist in the bargain. Moreover, he owed his election not to national support but rather to northern support. Thus he was a sectional president and much resented by the old Jeffersonian coalition.

From this morass emerged Andrew Jackson, a plantation aristocrat who made his fortune in the cotton fields of Tennessee and his reputation as a military chief at the Battle of New Orleans. Southerners who wanted to diminish the power of the federal government flocked to Jackson, as did northerners like Martin Van Buren who saw in the destruction of the old Jeffersonian-Federalist party system the seeds for disunion. These men reasoned that without party distinctions, the attention of the nation would settle on the issue of slavery. Better, they assumed, to have a two-party system with northerners and southerners in the same coalitions than one large party divided by sectional interests. Jackson's candidacy for the presidency caught fire, and in 1828 he was elected to that office principally due to the support of southerners and westerners. Jackson claimed that his principles were similar to Jefferson's and that he was guided by a belief that the agrarian vision of America should dominate over the pretensions of industry.

Despite such claims, Jackson was never a personal favorite of Jefferson, who once commented that

I feel much alarmed at the prospect of seeing General Jackson President, he is one of the most unfit men, I know of for such a place. He has had very little respect for laws or constitutions,—and is in fact merely an able military chief. His passions are terrible. When I was President of the Senate, he was a Senator; and he could never speak from the rashness of his feelings. I have seen him attempt it repeatedly, and as often choke with rage. His passions are no doubt cooler now;—he has been much tried since I knew him—but he is a dangerous man.

Such criticism is understandable. Despite the very important structural similarities between the pro-southern Jeffersonian and Jacksonian coalitions, real differences in personality existed between the two men. Jefferson was reflective and rational; Jackson operated from emotion and with great passion. Jefferson was suspicious of the military and Jackson was the early republic's greatest military hero. Jefferson was an aristocrat through breeding, education, and inheritance; Jackson acquired his standing in life through effort and sheer force of will. Moreover, Jefferson was first and foremost a product of the Enlightenment. True, he believed in popular democracy, but to a lesser extent than Jackson, who fancied himself a model of the "common man." Ultimately, Jefferson's form of democracy was more class-based and thus much more limited than Jackson's. Nevertheless, both men served to further a southern agenda for national development. Both failed. Andrew Jackson could no more limit the expansion of credit and speculation in the 1830s than Jefferson could in the 1790s. Each sought to bring back the virtue of an "Old Republic" that had long since ceased to exist.

See also:
Jackson, Andrew
States' Rights
Virginia Dynasty

Reference:

Watson, Harry. 1990. *Liberty and Power: The Politics of Jacksonian America*. New York: Noonday Press.

Jay's Treaty

The treaty that John Jay signed with Great Britain in November 1794 was attacked by Jefferson as a document that codified Alexander Hamilton's domestic policies on the stage of foreign diplomacy. Nevertheless, an agreement of some sorts with the British was badly needed. After the United States achieved its independence, Britain had refused to allow it into the lucrative empire to trade. Moreover, British forts in the American West, which were supposed to be evacuated and turned over to the United States, were still occupied. Further, America lacked commercial agreements with the British that would rationalize its economic relations with that nation and solidify the American economy. Yet Jefferson was

1796 painting by Gilbert Stuart of John Jay, chief justice of the U.S. Supreme Court.

hesitant to have any kind of rapprochement with Great Britain, a nation he viewed as perhaps irrevocably tainted by the curse of monarchy.

With Britain at war against a French nation undergoing the convulsions of a republican revolution, Jefferson believed the United States should maintain a friendly relationship with the French republic rather than the British Empire. Further, Jefferson understood that Hamilton's fiscal plans for America included steering the nation's basic economy away from agriculture and toward industry. To accomplish this, Hamilton would need access to British markets, capital, and credit. Jefferson concluded that such actions would promote speculation and corruption within the country.

Nevertheless, President Washington believed that to avoid war with Britain and provide Americans access to the empire's markets, a treaty between the two nations was vital. Hamilton wanted to lead the American mission to London, but his candidacy proved controversial and would have doomed the effort from the start. Instead, Washington chose John Jay, a New York Federalist. Jay was in basic sympathy with Hamilton's opinion, and the latter wrote out the plenipotentiary's orders.

In any case, the American position was weak. Britain was the strongest power on earth and the United States was a fledgling republic. Jay's purpose was to get the best deal he could for his nation, not to demand unreasonable access to British trade. He was successful in procuring a treaty that gave America peace with Britain in return for a pro-British view of world diplomacy. The United States received assurances that Britain would leave the western forts within a year and was awarded a commercial treaty that provided limited access to Indian and West Indian markets. In return, the United States was forced to renounce the principle of freedom of the seas, meaning it could not trade with France or France's allies. The treaty was a bitter pill for the nation to swallow, since it meant that Jay was agreeing that America would not trade with France. The treaty further granted Britain most-favored-nation status on all goods and produce, that is, Britain would receive the best prices on all merchandise sold to it.

Jeffersonians were livid over the treaty, contending that it placed the United States on the side of monarchy rather than republicanism. Jefferson lamented that the treaty was "an execrable thing" and "really nothing more than a treaty of alliance between England and the Anglomen of this country against the . . . people of the United States." Jefferson's dismay was shared by most Americans, who repudiated the treaty. Jay's handiwork was barely accepted by the Senate, with most of the negative votes coming from Jefferson's southern stronghold. Jay himself

remarked, upon his return from England, that he could travel across the country by the light of burning effigies cast in his likeness. From the press came the words "Damn John Jay! Damn every one that won't damn John Jay! Damn every one that won't put lights in his windows and sit up all night damning John Jay!" Yet the Senate's assent and Washington's signature made this very unpopular treaty law.

Jay's Treaty was a nail in the coffin of Federalism. Just five years after the treaty's acceptance, the Jeffersonian Republicans would come to power, partially due to their opposition to American subservience to Great Britain. "Though the Anglomen have in the end got their treaty through," Jefferson accurately concluded, "it has given the most radical shock to their party which it has ever received."

Cartouche engraving on "A map of the most inhabited part of Virginia . . ." drawn by Joseph Fry and Peter Jefferson in 1751, showing the selling of tobacco for shipment.

See also:
Anglo-French Wars
Hamilton, Alexander

Reference:
Bemis, Samuel Flagg. 1923. *Jay's Treaty, a Study in Commerce and Diplomacy*. New York: Macmillan.

Jefferson, Martha Wayles (1748–1782)

For ten years, Martha Wayles Jefferson was the beloved wife of Thomas Jefferson. An attractive widow at 23, Martha was in residence at her father's home in Williamsburg when she was courted by Jefferson. Contemporary accounts of Martha are few, but they show her to be a petite and genteel woman practiced in the arts expected of a Virginia belle. On a more practical note, as eldest child, Martha stood in line to inherit her father's vast landholdings and was thus a prize for any bachelor.

Martha and Thomas were married on New Year's Day in 1772 and began housekeeping at Jefferson's small quarters at Monticello. The marriage was by all accounts a happy one and produced six children, all but two of whom died before reaching adulthood. In Jefferson's Virginia, wives devoted themselves to husband, home, and children, and Martha was no exception. In 1782, after ten years of marriage and several difficult pregnancies, Martha died. Jefferson wrote in his *Autobiography* that Martha was "the cherished companion of my life, in whose affections unabated on both sides, I . . . lived . . . ten years in unchequered happiness." He never remarried.

See also:
Monticello

Reference:
Mayo, Bernard, ed. 1942. *Jefferson Himself: The Personal Narrative of a Many-Sided American.* New York: Houghton Mifflin.

Jefferson, Peter (1707/8–1757)

Peter Jefferson, the father of Thomas Jefferson, was born into a gentry family in Virginia in February 1707 or 1708. Upon reaching a suitable age, Peter inherited land, livestock, and two slaves from his father, which he used to develop a plantation. Over time the young man gained a reputation for running a prosperous agricultural enterprise. Taking his place among the local elites of his region, Peter became justice of the peace in 1734, sheriff in 1737, and three years later, county surveyor. In 1739, Peter married Jane Randolph, whose family was more prominent in Virginia society than his. Thomas was particularly proud of his father's skills as a surveyor. In the 1740s, Peter was part of an expedition that traveled throughout Virginia and made the first true map of the state. Thomas attributed his own interest in exploring to his father's example.

In many ways, Peter Jefferson's life anticipated and shaped his son's. Thomas became a local gentry figure of some importance, serving in the House of Burgesses as Peter had. Moreover, upon his death in 1757 at the age of 49, Peter left Thomas several thousand acres of land, more than 60 slaves, and some 300 hogs, cattle, and horses. Peter's generous bequest to his son, reminiscent of his own inheritance, ensured that Thomas would have the wealth to live as a country gentleman with ample time reserved for study. Peter himself was not a scholar, but he instilled in Thomas a love for learning and adventure. In praise of his benefactor, Thomas wrote, "My father's education had been quite neglected, but being of a strong mind, sound judgment, and eager after information, he read much and improved himself. . . . He placed me at the English school at five years of age and at the Latin at nine, where I continued until his death."

Reference:
Mayo, Bernard, ed. 1942. *Jefferson Himself: The Personal Narrative of a Many-Sided American.* New York: Houghton Mifflin.

Judiciary Act of 1801

Following the election of 1800, a lame-duck Federalist Congress passed the Judiciary Act of 1801, which created 23 new judicial positions and reduced the number of Supreme Court justices from six to five. The additional positions, complete with their attendant sinecures (marshals, attorneys, and bailiffs), were filled with Federalist partisans by outgoing Federalist president John Adams. To Jefferson, the incoming Republican party president, a great disservice had been foisted upon the American people who had voted Republican supporters into power. Now it seemed that the Federalists were trying to entrench themselves in the judiciary, the least democratic branch of government. Upon taking office, Jefferson successfully worked to have the Judiciary Act repealed.

See also:
Adams, John
Attack on the Judiciary

Reference:
McCloskey, Robert. 1960. *The American Supreme Court*. Chicago, IL: University of Chicago Press.

Kentucky Resolutions

*I*n 1798 a Federalist majority in Congress passed the Alien and Sedition Acts, which forbade public criticism of federal government officials and the policies they initiated. Vice President Jefferson understood that the intent of the act was to destroy the infant Republican coalition that he led. Jefferson warned that "if this goes down we shall immediately see attempted another act of Congress, declaring that the President shall continue in office during life, reserving to another occasion the transfer of the succession to his heirs, and the establishment of the Senate for life."

In response to the danger to civil liberties that he perceived, Jefferson took up his pen and drafted a series of resolutions denouncing centralized power while upholding the virtues of state sovereignty. Intending the document to be drafted by a state legislature in order to give it added force, Jefferson initially believed North Carolina would serve as the proper medium for his message. The resolutions, however, came to the attention of John Breckinridge, a former neighbor of the vice president who was now prominent in Kentucky politics. Breckinridge convinced Jefferson that Kentucky would serve as an ideal forum in the battle over local and national power. Jefferson agreed, and the Kentucky Resolutions were adopted in November.

Jefferson's resolutions articulated the classic argument that the Union should be recognized as a compact among the states rather than the people. While acknowledging that certain powers such as national defense and currency were the unquestioned prerogatives of a national government, Jefferson argued that acts beyond the central government's enumerated powers were unconstitutional and had no force in the states, which had, he noted, "an equal right to judge for itself, as well of the infractions as of the mode and measure of redress."

Thus Jefferson put forth a theory of local rights that would allow states to ignore federal laws that they believed were unconstitutional. In the original draft, which had been deemed too radical by the Kentucky legislature, Jefferson contended that "every State has a natural right in cases not within the compact . . . to nullify of their own authority all assumption of power within their limits." Had Kentucky appropriated the theory of nullification, it would have placed itself in a position of defiance of federal law. Fearful of such an encounter, the legislature refused to allow the word "nullification" to appear in the resolution they adopted.

Though the Kentucky Resolutions did not result in the repeal of the Alien and

Sedition Acts, they nevertheless succeeded in declaring them objectionable to many interests in the Union. Highlighting this fact was the Virginia legislature's adoption of a series of resolutions as well. These articles, authored by James Madison, condemned the recent actions by the Federalist Congress in language not quite as radical as Jefferson's. Beyond this, Jefferson would not go. He recognized that the tide of events was turning toward the Republicans and that political victory for himself and his party in 1800 was attainable. Jefferson remarked that "I would not do anything at this moment which would commit us further, but reserve ourselves to shape our future measures or no measures, by the events which may happen."

Finally, the Kentucky Resolutions served not only as a bulwark for First Amendment rights, but also as the intellectual currency behind southern attempts to nullify federal laws that endangered the institution of slavery. This argument was implicit in Jefferson's original resolutions and was passed down to proslavery advocates like John C. Calhoun, who used the theory of nullification and state sovereignty to weaken northern attempts to limit the extension of slavery.

See also:
Alien and Sedition Acts
Election of 1800

Reference:
Levy, Leonard. 1963. *Jefferson and Civil Liberties: The Darker Side*. Cambridge, MA: Harvard University Press.

King, Rufus (1755–1827)

This New Yorker opposed Jeffersonian democracy with nearly as much energy as the Federalist Colossus, Alexander Hamilton. Rufus King was born in Scarborough, Massachusetts (present-day Maine), in 1755. He attended Harvard College, graduated in 1777, and was admitted to the bar. A skillful orator, King was a member of the Continental Congress from 1784 to 1787 and gained a favorable reputation. His most significant achievement was the introduction of a resolution barring slavery in the Northwest Territory.

Settling in New York in 1788, King represented that state in the Senate from 1789 to 1796. He proved a most adept leader of the Federalist party, which championed a powerful central government that would give tone and discipline to the state governments. As reward for his efforts, King was appointed minister to Great Britain, where he served with great skill and distinction. Twice an unsuccessful candidate for the vice presidency, King was the last Federalist nominee for the presidency in 1816 and suffered a devastating defeat at the hands of James Monroe. King left the Senate in 1825 and died in New York City two years later.

See also:
Election of 1816
Federalist Party

Reference:
Elkins, Stanley, and Eric McKitrick. 1993. *The Age of Federalism: The Early American Republic, 1788–1800*. New York: Oxford University Press.

Lewis and Clark Expedition

Throughout his life, Jefferson was intensely interested in the American West. His father, Peter, surveyed much of Virginia's western territory, and early in his life Jefferson surmised that the nation's destiny lay in the frontier beyond the Appalachian Mountains. As the years passed, Jefferson championed various proposed excursions across the North American continent, most of which either failed to materialize or were limited in their effectiveness. Some have described Jefferson's interest in the West as merely scientific curiosity, which to a degree it was. It would be unfair to the complexity of the man, however, to leave unstated various other agendas that attracted him. Jefferson revealed some of them in a message to Congress in 1803, in which he declared that

the property and sovereignty of the Mississippi and its waters secure an independent outlet for the produce of

From a 1906 painting by Frederic Remington of the Lewis and Clark expedition.

the Western States, and an uncontrolled navigation through their whole course free from collision with other powers and the dangers to our peace from that source, the fertility of the country, its climate and extent, promise in due season important aids to our Treasury, an ample provision for our posterity, and a widespread field for the blessings of freedom and equal laws.

Shortly after this speech, Jefferson, who had never been more than 50 miles west of Albemarle County, planned an expedition to the Pacific and back by way of the Missouri and Columbia Rivers. The leaders of the expedition were two army veterans, Meriwether Lewis, who served as Jefferson's private secretary, and William Clark. The two explorers were ordered to find a useful road to the Pacific, study the geography of the region, and make commercial and diplomatic ties with the natives. Jefferson was particularly interested in tapping into the lucrative western fur trade.

The "Corps of Discovery" started up the Missouri River in the spring of 1804, nearly 50 strong. Traversing the Dakotas, where the explorers wintered, the expedition was fortunate in acquiring the navigational services of Sacajawea, a Shoshone girl married to a French trapper. In the spring the expedition started off again and by August had crossed the Continental Divide. Trips down the Snake and Columbia Rivers brought the party closer to the Pacific, which they reached in November. Clark memorialized the occasion by carving into a tree, "By Land from the U. States in 1804 & 5." After spending the winter there, the expedition returned by nearly the same route, completing the trip in September with their arrival in St. Louis.

In many respects, the project was a tremendous success. Unlike the superficial Spanish and French exploration in North America, the Lewis and Clark expedition took pains to ensure that plant and animal specimens were brought back and topographical calcu-

lations carefully recorded. In sum, the expedition awakened the American mind to the vastness and potential of the West. Jefferson was pleased with the efforts of his "discoverers," noting that "the expedition of Messrs. Lewis and Clark for exploring the River Missouri, and the best communication from that to the Pacific Ocean has had all the success which could have been expected."

See also:
Empire of Liberty
Louisiana Purchase

Reference:
Ambrose, Stephen. 1996. *Undaunted Courage: Meriwether Lewis, Thomas Jefferson, and the Opening of the American West.* New York: Simon & Schuster.

Library of Congress

During the War of 1812, a British invasion force set the capital on fire, destroying, among other buildings, the Library of Congress. Condemning the British action as one of "barbarism" not fitted "to a civilized age," Jefferson offered to sell Congress his library of 6,500 books, easily the best personal collection on the continent. Jefferson had planned for Congress to have access to his library at the time of his death, but the loss of the nation's library moved him to make the offer at that time. Along with an inventory, Jefferson sent to Congress his remarks on the invaluable collection that took him over 50 years to assemble. He had, he assured Congress, "spared no pains, opportunity or expense, to make it what it is." In summing up its contents, he noted that "it included what is chiefly valuable in science and literature generally, [it] extends more particularly to whatever belongs to the American statesman. In the diplomatic and parliamentary branches, it is particularly strong." Further, he cautioned Congress that his wishes were that the collection be taken as a whole: "I do not know that it contains any branch of sci-

Recapitulation of an estimate of the sum
necessary to carry into effect the Miss.ª
expedition. —

Mathematical Instruments	$. 217.
Arms Accoutrements extraordinary	, : 81.
Camp Equipage	, . 255.
Medicine & packing	, . 55.
Means of transportation	, . 430.
Indian presents	, . 696.
Provisions extraordinary	, . 224.
Materials for making up the various articles into portable packs	, . 55.
For the pay of hunters guides & Interpreters	, . 300.
In silver coin to defray the expences of the party from Nashville to the last white settlement on the Missourie	, . 100.
Contingencies	, . 87.
Total	**$. 2,500.**

19946

Letter sent by Meriwether Lewis to President Thomas Jefferson on April 20, 1803, itemizing estimated expedition expenses.

ence which Congress would wish to exclude from their collection." He concluded, "There is, in fact, no subject to which the member of Congress may not have occasion to refer." The payment, about which Jefferson was quite concerned because his own disheveled finances caused him considerable embarrassment, he would leave to the fair judgment of Congress.

To Jefferson's dismay, most members of Congress were unacquainted with his library and had only a dim perception of its true value. Moreover, members of the Federalist party viewed the acquisition of Jefferson's library through the prism of partisanship and ideology. They feared having the nation's library anchored by the kind of excessively democratic and libertarian works that they assumed filled Jefferson's library. "The grand library of Mr. Jefferson will undoubtedly be purchased with all its finery and philosophical nonsense," the Boston *Gazette* lamented. But despite Federalist opposition and various attempts to cripple the bill, the library

This engraving depicts the Congressional Library before the British burned it on August 24, 1814.

was purchased. The payment to Jefferson was $23,950 for his 6,487 volumes.

Jefferson oversaw the packing of the books, leaving them in the pine bookcases in which they were shelved at Monticello. Ten wagons were required to transport the material to the capital. Jefferson was proud that his library, now the nation's library, constituted "unquestionably the choicest collection of books in the U.S. and I hope it will not be without some general effect on the literature of our country." Yet the nation's gain was also a quiet loss for Jefferson, who wrote to John Adams after the last wagon had gone, "I can not live without books." Financed partially with the money he acquired from Congress to sell his original library, Jefferson's second collection soon began to take shape. At the time of his death just 12 years later, it would number some 1,000 volumes.

See also:
War of 1812

Reference:
Sanford, Charles. 1977. *Thomas Jefferson and His Library: A Study of His Literary Interests and of the Religious Attitudes Revealed by Relevant Titles in His Library*. Hamden, CT: Archon Books.

Linnaeus, Carl (1707–1778)

As a child of the Enlightenment, Jefferson believed in an orderly universe and, by association, an orderly society operating under "natural" principles founded on the tenets of republicanism, or rule by the people. Jefferson did not come to this worldview on his own; rather he was influenced by some of the best minds of the period. From Sir Isaac Newton, for example, Jefferson learned that there was order in the physical universe; from John Locke he understood the empirical foundations of knowledge and the operation of the mind; and from Carl Linnaeus, Jefferson learned that the world was not chaotic but operated from various principles that could be understood.

Linnaeus was born in Rashult, Sweden, in 1707. He studied botany at Harderwijk University in the Netherlands, where he obtained his M.D. In 1753, Linnaeus published *Species Plantarum,* which introduced the concept of binomial nomenclature for plants. Prior to Linnaeus, naturalists used various individualized diagnostic phrases to describe plant and animal life. In his *Systema Naturae,* for example, Linnaeus places under the category "Order of the Primates" the Homo (sapiens) diurnus, which includes all humankind, and Homo (troglodytes) nocturnus, represented by the orang-outang. This system was confusing because scientists dealing with the same species might use different names. Linnaeus's use of the binomial, which consisted of a Latin or Greek name followed by an epithet, made the naming of plant and animal life into a rational system. The American white oak, for example, became the *Quercus alba* and was acknowledged as such by all scientists, who now had a common scientific language. In sum, Linnaeus brought linguistic order to the natural world.

See also:
Enlightenment
Locke, John
Newton, Sir Isaac

Reference:
Boorstin, Daniel. 1948. *The Lost World of Thomas Jefferson.* Chicago, IL: University of Chicago Press.

Locke, John (1632–1704)

Jefferson's thinking on politics and society sprang from two main ideological sources. The first was the classical world in which Athenian democracy and Roman republicanism demonstrated how republics were formed, developed, and declined. The second source was the "country" or "liberal" writers of seventeenth-century England, who sought to reduce the power of the monarchy and enlarge the sphere of freedom for the general populace. The chief figure in this school of thought was John Locke, the most influential political theorist of his day.

Locke was born at Wrington, Somersetshire, in 1632. Educated at Christ Church at Oxford, Locke struck up acquaintances there with Robert Boyl, Robert Hooke, John Wilkins, and Isaac Newton. He received a medical degree at Oxford and joined the household of Lord Shaftesbury as secretary and family doctor in 1667. This relationship proved pivotal to Locke, as Shaftesbury's falling out with the Crown forced him and thus Locke to flee to Holland. Witnessing Charles II's purge of the Whig movement firsthand, Locke began to work on his masterpiece, *Two Treatises of Government,* which questioned the divine right of kings. Locke returned to England in 1689 when the Glorious Revolution ushered in the reign of William and Mary and signified a victory for Whig principles. Locke's interests in science, philosophy, and politics remained paramount until his death in 1704.

Jefferson found Locke's work useful because it provided a blueprint for revolution. The *Two Treatises* is nothing less than the foundational text of liberalism and represents the enlightened or "natural" perspective on the function of government. Until Locke's time, kings were believed to have been given authority to rule by God. To obey the king was thus not merely a civil but a spiritual imperative. Locke questioned such beliefs by tracing the genealogy of political authority, and his findings were revolutionary. Locke argued that if God did bestow the right of divine rule on any human, then it was on Adam, the first man who the Bible claimed held dominion over the land. The trouble, Locke argued, was that no one on earth could prove direct lineage to Adam or his immediate heirs, Cain and Abel. Thus, even if divine right existed at the inception of human history, it had no contemporary force because no individual could demonstrate claim to

Undated lithograph of John Locke.

great reason of men's putting themselves into society, and quitting the state of nature." In doing so, man does not give up his "natural" rights of life, liberty, and the pursuit of property, rather man joins in a community to enhance these rights. Thus, Locke contends, "the natural liberty of man is to be free from any superior power on earth, and not to be under the will or legislative authority of man, but to have only the law of nature for his rule. The liberty of man, in society, is to be under no other legislative power, but that established, by consent, in the commonwealth, nor under the dominion of any will, or restraint of any law, but what the legislative shall enact, according to the trust put in it." In other words, rulers receive their legitimacy from the people, not from any compact with God. Furthermore, the rights of the king, like those of his people, are enumerated and limited. The ruler is in place merely to protect property rights, and if he should fail in his obligation, the people are within their rights to remove him.

Locke's arguments were employed in the service of the Glorious Revolution, in which James II was removed as King of England by the Whigs in favor of a limited monarchy. Locke's ideas, however, provided more than justification for the replacement of one brand of monarchy for another. They bequeathed to the world the language of liberalism. By articulating the rights of individuals, Locke legitimized the notions of consent, right to resistance, and the value of constitutional government. In a famous passage, Locke argued that

God's favor through appeal to lineage. The real question, therefore, was where does political power come from if it does not emanate from God?

Locke contended that in the state of nature, all men were equal and enjoyed the same rights. He also recognized, however, that a state of nature could degenerate into a state of war when the strongest, smartest, or least ethical take property or power that does not belong to them. "In transgressing the law of nature," Locke argued, "the offender declares himself to live by another rule, than that of reason and common equity which is that measure God has set to the actions of men, for their mutual security: and so he becomes dangerous to mankind." In order to protect himself from such an "offender," man leaves the state of nature and voluntarily places himself in civil society to protect himself and his property. As Locke put it, "to avoid this state of war (wherein there is no appeal but to heaven, and wherein every the least difference is apt to end, where there is no authority to decide between the contenders) is one

> for all the power the government has, being only for the good of the society, as it ought not to be arbitrary and at pleasure, so it ought to be exercised by established and promulgated laws: that both the people may know their duty, and be safe and secure within the limits of the law, and the rulers too kept within their due bounds, and not to be tempted, by the power they have

in their hands, to employ it to such purposes, and by such measures, as they would not have known, and own not willingly. . . . The supreme power cannot take from any man any part of his property without his own consent. For the preservation of property being the end of government, and that for which men enter into society, it necessarily supposes and requires, that the people should have property, without which they must be supposed to lose that by entering into society, which was the end for which they entered into it, too gross an absurdity for any man to own.

The destruction of monarchical absolutism and the right to resist tyrants were ideas from Locke's work that heavily influenced Jefferson. Much of the Declaration of Independence revisits the principles embedded in the *Two Treatises*. Lockean liberalism provided Jefferson with the structure for an enlightened defense of individual rights that he would use to promote American independence.

See also:
Declaration of Independence
Enlightenment

Reference:
Locke, John. 1993. *Two Treatises of Government*. London: Everyman.

Louisiana Purchase

The area encompassing the Territory of Louisiana was deemed by Jefferson to be the future home of independent, republican farmers. Jefferson was not, however, the first person to prize this region. French exploration into the interior of the North American continent during the Age of Discovery gave that nation a strategically important foothold in the New World. Aside from Canada, the French domain consisted of a vast expanse of territory extending west of the Mississippi River to the Rocky Mountains and south to New Orleans. "New France" gave the French government an empire in the Americas that dominated the Trans-Appalachian economy. Agricultural produce was transported down the Mississippi River to the port of New Orleans and from there to Europe, the West Indies, or the Anglo-American seaboard. Great Britain defeated Franco-Spanish forces during the French and Indian War (1756–1763) and acquired territory from the defeated powers. The French lost Canada and, assuming that its days as a colonial power in North America were over, ceded to the Spanish government the Louisiana Territory as compensation for its efforts in the war. Two decades later, following the American Revolution, Great Britain ceded its land claims south of Canada and east of the Mississippi River to the United States.

The American government understood that access to the Spanish-controlled Mississippi River was one of the nation's most pressing issues. With farmers spilling into the West, adequate transportation for agricultural produce had to be secured. Some Americans feared that if the United States could not gain access to the interior river trade, then plantation owners and petty commercial farmers in the region would switch their allegiances to Spain. It was thus with much relief to the United States that Pinckney's Treaty of 1795 guaranteed America free navigation of the Mississippi and the right to deposit goods at New Orleans. In 1801, however, President Jefferson began to hear rumors that Napoleon had forced Spain to cede back the Louisiana Territory in the hopes of resurrecting the old French empire in North America. Startled by the prospect of having the aggressive French leader as a neighbor, Jefferson wrote to Robert Livingston, the new American minister in France, that "there is on the globe one single spot, the possessor of which is our natural and habitual enemy, it is New Orleans. . . . France placing herself in that door assumes to us the attitude of

H. C. Whorf painting depicting Monroe and Livingston completing negotiations with Talleyrand, April 30, 1803.

defiance." Jefferson instructed Livingston to find out if the retrocession had taken place and if it had, then offer to purchase the port of New Orleans so that American commerce in the West would still have an outlet. Failing this, Jefferson concluded, "we must marry ourselves to the British fleet and nation."

Livingston could make no headway in France, however, and after Spanish officials suspended the American right of deposit at New Orleans, the Federalist opposition in Congress pushed for military action against the important city. Jefferson refused to take such a belligerent position, correctly deducing that the uneasy peace between France and Great Britain was about to end, in which case the French would be more likely to bargain with the United States. To strengthen America's position, however, Jefferson concentrated troops on the Mississippi just north of the Spanish border and sent James Monroe to France to speed up negotiations. Monroe left the United States in March 1803

authorized to pay up to 50 million livres, that is, a little more than $9 million, for New Orleans and the Floridas.

While Monroe was on his way to Europe, the Federalists continued to agitate for aggressive action against the French. Alexander Hamilton suggested that the United States seize the Floridas and New Orleans and then allow Monroe to negotiate from a position of power. Jefferson believed that the Federalists were trying to use the French crisis as a means to return to power and resisted further action at this time. His patience was rewarded when he received word that the Spanish had ceded the Louisiana Territory back to the French. The right of deposit to New Orleans was not only restored but was preserved in the treaty of cession to France. Pleased with the outcome of events, Jefferson declared that "we have obtained by a peaceful appeal to justice, in four months, what we should not have obtained under seven years of war."

Meanwhile in Paris, negotiations for an American purchase of New Orleans began in earnest. In April, Livingston was finally permitted an audience with the French minister, Talleyrand, who startled the American by inquiring if the United States would be interested in purchasing the entire Louisiana Territory. Jefferson's information had been correct. Napoleon was about to commence war with Great Britain and needed money to finance his army. Additionally, the French leader's plans to construct an empire in North America foundered after his forces failed to conquer the former French colony of Santo Domingo. Napoleon understood that without this important island as a foothold in the Americas, France could not hope to be a power in the region. Moreover, he knew that France could not hold Louisiana against a British invasion and would thus lose the territory without compensation.

Livingston and Monroe, who had just arrived in Paris, quickly accepted Talleyrand's proposal, and on April 30 a treaty was concluded that ceded the Louisiana Territory to the United States for 60 million francs and the assumption by the United States of 20 million francs in claims of Americans against France. The total cost was $15 million for 825,000 square miles, more than doubling the size of the nation and constituting the largest peaceful acquisition of territory in American history.

Despite the stunning success in Paris, Jefferson had deep qualms about the legality of the treaty. He believed in a strict interpretation of federal laws, and the Constitution said nothing about annexing foreign territory into the United States. Jefferson considered an amendment to the Constitution but realized the process would take considerable time and Napoleon might change his mind. He submitted the treaty to the Senate, convinced that the unique circumstances required that Congress act quickly without the guidance of an amendment. Republican majorities in both houses ensured quick passage, and the ratification of the treaty was followed in December with a ceremony in New Orleans in which the French officially transferred the Louisiana Territory to the United States.

The Louisiana Purchase was the high point of Jefferson's presidency. "By enlarging the empire of liberty," Jefferson contended, "we . . . provide new sources of renovation, should its principles, at any time, degenerate, in those portions of our country which gave them birth." Thus, the American West would become the repository of republican values, a place where yeoman farmers preserved liberty and democracy through their economic independence. Ultimately, of course, Jefferson's empire of liberty was also an empire of conquest. Native American tribes in the region were forcibly removed, and slavery, which existed in the settled areas of Louisiana under Spanish and French occupation, was extended into what would become the states of Missouri, Arkansas, Louisiana, and Texas. The purchase thus proved a blessing for the Jeffersonians but quickly turned into a problem for future generations of Americans who questioned the social, economic, and moral feasibility of extending slavery in the West.

See also:
Empire of Liberty
Foreign Policy

Reference:
Tucker, Robert, and David Hendrickson. 1990. *Empire of Liberty: The Statecraft of Thomas Jefferson.* New York: Oxford University Press.

ℳ

Macon, Nathaniel (1758–1837)

Jefferson was the first president to use a political party to push his laws through Congress. In the House of Representatives, Nathaniel Macon was the man in charge of whipping Republicans together to make sure that party regularity was enforced and the tenets of Jeffersonian agrarianism were enacted into law. Thus Macon, with John Randolph and William B. Giles, proved to be the leading Jeffersonian lieutenants in Congress.

Macon was born in Warren County, North Carolina, in 1758. Like James Madison, he studied at the College of New Jersey (now Princeton University), after which he returned to North Carolina to study law. A proponent of limited government, Macon opposed the Constitution because he believed it centralized power in the hands of a few men. He joined the House of Representatives in 1791 and became, along with Jefferson, a vigorous opponent of Alexander Hamilton's attempts to enlarge the powers of the central government. He served as Speaker from 1801 to 1807 and left the House in 1815 to sit in the Senate until 1828.

See also:
Hamilton, Alexander
Macon's Bill Number Two
Randolph, John

Reference:
Malone, Dumas. 1948–1981. *Jefferson the President, First Term, 1801–1805,* vol. 4 of *Jefferson and His Time.* Boston: Little, Brown.

Macon's Bill Number Two

As president, Jefferson struggled to force the European powers to accept America's rights as a neutral shipping agent during the Napoleonic wars. When the chief aggressors in this conflict, Great Britain and France, refused to acknowledge American sovereignty, Jefferson responded with an embargo. The United States refused to ship its produce to foreign ports, hoping this measure would injure the European economy and force the acceptance of America's interpretation of commercial rights. The policy failed, however, and was rescinded in the final days of Jefferson's presidency. The new executive, James Madison, attempted a policy of "non-importation" that opened up American trade to all nations except Britain and France, but this measure also failed to influence those nations to cease their attacks on American shipping.

Finally, in the late autumn of 1809, after failing to accept an earlier discrimination bill from House member Nathaniel Macon, Congress passed Macon's Bill Number Two. It provided that the United States would trade with both Britain and France until one revoked its restrictions, whereupon the United States would cease trade with the other. In sum, it was an offer of national favor to the highest bidder. Madison had little confidence in the plan but was desperate to demonstrate to the nation that a Republican party government could secure the property rights of its citizens. Failing this, Madison feared, the Jeffersonian coalition might be removed from power and replaced by the Federalists.

Napoleon took advantage of the bill, authorizing his foreign minister to hand an ambiguous letter to the American minister that alleged the repeal of the French policy of picking up American ships. Though there was substantial evidence to the contrary, Madison chose to accept the French position, probably to put pressure on the British to do the same. When the British did not meet the American timetable for repealing their shipping acts, the War of 1812 resulted. Macon's Bill Number Two was consistent with the Jeffersonian party's attempt to shape Europe's relationship with the United States without going to war. The conflict that did eventually come is a testimony to both the intransigence of Britain and France and the unrealistic perceptions of Jeffersonian foreign policy.

See also:
Embargo of 1807
Non-Intercourse Act
War of 1812

Reference:
Perkins, Bradford. 1962. *The Causes of the War of 1812.* New York: Holt, Rinehart & Winston.

Madison, James (1751–1836)

James Madison was Jefferson's most intimate political colleague. The working relationship between the two Virginians proved to be perhaps the most fruitful and productive in the history of American government. Together they created the Democratic-Republican party, served a total of 16 years in the presidency, and shaped a political culture of southern rule that would last until the Civil War. Though perceived as Jefferson's junior apprentice, Madison was in fact the driving force behind the writing and drafting of the Constitution and took the lead in opposing the Federalist party. Though he deferred to the Sage of Monticello's reputa-

tion and experience, Madison deserves to be remembered as a leading light among the founding generation and certainly its most adept student of political philosophy. Perhaps more than any man of his age, Madison demonstrated a faith in republican principles even though he, much more than Jefferson, believed in the potential corruption of the human soul.

Madison was born in Port Conway, Virginia, in 1751 to a family of English ancestry. He was educated at home and then, unlike Jefferson, who remained in Virginia for college, traveled north to study at the College of New Jersey at Princeton. There he received a rigorous training in the classics and was awarded a bachelor of arts degree in 1771. Much like Jefferson, Madison was profoundly influenced during his college years by the best minds of the Enlightenment, including Isaac Newton, John Locke, and David Hume. Eschewing both the clergy and the legal professions, Madison found an outlet for both his energies and his education in the cause of American independence. In 1774 he served on Orange County's committee of safety and in 1776 was elected to the Virginia convention that declared the colony independent of Great Britain and produced a state constitution. Throughout the early war years Madison served in Williamsburg on the governor's council under both Patrick Henry and Jefferson. By the end of the Revolution, Madison was serving in the Continental Congress and becoming a proponent of a stronger national government.

Returning to the Virginia legislature in 1784, Madison helped Jefferson enact the latter's famous bill for religious freedom as well as various other reform measures designed to put behind them the colonial past of the Old Dominion. During Jefferson's removal to Paris as American minister, Madison became increasingly concerned that the weakness of the Confederation government, demonstrated best by its inability to draw tax revenues from the states, would destroy the republican experiment. In response, Madi-

"Death of the Embargo": metalcut from 1814 of James Madison cutting off the head of a turtle, representing the embargo.

son took the forefront in organizing a series of meetings that culminated in the Philadelphia Convention of 1787, in which he drafted the outlines of the U.S. Constitution. To ensure the passage of that document in the states, Madison joined with Alexander Hamilton and John Jay in producing *The Federalist*, a series of pamphlets that defended the Constitution and comprise this nation's greatest contribution to political philosophy.

Madison was elected to the first U.S. House of Representatives and pushed for discriminatory measures against British trade in an effort to coerce that nation into a commercial arrangement more favorable to the United States. To Madison's surprise, Hamilton, an ally in drafting the Constitution, opposed coercive acts aimed at England because he believed the United States needed access to British credit, markets, and naval protection. Hamilton produced a series of bills that brought the nation closer to the British orbit and strengthened the power of the central government to a degree that troubled Madison and Jefferson. In retaliation, Madison took the lead in creating the Democratic-Republican party, which would soon make Jefferson its leader.

Madison proved a capable political warrior throughout the 1790s, consistently opposing what he perceived to be Federalist attempts to limit local freedoms and enhance the powers and prerogatives of the central government. After Federalists passed the Alien and Sedition Acts in 1798, Madison and Jefferson wrote resolutions that condemned the government's attempt to curb civil liberties. Though defending the concept of states' rights, Madison never went so far as to advocate nullification, that is, the repeal of a federal law by a state, or secession. After all, this man so devoted to Virginia's sovereignty was the primary author of the nation's Constitution as well.

The overthrow of Federalism in 1800 with the election of Jefferson saw Madison rise to the position of secretary of state. Under his leadership, the Louisiana Territory was purchased in 1803, suppression of the Barbary pirates was carried out, and the nation was able to maintain an uneasy peace with Britain and France until the European wars encroached upon the United States in 1806. Jefferson's use of an embargo to force the warring powers to comply with America's interpretation of neutral rights failed, and upon Madison's election to the presidency in 1808, the question of American neutrality was predominant.

Madison's elevation to the presidency continued the Virginia Dynasty of southern-agrarian rule, but his eight years as chief executive proved to be the most trying of his career. Various attempts to negotiate a settlement with Britain and France that would recognize American neutrality failed, and the country drifted to war in 1812. Though he tried desperately to avoid the conflict, Madison ultimately came to believe that if the Republican party could not protect the property rights of its citizens, then it would be removed by the people at the next election. Such a situation, Madison presumed, would mean the end of the Republican party and thus, in his estimation, the end of republican government as well.

The war went badly for the nation, and Madison was forced to contend with serious divisions in Federalist New England. American attacks on Canada failed but were balanced by victories on Lake Erie and on the

Atlantic. Madison was personally humiliated in 1814 when a small British invasion force entered Washington and burned a few of the government's buildings. Madison watched the action from a nearby hillside, having escaped by only a few minutes the arrival of the British army. But later that year, when it was apparent that victory would come at too high a price, and with the defeat of Napoleon imminent, Britain decided to end the war with the United States.

The final two years of the Madison presidency saw a surge in nationalism stemming from the war. Under his guidance the National Bank, which he had opposed in the 1790s, was rechartered and a moderate protective tariff was instituted. Demonstrating a flexibility that often eluded Jefferson, Madison was able to set republican dogma aside to engage in a program of national development, which consequently enhanced the powers of the federal government. Retiring to his farm in Virginia, Madison lived out the remaining years of his life far from the stirrings of politics. Aside from participating in the Virginia Constitutional Convention of 1829 when his proposals to lessen the powers of the Tidewater aristocracy were repelled, Madison never again ventured onto the public stage. This most temperate and learned Founding Father died at Montpelier, Virginia, in 1836.

See also:
Federalist Party
Republican Party
War of 1812

Reference:
Koch, Adrian. 1950. *Jefferson and Madison: The Great Collaboration*. New York: Alfred A. Knopf.

Malthus, Thomas R. (1766–1834)

*B*orn into the upper middle class of English society, Thomas Malthus become one of the most influential thinkers of his generation. Malthus's study on population

disavowed the optimistic and progressive worldview that permeated the works of Enlightenment thinkers such as Jefferson. Rather, Malthus's 1798 study, *An Essay on the Principle of Population As It Affects the Future Improvement of Society,* argued that a natural tendency existed for population to outstrip all possible means of subsistence. Instead of the world becoming an increasingly rational, orderly, and perfectible entity, as Jefferson anticipated, Malthus posited that overpopulation would ensure an unremitting struggle for resources.

Malthus believed that humans tended to double their numbers every 25 years. Arable land, of course, could not be developed at the same pace, and thus the geometric growth rate of humans (1, 2, 4, 8, 16, 32, etc.) would soon overwhelm the subsistence crops, which grew at an arithmetical rate (1, 2, 3, 4, 5, 6, etc.). Malthus's study challenged Enlightenment thinkers such as Jefferson and Rousseau, who believed that the inception of popular government and the recognition of natural rights would lead to increased liberty. According to Malthus, the masses could not be counted on to regulate their reproductive rate. "The view has a melancholy hue," Malthus admitted, "the power of population is so superior to the power of the earth to provide subsistence . . . that premature death must in some shape or other visit the human race."

Consequently, Malthus believed that war, infanticide, disease, poverty, and famine were natural components of any society and served to enhance the quality of life for all by severely regulating population. Accordingly, he opposed poor relief and housing projects for the working classes, noting that such charity was only cruelty in disguise.

Jefferson read Malthus's work with enthusiasm but did not believe it was applicable in North America, where only a few million populated an entire continent. Ever the optimist, Jefferson retained a deep faith in the perpetual youth of America and assumed that as population increased along the East

Coast, successive waves of emigration would allow farmers to spill across the West. The Louisiana Purchase gave the nation a "safety valve" in the West, which Jefferson believed would provide enough land for the next 100 generations. The trans-Mississippi lands secured, Jefferson was sure that America had circumvented Malthus's dismal predictions on population.

See also:
Empire of Liberty
Louisiana Purchase
Urban Vices

Reference:
Heilbroner, Robert. 1953. *The Worldly Philosophers: The Lives, Times, and Ideas of the Great Economic Thinkers.* New York: Simon & Schuster.

Manufacturers

Jefferson's opinion of manufacturing was in constant flux throughout his life. As a son of Virginia, he could not help but be disposed to an agricultural lifestyle predicated upon the freedom and autonomy of the independent plantation owner or yeoman farmer. This vision was challenged in the early 1790s by Alexander Hamilton's "Report on Manufactures," which proposed a more industrial vision of American economic development. To Jefferson, such a system appeared to sow the seeds for speculation and loss of financial independence. Further, an industrial economy would prove far more beneficial to the commercial Northeast than to the slave-based labor system of Jefferson's beloved Virginia.

With the ascension of the Republican party and the end of the War of 1812, however, Jefferson demonstrated a more favorable opinion of manufacturers. He seemed to believe that as long as Jeffersonians controlled the federal government, they would not allow the industrial process to get out of hand. Moreover, with the Napoleonic wars spilling over into North America, Jefferson

believed that the United States could only be ideologically and politically independent of Europe if it enjoyed economic independence. Toward the latter years of his life, therefore, Jefferson approved of an industrial America, which he hoped would complement but not overwhelm the agricultural interests of the nation.

See also:
"Report on Manufactures"

Reference:
McCoy, Drew. 1980. *The Elusive Republic: Political Economy in Jeffersonian America.* Chapel Hill: University of North Carolina Press.

Marbury v. Madison

At the end of John Adams's presidency, a lame-duck Federalist Congress passed the Judiciary Act of 1801, which was designed to limit the powers of the incoming Republican Congress and executive, Thomas Jefferson. The act created new judicial positions that went to Federalist partisans who would then serve for life, allowing the defeated party to retain influence in governing. Jefferson thought the act unethical, and as president he refused to allow undelivered commissions to be given out to the new judges. Technically, commissions were to be distributed by the secretary of state, James Madison. When Madison's State Department would not hand over to William Marbury his commission, the Federalist judge went to the Supreme Court and asked for a writ that would compel Madison to do so.

This put the Court in a difficult position. Still in its infancy, the Supreme Court had not established the reputation it enjoys today, and Justice John Marshall feared that if he ordered Madison to give Marbury his commission, the ruling would be ignored by a powerful Jeffersonian administration. This incident would weaken the authority of the Court and perhaps make future unpopular rulings irrelevant. Seeking a way to chastise the Jeffersonians but not rule in favor of Marbury, which would pit the Court against the administration in a losing battle, Marshall found a brilliant alternative. He contended that Marbury improperly sought justice from the Court based upon the Judiciary Act of 1789, which gave that judicial body the power to issue writs in cases such as this.

But Congress, which created that 1789 act, had no power to do so, Marshall argued, because the Court's original jurisdiction is defined by the Constitution and can be neither enhanced nor diluted by act of Congress. Thus, Marshall created the precedent of judicial review. That is, the Supreme Court ruled that a law created by Congress was unconstitutional and carried no force. Marshall also chastised Jefferson's handling of the Marbury case, noting that even though the Court could not rule on the issue of Marbury's commission, the Federalist was deserving of his office.

To the end of his life, Jefferson never accepted the principle of judicial review. In his mind, the Constitution clearly stated that Congress and the executive branch checked one another through ballots, vetoes, and veto overrides. Nowhere was the court system given the power to nullify congressional law. In a broader sense, Jefferson interpreted *Marbury v. Madison* as an unethical attempt by the Federalist party to retain political power in America. Thrown out of elective positions by the people, the Federalists now appeared to be entrenching their principles in the judiciary, the most aristocratic branch of government. To withhold Marbury's writ, Jefferson believed, was to strike a blow for liberty and to validate the choice of the people by turning out the Federalists.

See also:
Judiciary Act of 1801
Midnight Appointments

Reference:
McCloskey, Robert. 1960. *The American Supreme Court*. Chicago, IL: University of Chicago Press.

Market Revolution

The final years of Jefferson's life witnessed the emergence of an economic transformation that historians have recently labeled the "market revolution." The capital-driven segment of the economy expanded tremendously, usurping the place of the subsistence, barter, and small-scale commercial economy of Jefferson's agrarian vision. The process was driven not by laws or regulations but rather by demographic pressures that could not be held back in a democratic society. By 1830, if not before, it was evident that a few major interests would dominate the business life of the nation.

Several factors must be accounted for in explaining the emergence of a broadly based capital economy. First, the growing population of the Ohio and Mississippi Valleys following the Louisiana Purchase brought millions of acres of land under cultivation. This expansion was particularly significant for the southern economy, since the majority of these lands, carved into the territories then states of Louisiana, Mississippi, Alabama, and Missouri, produced cotton. Second, the Northeast experienced the beginnings of an industrial revolution financed by the proliferation of the textile industry in New England. Following the War of 1812, the federal government offered northern factories protective tariffs to develop a factory-based system of production similar to Great Britain's. This development meant that industry gradually replaced commerce and agriculture as the Northeast's primary economic concern. Finally, the maturation of internal improvement projects—steamboats, turnpikes, canals, and railroads—linked peripheral markets in the American hinterland with national and international markets enjoined to major seaport cities.

The development of a truly national market forced an alteration in the Jeffersonian vision of independent yeoman farmers providing the backbone for the economy and character of the country. In the South, for example, the proliferation of new cotton lands meant that agricultural interests were now commerce driven rather than subsistence oriented. They were at the mercy of market prices that they could not control. Moreover, in order to purchase their lands, many farmers borrowed large sums of money and were hard-pressed, during lean years, to pay their debts. The American farmer, in other words, was no longer independent. A similar change affected those who lived in the cities. As the factory system became entrenched in the North, skilled artisans were no longer prized. Previously these independent craftsmen set their own schedule, worked at their own pace, and controlled their labor. With the influx of an industrial order that could produce finished products with unskilled labor very quickly and at minimal cost, the skilled artisan was no longer needed. His craft and his purse were lost, along with his independence.

It is doubtful that Jefferson would have approved of the change from moderate capital accrual to a more speculative, acquisitive, and predatory economy. It has been remarked of Abraham Lincoln that the "rail-splitter" was blessed never to have witnessed the economic excesses of the Gilded Age that followed the great moral crusade of the Civil War. So might it be said of Jefferson that he was fortunate not to have observed the rise of large-scale capital interests during the antebellum period.

See also:
Era of Good Feelings
Retirement
Transportation Revolution

Reference:
Sellers, Charles. 1991. *The Market Revolution: Jacksonian America, 1815–1846.* New York: Oxford University Press.

Marshall, John (1755–1835)

*T*hough a third cousin to Jefferson, John Marshall was a staunch supporter of centralized power and fought the Republi-

Undated painting of Chief Justice John Marshall.

can party's localist tendencies from his position as chief justice of the Supreme Court. Marshall was born in Prince William County, Virginia, in 1755 and took an active part in the American Revolution, serving with distinction at the battles of Brandywine, Monmouth, and Stony Point. In the winter of 1777–1778 he joined General Washington and suffered with the American contingent through the harsh winter at Valley Forge. After the Revolution, Marshall was admitted to the Virginia bar and began the most distinguished law career in the nation's history.

Throughout the 1780s and 1790s, Marshall served in various state and national offices. He achieved a measure of fame in 1797 for his refusal as part of an American negotiating team to accede to French demands for a bribe before work on a treaty could commence. In 1799, Marshall was elected to the U.S. House of Representatives, and in 1800 he accepted the office of secretary of state from President John Adams. One of Adams's last official acts was to appoint Marshall chief justice of the Supreme Court. Jefferson believed that with Marshall ensconced in the nation's court system, he would be removed from the political scene. But he underestimated both Marshall's intellect and the latent powers of the court system to effect change in the nation. As Supreme Court Justice Felix Frankfurter put it, "When Marshall came to the Supreme Court, the Constitution was essentially a virgin document. By a few opinions—a mere handful—he gave institutional direction to the inert ideas of a paper scheme of government. Such an achievement demanded an undimmed vision of the union of the States as a Nation and the determination of an uncompromising devotion to such insight."

As chief justice, Marshall assaulted the Jeffersonian position that the federal courts were somehow responsible for rendering decisions favorable to the majority of Americans. Rather, Marshall envisioned the federal courts as a bulwark against majority decisions that might hurt the interests of minorities. In *Marbury v. Madison*, the chief justice established the right of the Supreme Court to judge the constitutionality of congressional legislation. Jefferson never accepted this interpretation and viewed the federal court system as a dangerous vehicle that threatened the sovereignty of the states. In 1804, Jefferson gave his blessing to Republican attacks on Federalist judges through abuse of the impeachment clause of the Constitution. Though this effort ultimately failed, it did highlight the dramatic differences between the nation's elected officials and its federal court system. Jefferson lamented that "we had supposed we possessed fixed laws to guard us equally against treason and oppression. But it now appears we have no law but the will of the judge. Never will chicanery have a more difficult task than has been now accomplished to warp the text of the law to the will of him who is to construe it."

The Marshall Court continued to render decisions favorable to national power long after Jefferson's retirement in 1809. In the case of *Fletcher v. Peck*, for example, the Court declared its power to prevent a state from interfering with the property rights of individuals. In the 1819 case of *McCulloch v. Maryland,* Marshall wrote the majority opinion, which concluded that a state could not destroy a federally created institution (in this case, a bank) within its own borders. Such decisions legally empowered the federal government over the states much as Alexander Hamilton attempted to do in the area of finance. Marshall's lasting achievement was to raise the Supreme Court to the level of authority enjoyed by the executive and legislative branches of government.

See also:
Attack on the Judiciary
Burr Conspiracy
Marbury v. Madison

Reference:
Stites, Francis. 1981. *John Marshall: Defender of the Constitution.* Boston, MA: Little, Brown.

Mazzei Letter

Philip Mazzei was a native of Tuscany who emigrated to America and became Jefferson's neighbor. The two men shared a love of horticulture, with Mazzei providing Jefferson various Mediterranean vines and trees imported from Italy. They shared as well a love of liberty and a disgust for centralized power as personified by the Federalist party. In the spring of 1796, with Federalism at high tide, Jefferson wrote a private letter to Mazzei expressing his views on the political state of his country. Jefferson remarked that "in place of that noble love of liberty and republican government which carried us triumphantly through the war, an Anglican monarchical aristocratical party has sprung up." Though he took comfort in the fact that "the main body of our citizens . . . remain true to their republican principles," it grieved Jefferson that "against us are the Executive, the Judiciary, two out of three branches of the Legislature, . . . British merchants and Americans trading on British capital, speculators and holders in the banks and public funds." The

Virginian was optimistic, however, concluding that "we shall preserve it; and our mass of weight and wealth on the good side is so great, as to leave no danger that force will ever be attempted against us."

Jefferson intended his remarks to Mazzei to remain private, for he was not merely attacking a political faction but also the president. His reference to the executive office aimed "against us" was a direct attack on George Washington, who believed himself to be above the fray of partisan politics. Unfortunately for Jefferson, Mazzei had this passionate and highly combustible letter published in a Florentine newspaper. From there it found its way to the Paris *Moniteur*, and then to England, and finally, in the spring of 1797, to the American press.

Jefferson's private thoughts were now a point of debate among Federalists, who excoriated the Virginian for his attacks on the government and its beloved president. When the letter was published, Washington was settled into retirement at Mount Vernon, and Jefferson was newly sworn in as a Republican party vice president serving under the Federalist John Adams. The Federalists hoped to use the Mazzei letter to destroy Jefferson's political career. They believed that by exposing his critique of Washington, they would tarnish Jefferson's reputation and demonstrate that he was a duplicitous ingrate who wished to defame the great hero's well-earned reputation.

Jefferson did his best to weather the storm of criticism. He maintained a dignified silence and refused to engage his enemies in a debate that would have assuredly degenerated into an unseemly affair. Unfortunately, he did not communicate with Washington to explain the letter, and relations between the two men were never again picked up. Finally, the public exposure of the Mazzei letter was a shock to Jefferson, who considered each correspondence that left his desk a very private commodity. To a man who disdained confrontation, the publication of the letter proved a most painful episode.

See also:
Federalist Party
Washington, George

Reference:
Garlick, Richard. 1933. *Philip Mazzei, Friend of Jefferson: His Life and Letters*. Baltimore, MD: Johns Hopkins Press.

Midnight Appointments

In the waning weeks of John Adams's presidency, a lame-duck Federalist Congress passed the Judiciary Act of 1801, which allowed the president to make several appointments to the bench. Jefferson, the incoming president, charged the Federalists with attempting to subvert the will of the people, who had voted Republicans into power in 1800, by entrenching themselves in the federal judiciary. Jefferson was particularly dismayed that his old political friend, John Adams, would abuse this Judiciary Act by appointing Federalists to every post. The term "midnight appointments" comes from a letter to Henry Knox in which Jefferson describes his disgust over Federalist actions:

> The last day of [Adams's] political power, the last hours, and even beyond the midnight, were employed in filling offices, and especially permanent ones, with the bitterest Federalists, and providing for me the alternative either to execute the government by the enemies, whose study it would be to thwart and defeat all my measures, or to incur the odium of such numerous removals from office as might bear me down. This outrage of decency should not have its effect, except in the life appointments which are irremovable; but as to the others I consider the nominations as nullities, and will not view the persons appointed as even candidates for their office, much less as possessing it by any title meriting respect.

Thus, one is left with the ugly spectacle of President Adams working furiously through the final days and nights of his presidency to secure the appointments of Federalist partisans who could restrain the Republicans' rise to power, something Jefferson himself referred to as the "Revolution of 1800."

True to his word, Jefferson denounced the Judiciary Act and privately repudiated Adams's actions to all who would listen. Ultimately, Jefferson's anger over the midnight appointments and the Judiciary Act would lead him to declare war on the Federalist elements of the judiciary through use of the veto power. Moreover, he would not correspond again with Adams for a dozen years, providing testimony to how personally he took this attempt to circumvent his leadership through the nation's court system.

See also:
Attack on the Judiciary
Judiciary Act of 1801
Marbury v. Madison

Reference:
Brown, Ralph. 1975. *The Presidency of John Adams.* Lawrence: University Press of Kansas.

Milan Decree

The Milan Decree was issued by Napoleon in December 1807 to loosen Britain's hold on the world economy. With France and Great Britain at war, the United States served as a neutral carrier to both nations until British orders in council, that is, maritime laws, prohibited American ships from servicing France or its allies. In response, Napoleon issued a series of laws known collectively as the Continental System, which attempted to isolate Britain while enhancing the commercial power of continental Europe. The Milan Decree declared that American ships submitting to British blockade regulations or permitting searches by British vessels would be liable to seizure by French ships. In sum, Napoleon made it clear to the United States that if it did not protect its neutral status in the face of British aggression, then the French would not respect American neutrality either. The result of the various orders in councils and decrees coming from Europe and the British Isles would be war between America and Great Britain in 1812.

See also:
Anglo-French Wars
War of 1812

Reference:
Brown, Roger. 1964. *The Republic in Peril: 1812.* New York: Columbia University Press.

Minister to France

Jefferson arrived in Paris in August 1784 as a special envoy to the American mission to France. With the retirement of Benjamin Franklin as minister to France, Jefferson assumed the appointment and served until his return to the United States in the fall of 1789. These years were very good to Jefferson, and he counted them among his most enjoyable. As minister to France, Jefferson's duties consisted mainly of procuring preferential treatment for American commerce within France and its empire. Though at times he was distraught by the "present disrespect of the nations of Europe" toward the United States, he nevertheless took from his experiences a lifelong affection for the French people. To Abigail Adams he wrote, "I do love this people with all my heart, and think that with a better religion, a better form of government and their present governors, their condition and country would be most enviable."

Much of Jefferson's love of the French had to do with the charms of Parisian life. To someone of his intellect and breadth of interests, the artistic circles of Paris were irresistible. Moreover, the exploration of a different continent held intrinsic interest for an amateur scientist like Jefferson. Traveling through southern France and northern Italy, the American minister collected numerous samples of plant and animal life to take home with him to "colonize" the New World landscape with the flora and fauna of the Old World. Jefferson also carried on a platonic yet passionate relationship with a married woman while in Paris. His feelings for Maria Cosway, best expressed in a painfully correct letter to his love describing the compromising position their affections had placed them in [the famous "dialogue between my head and heart"], reveals an emotional side of Jefferson rarely glimpsed.

Jefferson's final year in Paris witnessed the onset of the French Revolution. The minister was elated at this event and presumed that America's own Revolution had precipitated events in France. He happily noted that "the American war seems first to have awakened the thinking part of this nation in general from the sleep of despotism in which they were sunk." Moreover, Jefferson found himself in the thick of the early revolutionary movement, a position he much enjoyed. "I was much acquainted with the leading patriots of the Assembly," he recalled. "Being from a country which had successfully passed through a similar reformation, they were disposed to my acquaintance, and had some confidence in me." But Jefferson was not destined to observe firsthand the course of the revolution. Events in the United States demanded that he return home. In his absence, a new and more powerful federal Constitution had been written, and it provided for an executive with a cabinet that included a secretary of state. Due in part to his years of service in Paris, the nation's first president, George Washington, chose Jefferson to serve in the country's highest foreign policy post, a position the Virginian now returned home to assume.

See also:
Cosway, Maria
French Revolution

Reference:
Malone, Dumas. 1948–1981. *Jefferson and the Rights of Man*, vol. 2 of *Jefferson and His Time*. Boston: Little, Brown.

Missouri Compromise

*I*n 1819 the Territory of Missouri petitioned the federal government for statehood. Because the practice of slavery existed in Missouri, many northerners opposed statehood for Missouri, contending that the area in question, part of Jefferson's Louisiana Purchase, should be preserved for free labor. Jefferson believed that the North's unwillingness to accept a new slave state in the West would precipitate an irreparable division between the sections. "This momentous question," he wrote, "like a fire-bell in the night, awakened and filled me with terror. I considered it at once as the knell of the Union." But Jefferson's fears were not immediately realized. In the congressional compromise that followed, Missouri was allowed to enter the Union as a slave state, provided that a new free territory, Maine, also successfully petition for statehood. Moreover, to ensure that such dissension did not arise in the future, it was established that, in the territories encompassing the Louisiana Purchase, slavery could not exist above the latitude of 36 degrees 30 minutes, that is, above the southern border of Missouri.

The Missouri crisis involved much more than a congressional solution, however. It also shaped the transformation of party politics in America. A truism in southern history prior to the Civil War was that the South must be left alone to deal with the issue of slavery, a subject too critical and potentially perilous to allow the North any say. Jefferson formed the Republican party in the 1790s in response to the Federalist party's attempts to enlarge the powers of the Constitution to bring about a more industrial, capital-oriented economy. Jefferson feared that such an economy would work against the interests of the agricultural South. Further, he feared that a powerful central government, one that could create a national bank or fund internal improvements, could be used someday by a northern majority to eradicate slavery. Thus Jefferson wanted to

ENUMERATION
OF THE INHABITANTS
OF THE
STATE OF MISSOURI.

COUNTIE	Free white males	Free white females	Free per- sons of color	Slaves	Persons bound to service for a term of years	Total	Representatives
Boone,	1679	1486	1	576		3696	3
Cooper,	1612	1419	19	446		3483	3
Callaway,	718	642		445		1797	1
Cole,	559	444		59		1028	1
Chariton,	885	841	7	290	5	1446	2
Cape Girardeau,	5526	5200	44	1088		7852	6
Franklin,	860	853	9	186		1928	1
Gasconade,	650	463	1	60		1174	1
Howard,	5210	2600	2	1409	3	7321	5
Jefferson,	875	749	4	200	1	1838	1
Lincoln,	823	656	2	211	2	1614	1
Lillard,	695	515		150		1340	1
Montgomery,	908	802		209		2032	2
Madison,	858	715	7	344	3	1907	1
New madrid,	1155	972	7	510		2449	2
Pike,	1286	1014	2	405		2607	2
Perry,	740	683	1	099	6	1593	1
Ralls,	742	581	1	358	2	1654	1
Ray,	913	730	2	141	2	1730	2*
St. Louis,	3564	5858	141	1608	24	8190	7
St. Charles,	1826	1443	11	739	5	4058	3
St. Genevieve,	1317	1081	62	717	4	3181	
Saline,	510	476	2	179	1	1142	1
Washington,	1816	1309	2	760		4...	
Wayne,	729	615	1	246	2	1614	1
	32120	96093	361	11254	60	70647	54

*County divided.   County of St. Francois   1
——
55

This enumeration of the inhabitants of the state of Missouri appeared in the St. Louis, Missouri, Gazette in 1822.

create a political coalition that would encompass a statistical majority of both southerners and northerners in order to take power, yet serve the bidding of a minority interest, the South.

The Jeffersonian party was successful due to circumstances. In the South, wealthy plantation owners were able to unite with poor "mudsill" whites on the race issue. That is, most southerners, be they rich or poor, wanted a weak central government that could not touch slavery. Thus most citizens in that section rallied around Jefferson. In the North, the largest class of people were not commercial farmers but rather subsistence farmers who feared the encroachments of the central government, made very real by the Federalist party's intrusive tax policies and by the government's penchant for using the military to force farmers to pay duties. These men, hardly supporters of slavery, nevertheless rallied to the Jeffersonian coalition over the issue of liberty, that is, freedom from the federal government. Though they had different reasons for doing so, a majority in both the North and the South could unite in Jefferson's Republican party in order to preserve personal or state autonomy.

In 1800, Jefferson was elected president. The South now controlled the reins of government and would do so, more or less, until the Civil War. Until the Missouri crisis, Republican control was unquestioned. The Federalist coalition was still in the field, and though it was now a minority party, it nevertheless forced the Republicans to remain united in order to win elections. Following the War of 1812, however, this situation changed. The Federalists had opposed the war, and with its successful conclusion in 1815, the party was destroyed. Now, with every politician in the nation claiming affiliation with the Jeffersonian-Republican party, the coalition was simply too large and encompassed too many disparate interests to serve its primary function: control of the federal government by the South. This amalgamation of political interests brought up a critical question: if everyone is a Jeffersonian, then what does it mean to be a Jeffersonian?

The Missouri crisis brought this situation to light. Southern Jeffersonians were shocked when northern Jeffersonians blocked the statehood bill for Missouri. Future events would be even more disconcerting. The compromise bill that resolved the crisis closed off the vast majority of the Louisiana Purchase territory to future slave states. Thus vast expanses of the American West would be shut off to southern slaveholders and the southern way of life. At the same time the Missouri issue was before Congress, Secretary of State John Quincy Adams was concluding a treaty with Spain that would allow the U.S. to purchase Florida and the Oregon territory at the price of giving up claims to Texas. Southerners had lusted after Texas for years, envisioning a new slave empire in the Southwest. That Adams, a former Federalist and resident of New England, would give away "southern" territory was anathema to the old Jeffersonian party. Finally, the election of

Adams to the presidency in 1824 was the last straw. Andrew Jackson was the favorite candidate of most southerners that year, and in fact Jackson received more popular and electoral votes than Adams or his other competitors. But because no candidate received a majority of electors, the contest went to the House of Representatives. There Adams received the necessary votes and defeated Jackson. This new "minority" president proceeded to call for the federal government to become involved in the economy in ways that made southerners think of Alexander Hamilton's fiscal policies of the 1790s.

To southerners one thing was evident: the control they had exercised over the federal government and thus the nation in the period between Jefferson's inaugural and the Missouri Compromise (1800–1819) was now being successfully countered by northern rule. During Adams's presidency, southerners and northern interests, weary of encroaching federal power, resurrected the old Jeffersonian coalition and found the successor to the Sage of Monticello to be Andrew Jackson. With the election of Jackson in 1828, southerners once again claimed control of the government and would not give it up until the election of Abraham Lincoln in 1860.

See also:
Adams, John Quincy
Jackson, Andrew
Retirement

Reference:
Brown, Richard. 1966. "The Missouri Crisis, Slavery, and the Politics of Jacksonianism." *South Atlantic Quarterly* 65 (Winter): 55–72.

Monroe, James (1758–1831)

The fifth president of the United States, James Monroe was one of Jefferson's most able political lieutenants. Along with James Madison, Monroe and Jefferson made up the Virginia Dynasty that controlled the executive office for a quarter of a century

1817 engraving of James Monroe by Goodman and Piggot after a painting by C. B. King.

and promoted a southern agrarian vision of national development. Like Jefferson, Monroe's political life was shaped by the American Revolution, opposition to the Federalist party, and residency in Paris as American ambassador. In sum, Monroe was a thorough Republican who battled the forces of what he perceived to be despotism, both at home and abroad. In many ways he was a more consistent Jeffersonian than Jefferson.

Monroe was born in Westmoreland County, Virginia, in 1758. Like Jefferson he attended William and Mary College but because of the onset of the American Revolution, did not finish. Rather, he joined the Third Virginia Regiment and distinguished himself in several engagements in New York. Seriously wounded at the battle of Trenton, Monroe later participated in the Battle of Monmouth and was present at Valley Forge. Unable to secure a command in the field, he returned to Virginia and studied law under Jefferson.

After Jefferson left for Paris in 1784, Monroe emerged as one of the Old Dominion's leading proponents of state and southern interests. While sitting in the Confederation congress, he organized opposition to a treaty with Spain because it would have yielded American claims to the right of access to the Mississippi River. The loss of access would have harmed the southern economy, which used the river as an artery for transporting commerce. In 1787, Monroe further enhanced his reputation as a localist by opposing the Constitution, which he believed granted excessive powers to the Senate and the executive. At this point in his life Monroe had married and settled in Albemarle County to be close to Jefferson. His consistent republicanism was rewarded in 1790 when the state legislature sent him to the U.S. Senate. There he joined Congressman James Madison in opposing the Federalist party's attempts to centralize political power in the federal government. Monroe emerged at this time as a major opponent of American foreign policy, which, under President George Washington, favored close ties with Great Britain. Monroe believed that the United States should ally itself with France, which had recently christened itself a republic. To institutionalize his position, Monroe joined Jefferson and Madison in creating the Republican party, the first opposition party in the nation's history.

Because of his well-known affection for the French Revolution, Monroe was made American minister to France in 1794. Unfortunately, Monroe operated in Paris more as a Republican party spokesman than as the representative of a nation. He embarrassed Washington with frequent outbursts against the British government and gave the impression that the president's administration was at odds with public opinion, which, he contended, favored an alliance with France. For his indiscretion, Monroe was recalled. After serving as governor of Virginia from 1799 to 1802, Monroe returned to Paris in 1803 as President Jefferson's special envoy to assist Minister Robert Livingston in purchasing the port of deposit on the lower Mississippi River, that is, the city of New Orleans. The subsequent purchase of not only New Orleans but the entire Louisiana Territory established Monroe as a national figure and put him in line for the presidency.

Monroe served as minister to Britain from 1803 to 1807, during which time he secured a treaty that would have relaxed Britain's commercial restrictions against the United States. Because the treaty did not end the illegal impressment of American seamen, however, Jefferson refused to sign it. Monroe, believing he had attained the best terms possible, was furious with the president. As a form of protest, he briefly challenged Madison for the presidency in 1808 but received little support. Friendship was restored among the Republican elite, however, and in 1811, Madison made Monroe his secretary of state. Following the War of 1812, Monroe was the obvious choice for the presidency, which he won with an easy victory over Senator Rufus King of New York. Monroe adopted a conciliatory tone toward the declining Federalist party because of his belief that political factions damaged the nation. As president he relied on personal contacts with congressmen as well as the support of a very distinguished cabinet to achieve his goals. For his efforts, a Boston newspaper referred to Monroe's tenure as the "Era of Good Feelings."

Monroe's greatest achievements as president were in the area of foreign policy. In 1819, under the very capable guidance of Secretary of State John Quincy Adams, the United States purchased Florida and parts of the Pacific Northwest from Spain. In 1822, also at the behest of Adams, Monroe announced that the Americas were no longer available for European colonization. Though largely symbolic at the time, this Monroe Doctrine asserted American independence in foreign policy and dramatized the seriousness of the republican experiment in the United States.

Domestically, President Monroe believed in limited government and refused to approve federal aid for internal improvements without a prior amendment of the Constitution. Though he easily won reelection in 1820, Monroe's second term proved difficult. The Federalist party was destroyed after the War of 1812 and thus Republicans no longer saw the need for strict party discipline. Without party machinery in place to promote a candidate (as the Republican party had promoted the candidacies of Jefferson, Madison, and Monroe), politicians who aspired to the presidency were forced to attack administration policies.

When he retired from public service in 1825, Monroe was deeply in debt and engaged in a bitter debate with Congress over money owed to him for previous services rendered. Due to age and infirmity, Monroe moved to the home of his daughter in New York City, where he died on July 4, 1831.

See also:
Monroe Doctrine
Virginia Dynasty

Reference:
Ammon, Harry. 1971. *James Monroe: The Quest for National Identity*. New York: McGraw-Hill.

Monroe Doctrine

*I*n one of his final statements on international politics, Jefferson advised President James Monroe to use American power to limit European influence in the Western Hemisphere. Beginning with the French removal from Canada in the early 1760s, European hegemony in the New World appeared to be coming to an end. The American Revolution encouraged this trend, while the French Revolution unwittingly furthered the process of liberty as the occupation of Spain by Napoleon's armies induced successful colonial rebellions in Central and South America. Following Napoleon's defeat at Waterloo and subsequent exile, the European powers sought to limit the expansion of liberal ideas by creating the Holy Alliance.

This conservative reaction to the French Revolution encompassed Europe's leading powers with the exception of Great Britain. As European armies employed by the Holy Alliance commenced the business of destroying popular democratic movements on the Continent, Americans like Jefferson feared that Europe would soon cast a covetous eye on the infant republics south of the United States, trying once again to carve out European spheres of influence in the Americas.

To Jefferson, the Holy Alliance represented Old World despotism at its worse, and he encouraged Americans to resist future European incursions in the New World. To a colleague he remarked that "I hope [to see] a cordial fraternization among all the American nations, and . . . their coalescing in an American system of policy totally independent of and unconnected with that of Europe." Offering aid to Jefferson's vision was, ironically, Great Britain, the world's greatest colonial power. The British preferred that the former Spanish empire remain independent of Europe, though for decidedly different reasons than Jefferson. Britain understood that if the European powers dominated the lower Americas, it would loose lucrative markets in the region. The British government thus proposed a joint Anglo-American agreement to preserve the autonomy of the Americas from future European colonization.

President Monroe was pleased with the British overture and asked Jefferson for his opinion on the subject. Jefferson responded that, although he detested the monarchical system of British politics and hoped to see the French Revolution destroy the Anglo system, he now recognized the British as a potential ally in a world increasingly hostile to republics. To Monroe he advised that

> our first and fundamental maxim
> should be, never to entangle ourselves
> in the broils of Europe. Our second,
> never to suffer Europe to intermeddle
> with cis-Atlantic affairs. . . . One
> nation, most of all, could disturb in

this pursuit; she now offers to lead, aid, and accompany us in it. By acceding to [Great Britain's] proposition we detach her from the bands, bring her mighty weight into the scale of free government, and emancipate a continent at one stroke. . . . Great Britain is the nation which can do us the most harm of any one, or all, on earth; and with her on our side we need not fear the whole world.

Ultimately, Secretary of State John Quincy Adams convinced Monroe that the United States could make a singular statement on the protection of the New World from future European expansion. More so than Jefferson, Adams knew that the British fleet, and perhaps more importantly British merchants, would back up American resolve even without a formal alliance. It would simply be in Britain's commercial and diplomatic interests to do so. Thus, the Monroe Doctrine was not a joint Anglo-American statement on the protection of New World republics as Jefferson had advocated. Yet, Monroe's contention in that doctrine that "the American continents, by the free and independent condition which they have assumed and maintain, are henceforth not to be considered as subjects for future colonization by any European power," echoes a Jeffersonian optimism about the natural rights of humanity and a faith in the redemptive power of the future.

See also:
French Revolution
Monroe, James

Reference:
Cunningham, Noble. 1996. *The Presidency of James Monroe.* Lawrence: University Press of Kansas.

Montesquieu, Baron de (1689–1755)

*T*his French political philosopher developed several theories on the evolution of republican states that greatly influenced

Jefferson. Born Charles Louis de Secondat in 1689, Montesquieu attended the Oratorian College of Juilly and studied law in Bordeaux. He assumed his titles in 1713 and 1716 upon the deaths of his father and uncle. In 1734, Montesquieu published his first significant political treatise, *Considerations on the Causes of the Greatness of the Romans and Their Decline.* The work evaluated the broad expanse of Roman history, from its earliest form of monarchy through the years of the republic and empire to the invasion of the Eastern tribes.

Montesquieu suggested that only small republics could be long lasting, because the swell of various social and ethnic groups in one state brings about a multiplicity of diverse and often conflicting interests. In Rome, for example, the infusion of Christianity and its different sects brought about a disastrous relationship between the church and state that fatally weakened the latter.

Montesquieu's most famous work, *The Spirit of the Laws,* was published in 1748 and greatly attracted Jefferson, who read the work around 1770. The Virginian admired Montequieu's assertion that civic virtue was required of citizens in order that the social organism operate at its most efficient level. Thus common citizens rather than elite rulers were responsible for the health of a nation. Further, Montesquieu advocated civil liberties, religious toleration, and a more humanistic interpretation of crime and punishment, all of which found favor with Jefferson.

The Virginian did, however, harbor certain reservations about Montesquieu's ideal society. Jefferson envisioned a large, agrarian republic that would be repeatedly energized by the virtue of its citizens. Montesquieu entertained more elitist thoughts. He presumed, for example, that while common citizens would be expected to demonstrate virtue, they would have no voice in the actual process of governing. Governing would be done, as it always had been, by an aristocracy infused by the spirit of liberty. In other

J. C. Buttre engraving of Monticello, which was in a state of continual construction and rebuilding over the course of 40 years. Jefferson noted that "architecture is my delight, and putting and pulling down, one of my favorite amusements."

words, hierarchy rather than social mobility would still predominate. Moreover, in the age of the American Revolution, neither Jefferson nor his peers could accept Montesquieu's assertion that the English system of government was the most perfect in the world. Finally, Jefferson rejected Montesquieu's claim that only a small republic could survive. The Virginian believed that the vastness of the American landscape would provide for a continual rejuvenation of republican values as generations of citizens became independent yeoman farmers.

See also:
Enlightenment
Louisiana Purchase

Reference:
Pangle, Thomas. 1974. *Montesquieu's Philosophy of Liberalism*. Chicago, IL: University of Chicago Press.

Monticello

Jefferson's home at Monticello took four decades to complete. It was an extension of Jefferson himself, absorbing the Virginian's scientific, domestic, ideological, and intellectual interests in a common cause, the shaping of a physical expression of reason and enlightened construction. Jefferson built his home on lands staked out by his father, Peter Jefferson, in the 1740s. By the late 1760s, Jefferson located an ideal site for his home just across the Rivanna River on the summit of a mountain that he called "Monticello," Italian for "little mountain."

The top of the mountain was cleared and leveled in 1768, and in late 1770, Jefferson moved into a one-room brick cottage until the rest of the house was ready. During Jefferson's lifetime, Monticello was in an almost perpetual state of construction. An avid student of architectural design, Jefferson anticipated using native structures as a model for his future home. To his disappointment, however, Williamsburg, the most cosmopolitan city in colonial Virginia, offered no suitable models. Jefferson was disdainful of the provincial styles and wooden structures that distinguished the capital. In time, he turned toward European designs, and soon his library was filled with some of the most important works on the subject. From James Gibbs's *Book of Architecture* Jefferson was introduced to the work of the Italian master Andrea Pallid, whose magisterial work, *Four Books of Architecture*, would influence Jefferson's thinking substantially.

By the mid-1770s, the essential contours of Monticello were complete. One student described Jefferson's home as "a two story brick pavilion with wings, entered front and back by columned porticoes, connected with its service buildings by hidden passageways; a house which commanded a magnificent view of the Blue Ridge Mountains to the west, the hamlet of Charlottesville in the valley immediately below, and on the east a stretch of red-clay farmlands which Jefferson called his sea-view." Probably the most distinctive feature of Monticello was Jefferson's plan to group under a single roof all the functions of the household. Thus, the scattered outbuildings—kitchen, laundry,

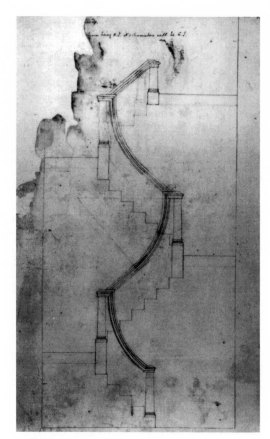

Working drawing by Thomas Jefferson for the main stairs of Monticello, probably sketched around 1775.

This stand has adjustable rests to hold sheet music for up to five musicians. Believed to be designed by Thomas Jefferson, the device was likely constructed in the cabinet shop at Monticello by one of Jefferson's workers.

woodhouse, and various storage rooms—were connected to the main structure through a series of passages. The landscaping of the home also reflected Jefferson's eclectic tastes. The roundabout walks and terraced gardens were embellished by domestic and imported trees and plants. In this happy world, Jefferson once remarked, he was content to spend "philosophic evenings and rural days."

Jefferson's home was also a plantation, that is, an insular economic and social community. While Jefferson housed his books, played the violin, and carried on correspondences at Monticello, the grounds were being worked by African-American slaves. Aside from laboring in the fields, orchards, and pastures of Monticello, slaves also worked in the infant industrial world that Jefferson had created just outside his doorstep. The gristmill, sawmill, and workshop are testimony that

Jefferson did not view Monticello merely as a retreat from the outside world. Rather, it was more akin to a village that Jefferson could constantly shape, create, wipe away, and start over. Monticello, in other words, provided Jefferson with the land and leisure to put his ideas into practice.

Finally, Monticello was Jefferson's home and served as a respite from the pressures of being one of the nation's most public figures. "I am savage enough to prefer the woods, the wilds, and the independence of Monticello to all the brilliant pleasures of this gay capital," he once remarked. "I shall, therefore, rejoin myself to my native country with new attachments and with exaggerated esteem for its advantages; for though there is less wealth there, there is more freedom, more ease, and less misery. I am as happy nowhere else, and in no other society, and all my wishes end, where I hope my days will end, at Monticello."

See also:
College of William and Mary

Reference:
Bear, James. 1967. *Jefferson at Monticello: Recollections of a Monticello Slave and a Monticello Overseer*. Charlottesville: University Press of Virginia.

National Bank

*I*n December 1791, Alexander Hamilton submitted a report to Congress that called for a national bank to serve as the federal government's chief fiscal agent. Jefferson's opposition to this bank helped crystallize the climate of dissent toward "Hamiltonianism," that is, the subservience of the states to the national government, and played a part in the formation of the Republican party.

Hamilton proposed that the bank be capitalized at $10 million, more capital than all existing banks in the country combined. Of this sum, $2 million would be paid by the federal government while the remaining $8 million would be sold to private investors, who would pay either in specie or by purchasing federal securities. The bank would assist in the collection of taxes, provide a universally acceptable currency for an economy short of specie, and perhaps most importantly, serve as a dependable source of credit for expanding business interests. In short, Hamilton's bank would unify the nation by funding internal improvements and creating a common currency.

Many Americans feared the proposed bank, however, and some, such as James Madison, believed that a powerful centralized financial structure might someday overawe the power of the people and their republican government. Madison's opposition to Hamilton's bank placed President George

Washington in a difficult position. The Bank Bill had passed through Congress and awaited only the president's signature to make it law. Washington respected Madison's opposition, however, and was wary of signing a bill of doubtful constitutionality. In such cases, Washington habitually turned to trusted colleagues to register opinions. In this matter, he asked that both Hamilton and Jefferson express their ideas on the subject.

Jefferson's opinion arrived first. It contained a classic argument for a strict, that is, narrow, interpretation of the Constitution. Jefferson argued that the only powers given to the federal government were those specifically enumerated in the Constitution. That document, he continued, did not give Congress the power to create a national bank. In seeking to limit the prerogatives of the government, Jefferson warned, to "take a single step beyond the boundaries thus specially drawn around the powers of Congress, is to take possession of a boundless field of power, no longer susceptible of any definition." As for the "necessary and proper" clause allowing Congress to extend its powers in a time of crisis, Jefferson argued that no such crisis existed. Including the colonial period, the country had operated for over 150 years without a national bank and could continue to do so without one. The fact that some citizens thought a bank would be expedient, Jefferson argued, was not cause enough to enlarge the interpretation of the Constitution, which in turn would enlarge the powers of the federal government.

The tension over expansion of federal power formed the heart of the issue for southerners like Jefferson and Madison. Both men feared that if Congress were empowered, through a liberal interpretation of the Constitution, to create a federal banking system, then Congress might also find within its powers the prerogative to declare slavery unconstitutional. Thus Jefferson's opinion to Washington sought to strike a death blow to the movement toward expanding the federal government by strictly confining its powers to those named in the Constitution.

Hamilton's argument to Washington was nearly the opposite of Jefferson's. He sought to expand the powers of the federal government to accommodate his banking plan. He suggested to the president that the "necessary and proper" clause be interpreted in a more liberal way than Jefferson suggested. To Hamilton, "necessary" meant "useful," and in his opinion, the bank would serve a useful function to bind the nation more closely together. Moreover, Hamilton successfully argued that if Jefferson's definition of "necessary" won out, then it would bind future generations of leadership to a rigid and inflexible interpretation of the Constitution, which would undoubtedly endanger the existence of that document.

Washington, who as president saw the need for a liberal interpretation of executive and congressional power, sided with Hamilton and signed the Bank Bill in February 1792. The national bank had a 20-year charter and thus operated throughout Jefferson's presidency. Though he was forced to accommodate the bank, Jefferson was never comfortable with it and looked forward to its eventual demise. To a foreign observer of American life, Jefferson wrote that

> this institution is one of the most deadly hostility existing against the principles and form of our Constitution. The nation is at this time so strong and united in its sentiments that it cannot be shaken at this moment. But . . . an institution like this, penetrating by its branches every part of the Union, acting by command and in phalanx, may, in a critical moment, upset the government. I deem no government safe which is under the vassalage of any self-constituted authorities, or any other authority than that of the nation or its regular functionaries.

See also:
Assumption
Hamilton, Alexander

Reference:
Hammond, Bray. 1957. *Banks and Politics in America from the Revolution to the Civil War.* Princeton, NJ: Princeton University Press.

National Debt

*T*hough Jefferson consistently owed large sums of money to banks and creditors throughout his adult life, he believed that the nation must be free from the burden of debt in order to preserve its independence. In Jefferson's opinion, the ideal republican citizen was a subsistence farmer or skilled artisan who owned his land and the means of production. This financial freedom would place the citizen beyond the encroachments of institutions that would inhibit his liberty. So too, Jefferson argued, must the federal government operate free from the influence of speculators or lending institutions that would compromise the virtue of government. He concluded that a national debt was a national burden and must be erased. "I am for a government rigorously frugal and simple," Jefferson argued,

> applying all the possible savings of the public revenue to the discharge of the national debt; and not for a multipli-

cation of officers and salaries merely to make partisans, and for increasing by every device the public debt on the principle of its being a public blessing. I am for relying for internal defense on our militia solely, till actual invasion, and for such a naval force only as may protect our coasts and harbors from such depredations as we have experienced; and not for a standing army in time of peace which may overawe the public sentiment, nor for a navy which, by its own expenses and the eternal wars in which it will implicate us, will grind us with public burdens and sink us under them.

Toward this end, Jefferson continually advocated a frugal, even tiny, federal influence in public affairs. As president, he slashed the budgets of the army and navy while recalling every American minister but those in Madrid, Paris, and London. Jefferson believed such frugality would usher in an era of governmental austerity that would ensure the honesty of public servants and private citizens.

The Jeffersonians never succeeded in erasing the national debt, though they did go a long way in reducing it. The price the country paid, however, was considerable. The nation's poor showing in the War of 1812, in which the capital was burned and various invasions of Canada were rebuffed, might properly be blamed on the weakened condition of the military. Following the war, Republican presidents James Madison and James Monroe championed a more aggressive, and thus more costly, federal government, largely with Jefferson's blessing. As for the national debt, only once, in the 1830s, did the government manage to retire its financial obligations. In retrospect, Jefferson seems to have been both right and wrong on this issue. Certainly excessive debt can chip away at a nation's sovereignty, character, and force, yet a manageable debt can serve, as Hamilton once suggested, as a "national blessing."

See also:
Madison, James
War of 1812

Reference:
Frisch, Morton, ed. 1985. *Selected Writings and Speeches of Alexander Hamilton.* Washington, DC: American Enterprise Institute for Public Policy Research.

National Road

The Cumberland or National Road was designed to link the Potomac River with the Ohio Valley, allowing the region bordering the Chesapeake Bay access to the vast resources of the West and providing a path for migration. The road was authorized in 1806, when Congress empowered President Jefferson to appoint commissioners to oversee the project. Jefferson believed that the federal government should encourage the development of the western road through land grants to territories. It should not, however, be involved in granting states federal money for "internal improvements," which would enhance the power of the federal government at the expense of the states. With this principle in mind, Jefferson arranged for territories like Ohio to use a percentage of the proceeds from the sale of its public lands to finance the portion of the national road that cut through its borders.

Though some "national" Republicans wanted the federal government to more actively finance the road, claiming that its presence would enhance the economic and military capabilities of the nation, Jefferson and his presidential successors from Virginia, James Madison and James Monroe, largely allotted the responsibility for the progress of the road to the states. By 1818, Wheeling, Virginia, had been reached, and in 1833, Columbus, Ohio, was connected to the Cumberland Road. Finally, by the middle of the eighteenth century, Vandalia, Illinois, became the westernmost terminus. Plans for further extension were disrupted by the emerging sectional conflict between North and South as well as the changing contours of antebellum transportation. By 1850, the National Road was eclipsed by the proliferation of canals and the invention of the railroad.

See Also:
States' Rights

Reference:
Taylor, George. 1951. *The Transportation Revolution, 1815–1860.* New York: Holt, Rinehart & Winston.

Native Americans

To Jefferson, the native peoples of North America lived in the original free relationships that he presumed all people once enjoyed. These "children of nature," living in rational, orderly societies without the intrusive power of a large central government to keep them in line, appeared to exemplify the political theories of the Enlightenment. Jefferson believed their societies provided a contemporary example of John Locke's writings in *The Second Treatise of Government.* Locke posited that all civilization evolved from a natural condition where men were free (state of nature) to a possession culture stimulated by material items that needed to be protected (state of war). From Jefferson's perspective, Native Americans were still living in a pure "republican" condition, the state of nature.

The natives' "happy" existence free from the hand of an intrusive society was due, Jefferson believed, to "their having never submitted themselves to any laws, any coercive power, any shadow of government." Guiding their behavior, he suggested, was an innate sense of manners and morality heightened by the conditions of life in the natural environment. Though this type of social justice could be abused, Jefferson found that "imperfect as this species of coercion may seem, crimes are very rare among them."

Moreover, Jefferson could not help but admire a society that ran, in his mind, along "natural" principles. In a famous passage comparing Native American and Anglo-American governmental principles and bodies of law, Jefferson noted that "insomuch that were it made a question, whether no law, as among the savage Americans, or too much law, as among the civilized Europeans submits man to the greatest evil, one who has seen both conditions of existence would pronounce it to be the last." The "sheep," he concluded, were happier under their own care "than under care of the wolves."

In addition to his sociopolitical interest in the natives peoples of North America, Jefferson demonstrated an anthropological interest as well. He believed the Indians to be the equal of whites in mental and physical endowments. "We shall probably find," Jefferson offered, "that [the natives] are formed in mind as well as in body on the same module with the Homo sapiens Europaeus." This statement is complimentary, considering that Jefferson viewed other non-Anglo-Europeans, such as the African and the African-American, as a decidedly inferior species. In the Native Americans, however, Jefferson saw primitive republicans who lived an essentially agrarian lifestyle. Such peoples, he presumed, could be "civilized" and incorporated into white society by amalgamating Indian culture and the dominant British-American culture. Thus Jefferson seemed to be calling for the preservation of the Native Americans through the high price of losing their cultural identity.

Jefferson's praise for Native Americans was highly qualified, of course. His perspective was based not on contact or intimate investigation, but on conjecture. In fact, it would not be going too far to say that Jefferson's sympathy for the native peoples was embedded in environmental rather than humanitarian concerns. To praise the Native Americans and their lifestyle was in essence to praise the American environment, which provided the natural conditions of plenty that allowed such societies to exist. For a student of the Enlightenment like Jefferson, the cult of environmentalism was powerful, and to condemn the native peoples would be tantamount to condemning the American experiment in self-government in the New World. Consistency dictated that Jefferson find redeeming qualities in the Native American that he did not find in the African.

In practical terms, Jefferson believed that Indians and whites were best distanced from one another. The failure of "acculturation," that is, the grafting of native practices to a Euro-American economy of independent landholders, induced most Americans to advocate the removal of the eastern tribes. Thus Jefferson's purchase of the Louisiana Territory in 1803 represented more than an "Empire of Liberty" for free whites; it also served as a potential reservation for the displaced native peoples. "If our legislature dispose of [Louisiana] with the wisdom we have a right to expect," Jefferson explained, "they may make it the means of tempting all our Indians on the east side of the Mississippi to remove to the west, and of condensing instead of scattering our population."

Nevertheless, Jefferson retained to the end of his life the romantic notion that the Indians could find a place, albeit limited, in white society. At the conclusion of his presidency, for example, he wrote to a colleague that the main problem with the "civilizing" process was that whites attempted to Christianize the Indians before inculcating in them the proper intellectual and economic values. To Jefferson, the native should be taught to "raise cattle . . . and thereby acquire a knowledge of the value of property." Following this, arithmetic, reading, and writing should be introduced, particularly *Aesop's Fables* and *Robinson Crusoe,* since they are the natives' "first delight."

Anglo-America's romantic view of the natives was eclipsed by their quest for westward expansion. With families moving into the Ohio and Mississippi Valleys looking for land, gold, and independent homesteads, the natives were viewed as little more than impediments to progress. The "primitive republicans" that Jefferson admired were removed west of the Mississippi by Andrew Jackson on the infamous Trail of Tears.

See also:
Jackson, Andrew
Louisiana Purchase

Reference:
Sheehan, Bernard. 1973. *Seeds of Extinction: Jeffersonian Philanthropy and the American Indian.* Chapel Hill: University of North Carolina Press.

Natural Aristocracy

Jefferson believed that the Creator intended for each generation to rule its own affairs. Within this framework, he presumed that a natural aristocracy, that is, individuals with an abundance of talent and virtue, would emerge as the leaders of their societies. "It would have been inconsistent in creation," Jefferson remarked, "to have formed man for the social state, and not to have provided virtue and wisdom enough to manage the concerns of the society." Through education, culture, or innate competence, a select group of individuals comprised the dynamo that made society run in an orderly fashion. Unlike Plato's vision of the philosopher-king, Jefferson's natural aristocracy did not create laws for others to conform to, for those laws were "natural" and had already been defined by mankind. As the Enlightenment made such laws self-evident, the natural aristocracy merely functioned as agents to ensure that such laws were upheld.

The natural aristocracy also provided Jefferson a way to rationalize the development of the American republic in "scientific" terms. After the Revolution, the new nation was forced to design a republican form of government. With sovereignty invested in the "people," commoners were entrusted with their own welfare. In lieu of a hereditary aristocracy based on custom and force, Jefferson believed that the American environment, with its abundance of land allowing for relatively liberal political institutions, encouraged a natural aristocracy. Thus, though the people would be the repository of republican values, a small cadre of virtuous elites would do the actual governing. To John Adams, Jefferson remarked:

> I agree with you that there is a natural
> aristocracy among men. The grounds
> of this are virtue and talents. Formerly,
> bodily powers gave place among the
> aristoi. But since the invention of
> gunpowder has armed the weak as
> well as the strong with missile death,
> bodily strength, like beauty, good
> humor, politeness and other accom-
> plishments, has become but an auxil-
> iary ground of distinction. There is
> also an artificial aristocracy, founded
> on wealth and birth, without either
> virtue or talents; for with these it
> would belong to the first class. The
> natural aristocracy I consider as the
> most precious gift of nature, for the
> instruction, the trusts, and government
> of society. . . . May we not even say,
> that that form of government is the
> best, which provides the most effectu-
> ally for a pure selection of these
> natural aristoi into the offices of
> government? The artificial aristocracy
> is a mischievous ingredient in govern-
> ment, and provision should be made
> to prevent its ascendancy.

Adams made clear that in his opinion, aristocracies that relied on force or wealth were inferior to the kind of leadership that arises from a pool of talent. In sum, Jefferson believed that republican government, liberal values, and social, political, and economic equality provided the climate from which the natural aristocracy emerged. These values, he presumed, would spread beyond the United States and serve as the backbone for a new world order of talented citizen-leaders displacing hereditary monarchies.

See also:
Enlightenment
Nature

Reference:
Boorstin, Daniel. 1948. *The Lost World of Thomas Jefferson.* Chicago, IL: University of Chicago Press.

Nature

Though Jefferson is viewed primarily as an intellectual, a current of pragmatism runs throughout his vision of nature and man's place in the natural world. Unlike Europeans, Americans in Jefferson's time were not living in a settled and cultivated civilization. The drive to manipulate and master the American environment, to create a republican world, drew a distinct line between the contemplative and active sides of human nature, with Jefferson more often than not fitting into the latter category.

The earliest manifestation of naturalism was the American Philosophical Society, organized by Benjamin Franklin in 1743, the year Jefferson was born. The society reflected the pragmatic side of eighteenth-century American thought. Action, not ideas, made up the code of the organization, and experimentation was carried on at a feverish pitch. The society's members, which eventually included Jefferson, were united by a common challenge: to subdue the primitive American landscape and exemplify New World art, architecture, and literature. Society men were observant and practical, not bent toward undo reflection. They were republican in their political practices and cosmopolitan in their worldview. They sought to understand the environment and then to alter it to fit the needs of a burgeoning nation.

Earthly justification for an assault on nature was reinforced by the Jeffersonians' successful secularization of God. Whereas the Puritan concept of the divine Being stressed individual accountability to a wrathful judge, Jeffersonians believed that God served the earthly as well as spiritual needs of humans. Accordingly, they created a God in their own image, de-emphasizing the austere Calvinistic features and replacing them with the conception of a divine Creator. In such a view, the universe represented an orderly reflection of God the architect and God the builder. The Jeffersonian deity, in the words of one historian, thus resembled the "Supreme Workman," that is, the spiritual model for the practical, agrarian, republican citizen.

To better understand the celestial mysteries of the world, the Jeffersonians looked to natural history as the physical testimony of the Creator. The American Philosophical Society devoted considerable time to the search for "missing links," what we know today to be extinct species. To the Jeffersonians, however, it was inconceivable that the Creator would waste energy and material producing a plant or animal that no longer exists. This would be a violation of the principle of the economy of nature: the idea that the physical world was perfect, reflecting the Creator who made it. Yet the immaturity of American society required an active deity, which encouraged the Jeffersonians to project their own beliefs onto their God. For example, the machinelike Creator of the Jeffersonians displayed workmanship and frugality—traits that would aid humans in their efforts to subdue the environment. Just as the physical world's perfect order of clouds, rain, and sun produced flowers and fruit, so too could the proper mixture of hard work, diligence, and discipline produce a new material world.

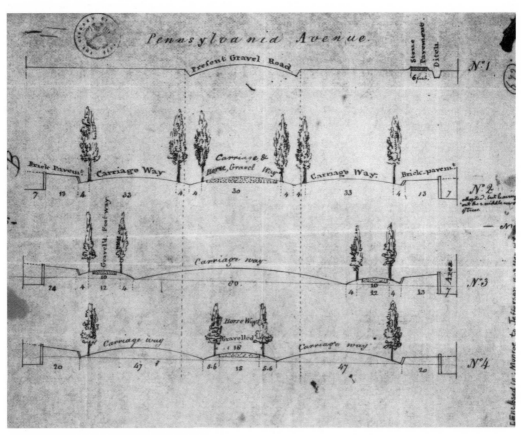

Jefferson's plans for the District of Columbia.

Jefferson's deity, therefore, epitomized the cult of a perfect physical world as a model for man and his institutions. Discarding the idea of a personal Puritan God, Jeffersonians viewed the Creator in an impersonal, cosmopolitan sense, interested more in the workings of the universe than in individual salvation. Thus man was not unique in the Jeffersonian worldview, but rather a small part of the natural world that surrounded him. From this perspective the argument for natural design made perfect sense to the Jeffersonians. In their view, life and death held no otherworldly significance. All that happened, be it benign or malignant, was "natural" and through a variety of means—population control or conservation, illness, death, or simply bad luck—worked toward the benefit of society as a whole. Like the perfect symmetry of the seasons or the patterns of constellations, human behavior contained a natural rhythm that ultimately reflected the order of the world.

In his conception of nature, Jefferson sought reassurance that divine assistance was secured in the development of American civilization. It was not important that man was insignificant in the larger scheme of the Creator's universe, because by understanding the order of nature, man became one with his environment. If this vision of humans finding harmony with the natural order of the world around them sounds similar to the Chinese practice of Taoism or to various Native American faiths, it should be remembered that for Jefferson, faith was clearly leading toward material rather than spiritual ends. Nature was neatly tied to the Christian God in order to ease the transition toward a more ambitious and complex society.

See also:
American Philosophical Society
Religion

Reference:
Boorstin, Daniel. 1948. *The Lost World of Thomas Jefferson*. Chicago, IL: University of Chicago Press.

Navigation Acts

The navigation acts shaped British colonial policy during the period 1650–1820 and would be the cause of Jefferson's animosity toward Britain during both the American Revolution and the War of 1812. The first acts predated Jefferson's birth by nearly a hundred years. In the latter half of the seventeenth century, British navigation acts were aimed at Dutch dominance over major lines of English trade. England ordered that imports brought within its borders must be carried in English ships or ships made in England. It also placed various duties, or tariffs, on Dutch commodities. These taxes made it difficult for the Dutch to sell their wares in the British Empire.

As the years passed, the navigation acts were extended to include other nations and to codify production and trade in British North America. By and large, Americans like Jefferson acquiesced to the regulation of their trade because they accrued certain benefits in the bargain. The British Royal Navy, for example, protected American exports on the seas while the colonials were allowed to trade within the empire, ensuring the Americans of trade that was closed to other nations. The expansion of the acts to include direct forms of taxation in the 1760s and 1770s, however, precipitated the revolutionary movement that Jefferson embraced. The successful culmination of the war of independence, however, did not end America's relationship with either Great Britain or its navigation acts.

As president, Jefferson wanted the United States to remain neutral in the wars of the French Revolution, which pitted a British-led coalition against France and its allies. Neutrality proved impossible, however, when Britain introduced several acts, Orders in Council, in the years 1805–1812 that attempted to force the United States into service as a carrier for British goods. Jefferson repudiated the British system of militarism, finance, and speculation and refused to recognize England's right to dissuade America from trading with its enemies. At stake for Jefferson was a very important issue: either the United States would accede to the British acts and trade only with that nation, thus helping it defeat its enemies, or the country would resist British intrusions on American rights, deny the legality of the acts, and operate as an autonomous nation. Jefferson chose the latter course. He placed an embargo on American goods, thereby keeping U.S. ships at home and refusing to sell goods to either of the warring sides. Unfortunately for Jefferson, this response was not enough to persuade Britain to recognize American rights, and the War of 1812 resulted. With the defeat of Napoleon in 1815, over a century of conflict between Great Britain and France ended, and with it ended the navigation acts.

See also:
Embargo of 1807
Macon's Bill Number Two
Non-Intercourse Act

Reference:
Appleby, Joyce O. 1978. *Economic Thought and Ideology in Seventeenth Century England.* Princeton, NJ: Princeton University Press.

Navy

*I*n the 1780s, Jefferson spoke for many Americans when he declared "we ought to begin a naval power if we mean to carry on our own commerce." Yet it was not until 1794 that Congress founded the United States navy, and the size of that fleet was woefully inadequate to perform its true function: coercing European powers to recognize American commercial policy. As president, Jefferson sought to erase the nation's debts by cutting taxes and slashing the military budget. The shrunken navy found some success in combating North African pirates who confiscated American ships in the Barbary War but simply could not compete against the larger and superior British and French fleets.

Complicating Jefferson's position were various philosophical prejudices against a large naval force. First, he believed they tended to breed wars, absorbed the labor of thousands of seamen, and enriched the merchant class. Further, a navy was expensive to maintain and tended to decay while staying in dry dock during peacetime. "It has been estimated in England," Jefferson reflected, "that, if they could be sure of peace for a dozen years it would be cheaper for them to burn their fleet, and build a new one when wanting than to keep the old one in repair during that term." With such considerations in mind, Jefferson preferred gunboats—a "mosquito fleet"—rather than expensive ships of the line. A single gunboat cost a mere $5,000, which meant that 100 such vessels could be constructed for the price of a single ship of the line.

Jefferson's gunboat policy, which commenced in 1805, ran into practical difficulties. The vessels were structurally unsuited for the rough seas of the Atlantic, and even the task of harbor defense proved beyond their means. On one occasion, a vigorous storm off the coast of Georgia blew several of the gunboats from the sea into a cornfield. At the end of Jefferson's presidency, only 180 of these small craft were stationed in American ports. Jeffersonian naval frugality contradicted the Jeffersonian economic vision that sought to transport American produce around the globe. Such an aggressive commercial vision required a more substantial naval presence than Jefferson was willing to invest in. This would be demonstrated in the period 1805–1812, when American commercial shipping fell prey to raids by British and French vessels. It was only after the War of 1812, when a general peace ensued, that American shipping was left alone by the European powers.

See also:
Anglo-French Wars
War of 1812

Reference:
Love, Robert. 1992. *History of the U.S. Navy.* Harrisburg, PA: Stackpole Books.

Neutral Rights

From the moment America proclaimed its independence in 1776 to the conclusion of the War of 1812, Jefferson labored to achieve recognition of the nation's rights as a neutral power. At stake was the country's right to carry American goods by ship at home and abroad and to carry British and French goods that could not be transported by the home country. So significant was this right that at the conclusion of the American Revolution, Jefferson contended:

> Our first employment was to prepare a general form to be proposed to such nations as were disposed to treat with us . . . an article exempting from capture by the public or private armed vessels and their cargoes employed merely in carrying on the commerce between nations, . . . with a provision against the molestation of fishermen, husbandmen, citizens unarmed and following their occupations in unfortified places; for the humane treatment of prisoners of war; the abolition of contraband of war, which exposes merchant vessels to such vexatious and ruinous detentions and abuses; and from the principle of free bottoms, free goods.

Jefferson's faith in free trade, or the principle that "free bottoms" equals "free goods," never wavered and was, in fact, a vital component of his vision of a republican political economy. Because he believed that the nation would stay virtuous only if agricultural interests dominated, Jefferson was convinced that the United States had to maintain a viable commercial fleet capable of transporting American produce to national and international markets. A disruption of such trade could mean a disruption in the American experiment of self-government.

As the world's largest neutral carrier, the United States made great profits in the early 1790s during the Anglo-French Wars. America serviced much of the world's trade, transporting colonial goods to Europe at excellent prices. America's commercial development, however, threatened Great Britain, which had the largest carrier fleet in the world. Beginning in 1793, that nation began to confiscate American ships carrying French cargo. In retaliation, the French did the same with American vessels transporting British cargo. Jefferson lamented the emergence of antagonistic relations in Europe, remarking that

> I do sincerely wish . . . that we could take our stand on a ground perfectly neutral and independent towards all nations. It has been my constant object through my public life; and with respect to the English and French, particularly, I have too often expressed to the former my wishes and made to them propositions verbally and in writing, officially and privately, to official and private characters, for them to doubt of my views, if they would be content with equality. . . . But they have wished a monopoly of commerce and influence with us; and they have in fact obtained it. Peace is undoubtedly at present the first object of our nation. . . . The insults and injuries committed on us by both the belligerent parties from the beginning of 1793 to this day, and still continuing, cannot now be wiped off by engaging in war with one of them. . . . Our countrymen have divided themselves by such strong affections to the French and the English that nothing will secure us internally but a divorce from both nations.

As president, Jefferson did in fact seek a "divorce" from both Britain and France. Continued refusal to respect America's neutral rights prompted Jefferson in 1807 to levy an embargo on the world, refusing to sell its surplus agricultural produce in Europe. The embargo proved ineffective, however. American rights would not be respected until the conclusion of the War of 1812, when the defeat of Napoleon and revolutionary France ushered in a new era of stability in Europe.

See also:
Anglo-French Wars
French Revolution
War of 1812

Reference:
Horsman, Reginald. 1972. *The Causes of the War of 1812.* New York: Octagon Books.

Newton, Sir Isaac (1642–1727)

A student of natural philosophy, Sir Isaac Newton of England was one of the most influential figures in the history of science. His invention of infinitesimal calculus, his theories of light and color, and his discovery of the laws of motion and gravity formed the core of the seventeenth-century scientific revolution. Jefferson was strongly influenced by Newton's work and its inference that the world operated in an orderly, rational way. In the Newtonian model, the physical world observed the laws of nature, just as Jefferson expected men and governments to do as well. In Newton's system, nothing in nature could be out of place or disharmonious with the whole. In other words, man could begin to feel at home in the world, rather than simply looking upon his surroundings as a temporary and sinful waystation in the soul's journey to heaven or hell. Newton's classical mechanics posited that the natural world operated in predictable and understandable ways, and thus man was freed from both superstition and the church.

See also:
Enlightenment

Reference:
Hart, Michael. 1992. *The 100: A Ranking of the Most Influential Persons in History.* Secaucus, NJ: Carol Publishing Group.

Non-Intercourse Act

When Great Britain and France went to war during Jefferson's presidency, both nations began to confiscate American ships carrying goods to their enemy's ports. With America too weak to combat these abuses, Jefferson placed an embargo on trade abroad, hoping that European and British needs for American foodstuffs and cotton would force a more lenient policy. The embargo did not work, however, and nearly destroyed the economy of New England in the bargain. Jefferson decided in the final days of his presidency that he could not leave the failed embargo policy for his handpicked successor, James Madison, to deal with. Thus, in March 1809 a Republican Congress repealed the act. At this point it seemed that the only honorable solution was war.

Even so, Congress, eager to avoid a war against the major European powers, demurred. Instead of declaring war, it passed the Non-Intercourse Bill, which barred British and French ships from entering American ports and kept an embargo against those two countries while opening trade with the rest of the world. The virtue of the bill was that it opened some markets for New England shipping while simultaneously keeping economic pressure on the aggressor nations. In private, Jefferson confided that he was pressured into accepting the end of the embargo and felt dismayed at leaving Madison with the unenviable task of attempting to coerce Europe into accepting American commercial sovereignty. "I thought Congress had taken their ground firmly for continuing their embargo till June," he wrote,

> but a sudden and unaccountable
> revolution of opinion took place . . .
> chiefly among the New England and
> New York members, and in a kind of
> panic they voted the 4th of March for
> removing the embargo, and by such a

majority as gave all reason to believe they would not agree either to war or non-intercourse. This, too, was after we had become satisfied that the Essex Junto [extremist Federalists in New England] had found their expectation desperate of inducing the people there to either separation or forcible opposition. The majority of Congress, however, has now rallied to the removing of the embargo . . . non-intercourse with France and Great Britain, trade everywhere else, and continuing war preparations. Our embargo has worked hard. . . . We have substituted for it a non-intercourse with France and England and their dependencies and a trade to all other places. It is probable the belligerents will take our vessels under their edicts, in which case we shall probably declare war against them. After using every effort which could prevent or delay our being entangled in the war of Europe, that seems now our only resource. . . . Fifty millions of exports, annually sacrificed, are the treble of what war would cost us; besides that, by war we should take something and lose less than at present. . . . But all these concerns I am now leaving to be settled by my friend Mr. Madison.

A weary Jefferson left the White House, his embargo policy repudiated and his closest political friend, James Madison, left to cope with a conflict that Jefferson could not successfully resolve.

See also:
Anglo-French Wars
Embargo of 1807

Reference:
Brant, Irving. 1956. *James Madison: The President, 1809–1812*. Indianapolis, IN: Bobbs-Merrill.

Nootka Sound Controversy

As the nation's first secretary of state, Jefferson's initial international controversy involved the Spanish and British struggle for control of western Canada. In the years following the French and Indian War, Spain was well on its way to recouping much of its lost empire in North America, having gained Louisiana from France in 1763 and Florida from Great Britain in 1783. Looking to extend its authority further, Spain laid claim to the Pacific Northwest as well. This claim was disputed by Britain, which enjoyed a vigorous trade in furs from the Columbia River region. In 1789 a vessel carrying British traders sailed into Nootka Sound on Vancouver Island, where the traders proceeded to build a trading post. Spain responded by capturing the British vessels and arresting their crews.

Jefferson was interested in the Nootka Sound controversy as an opportunity to advance American interests. At this time both Spain and England presented serious obstacles to American expansion. Spain would not allow the United States access to the Mississippi River, which meant that American farmers in the West had no way to transport their produce to market. The British retained military posts on American soil in the West in violation of the Treaty of Paris, which ended the American Revolution. Jefferson believed that Britain used these forts to maintain alliances with the native peoples in order to keep their former colonists out of the region. In short, both European powers threatened American sovereignty and seemed intent on keeping the United States in a colony-like status. Jefferson hoped that his state department could use the present controversy to solve America's western problems.

A more pressing issue was at hand, however. The possibility of hostilities made it seem likely that Britain would prevail upon the United States for permission to cross neutral American soil in the West to conquer Louisiana. Secretary of the Treasury Alexander Hamilton commented that if such a situation arose, the government should allow British armies to pass. His response was a predictable one, for as America's chief financial officer he was in the midst of constructing a national economy reliant upon British credit, markets, and goodwill. Jefferson, on the other hand, was against such a clear violation of American neutrality and advised President Washington to say nothing on the matter. Ultimately the question proved moot. Spain was forced to recognize British power in the Pacific Northwest and, unfortunately for Jefferson, the controversy did not provide the United States an opening to remove foreign interests in the West.

See also:
Anglophobia
Secretary of State

Reference:
Horsman, Reginald. 1985. *The Diplomacy of the New Republic, 1776–1815.* Arlington Heights, IL: Harlan Davidson.

Northwest Ordinance of 1784

In January 1781, Governor Thomas Jefferson ceded Virginia's western land claims encompassing the present-day Ohio Valley to the national domain. The Virginian stipulated, however, that any territories carved out of the West should eventually be brought into the Union as republican states on equal footing with the original 13. In essence, Virginia was giving away an empire in the hopes that the United States would be strengthened by the expansion of republicanism and the proliferation of statehood.

Jefferson's actions in the Ohio Valley in the 1780s foreshadowed his much more famous purchase of the Louisiana Territory in 1803. In both cases, Jefferson sought to create a western reserve where citizens could practice independent living far from the intrusive reach of cities or central governments. However, several hurdles stood in the way of Jefferson's 1784 vision. Land-hungry settlers had pushed across the Appalachian mountains in the years immediately following the American Revolution, and their needs had to be met; treaties with the Native Americans in the region were needed to codify relations between the two peoples and keep peace; provisions for territorial government had yet to be worked out; and an orderly system of land survey and distribution was not yet in place.

The plan that Jefferson submitted to Congress was adopted as the Ordinance of 1784. Jefferson claimed for the United States the entire western country between the Mississippi and the British northern and Spanish southern borders, though at the time, nearly half of this area was not under congressional jurisdiction. Jefferson divided the region into 14 states, each state covering two degrees of latitude from north to south. Congress approved of Jefferson's division but not the names that he proposed for the new states. Jefferson wanted the American West to reflect both the spirit of classical scholarship in the Old World and the unpredictable wilderness of the New World. Thus, he proposed that western states be named Cherronesus, Assenenisipia, Metropotamia, Polypotamia, Pelisipia, and so on, a uniting of Native American derivatives with Roman endings. Mercifully, Congress did not agree.

Jefferson's plan also proposed that western territories would become states in three stages. In the first stage, the free adult males of a territory would meet to form a temporary government based on republican principles. When the free inhabitants numbered 20,000, they would draw up a constitution and work toward self-government. When the population equaled the total of the least numerous state in the Union, statehood would be attained.

Jefferson's plan was exceedingly democratic for its day, in that the ordinance guaranteed male suffrage in ways that the original states did not. Jefferson's draft emphasized that each new state would have to establish a republican form of government before being admitted to the Union. States would also be subject to the jurisdiction of Congress and liable for payment of federal debts, and once a state entered the Union, it would not be allowed to secede. Finally, Jefferson's draft of the Ordinance of 1784 declared that "after the year 1800 of the Christian era, there shall be neither slavery nor involuntary servitude" in the West. Unfortunately this clause was taken out of the document's final draft.

Ultimately, Jefferson's ordinance was not adopted by Congress because of the practical problems it presented. The low ratio of land to people in Jefferson's division of territory would delay statehood for generations. Moreover, while carving up the region into proposed states, Jefferson placed dividing lines inconveniently along mountains rather than rivers. Yet the heart of Jefferson's 1784 proposal found its way into the Northwest Ordinance of 1787, which was accepted by Congress and did allow for the creation of republican states in the West.

See also:
Confederation Period
Empire of Liberty

Reference:
Morris, Richard B. 1987. *The Forging of the Union, 1781–1789.* New York: Harper & Row.

Notes on the State of Virginia

For all his education, imagination, and inquisitiveness, Jefferson wrote but a single book in his lifetime. Remarkably, the treatise composed by the author of the Declaration of Independence had little to do with political philosophy. Rather, Jefferson's *Notes on the State of Virginia* is a natural history of the Old Dominion. The monograph began as a response to a query from François de Marbois, secretary of the French legation sta-

tioned at Williamsburg during the American Revolution. The Frenchman asked Jefferson for a description of the plant and animal life in the region encompassing the James and York Rivers. Freed from his duties as governor, Jefferson eagerly took this opportunity to write a detailed treatise on Virginia. Jefferson turned his work over to de Marbois in December 1781 and considered the project complete.

Shortly thereafter, however, word of Jefferson's *Notes* reached the ears of Charles Thomson, secretary of Congress and a member of the American Philosophical Society. Thomson encouraged Jefferson to present his material to a broader audience by making several copies of the work. Jefferson hesitated, deciding that the *Notes* needed additional polishing. Following three years of revisions, he wrote that the project had "swelled to nearly treble bulk." This bulk was a problem for Jefferson. It meant that the only practical way to produce copies for friends was through printing. Jefferson feared a mass publication because of the *Notes*' despairing view of slavery, the bread and butter of the Virginia economy. Planning for a limited edition, Jefferson had 200 copies printed and distributed in the spring of 1785 for private consumption only. Hopes for anonymity were dashed, however, when a copy fell into the hands of a French bookseller. It was badly translated into French and then badly retranslated into English when a French copy found its way to Great Britain. At that point, Jefferson saw little choice but to arrange for the publication of the *Notes* in English. Moreover, Jefferson's friends in Virginia had been less than secretive with their "private" editions. James Madison, for example, sent 37 copies of the book to George Wyth to distribute to his law students. The first American edition, unauthorized, appeared in Philadelphia in 1788, and the book has never been out of print since.

The best introduction to the *Notes* is Jefferson's own. Composing an advertisement for the work in 1787, he wrote that

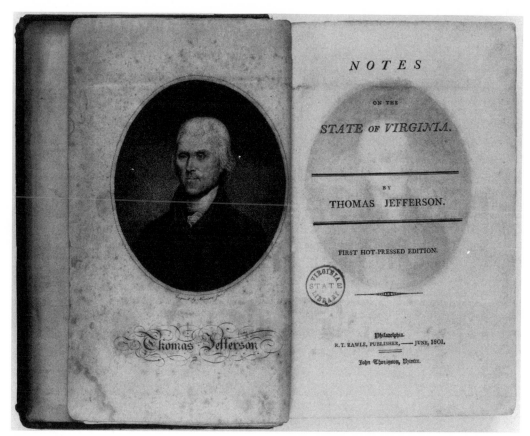

NOTES

ON THE

STATE OF VIRGINIA.

BY

THOMAS JEFFERSON.

FIRST HOT-PRESSED EDITION.

Philadelphia.
R. T. RAWLE, PUBLISHER,——JUNE, 1801.

John Thompson, Printer.

Title page and frontispiece of the 1802 edition of Jefferson's **Notes on the State of Virginia.**

the following Notes were written in Virginia in the year 1781, and somewhat corrected and enlarged in the winter of 1782, in answer to Queries proposed to the Author, by a Foreigner of Distinction then residing among us. The subjects are all treated imperfectly; some scarcely touched on. To apologize for this by developing the circumstances of the time and place of their composition, would be to open wounds which have already bled enough. To these circumstances some of their imperfections may with truth be ascribed; the great mass to the want of information and want of talents in the writer. He had a few copies printed, which he gave among his friends: and a translation of them has been lately published in France, but with such alterations as the laws of the press in that country rendered necessary. They are now offered to the public in their original form and language.

Jefferson's customary modesty cannot hide the fact that the work is a brilliant piece of writing that fits in nicely with the worldview promoted by the French physiocrats that Jefferson admired. Above all, *Notes* is a systematic categorization of the natural world in Virginia. Demonstrating the influence of Enlightenment thought, Jefferson framed his book around individual queries concerning the rivers, mountains, landscapes, and other natural phenomena in the Old Dominion. Like a scientist, he further dissected the inner workings of Virginia by examining how its social institutions—slavery, the church, the militia, and so on—developed in the community organism. Jefferson was seeking a grand synthesis, a natural history that explained how plant and animal life changed over time and were shaped by their environment.

Jefferson was no mere disinterested scientist, however. The *Notes* are infused with Jeffersonian values and Jeffersonian optimism. The author took obvious satisfaction, for example, in attacking the belief generally held by Europeans that the plant and animal life in the Americas was of a lower grade than that found in Europe, indicative of the inferiority of the New World. Composing a chart that he titled "A Comparative View of the Quadrupeds of Europe and of America," Jefferson argued that four-legged animals in America were actually larger than their European counterparts. An adult American bear, for example, was recorded by Jefferson as averaging 410 pounds, while its European counterpart tipped the scales at a mere 153.7 pounds. The American beaver averaged nearly 27 pounds more than a European beaver, while American cows were some three times larger than their European cousins. Jefferson, in other words, attempted to use science for ideological purposes. The Virginian argued, for example, that a superior plant and animal life in the United States was an indication of God's favor for a land that held both Christian and Republican values. The continued rise of America seemed certain, and from this perspective, *Notes* evokes not the spirit of science, but rather that of prophecy.

See also:
Enlightenment
Physiocrats

Reference:
Jefferson, Thomas. 1972. *Notes on the State of Virginia*. New York: W. W. Norton.

Paine, Thomas (1737–1809)

An Anglo-American pamphleteer and professional revolutionary, Thomas Paine believed that the experiment in republican government in the United States would serve as a model for future revolutionary activity around the world. Thus he, like Jefferson, believed in the concept of American exceptionalism and eagerly anticipated the redemption of the Old World by the New. Paine's faith in reason over the admonitions of the clergy further endeared him to Jefferson, as both men presumed that the political independence of America should be accompanied by an independence from ignorance and superstition. In sum, Paine, though more radical than Jefferson, articulated in his treatises and papers an enlightened perspective for human conduct and behavior that the Virginian found refreshing.

Paine was born in England in 1737. A restless man, he drifted from position to position, trying out the vocations of, among other things, corset maker, schoolteacher, and government official. In 1774, Paine came to America, where he contributed essays and poems to the *Pennsylvania Magazine*. He became well known in the colonies in early 1776 when his pamphlet *Common Sense* was published. This short treatise called for American independence from the British Crown and articulated many of the arguments that men like Jefferson had made in private discourse.

It was not the originality of Paine's essay that made him popular; it was his ability to put the feelings of his newfound countrymen into a readable and powerfully emotional summary. Throughout the Revolutionary War, Paine aided the American cause by publishing a steady stream of propaganda pieces.

After the successful conclusion of the Revolution, Paine returned to England, where he became involved in the French Revolution. In defense of this cause, he authored *The Rights of Man*, a powerful exposition that advocated the removal of royal influence in France. "Aristocracy," he argued, "is kept up by family tyranny and injustice. . . . Nature herself calls for its destruction." In the United States at this time, Secretary of State Jefferson was in the midst of an ideological battle with Secretary of the Treasury Alexander Hamilton concerning the powers and prerogatives of the federal government. Jefferson wished to limit central authority in America and recognized that Paine was fighting the same battle in Europe. The Virginian wrote to Paine:

> Would you believe it possible that in this country there should be high and important characters who need your lessons in republicanism, and who do not heed them? It is but too true that we have a sect preaching up and pouting after an English constitution of king, lords, and commons, and

whose heads are itching for crowns, coronets, and mitres. But our people, my good friend, are firm and unanimous in their principles of republicanism, and there is no better proof of it than that they love what you write and read it with delight. The printers season every newspaper with extracts from your last, as they did before from your first part, of the *Rights of Man*. They have both served here to separate the wheat from the chaff, and to prove that though the latter appears on the surface, it is on the surface only. The bulk below is sound and pure. Go on then in doing with your pen what in other times was done with the sword: show that reformation is more practicable by operating on the mind than on the body of man.

The British government did not look as favorably on Paine's work as Jefferson did, and he was forced to leave England for France, where he was granted citizenship and elected to the National Convention. In 1793 the revolution took a radical turn with the execution of the King and Queen. Paine voted against the executions and was imprisoned for nearly a year. While confined, he wrote a declaration of his political beliefs. *The Age of Reason* is a profound statement on natural theology and the deist position on the supernatural. Wrongly condemned as atheistic by Christian theologians, it was accepted by Jefferson. Paine returned to America where he devoted his energies to promoting president Jefferson's programs. In 1809, the year Jefferson retired from the presidency, Paine died and was buried on his farm in New York.

See also:
American Revolution
Deism
French Revolution

Reference:
Foner, Eric. 1977. *Thomas Paine and Revolutionary America*. New York: Oxford University Press.

Panic of 1819

The Panic of 1819 nearly ruined Jefferson, whose financial situation was already fragile, and reinforced his belief that an economy based upon speculation and paper money was a danger to the health of the republic. Following the War of 1812, the nation's economy expanded dramatically as farmers flooded into the Ohio and Mississippi Valleys in search of profitable farmland. The growth of the cotton market created a rapid expansion of credit in the South, while northern financiers were eager to lend large sums of largely unsecured capital to those who speculated in the futures of western lands. The Second Bank of the United States, which was supposed to constructively regulate the nation's money supply, instead fed the economic boom through a reckless extension of loans to state banks, which made credit widely available.

By 1819 the market for cotton was nearly saturated, and it was evident that the economic "bubble" constructed from credit, paper money, and public confidence would not survive a fall in the price of western lands. The national bank understood this first and began to restrain credit and call in outstanding loans. The bank saved itself, in other words, by putting heavy pressure on the state banks. They, in turn, were forced to put pressure on their debtors, who suddenly could no longer renew old loans or get new ones. Debtors like Jefferson blamed the national bank for its tight money policy and for the resulting three years of economic dislocation.

Though Jefferson's terrific private debt was mainly of his own making, the Panic of 1819 reaffirmed his belief that the banking system of the country, a system he associated with speculation, cities, and loss of virtue, was undermining individual independence. He noted, for example, that never before had any nation "abandoned to the avarice and jugglings of private individuals to regulate, according to their own interests, the quantum of circulating medium for the nation."

To alleviate this situation, Jefferson proposed a "hard money" or specie economy of gold and silver in place of paper currency. Though most Americans would never have agreed to such a "radical" proposal, in the 1830s the agrarian wing of the Jacksonian party came close to creating an all-metal money system. Moreover, aside from the Civil War when the North printed "Greenbacks" to finance the war effort, the latter decades of the nineteenth century and the first three decades of the twentieth century saw an American money supply based upon the gold standard. To Jefferson, the financial crash of 1819 seemed to vindicate his criticisms of a speculative economy, something he had been decrying since the 1790s.

See also:
Market Revolution
Transportation Revolution
War of 1812

Reference:
North, Douglass C. 1961. *The Economic Growth of the United States, 1790–1860*. New York: Prentice Hall.

Party Politics

Jefferson viewed himself as a "philosopher-king" or natural aristocrat who ruled the nation as president because a majority of American citizens believed his social, economic, and political views were beneficial to the nation. In reality, however, Jefferson was closer to a political "boss" who used party discipline as a means to attain power. This fact is ironic, since the Constitution made no mention of political parties, considering them an evil. How could individuals have the nation's interests first in their hearts if they belonged to an organized faction? Such membership implied allegiance to party rather than nation. Jefferson believed this and was very critical of political or pseudopolitical organizations that cropped up in America. He presumed that his own Re-publican "party" in fact represented the true interests of the country.

Jefferson's friend, James Madison, began to organize the Republican coalition in 1789 to protect southern interests. Hoping to expand the southern agricultural economy, Madison proposed discriminatory measures against Great Britain, which did not allow American goods into its empire. Opposing Madison was Alexander Hamilton, a nationalist from New York who served as secretary of the treasury. Hamilton did not want the United States to discriminate against British products because the country needed access to British loans and markets. He promoted a pro-northern foreign policy that emphasized a close relationship with the former mother country.

In 1790, Hamilton introduced a series of bills that sought to dramatically increase the power of the federal government, a policy he believed was necessary to circumvent the inherent dangers of public power in a mass democracy. Madison's objections to Hamilton's agenda were brushed aside. Madison then persuaded Jefferson to put himself into the fray and take up the standard for agrarian rights, which were broadly interpreted in the South as American rights. Jefferson did in fact take up his pen to oppose "Hamiltonianism," and his popularity throughout the South and West ensured that he would be the symbol for Americans discontented with the kind of centralized government Hamilton proposed. Supporters of Hamilton, who tended to come from New England or New York, took the moniker "Federalists." Throughout 1793 a newspaper war in Philadelphia between Hamilton's Federalist newspaper and Jefferson's Republican newspaper brought the two factions' political differences to the public's attention, and the first party system in the nation's history was created.

Jefferson spent the second half of the 1790s challenging Federalist rule on the national level, unsuccessfully opposing Federalist candidate John Adams for the presidency in 1796. At no time did Jefferson accept Federalism as a national party. Rather, he believed

Federalism retained power through intrigue and speculation. In 1800, however, Republicans swept Jefferson into the presidency. At his inaugural, Jefferson described the party warfare of the previous decade in terms of consensus conflict. In doing so, he demonstrated his inability to take seriously the concept of parties in the United States. "We have called by different names brethren of the same principle," Jefferson proclaimed.

> We are all Republicans—we are all Federalists. If there be any among us who would wish to dissolve this Union or to change its republican form, let them stand undisturbed as monuments of the safety with which error of opinion may be tolerated where reason is left free to combat it. I know, indeed, that some honest men fear that a republican government cannot be strong; that this government is not strong enough. But would the honest patriot, in the full tide of successful experiment, abandon a government which has so far kept us free and firm, on the theoretic and visionary fear that this government, the world's best hope, may by possibility want energy to preserve itself? I trust not.

Thus Jefferson repudiated partyism in America and maintained that he served national rather than sectional or economic interests. Toward the end of his life, when it was evident that the party system would not dissipate, Jefferson took a different approach to partyism, calling partisans "useful watchmen for the public" because they served as the "censors of the conduct of each other." Drawing upon his belief in the "natural" laws of Enlightenment thought, Jefferson contended that

> men by their constitutions are naturally divided into two parties: 1. Those who fear and distrust the people, and wish to draw all powers from them into the hands of the higher classes.

> 2. Those who identify themselves with the people, have confidence in them, cherish and consider them as the most honest and safe, although not the most wise, depository of the public interest. In every country these two parties exist, and in every one where they are free to think, speak, and write, they declare themselves. Call them, therefore, . . . Whigs and Tories, Republicans and Federalists, Aristocrats and Democrats, or by whatever name you please, they are the same parties still, and pursue the same object.

Thus, by the end of his life, Jefferson accepted party politics as a natural and useful function of republican society.

See also:
Election of 1800
Hamilton, Alexander

Reference:
Hofstadter, Richard. 1969. *The Idea of a Party System: The Rise of Legitimate Opposition in the United States, 1780–1840.* Berkeley: University of California Press.

Peace of Paris (1763)

*I*n 1763 the French and Indian War concluded, and Great Britain descended upon the Paris peace conference as the major victor in the conflict. The treaty produced at that conference shaped the future of the 20-year-old Thomas Jefferson in ways that the Virginian could not imagine. First and foremost, the treaty gave to Britain France's empire in Canada. This new territory extended the physical contours of Britain's colonial possessions, but it also meant that England would have to institute new tax policies in order to cover the cost of administering its increased landholdings in North America. The psychological effect of the treaty on the colonists was important as well. Previously, they had acceded to the wishes of the mother country, in part because they feared their

French-Catholic neighbors to the north. With French governance of Canada removed, British subjects in North America no longer needed England to champion its defense.

When Great Britain began to propose new taxation measures in North America to pay for the upkeep of its empire, Jefferson and other members of the founding generation took umbrage, and over a period of 13 years, from 1763 to 1776, the colonists moved toward independence from Great Britain. Had the British not taken Canada in 1763 and taken instead the French sugar islands in the Caribbean, there would have been no reason for new tax measures and the British might well have kept their colonies in North America into the nineteenth century. The Treaty of Paris enlarged the British Empire to an unprecedented degree and simultaneously put into motion the forces that would shape Jefferson's career.

See also:
American Revolution
Anglo-French Wars
French and Indian War

Reference:
Olson, Alison. 1973. *Anglo-American Politics, 1600–1775*. London: Oxford University Press.

Peace of Paris (1783)

At the conclusion of the American Revolution, Congressman Jefferson was faced with the task of ratifying the Treaty of Paris, which officially concluded the Anglo-American conflict. Congress met in December 1783 at Annapolis and initially failed to reach a quorum. In order to conduct business concerning issues of importance, nine states had to be present. Jefferson wrote to Madison, "there are eight states in town, six of which are represented by two members only. Of these two members of different states are confined by the gout so that we cannot make a house. We have not sit

above three days I believe in as many weeks. Admonition after admonition has been sent to the states, to no effect." Jefferson contended that the states simply did not have the funds to send large delegations, or, in the case of a few states, any delegations at all to Annapolis. There is evidence, however, that Jefferson was too generous to the states that simply wanted to protect their own sovereignty and were fearful of what the Confederation government might do in Annapolis.

Jefferson was appointed to a committee to report on the Treaty of Paris, which was recommended by that group in a report submitted in his hand. Yet, with only seven states present at that time, the proceedings bogged down. This delay caused real concern on the part of the delegates, since the treaty, which was signed on September 3, 1783, provided for the exchange of ratifications to take place within six months or no later than March 3, 1784, a date fast approaching. Several delegates attempted to argue that seven states were enough to ratify the treaty, since that number constituted a majority of the states. But Jefferson found such actions "a dishonorable prostitution of our seal," and he was successful in defeating the push for immediate ratification. He did, however, meet his opponents on what he called the "middle ground" by preparing a resolution declaring ratification by seven states to be legitimate as long as it was legally passed through the Congress. In this way, the integrity of the Confederation government would be unsoiled and fears of congressional usurpation would be avoided.

Jefferson's compromise ultimately proved inconsequential as, on January 13, the delegations from Connecticut and New Jersey took their seats. Just one day later, the nine state delegations sitting in Annapolis ratified the Peace of Paris. The public was notified of Congress's actions by a public proclamation authored by Jefferson. Thus the author of the Declaration of Independence, which had announced to the world America's intent to achieve independence, also had the happy

C. Seiler painting of the signing of the preliminary Treaty of Peace at Paris, November 30, 1782, by the joint Commissioners of the United States and England.

task of informing the world of the success of America's revolution.

See also:
American Revolution
Articles of Confederation

Reference:
Morgan, Edmund S. 1977. *The Birth of the Republic, 1763–1789.* New York: Harper & Row.

Peale, Charles Wilson (1741–1827)

Charles Wilson Peale was a leader in the movement to develop the nation's arts and sciences along "republican" principles following the American Revolution. Jefferson promoted Peale's interests because he saw in the artist a kinship grounded in a mutual desire to bring about a republican social order. Jefferson's talents led him to work to-ward this goal in the realm of public policy while Peale pursued a democratic form of artistry, free from the trappings and patronage of monarchical society.

Peale was born in Maryland in 1741. He became a saddler's apprentice and by the time he was 20, opened his own shop. In 1763 he traded a saddle for art lessons from the painter John Hesselius. Four years later Peale traveled to London, where he studied with Benjamin West. He returned to the colonies in 1769 and moved to Philadelphia in 1776. Along with John Trumbull and Gilbert Stuart, Peale was one of America's greatest portraitists. Peale put his talents to use for the patriot cause during the Revolution, painting portraits of the Revolution's leading lights. George Washington posed for him no less than seven times, and in 1782, Peale opened a gallery devoted to his artistic interpretation of the Revolution. In later years, Peale developed an interest in science and, much to Jefferson's admiration, synthesized the best of American art and natural history in his displays. Peale was not merely a champion of the American Revolution, he was, more importantly, the proponent of a republican form of art.

See also:
Enlightenment

Reference:
Plate, Robert. 1967. *Charles Wilson Peale: Son of Liberty, Father of Art and Science.* New York: McKay.

Personal Popularity

Jefferson's popularity was essentially a regional phenomenon. The South and the West championed his policies and various candidacies to national office, while New England approached Jefferson with suspicion. The reasons for Jefferson's popularity in the South are easy to discern. He was a slaveholder, and southerners were rarely comfortable unless a plantation aristocrat occupied the White House. Second, while serving as president, Jefferson concluded the Louisiana Purchase, which awarded millions of acres of land to both farm and plantation economies. Moreover, individual areas of the new territory were settled during a period when Republicans controlled Congress, ensuring that their territorial and eventually their state governments would become Republican. Finally, Jefferson assuaged the fears of Americans. The Jeffersonian "persuasion"—advocacy of states' rights, enhanced liberty for white males, and the interests of independent small farmers—played well in a country fearful of centralized power.

See also:
Empire of Liberty
Louisiana Purchase

Reference:
Peterson, Merrill. 1960. *The Jefferson Image in the American Mind.* New York: Oxford University Press.

Personality

Jefferson's disposition was good-humored, cheerful, and, one historian has argued, "sunny." Certainly Jefferson's environment contributed to his contented nature. A country squire with wealth and leisure time, Jefferson did not want for material possessions. Moreover, his health was excellent. "He was strong," one observer has noted, "and, except for periodic headaches, very healthy; his admirable digestion helped him attain the serenity he sought." Throughout a very long life, punctuated at times by the death of family members and public attacks on his personal character, Jefferson never wavered from his fundamental optimism concerning the potential of humans and the institutions they created.

Yet to describe Jefferson simply as an optimist overlooks the complexity of his personality. Though he often referred to his affection for "the people," he was quite shy and rarely addressed large audiences. He preferred the intimacy of small groups and conducted much of his public business not

Pencil sketch, probably drawn from life, attributed to Benjamin Latrobe, circa 1799.

through direct command but rather through his persuasive letters. He preferred the security of letter writing to the uncertainty of public speaking and broke with precedent by not delivering oral messages to Congress as George Washington and John Adams had done. Jefferson's well-crafted messages were read by a simple clerk. One contemporary found Jefferson's disposition surprisingly resigned, noting that he was "so meek and mild, yet dignified with a countenance so benignant and intelligent."

Jefferson must have suffered terribly from the death of his wife and four of his children, who had all died by the time he was 39. After his family life had virtually disintegrated, politics, intellectual discourse, and scientific investigation alleviated his despair. That Jefferson was able to endure such personal tragedy is testimony to his faith in redemption and to his most eclectic interests and most admirable character.

See also:
Jefferson, Martha Wayles
Monticello
Personal Popularity

Reference:
Malone, Dumas. 1948. *Jefferson the Virginian.*
  Boston: Little, Brown.

Physiocrats

The physiocrats were part of an intellectual community in Europe that shaped Jefferson's conception of social and economic conditions in America. The movement originated in France with François Quesnay's 1758 publication, "Economic Picture." Quesnay and other French physiocrats spoke of the "Rule of Nature" that opposed government intrusion into the economy. Scotland's leading physiocrats, Adam Ferguson, John Millar, Lord Kames, and Adam Smith, agreed and concluded that it was best to allow the "invisible hand" of the market to serve as the natural regulator of economic activity.

Primary in the minds of these French and Scottish thinkers was a concern for the dramatic expansion of state power Great Britain experienced during its "financial revolution" of the early eighteenth century. On the foundation of mercantilist policy the British government had created a stock market, a national bank, and subsidized manufactures. This system produced great wealth but also great inequality. In the physiocrats' conception of the ideal economic order, free trade would reign in a predominately agricultural society. From this perspective they articulated very clearly the fears and concerns that were to grip many Republican agrarians in the 1790s.

A student of the physiocrats, Jefferson could not help but suspect that Hamilton's plans to centralize the locus of power in the national government were an attempt to emulate British mercantilist policies. By encouraging speculation, promoting manufactures, and creating a national bank, Hamilton appeared to be creating the worst edifices of the bureaucratic state. When he opposed Hamilton's programs, Jefferson did so from the perspective of a physiocrat who believed that most forms of economy were best left not to the calculations of government, but rather to the natural rhythms of the marketplace.

See also:
Ferguson, Adam
Smith, Adam

Reference:
Meek, Ronald. 1967. *Economics and Ideology and Other Essays: Studies in the Development of Economic Thought.* London: Chapman & Hall.

Pickering, Timothy (1745–1829)

A staunch Federalist from New England, Timothy Pickering was at odds with Jefferson's agrarian vision of America.

Pickering was born in Salem, Massachusetts, in 1745 and graduated from Harvard

College at the age of 18. He was admitted to the bar in 1768 and quickly became a figure of some prominence, signified by his commission in the Massachusetts militia as a colonel. He actively supported the American cause for independence and served during the Revolution as both a military commander and an administrator. Following his relocation to Pennsylvania, Pickering was active in procuring that state's acceptance of the United States Constitution.

Due more to his military background than to any discernible talent, Pickering was awarded several key positions in George Washington's and John Adams's cabinets. Starting out as postmaster general in 1791, Pickering soon was appointed secretary of war and by 1796, secretary of state, a position that he kept until he was removed for insubordination in 1800. Pickering was not a supporter of the president but instead championed the policies of Alexander Hamilton. Though he "served" Adams, Pickering reported cabinet business to Hamilton and took advice from him.

The most perplexing problem of Adams's presidency was whether to go to war with France over that nation's refusal to allow the United States to operate as a neutral in the Anglo-French War. Adams pursued a policy of reconciliation while Hamilton, and thus Pickering, maneuvered for war. In a last-ditch effort for peace, Adams ordered an American team of negotiators to seek peaceful terms with France. Adams then left Washington and returned home to Massachusetts where, remarkably, he stayed for the next several months. With Adams out of the capital city, Pickering impeded the mission by delaying its travel to the continent. Pickering's obstructiveness cost him his position when Adams returned.

Pickering returned to Massachusetts and served in the U.S. Senate from 1803 to 1811 and in the House of Representatives from 1813 to 1817. It was during his tenure in the Senate that he attempted to sever New England from the Union. His grievances centered around the election of Jefferson in 1800. As a Federalist, Pickering was uncomfortable with the increasing democratic tone in America and viewed Jefferson's victory with disgust. Furthermore, Jefferson's purchase of the Louisiana Territory meant that the new western territories and states that were to be carved out of the region would owe their livelihood to the Jeffersonian party and would in turn become Jeffersonian states. That turn of events would ensure that Federalism, which had dominated the political life of the nation of the 1790s, would never again return to power. Such awful premonitions caused Pickering and other disgruntled Federalists to attempt a peaceful separation from the Union. Their plan, joining New York and New Jersey to a "Northern Confederacy," came to naught, and Pickering was forced to live out the remainder of his days in a democratic country far different from the one he envisioned.

See also:
Adams, John
Essex Junto
Hamilton, Alexander

Reference:
Clarfield, Gerard. 1980. *Timothy Pickering and the American Republic.* Pittsburgh, PA: University of Pittsburgh Press.

Pinckney, Charles Cotesworth (1746–1825)

Charles Cotesworth Pinckney opposed Jefferson for the presidency in 1804 because he believed the Republican party was too democratic.

Pinckney was born in Charles Town, in the colony of South Carolina, in 1746. He was taken to England and educated at Oxford and then at Middle Temple in France. After returning to America in 1770, Pinckney practiced law and sided with the patriot cause in the Revolution. During the war, Pinckney was first an officer in a South Carolina regiment and then became an aide to General George Washington. Later Pinckney commanded American forces in Florida and Georgia and was taken prisoner in 1780, when the British captured Charles Town. Freed upon the war's end in 1783, he was made brigadier general.

Pinckney played a vital role in the process of drafting and implementing the United States Constitution. At the convention, he opposed religious tests for officeholders and urged, unsuccessfully, that slaves be counted equally with whites in order to determine representation in the House of Representatives. He also wanted senators to serve without pay. Had this idea been accepted, then only men with independent incomes, that is, wealthy men, would have been able to serve. Though the delegates did not incorporate all his suggestions into the final document, Pinckney worked diligently in South Carolina to ensure that his home state ratified the document.

In 1797, Pinckney was sent to France as part of a negotiating team empowered to end Franco-American hostilities. This effort proved unsuccessful, and a disgruntled Pinckney returned home. He served as the Federalist candidate for vice president in 1800. In 1804 and 1808 he opposed Jefferson and Madison for the presidency. In each case he was defeated. Pinckney practiced law in Charleston until his death in 1825.

See also:
Election of 1804
Election of 1808
XYZ Affair

Reference:
Fischer, David Hackett. 1965. *The Revolution of American Conservatism*. New York: Harper & Row.

Pinckney's Treaty

*T*his treaty between the United States and Spain would have been known to posterity as "Jefferson's Treaty" had the Virginian accepted President Washington's invitation to conduct negotiations for the American side.

The United States desperately wanted access to the Mississippi so that Americans living in the territories of Kentucky and Tennessee could transport their produce to market. Without access, westerners might lose their affection for the Union and join a Spanish empire that could guarantee the transit of their produce to the port of New Orleans and from there to regional and international markets. Another pressing issue was a boundary dispute. Spanish Florida demanded that its northern border be fixed well into present-day Georgia, and the United States refused. Furthermore, Native Americans in northern Florida successfully carried out raids on American soil, demonstrating Spain's inability to police its North American empire. Too, the success of the raids, along with the proximity of "foreign" soil, induced many slaves in Georgia to escape their masters by crossing into Spanish territory.

Thus the United States was eager to enter into a treaty with Spain that would address such concerns. In 1785, John Jay was dispatched to Madrid and concluded a treaty that would have furthered economic contact between the two nations. But because the treaty did not open the Mississippi to American navigation, the southern states, which were connected economically to the Mississippi trade, killed it.

Ten years later, however, circumstances favored a new mission that would achieve open transport on the Mississippi and resolve the remaining issues. By 1795, Spain was linked with France in a major European war against Great Britain and its allies. Spain understood that Britain looked to injure its colonial interests in North America and would be most likely to strike at the Louisiana Territory, a vast and sparsely held province of "New Spain." Furthermore, John Jay was at that moment concluding a treaty with Great Britain that would bring the

United States into a pro-British stance concerning commercial relations. Spain feared that this Anglo-American rapprochement might have military implications: a unified assault on Spanish possessions in the West. For these reasons, the government in Madrid was eager to settle its disputes with the United States.

Jefferson, who had recently retired as secretary of state, was asked by Washington to conduct negotiations. Citing health concerns, Jefferson declined the offer. To Edmund Randolph, however, Jefferson confided that attacks on his personal character by the Federalist party had soured him on public service for the time being. "No circumstances, my dear Sir," he wrote to Randolph, "will ever more tempt me to engage in anything public. I thought myself perfectly fixed in this determination when I left Philadelphia, but every day and hour since has added to its inflexibility."

Washington's eventual plenipotentiary, Thomas Pinckney, proved a good choice. Pinckney's Treaty, or the Treaty of San Lorenzo, gave the United States access to the Mississippi River and right of deposit at New Orleans for a term of years with the promise of renewal. In addition, the boundaries of Georgia and Florida were settled on the American side of the issue and agreements were made to end Native American raids in the Southwest. Pinckney's Treaty was the jewel in Washington's foreign policy. Ironically, this pro-Federalist administration fulfilled a very Jeffersonian diplomatic objective: opening the trans-Appalachian West to millions of American settlers. Jefferson himself could not have done more.

See also:
Anglo-French Wars
Federalist Party
Jay's Treaty

Reference:
Bemis, Samuel Flagg. 1926. *Pinckney's Treaty: A Study of America's Advantage from Europe's Distress, 1783–1800*. Baltimore, MD: Johns Hopkins Press.

Plantation System

Jefferson's worldview was shaped by the plantation system that dominated Virginia before, throughout, and beyond his lifetime. As a master, Jefferson was representative of his class in that he supposed himself to be a fair and kind slaveholder. Such images, or perhaps illusions, were not always easy to maintain. During the American Revolution, for example, some 30 slaves escaped Monticello and were "rescued" by the British army. Their unwillingness to content themselves with life at Monticello is a moving testimony to what Jefferson would consider, when speaking of whites, to be a natural desire for liberty. Jefferson prided himself on his benevolent, even paternal compassion toward his slaves. Ironically, he found such behavior patronizing when directed toward whites and practiced by aristocrats and the clergy, believing that it stunted the natural development of the free individual. Jefferson's racial views, however, allowed him to believe that plantation slavery benefited the slave, who acquired the rudiments of Christianity and enjoyed daily intercourse with a superior civilization and race. Moreover, Jefferson believed that the treatment his slaves received was comparable to that received by "the laborers of other countries."

There is some evidence that Jefferson was a benevolent master in comparison with his southern counterparts. One visitor to Monticello remarked that Jefferson's slaves were "nourished, clothed and treated as well as white servants could be." Jefferson certainly agreed with such observations, describing the environment at Monticello as a place "where all is peace and harmony, where we love and are loved by every object we see." But Jefferson's idea of his slaves' peaceful, harmonious existence might be due in part to his long absences from home. Public service often required Jefferson to be elsewhere, and the daily running of his grounds was left to overseers and stewards. Thus, as one historian has noted, "Jefferson was more or less insulated against the grosser aspects of slavery." His most intimate contact with slaves was reserved for house servants, who were considered superior to the field hands. The lash, therefore, never was wielded by Jefferson personally, though he left instructions that the most temperamental slaves be dealt with in such a fashion.

A comparison between Jefferson and Washington on this subject is revealing. Unlike Jefferson, who maintained that plantation agriculture was a profitable enterprise, Washington harbored no such delusions, regarding slave labor as a historical misfortune of the southern economy. As a master, Washington was often severe with his slaves and had the reputation of a strict disciplinarian. Yet Washington refused to sell his slaves "as you would do cattle at a market," as he once put it, and considered breaking up families a dirty business. Without such qualms, Washington probably would have sold all of his slaves and been done with the practice. As things stood, he waited until death, when his will ordered the manumission of every slave in his possession upon the death of his wife. Jefferson, however, actively engaged in the buying and selling of slaves throughout his life, even while serving as president. Moreover, while Jefferson often reflected on the ills of slavery for both bondsman and master, he freed very few of his slaves.

The occupations of Jefferson's slaves came to reflect his interests and tastes. Many were artisans and shared their master's penchant for construction and architecture. A significant number were blacksmiths, bricklayers, and carpenters. Moreover, Jefferson's desire to lead an aristocratic lifestyle ensured that many of his slaves would work in or around the home as coachmen, grooms, and attendants. Regarding the "productive" labor force at Monticello, another irony arises. Jefferson condemned Alexander Hamilton's plans to employ white women and children in factory work, yet he felt no qualms about using black women and their children in such endeavors. At Monticello, for example, slave women and children ran a small textile factory, mill, and nail manufactory. This supplement to the traditional plantation economy was merely a diversion, however, and certainly could not challenge the dominance of the agrarian element.

See also:
Slave Trade
Slavery
Washington, George

Reference:
Bear, James, Jr. 1967. *Jefferson at Monticello: Recollections of a Monticello Slave and a Monticello Overseer.* Charlottesville: University Press of Virginia.

Priestley, Joseph (1733–1804)

An English scientist and religious freethinker, Joseph Priestley epitomized the rational approach to understanding the natural world. Much like Jefferson's, Priestley's career was devoted to the pursuit of reason and the destruction of superstition and dogma. His early education prepared him for a career in the ministry, but Priestley turned away from orthodox Calvinism and accepted the more lenient strictures of the Arminian faith. At 19 he entered an academy in Daventry and studied natural philosophy. He then took a teaching position in Warrington, where he struck up what would prove to be a lifelong friendship with Benjamin Franklin. At Franklin's encouragement, Priestley wrote *History of Electricity,* which marked his initial foray into the sciences.

By the 1770s, Priestley had abandoned electrical studies in order to concentrate on chemistry. Experiments in the heating of mercuric oxide in 1774–1775 led Priestley to discover oxygen and make a name for himself. In all, Priestley discovered nine gases, including nitrogen, hydrogen chloride, and sulfur dioxide. Justly famous for his insights into the natural world, Priestley's involvement in religious controversy proved to be his downfall in England. Specifically, his support for Unitarianism made him an enemy of the Anglican Church. In 1791 his home and laboratory were destroyed by a mob, and he was urged by his wife to live out the remainder of his life in America, where his three sons had already emigrated.

Jefferson was ecstatic that such an eminent scientist would come to the United States to live. It seemed to prove Jefferson's belief that the New World, free of cant and hypocrisy, would regenerate Europe. In a letter to Priestley, Jefferson wrote that

the barbarians [English] really flattered themselves they should be able to bring back the times of Vandalism, when ignorance put everything into the hands of power and priestcraft. . . . Those who live by mystery and charlatanerie, fear you would render them useless by simplifying the Christian philosophy—the most

sublime and benevolent but most perverted system that ever shone on man—endeavored to crush your well-earned and well-deserved fame.

For Jefferson, Priestley's leaving England highlighted the enlightened views of America's republic, which welcomed dissenters to its shores. "I can hail you with welcome to our land," Jefferson remarked, promising that the nation would "cover you under the protection of those laws which were made for the wise and good like you." Priestley settled in Northumberland, Pennsylvania, where he maintained a laboratory until his death in 1804.

See also:
Enlightenment

Reference:
Boorstin, Daniel. 1948. *The Lost World of Thomas Jefferson.* Chicago, IL: University of Chicago Press.

Quasi War

During the period 1795–1800, a Quasi War was fought between the United States and France over the signing of Jay's Treaty, which brought America into closer relations with France's greatest enemy, the British Empire. Jefferson was disturbed by this undeclared naval war. He had always preferred an alliance with the French rather than the British. Like the United States, France was a predominately agricultural nation with a republican form of government. Great Britain, on the other hand, was an industrial nation ruled by a monarchy. Jefferson hoped that France and the United States would develop a republican-agricultural political economy that would rule the Atlantic and isolate the British Isles. The Quasi War shattered this dream.

Jefferson tended to blame the Quasi War on the Federalist party. It had pursued close ties with Britain in order to acquire English loans and credit to fuel manufacturing in Federalism's stronghold, New England. More ominous to Jefferson was the Federalist response to the Quasi War at home. Though President John Adams resisted a declaration of war, he put the country on a wartime footing by raising taxes to pay for an enlarged military of approximately 10,000. Even more disturbing were the Alien and Sedition Acts that the Federalist party passed in 1798 to limit freedom of speech and the press in order to encourage a patriotic consensus against the French. Jefferson interpreted these actions as blatantly unconstitutional and suspected that the Federalists were trying to protect their party from internal dissent rather than strengthen the nation against an external enemy.

Still, Jefferson was dismayed at France's aggressive actions against American shipping and came down on the side of preparation. "It is our duty still to endeavor to avoid war; but if it shall actually take place, no matter by whom brought on, we must defend ourselves. If our house be on fire, without inquiring whether it was fired from within or without, we must try to extinguish it. In that, I have no doubt we shall act as one man." With the United States vigorously opposing the French, who had other concerns in Europe, the Convention of 1800 officially ended the unofficial war.

See also:
Adams, John
Alien and Sedition Acts
Jay's Treaty

Reference:
De Conde, Alexander. 1966. *The Quasi-War: The Politics and Diplomacy of the Undeclared War with France, 1797–1801.* New York: Scribner.

Randolph, Edmund
(1753–1813)

During the bulk of his public service, Edmund Randolph was a distinguished member of the inner circle of Virginia Republicans. His tendency to stray from strict party orthodoxy, however, engendered Jefferson's ill will and forced him from the Republican fold.

Randolph was born in Williamsburg, Virginia, in 1753. He was ten years younger than Jefferson and viewed him as something of a mentor. Like Jefferson, Randolph attended William and Mary College and studied law. At the beginning of the war for independence, Randolph served as an aide to General George Washington and thus experienced the Revolution in a different way than Jefferson, who took no active military role in the affair. Randolph returned to the Old Dominion in 1776, where he was a member of the state's constitutional convention and served as Virginia's first attorney general from 1776 to 1786.

Randolph was elected governor of Virginia in 1786 and was a delegate to the federal Constitutional Convention the following year. Though he was an early backer of the Constitution while it was being drafted, he grew concerned about the lavish commercial powers and the centralized executive authority it authorized and refused to sign it. In the state ratification convention that followed, however, Randolph reluctantly defended the Constitution as the best the nation could hope for.

In 1789, President Washington chose Randolph to serve as the nation's first attorney general. Though most historians believe that Randolph acted as an impartial member in the cabinet, Secretary of State Jefferson presumed that Randolph sided with his enemy, Alexander Hamilton. This alliance disappointed Jefferson, who believed that Hamilton and Secretary of War Henry Knox, both northerners eager to develop the nation's latent industrial capabilities, were critical of his promotion of states' rights agrarianism. But from Randolph, his fellow-Virginian, Jefferson expected the utmost support. He wrote to James Madison in reference to Randolph that "everything . . . now hangs on the opinion of a single person, and the most indecisive one I ever had to do business with. He always contrives to agree in principle with one [Jefferson] but in conclusion with the other [Hamilton]." For his imagined sins Randolph was cast out of the Republican fold, and any hopes he may have entertained of following Jefferson or Madison as the leader of the Republican faction were now extinguished. In reality, Randolph was probably following the precedent set by Washington, who conducted cabinet business in a neutral, dispassionate manner. Jefferson, however, expected nothing shy of absolute obedience from his junior colleague.

In reward for his services to the cabinet, Randolph was elevated to the position of secretary of state in 1794 following Jefferson's retirement. He quickly ran afoul of Washington, however, when he opposed many of the instructions given to John Jay, who was about to travel to Great Britain to negotiate a treaty that would ease tensions between the two nations but divide Federalists and Republicans at home. In particular, Randolph was offended by the treaty's commercial provisions, which he believed were too favorable to the British. His troubles were compounded in 1795, when he was accused of soliciting bribes from the French and forced to resign. Though these charges were later proven false, Randolph's reputation was irreparably damaged. He devoted the rest of his life to private law practice and died on his estate in Clark County in 1813.

See also:
Jay's Treaty
Washington, George

Reference:
Rearden, John. 1974. *Edmund Randolph: A Biography.* New York: Macmillan.

Randolph, John (1773–1833)

Though 40 years Jefferson's junior, John Randolph was actively involved in shepherding Jefferson's presidential programs through Congress. Like Jefferson, Randolph was a Virginian, born in Prince George County in 1773. He studied briefly at Princeton, Columbia, and William and Mary and also read law. Following a move to the Roanoke River, he became known as John Randolph of Roanoke. In 1799, Randolph was elected to the House of Representatives and in 1801 became chairman of the Ways and Means Committee and thus the leader of the Jeffersonian faction in the House.

In many ways Randolph was a more consistent Jeffersonian than Jefferson himself, because he was caustic, rigid, and unyielding where Jefferson was flexible, optimistic, and generally receptive to new solutions. Thus Randolph, unwilling to give ground on Republican principles, became the defender of a particularly "pure" strain of Republicanism. The differences between the two men became evident during Jefferson's presidency and split their political partnership. The most damaging episode involved the president's attempt to obtain money from Congress to enlist French aid in America's efforts to acquire Florida from Spain. Where Jefferson saw this maneuver as little more than greasing the gears of the international diplomacy machine, Randolph saw a bribe. His shrill opposition ensured that the motion was rejected.

Finding himself in opposition to a Jeffersonian party that he believed to be losing its ideological purity, Randolph formed a separate faction known as the Tertium Quid ("third something"). The Quid believed in states' rights and in strict construction of the Constitution. As the Jeffersonian party became more nationalistic, Randolph stepped up his attacks, denouncing the Republican-backed national bank and protective tariffs. He was also a vigorous opponent of the War of 1812, believing that malignant Republican leadership and a desire to acquire territory were the primary motives behind American involvement in the conflict. In a congressional speech, Randolph claimed that "gentlemen from the North have been taken up to some high mountain and shown all the kingdoms of the earth; and Canada seems tempting in their sight. That rich vein of Gennesee land, which is said to be even better on the other side of the lake than on this. Agrarian cupidity, not maritime rights, urges the war." He concluded that this was to be a "predatory war," not "a war for our homes and firesides—a war that might generate, or call forth manly and honorable sentiment—but, a war of rapine, of privateering, a scuffle and scramble for plunder."

Randolph's alienation from the Republican party did not hinder his congressional career, which continued to flourish in both the House and the Senate. Following Jefferson's retirement, Randolph maintained his self-appointed position as defender of "pure" Republicanism. Though he was popular in his home state of Virginia, Randolph's acerbic wit and obstructionist tactics prohibited him from any constructive activity during his final years in Congress. He is remembered today as a gadfly rather than a statesman. During his final years Randolph enjoyed a well-earned reputation for eccentric behavior. On more than one occasion he entered sessions of Congress in boots and spurs, carrying a riding whip. In response to poor health, Randolph turned to alcohol and opium, which exacerbated his condition. He died in Philadelphia in 1833 and was buried facing west so that, legend has it, he could keep an eye on Henry Clay, a political enemy from Kentucky.

See also:
States' Rights
Tertium Quid

Reference:
Adams, Henry. 1882. *John Randolph by Henry Adams.* New York: Houghton, Mifflin.

Religion

Thomas Jefferson lost his faith in traditional Christianity at an early age. Though he patronized churches of different denominations in Virginia and often attended their services, he belonged to no organized religious order. Jefferson could not escape the influence of rationalism inspired by the Enlightenment. To him, the Christian God made no sense. Rather, Jefferson believed in a benign Creator, a dynamic entity that allowed the world to operate to its own conclusions, much as a watchmaker allows a timepiece to run independently after it has been wound. This conception allowed Jefferson to retain a sense of the mysterious by subscribing to belief in a Creator yet make his views conform to Enlightenment thinking. Though his spirituality is difficult to pinpoint, Jefferson seemed to desire a consensus uniting men of reason and liberality around a moral center.

The moral branch of religion alone interested him. The question of Christ's humanity or divinity, the debate over the virgin birth, and postulations on issues such as original sin, miracles, and the like seemed nonsensical to Jefferson. Instead, Christianity attracted him because it offered a moral code that was liberal and useful as well as rational. Moreover, as Jefferson's political career developed, he became increasingly disenchanted with clergymen, who often attacked him from the pulpit for his "atheism." By promoting a rational God, one that operated from reason and disinterestedness rather than emotion, mystery, or even wrath, Jefferson sought to weaken organized religion, dominated, he argued, by the "priest and the infidel," and make Christ accessible to all. In sum, Jefferson proposed to tie the teachings of Jesus to the principles of the Enlightenment. In the natural world all men were created equal and shared equal rights; so, too, they could find universal salvation in the supernatural world.

In 1803, Jefferson wrote one of his most memorable letters. To Dr. Benjamin Rush he sought to make clear his "religious views." Not designed for a wide audience, Jefferson's letter was intended to demonstrate that he shared faith in a Creator with most of his fellow citizens, although the letter makes clear that Jefferson's God is less powerful than most Christians would accept.

My views . . . are the result of a life of inquiry and reflection, and very different from that anti-Christian system imputed to me by those who know nothing of my opinions. To the corruptions of Christianity I am indeed opposed, but not to the genuine precepts of Jesus himself. I am a Christian in the only sense in which he wished anyone to be, sincerely attached to his doctrines in preference to all others, ascribing to himself every human excellence, and believing he never claimed any other. . . . His parentage was obscure, his condition poor, his education null; his natural endowments great; his life correct and innocent: he was meek, benevolent, patient, firm, disinterested, and of the sublimest eloquence. The disadvantages under which his doctrines appear are remarkable.

1. Like Socrates and Epictetus, he wrote nothing himself.

2. But he had not, like them, a Xenophon or an Arrian to write for him. I name not Plato, who used the name Socrates to cover the whimsies of his own brain. On the contrary, all the learned of his country, entrenched in its power and riches, were opposed to him, lest his labors should undermine their advantages; and the committing to writing his life and doctrines fell on unlettered and ignorant men who wrote, too, from memory, and not till long after the transactions had passed.

3. According to the ordinary fate of those who attempt to enlighten and reform mankind, he fell an early victim to the jealousy and combination of the altar and the throne, at about thirty-three years of age, his reason having not yet attained the maximum of its energy, nor the course of his preaching, which was but of three years at most, presented occasions for developing a complete system of morals.

4. Hence the doctrines which he really delivered were defective as a whole, and fragments only of what he did deliver have come to us, mutilated, misstated and often unintelligible.

5. They have been still more disfigured by the corruptions of schismatizing followers, who have found an interest in sophisticating and perverting the simple doctrines he taught, by engrafting on them the mysticisms of a Grecian sophist, frittering them into subtleties, and obscuring them with jargon, until they have caused good men to reject the whole in disgust and to view Jesus himself as an impostor.

Notwithstanding these disadvantages, a system of morals is presented to us which, if filled up in the style and spirit of the rich fragments he left us, would be the most perfect and sublime that has ever been taught by man.

Thus to Jefferson, the moral system and Christ's place as its center remain. Yet the Virginian made it clear that Christ's legacy is limited, like a human's. Rather than celebrate Jesus as the founder of traditional Christianity, Jefferson placed Christ within his own spiritual world, alongside Socrates and Epictetus, as the repositories of reason and justice. Jefferson's spirituality was complete, but in alliance with a healthy skepticism, it provoked doubt among those around him. As one historian noted, Jefferson "did not even accept Jesus on his own terms, for Jesus was a spiritualist by the grace of God and he was a materialist by the grace of science."

See also:
Deism
Virginia Statute of Religious Freedoms

Reference:
Cousins, Norman, ed. 1958. *In God We Trust: The Religious Beliefs and Ideas of the American Founding Fathers*. New York: Harper.

Repeal of the Judiciary Act of 1801

After losing political power to the Republican party following the elections of 1800, a lame-duck Federalist Congress passed the Judiciary Act of 1801. The act enlarged the federal judiciary, providing outgoing President John Adams the opportunity to appoint Federalist partisans to the bench and thus limit the effects of the Republican victory. Jefferson was appalled by this attempt to thwart the public will and immediately set out to repeal the act. However, he shrewdly refused to attack the judiciary itself, which would have cost him popularity, contending instead that the new courts were not necessary because the existing system could take care of the workload.

Evidence demonstrates that Jefferson was probably correct. Of the over 8,000 cases heard during the previous ten years, only approximately 1,600 were still pending. Moreover, there were indications that the federal judiciary's docket would actually shrink over the next several years. Claims made by British creditors against American debtors going back as far as the colonial period were now being referred to an Anglo-American commission that would soon end its proceedings by making a lump-sum payment to Britain. Further, the Supreme Court generally completed its session in Washington in five to six weeks, leaving the justices plenty of time to preside over legal matters in their appointed districts. While Jefferson feared the extension of Federalism in the judiciary, his campaign against it shrewdly emphasized the issues of cost and efficiency.

Under the auspices of Jefferson's friend John Breckinridge, the Repeal Act passed through the Senate in February 1802 and the House one month later. Federalists decried this "executive usurpation" on the part of Jefferson and his allies in Congress. Referring to what he considered an overthrow of legal principles, Gouverneur Morris mournfully declared of the Constitution, "It is dead, it is dead." Republicans, however, were pleased with their efforts in limiting Federalist influence. One Republican newspaper proclaimed that the act "demonstrates the inflexible determination of those who now hold the reigns of authority, to adhere in power to the same principles, avowed by

them out of power." Though Jefferson never doubted the correctness of his actions, he was nevertheless pleased when, in 1803, the Supreme Court upheld the Repeal Act and gave legal sanction to the Republican party's removal of Federalism from the most aristocratic estate of government.

See also:
Attack on the Judiciary
Judiciary Act of 1801

Reference:
Ellis, Richard. 1971. *The Jeffersonian Crisis: Courts and Politics in the Young Republic.* New York: Oxford University Press.

"Report on Manufactures"

The "Report on Manufactures," submitted to Congress in December 1791, was Alexander Hamilton's most thorough summation of his argument for a more industrial and less agrarian vision of American development. It incurred the wrath of Jefferson, who interpreted Hamilton's report, along with his creation of a national bank, an attempt to secure power for the federal government at the expense of the states. In his report, Hamilton clearly defines the type of society he envisioned for America. Unlike Jefferson, who believed that rationality and civic responsibility would influence the public actions of citizens, Hamilton's treatise emphasized people's acquisitive nature. Given enough room, he suggested, individuals would pursue private fortunes in an enlarged national economy and, through paying taxes and creating jobs, economic benefits would accrue to the entire nation. From this perspective, Hamilton argued that private interests in a community could not be separated from the larger political society.

The heart of Hamilton's report attempted to show the intrinsic advantages of an economy based on industrial manufacturing. He argued, for example, that European curtailment of American trade made the United States weak and dependent. The only alternative to subservience was industrial independence. There existed, he continued, a prejudice against manufacturing in America because of the nation's traditionally agrarian heritage.

To offset ingrained patterns and best serve the country, he offered the aid and patronage of the federal government. Hamilton called for inducements to bring foreign capital to America; the expansion of the national banking system to make provisions for investment capital; the employment of immigrants, women, and children in factories to make up for the shortage of laborers created by white males' habit of seeking their employment in the agrarian economy; roads and canals to facilitate market expansion; modest protective duties to induce infant capitalists in America to invest in competitive industries; and finally bounties awarded to inventors who received patents for articles of practical use in the industrial process. Hamilton concluded that such measures were constitutional under the "necessary and proper" clause. Further, the treasury secretary attempted to eliminate criticism of his report by portraying the alternative, an agriculture-based economy, in bleak terms, as endangering the future of the republic.

It has been maintained that agriculture is, not only, the most productive, but the only productive species of industry. The reality of this suggestion in either aspect, has, however, not been verified by any accurate detail of facts and calculations; and the general arguments, which are adduced to prove it, are rather subtle and paradoxical, than solid or convincing. . . .

The expediency of encouraging manufactures in the United States, which was not long since deemed very questionable, appears at this time to be pretty generally admitted. The embarrassments, which have obstructed the progress of our external trade, have led to serious reflections on the necessity of enlarging the sphere of our domestic commerce: the restrictive regulations, which in foreign markets abridge the vent of the increasing surplus of our agricultural produce, serve to beget an earnest desire, that a more extensive demand for that surplus may be created at home: And the complete success, which has rewarded manufacturing enterprise, in some valuable branches, conspiring with the promising symptoms, which attend some less mature essays, in others, justify a hope, that the obstacles to the growth of this species of industry are less formidable than they were apprehended to be; and that it is not difficult to find, in its further extension; a full indemnification for any external disadvantages, which are or may be experienced, as well as an accession of resources, favorable to national independence and safety.

Predictably, Hamilton's report inspired vigorous dissent from Jefferson. To the Virginian, the championing of manufactures would bring about speculation and corruption rather than liberty and freedom. Jefferson's own vision of the "good society" called for the rapid expansion of the farming class across the western frontier—the antithesis of Hamilton's call to keep industrial workers bottled up along the Eastern Seaboard toiling in factories. In such case, Jefferson offered, the "pursuit of happiness" was sacrificed to the industrial machine. In a remarkable letter to George Washington, Jefferson argued that Hamilton's "system flowed from principles adverse to liberty, and was calculated to undermine and demolish the republic, by creating an influence of his department over the members of the legislature." Jefferson concluded that Hamilton

. . . expressly assumed that the general government has a right to exercise all powers which may be for the general welfare, that is to say, all the legitimate powers of government: since no government has a legitimate right to do what is not for the welfare of the governed. There was indeed a sham-limitation of the universality of this power to cases where money is to be employed. But about what is it that money cannot be employed? Thus the object of these plans taken together is to draw all the powers of government into the hands of the general legisla-ture, to establish means for corrupting a sufficient corps in that legislature to divide the honest votes and prepon-derate, by their own, the scale which suited, and to have that corps under the command of the Secretary of the Treasury for the purpose of subverting step by step the principles of the constitution, which he has so often declared to be a thing of nothing which must be changed.

For all the sound and fury in Jefferson's indictment, the "Report on Manufactures" was never seriously considered by Con-gress. Its breadth and scope, while brilliant, were simply too radical for the young re-public. Moreover, Hamilton's plans were wildly optimistic and ultimately impracti-cal. The kind of economy that Hamilton hoped to encourage in America in the 1790s would not be possible until the 1820s. In other words, Jefferson never had to grapple with the practical aspects of industrialism as heralded by Hamilton. Yet his forceful cri-tique of Hamilton's report leaves no doubt that he feared a political economy admin-istered along northern, industrial, and na-tional values.

See also:
Hamilton, Alexander
Manufacturers
National Bank

Reference:
Frisch, Morton, ed. 1985. *Selected Writings and Speeches of Alexander Hamilton*. Washington, DC: American Enterprise Institute for Public Policy Research.

Republican Party

The Republican party was also known as the Democratic-Republican party or the Jeffersonian-Republican party to de-note both the faction's commitment to democratic rule and Jefferson's central lead-ership position in the party. The Republican party was created by James Madison in the wake of Alexander Hamilton's efforts to cen-tralize power in the federal government and thus weaken state sovereignty. By 1791, Jef-ferson was the recognized leader of the coa-lition. Through its support he won the presidency in 1800 and 1804.

The Republican party was as much a sec-tional coalition as it was a political one. Re-publicans tended to come from the South and the West, and the party was weakest in the Federalist stronghold of New England. Domestically, Republicans promoted the cause of democracy and states' rights while Federalists advocated a more limited kind of democracy and a powerful federal govern-ment. In foreign policy, Republicans tended to support the French Revolution and the fortunes of that nation while the Federalist party pushed for closer ties with Great Brit-ain, whose markets and credit New England needed in order to prosper. Throughout the 1790s, the Federalists controlled the national government, and Republicans were forced to operate as an opposition party. Jefferson explained his coalition's initial setbacks by noting that

the Republican part of our Union comprehends 1. The entire body of landholders throughout the United States. 2. The body of laborers, not being landholders, whether in husbanding or the arts. The latter is to the aggregate of the [Federalists] probably as five hundred to one; but their wealth is not as disproportionate, though it is also greatly superior, and is in truth the foundation of that of their antagonists.

Trifling as are the numbers of the anti-Republicans party there are circumstances which give them an appearance of strength and numbers. They all live in cities together and can act in a body readily, and at all times, they give chief employment to the newspapers, and therefore have most of them under their command.

Even after assuming the presidency in 1800, Jefferson worried about the fortunes of the newly elected Republican party. "My great anxiety at present," he commented, "is to avail ourselves of our ascendancy to establish good principles and good practices; to fortify Republicanism behind as many barriers as possible, that the outworks may give time to rally and save the citadel, should that be again in danger." Toward this end, Jefferson's Republican coalition championed the rapid expansion of western lands, cut taxes, and offered a vision of national development that relied more on state initiative than federal government planning.

These components of Republicanism proved very popular with a constituency wary of institutional restraints, and between 1800 and 1824 the party was perhaps more successful than any in American history in implementing its governing vision. More than a party, Republicanism represented a vision of how the nation should develop. It was predicated on the virtues of agrarianism, it looked with suspicion on large cities and the manufacturing system, and it stood by the rights of southerners to hold slaves as property.

See also:
Virginia Dynasty

Reference:
Cunningham, Noble. 1963. *The Jeffersonian Republicans in Power.* Chapel Hill: University of North Carolina Press.

Retirement

*J*efferson spent the final 17 years of his life out of public office, but his retirement was never as peaceful or uneventful as he wished. Upon leaving the presidency, Jefferson remarked that "I shall retire to my family, my books and farms. . . . Never did a prisoner released from his chains feel such relief as I shall on shaking off the shackles of power." Yet much remained for Jefferson to accomplish. In the words of one historian, Jefferson became not merely a former president or party leader but the "Sage of Monticello," living on his "little mountain" in Virginia and dispensing wisdom to the public officials and private citizens who made the pilgrimage to Albemarle County to hear the arch apostle of republicanism speak. Though professing a love for horseback riding and long walks around his property, Jefferson never repudiated his former political lifestyle completely and generally spent each morning corresponding with important men around the country in hopes that he might influence the course of national events.

Happily, Jefferson's final years included a renewal of his old friendship with John Adams. The two men had been estranged for several years over political differences, but the letters they wrote to one another after resuming their friendship are among the most profound descriptions of republican theory and political culture that this nation has produced. Around the time his correspondence with Adams commenced, Jefferson was invited to lend his name to an emancipation organization. For both personal and public reasons he declined leadership. He reasoned that the extinction of slavery was inevitable; agitation would only serve to prolong the

A view of the University of Virginia. "This institution of my native state, the hobby of my old age, will be based on the illimitable freedom of the human mind." Engraving published by C. Bohn, 1856.

practice. Ever the optimist, Jefferson counted on time to cure the social ills that perplexed humanity.

The last eight years of Jefferson's life were not as happy as he deserved. Personal debt followed him at every turn. A lifetime of living beyond his means to fund his plantation aristocrat lifestyle had forced Jefferson into a precarious financial position. However, he blamed his condition on external issues. "Had crops and prices for several years been such as to maintain a steady competition of substantial bidders at market," he declared to James Madison, "all would have been safe." Over the years, Jefferson had resorted to selling off land or borrowing money to pay off loans that were in danger of going into arrears. In 1815 he sold what was perhaps his most cherished material possession, his library of 6,500 volumes, to the United States to replace the Library of Congress collection that had been destroyed by the British during the War of 1812. Subsequent financial

reversals forced Jefferson to launch a lottery scheme shortly before his death that would have auctioned off many of his possessions so that he could retain Monticello and at least a minor legacy, a "farm free," as he described it, for his dependents.

Jefferson's retirement years were also a time of wrapping up lifelong projects and simplifying his life. In 1818, for example, this avid reader canceled newspaper subscriptions to all but the *Richmond Enquirer* and began to sum up his weather records, analyzing decades of observation of the natural environment around Monticello. These years were also consumed by Jefferson's efforts to establish the University of Virginia and bring to fruition a lifelong dream of centering the scholarly culture of the South in his own backyard. To John Adams he noted that "I am fortunately mounted on a hobby, which, indeed, I should have better managed some thirty or forty years ago; but whose easy amble is still sufficient to give exercise and amusement to an octogenary rider. The University will give employment to the remaining years, and quite enough for my senile faculties. It is the last act of usefulness I can render, and could I see it open I would not ask an hour more of life." Jefferson's project was completed shortly before his death.

See also:
University of Virginia
War of 1812

Reference:
Malone, Dumas. 1948–1981. *The Sage of Monticello,* vol. 6 of *Jefferson and His Time.* Boston: Little, Brown.

Revolution of 1800

Thomas Jefferson referred to his electoral victory in 1800 as a "revolution." He believed the American public had repudiated the Federalist party, which he associated with monarchy, and embraced the more democratic Republican coalition. As one pro-Jefferson paper put it:

> Rejoice! Columbia's sons rejoice!
> To tyrants never bend the knee,
> But join with heart, and soul, and voice,
> For JEFFERSON and LIBERTY.

In his memoirs, Jefferson added that

> the Revolution of 1800 . . . was as real a revolution in the principles of our government as that of 1776 was in its form; not effected indeed by the sword, as that, but by the rational and peaceable instrument of reform, the suffrage of the people. The nation declared its will by dismissing functionaries of one principle and electing those of another in the two branches, executive and legislature, submitted to their election.

And yet the victory was not complete, for, as Jefferson lamented, "over the judiciary department the Constitution had deprived [the people] of their control." Jefferson was satisfied, though, that "the nation at length passed condemnation on the political principles of the Federalists by refusing to continue Mr. Adams in the presidency." While most historians scoff at the notion that Jefferson's election resembled anything so radical as a "revolution," the Republican party was now in position to sweep away the last vestiges of Federalism and usher in a new era of popular government.

See also:
Adams, John
Election of 1800
Republican Party

Reference:
Sisson, Daniel. 1974. *The Revolution of 1800.* New York: Alfred A. Knopf.

Ritchie, Thomas (1778–1854)

Thomas Ritchie was the editor of the Richmond *Enquirer* and a member of the Virginia Junto, an informal group of states' rights activists who promoted the interests of the Old Dominion in particular and the South in general. Ritchie was a staunch Jeffersonian and used his paper to champion Republican causes. The *Enquirer* was by far the most important newspaper in Virginia and one of the most influential in the country. Late in his life, Jefferson cut back on his correspondence and subscribed to fewer and fewer newspapers until Ritchie's was the only one he received. Jefferson noted that he subscribed to "every tittle [in the *Enquirer*] . . . they contain the true principles of the revolution of 1800 [the year he was elected president]." In sum, Jefferson viewed Ritchie's paper as a true friend of republican ideology in America.

Jefferson's uncritical patronage of the *Enquirer* had a negative side, however. In the last years of the Virginian's life, the federal government began to assume a host of powers that many southerners believed threatened state sovereignty. Following the War of 1812, a new national bank was chartered, a federal tariff was instituted, the Supreme Court became a major figure in the governing process, and the Missouri crisis, which brought up the issue of slavery's extension into the West, nearly wrecked the nation. To southerners like Jefferson and Ritchie, it appeared that Virginia and its slaveholding neighbor states were under attack from an increasingly powerful central government. Ritchie fought back through the pages of the *Enquirer,* where other members of the Virginia Junto, including John Randolph and John Taylor, contributed essays. Jefferson's main source of information was the Richmond paper, and his sense of the purity of local rule was heightened by the influence of the *Enquirer.* Though it is difficult to measure the impact of such things, Jefferson's pessimistic outlook on the Missouri affair and his fears of an oncoming war between slaveholding and nonslaveholding interests may have come largely through his devotion to a single partisan newspaper.

See also:
Randolph, John
Revolution of 1800
Taylor, John

Reference:
Risjord, Norman. 1965. *The Old Republicans: Southern Conservatism in the Age of Jefferson.* New York: Columbia University Press.

Rush, Benjamin (1745–1813)

B enjamin Rush was a Philadelphia physician and patriot during the American Revolution who became a supporter of Jefferson's brand of republicanism in the 1790s.

Like Jefferson, Rush was brought up on the tenets of the Enlightenment and sought connections between the "natural" physical world and the human condition. Choosing medicine as his vocation, Rush became enamored of the notion that the American movement for independence was somehow related to the health of individual Americans. In his "Account of the Influence of the Military and Political Events of the American Revolution upon the Human Body," Rush drew parallels between individual and social well-being as well as private virtue and correct political principles. He argued, for example, that the political anxieties endured by the citizens of Philadelphia during the period 1774–1775 brought on an epidemic of apoplexy. Loyalists, on the other hand, suffered from what he termed "revolutiana," an ailment induced by alienation from one's broader culture. Though Rush's diseases seem far-fetched today, they were based on plausible assumptions. A loyalist could, for example, find his or her wealth and status undermined during the patriot movement and thus experience a real loss in position. And such a loss might induce both physical and psychological reactions, which Rush crudely but correctly diagnosed as coming from an unwillingness to accept change in the social order.

Rush's faith in the Revolution as a cure-all, however, tended to drift into the ridiculous. For example, his theories that the Revolution was an elixir for hysteria and infertility in women or that men experienced increased physical stamina and became more virile through support of the patriot cause played more upon traditional myths and stereotypes than on "modern" Enlightenment thought. However, Rush's broader thesis—that the Revolution produced the kind of environment in which people could flourish—resonated deeply with the American soul. It also fit squarely into Jefferson's conception of the American Revolution as a movement that would induce liberal reform throughout the world. Rush shared this vision, contending that a republican body of government could bring benefits not simply to a community or region, but to an entire continent. In his "Inquiry into the Cause of Animal Life," Rush observed that

in no part of the human species, is animal life in a more perfect state than in the inhabitants of Great Britain, and the United States of America. With all the natural stimuli that have been mentioned, they are constantly under the invigorating influence of liberty. There is an indissoluble union between moral, political, and physical happiness; and if it be true, that elective and representative governments are most favourable to individual, as well as national prosperity, it follows of course, that they are most favourable to animal life. But this opinion does not rest upon an induction derived from the relation, which truths upon all subjects bear to each other. Many facts prove animal life to exist in a larger quantity and for a longer time, in the enlightened and

happy state of Connecticut, in which republican liberty has existed above one hundred and fifty years, than in any other country upon the surface of the globe.

Rush put his faith in republicanism to the test, becoming an active Jeffersonian partisan. He attacked Federalist financial bills on medical grounds, arguing that the infusion of capital they injected into the economy produced a "paroxysm of avarice" and caused "febril diseases." Rush's social discourse and political support of Jefferson give evidence of the Virginian's varied circle of republican friends and Enlightenment partisans.

See also:
Enlightenment
Hamilton, Alexander

Reference:
D'Elia, Donald. 1974. *Benjamin Rush: Philosopher of the American Revolution*. Philadelphia, PA: Transactions of the American Philosophical Society.

S

Santo Domingo

A slave rebellion in the French colony of Santo Domingo was an important factor in Napoleon's decision to sell the Louisiana Territory to the United States. The seeds of the rebellion can be traced to the beginning of the French Revolution, when the National Assembly issued the Declaration of the Rights of Man and Citizen in 1789. This statement, in language reminiscent of Jefferson's Declaration of Independence, focused on the equality of humans irrespective of race and was cause for concern among white planters on Santo Domingo.

The rhetoric coming from Paris divided the colony's 40,000 whites from the 28,000 free blacks and mulattos, who suffered social and political oppression on the island. The National Assembly put forth a series of contradictory decrees, which at first gave political equality to mulattos, but then took it away. In 1791 the first mulatto rebellion occurred, and though ruthlessly put down, it served as a lesson for the slave population in Santo Domingo. Later that year a more aggressive assault on French power took place, this time by the slaves on the island. The following ten years witnessed a firestorm of brutal violence, with blacks, whites, and mulattos each attempting to gain the upper hand. Finally in 1801, forces loyal to the former slave Toussaint L'Ouverture controlled the entire island. Subsequent efforts by the French to retake Santo Domingo failed. In 1804 the island was renamed Haiti, and the first black republic was born.

Prior to L'Ouverture's victory, Napoleon had anticipated the revitalization of the French empire in North America. In 1802 he forced Spain to cede the Louisiana Territory to France, hoping the region would serve as a base from which his armies might challenge the British presence in Canada. At a minimum, a French presence in the West would keep the United States from expanding and developing into a significant international power. The French army's failure to retake Santo Domingo, however, demonstrated to Napoleon that his dream of a great empire in the Western Hemisphere was unrealistic, and when President Jefferson sent ministers to France to negotiate for the purchase of the port of New Orleans, the French leader offered instead the entire Louisiana Territory.

Though the slave insurrection in Santo Domingo was in some ways reminiscent of America's own colonial rebellion, the United States government would not recognize the republic of Haiti because it was created by blacks. Southern congressmen feared that if slaves in America heard of the rebellion and overthrow of the French planter class in Santo Domingo, they would attempt to replicate this feat in the South. Moreover, Americans like Jefferson accepted slavery partially on the assumption that blacks were inferior to whites. The creation of a black republic whose fundamental laws shared many of the principles underlying American laws seemed to give the lie to the notion that blacks could not organize and operate their own form of government.

See also:
Empire of Liberty
Louisiana Purchase

Reference:
Jordan, Winthrop. 1968. *White over Black: American Attitudes toward the Negro, 1550–1812.* Chapel Hill: University of North Carolina Press.

Second Administration

Jefferson's second presidential administration held much promise. His first four years in office had produced a fiscally prudent federal government that cut taxes, shrank the national debt, and expanded territorially through the Louisiana Purchase. Jefferson and his party were rewarded in the autumn of 1804 with smashing electoral victories over their Federalist opposition. Yet, at the peak of power, Jefferson's second term proved a disappointment.

In 1806, former vice president and Jefferson's personal enemy Aaron Burr put in motion a complicated plot to sever the western territories from the Union. The scheme fell apart, but Jefferson watched with dismay as Supreme Court Justice John Marshall, another enemy, freed Burr on the grounds that treason had not been proven. Later that year, Jefferson encountered a division within his own party as the radical agrarian Tertium Quids broke with the Republicans, who they believed were becoming corrupted by power. Though this party fissure was relatively small, it weakened the Jeffersonians politically and aided their Federalist opposition.

The latter half of Jefferson's second term was dominated by foreign policy concerns. The resumption of warfare between Great Britain and France found neutral American ships picked up on the high seas by the aggressor nations. Jefferson's initial efforts to make the warring powers respect the rights of American shipping and property were ineffective. The president responded in December 1807 with an embargo stipulating that the United States would purchase but not sell on the international market. This attempt at "peaceable coercion" failed, however, when smugglers violated the embargo. In New England, the reduction in trade nearly destroyed the maritime economy, and there was talk of secession. Admitting failure and not wishing to saddle his successor with unpopular policy, Jefferson lifted the embargo in the final days of his presidency. Following such tribulations, Jefferson was eager to leave public office. To his daughter he wrote, "I look with infinite joy to the moment when I shall be ultimately moored in the midst of my affections, and to follow the pursuits of my choice." With such emotions in his heart, Jefferson rode down Pennsylvania Avenue in March 1809 with his grandson by his side, eager to watch the swearing-in ceremony of his successor, James Madison. It signified his imminent return to Monticello.

See also:
Election of 1804
Embargo of 1807
Tertium Quid

Reference:
Malone, Dumas. 1948–1981. *Jefferson the President: Second Term, 1805–1809,* vol. 5 of *Jefferson and His Time.* Boston: Little, Brown.

Secretary of State

While serving as the American minister to the French court in the fall of 1789, Jefferson learned that his appointment to the post of secretary of state had been approved by the Senate. Jefferson immediately left Paris and returned to the United States where, in February of the following year, he became the first head of the State Department. Jefferson served in this capacity for just under four years, which proved to be one of the most difficult and frustrating periods of his life.

Upon assuming his duties, Jefferson was confronted not by an international crisis, but by an internal one. Secretary of the Treasury Alexander Hamilton introduced into Congress various financial bills and propositions designed to secure the government's and therefore the public's credit by significantly enhancing the power of the central government. Jefferson was adamantly opposed. For the next several months, aside from his "official" duties, such as reporting to Congress on international relations or the feasibility of expanding American cod and whale fisheries, Jefferson attacked Hamilton's programs with vigor. In order to expand the opposition to "Hamiltonianism," Jefferson and James Madison visited New York in the spring of 1791 to rally support among that state's infant Republican coalition. Later that year Jefferson started up a newspaper whose chief function was to attack Hamilton. Jefferson was able to secure the services of Philip Freneau, a noted poet, to edit the paper by providing him a position in the State Department. The result was a newspaper war between Jeffersonian and Hamiltonian scribes that left both Jefferson and Hamilton publicly abused and privately embittered.

Jefferson's final months as secretary of state proved wearisome. With the war against Hamilton in abeyance, Jefferson's attention turned to the question of how the United States should respond to the French Revolution. In August 1792, France declared itself a republic and expected to receive aid and recognition from its ideological sister state, the republic of the United States of America. Matters were complicated, however, when in the first months of the following year, the French executed the members of its defunct monarchy and declared war against England and the Netherlands. This extremist turn in the revolution, while not troubling to Jefferson, cost France a great deal of support in America. Complicating matters was the arrival of Edmond Genet, the new French minister to America, who planned to make the United States an ally in France's war against the "monarchical" powers of Europe. Jefferson was sympathetic to his plans, since he was personally working to have America take a pro-French position against the ancient enemy, Great Britain. To this end, Jefferson championed Genet's cause and helped him make important contacts in America. But Genet quickly grew annoyed by American neutrality and began to illegally outfit French privateers in American ports to send against the British. Genet's actions cost him his position, and Washington demanded that he be recalled. With the dismal end of the Genet affair, and Jefferson's hope of promoting a rapprochement between France and the United States all but extinguished, he formally resigned his position in December 1793 and returned to Monticello.

See also:
Federalist Party
Freneau, Philip
Genet, Edmund Charles

Reference:
Malone, Dumas. 1951. *Jefferson and the Rights of Man.* Boston: Little, Brown and Company.

Sectionalism

The North-South split that divided America socially, culturally, economically, and politically helped to shape and define Jefferson's vision of America. First and foremost, Jefferson was a citizen of the state of Virginia. References to "my country" in his letters and correspondences were allusions to the Old Dominion rather than the United States. While championing the cause of nationalism during times of external crisis such as the American Revolution and the War of 1812, Jefferson remained primarily an advocate of southern principles. He split with the Federalist party when it promoted an economic vision that would aid New England manufacturers and financiers while providing little reward for southern agrarians. He sided with France against Great Britain in his foreign policy, not merely because the French Revolution spread republicanism but also because closer ties with Britain would nurture the strength of the North, whose economy was closely allied with that of London.

The Democratic-Republican party that Jefferson created reflected the sectional disparities in America. Though it had a northern wing, the party was successful because it dominated below the Mason-Dixon Line. The party system ushered in by Jefferson in 1800 reflected the values of southernism. From that year to 1824, three Virginia slaveholders controlled the presidency while Republicans ruled Congress. This southern-oriented government abandoned the nationalism of the Federalists and promoted states' rights instead. By limiting the powers of the central government, Jefferson's party attempted to ensure that slavery would be safe from institutional attacks. At the same time, the absence of a strong central government meant that internal improvements, which the rapidly developing northern economy needed, would not be forthcoming from the national government.

Interpreted in this light, Jefferson can be seen not so much as the president of a nation, but as the advocate or the partisan of a section. He wished to promote the interests of the southern agrarian way of life while simultaneously limiting what he interpreted to be the debilitating characteristics of northern culture: overcrowded cities, speculation, and abolitionism.

See also:
Missouri Compromise
Urban Vices
Virginia Dynasty

Reference:
Smelser, Marshall. 1968. *The Democratic Republic, 1801–1815.*

Shays' Rebellion

This insurrection by New England farmers frightened those Americans who believed the republic was becoming too democratic and too susceptible to internal dissent. To Jefferson, however, the rebellion reflected the spirit of liberty and the inherent right of man to protest unreasonable conditions.

Throughout the 1780s, Massachusetts politics was controlled by a rigidly conservative regime. The state incurred heavy debts during the American Revolution, and the government attempted to meet these obligations by levying high taxes on agricultural land and products, including sheep, pork, and other commodities produced in the farming counties of western Massachusetts. When the state legislature adjourned in 1786 without providing some measure of tax relief, the western counties erupted in revolt against their oppressors in the East.

Armed bands of farmers proceeded to close the local courts and thus prevent the foreclosure of farms belonging to friends and neighbors who could not meet the state's stiff tax requirements. Over a short period of time the farmers coalesced around the leadership of Daniel Shays, a destitute farmer and Revolutionary War veteran. This citizens' or farmers' "army" of some 1,200 advanced upon the federal arsenal at Springfield in early 1787 to collect munitions. The "Shaysites" were routed by a large army privately financed by men of property, however, and melted into the countryside or returned home, never to challenge the state government again. Yet even in their retreat the rebels could claim a victory of sorts. Following the insurrection, the state legislature reduced the number of taxable items and thus alleviated the tax burden of western Massachusetts. On the national level, the rebellion stimulated interest in creating a more vigorous central government that could stop public insurrections before they got out of control. Toward this end the Constitutional Convention met during the summer of 1787 and drafted a document that was significantly more powerful than the Confederation Constitution it replaced.

Jefferson did not participate in this upsurge of nationalism. In fact, he was not even in the country during Shays' Rebellion. He was in Paris serving as American minister to France. While there, he received word of the rebellion and expressed sympathy for the farmers. He commented to a friend:

> Some tumultuous meetings of the people have taken place in the Eastern States, their principle demand was a respite in the judiciary proceedings. No injury was done . . . [and] these people are not entirely without excuse. The way to prevent these irregular interpositions of the people is to give them full information of their affairs. . . . If once they become inattentive to the public affairs, . . . Congress and Assemblies, judges and governors shall all become wolves. It seems to be the law of our general nature, in spite of individual exceptions; and experience declares that man is the only animal which devours its own kind, for I can apply no milder term to the governments of Europe, and to the general prey of the rich on the poor. I hold it that a little rebellion now and then is a good thing, and as necessary in the political world as storms in the physical. . . . It is a medicine necessary for the sound health of government.

Just as lightning, wind, and rain purify the natural world through destruction, Jefferson maintained, internal dissent works to overthrow tyranny through a show of righteous force. Ever the optimist, he believed that rebellions work on the side of liberty as they, by nature, challenge established avenues of power and purify whatever they touch. "God forbid we should ever be twenty years without such a rebellion," Jefferson concluded. "What signify a few lives lost in a century or two? The tree of liberty must be refreshed from time to time with the blood of patriots and tyrants. It is its natural manure."

See also:
Articles of Confederation
Constitution

Reference:
Szatmary, David P. 1980. *Shays' Rebellion: The Making of an Agrarian Insurrection.* Amherst: University of Massachusetts Press.

Slave Insurrections

Thoughts of slave insurrections in the American South were ever present in Jefferson's mind throughout his life. Too much a believer in freedom to assume that slaves would settle for anything less, Jefferson presumed that someday their natural inclination toward liberty would inspire African-American slaves to risk everything to gain their liberty. While Jefferson often deprecated the innate abilities of slaves, he credited blacks with the same instinct toward freedom that had driven Euro-Americans to fight the Revolution. Moreover, Jefferson was a student of the past, and he uncomfortably observed that in the Roman republic, hitherto the closest example to America's own experiment in republican governing, wars over slavery had destroyed the civic virtue of Rome's citizens and paved the way for the empire's decline. Further, the French Revolution brought Enlightenment thought into a more central role in determining how governments conducted their state affairs. If the Enlightenment was correct and all men were created equal, then where did that leave slavery?

Although slave insurrections occurred infrequently, the hysteria they produced among southerners could linger for years. Aside from a brief insurrection during the colonial period, Jefferson's Virginia had been spared from the specter of a black uprising until 1800, the year Jefferson was elected president. In that year, thousands of blacks were reported to have joined a free black named Gabriel, who planned an attack on Richmond, the state's capital. Presumably after torching the city and murdering the inhabitants, the former slaves would escape to the West. The plot never unfolded, however, as a slave warned authorities of the plot. Hundreds of slaves were arrested and over 30 were executed.

Jefferson responded to the news of Gabriel's rebellion with sympathy for the white inhabitants of Virginia. "We are truly to be pitied!" he remarked, alluding to his belief that the slaveholders in his home state were performing the difficult and necessary task of keeping potentially dangerous blacks in order. Yet Jefferson had no desire to see the slaves involved executed. After all, he reasoned, no white was actually harmed in the failed insurrection, and perhaps more importantly, Jefferson had no desire to make martyrs out of blacks. He was quite content to allow that the tree of liberty must from time to time be watered by the blood of white patriots, which would, in turn, consecrate their dedication and right to freedom. The deaths of the black insurrectionists, he reasoned, would only enhance their moral cause. For these reasons he recommended to Governor James Monroe that the accused slaves be removed from Virginia rather than executed. Upon assuming his duties as president a few months later, Jefferson advanced the possibility of sending the rebellious slaves to Sierra Leone, a colony for free blacks on the west coast of Africa. Despite Jefferson's plea to the company involved in colonizing the area that it was being asked to accept men who had fought for their freedom, his request was denied. Ultimately, most of the slaves involved in Gabriel's aborted rebellion were sold as slaves in the Spanish and Portuguese colonies.

Jefferson hoped the upheaval would induce Virginians to emancipate and deport their slaves. Quite the opposite response occurred, however, as the Old Dominion proceeded to tighten the screws of the slave system. The Virginia militia grew in number, night riders patrolled more frequently, and freedoms of speech and press were limited to thwart the distant rumblings of abolitionists. The social anxiety over slave insurrections continued throughout the antebellum period in Virginia, and the hopes of moderates like Jefferson to put the Old Dominion on the road to emancipation faded in the light of white fears.

See also:
Slave Trade
Slavery

Reference:
Davis, David Brion. 1975. *The Problem of Slavery in the Age of Revolution*. Ithaca, NY: Cornell University Press.

Slave Trade

Jefferson viewed slavery as an unfortunate practice that contaminated the American experiment in republican government. In his eyes, the true culprit was not southern plantation owners but the British government, which foisted slavery upon its North American colonies through the lucrative Atlantic slave trade. Jefferson's original draft of the Declaration of Independence excoriated Britain's king for waging

cruel war against human nature itself, violating its most sacred rights of life and liberty in the persons of a distant people who never offended him, captivating and carrying them into slavery in another hemisphere, or to incur miserable death in their transportation hither. This piratical warfare, the opprobrium of INFIDEL powers, is the warfare of the CHRISTIAN king of Great Britain. Determined to keep open a market where MEN should be bought and sold, he has prostituted his negative for suppressing

RUN away from the subscriber in *Albemarle*, a Mulatto slave called *Sandy*, about 35 years of age, his stature is rather low, inclining to corpulence, and his complexion light; he is a shoemaker by trade, in which he uses his left hand principally, can do coarse carpenters work, and is something of a horse jockey; he is greatly addicted to drink, and when drunk is insolent and disorderly, in his conversation he swears much, and in his behaviour is artful and knavish. He took with him a white horse, much scarred with traces, of which it is expected he will endeavour to dispose; he also carried his shoemakers tools, and will probably endeavour to get employment that way. Whoever conveys the said slave to me, in *Albemarle*, shall have 40 s. reward, if taken up within the county, 4 l. if elsewhere within the colony, and 10 l. if in any other colony, from

THOMAS JEFFERSON.

Ad placed by Thomas Jefferson seeking the whereabouts of his runaway slave. It appeared in the September 14, 1769, Virginia Gazette of Williamsburg.

every legislative attempt to prohibit or to restrain this execrable commerce. And that this assemblage of horrors might want no fact of distinguished die, he is now exciting those very people to rise in arms among us, and to purchase that liberty of which he has deprived them by murdering the people of whom he also obtruded them: thus paying off former crimes committed against the LIBERTIES of one people, with crimes which he urges them to commit against the LIVES of another.

During the Revolution, Jefferson served as governor of Virginia and played a major part in liberalizing the slave system in that state. An act of 1778 abolished the slave trade in the Old Dominion, though Jefferson's attempts to free and then deport slaves were less successful. Jefferson concluded that he had "stopped the increase of the evil by importation" but would have to leave "to future efforts its final eradication." As president, Jefferson was most proud of his efforts in acquiring the Louisiana Territory and abolishing the slave trade in America. Jefferson hoped to use the vast western territory as the repository of white free labor. By shutting down the African slave trade during his second term, Jefferson believed that this would be the first step toward emancipation

and removal of the black race in North America. At the very least, he anticipated that with the flow of Africans stopped, white labor, rather than plantation labor, would predominate in the West.

See also:
Declaration of Independence
Slavery

Reference:
Du Bois, W. E. B. 1896. *The Suppression of the African Slave Trade.* New York: Schocken Books.

Slavery

The Enlightenment sought to advance the study of man to a science, and human behavior was presumed to be based on predictable laws that could be understood by the investigator. Jefferson tried to apply the scientific method in *Notes on the State of Virginia* in a variety of ways, none more important than his discussion of the differences between blacks and whites and whether they were attributable to environmental or biological factors. Though he certainly believed otherwise, Jefferson was not an impartial investigator.

The master of over 100 slaves, Jefferson began his study on race from the premise that white is a more pleasing color than black. He spoke of the "eternal monotony . . . that immovable veil of black which covers all the emotions." To the black race he conceded musical superiority and argued that blacks' moral deficiencies were attributable to slavery, which degraded its victims. Nevertheless, Jefferson refused to believe that slaves were merely white men with black skins. He found them lazy and often expressed dismay at their reluctance to be "uplifted" by the dominant white culture. Jefferson could discern in them no affinity toward manners, culture, poetry, or mathematics. In sum, he found them "dull, tasteless, and anomalous." He even conjectured that blacks might have emerged from a separate creation, holding more in common with the recently discovered simians, that is, orangutans, than whites. By grounding the distinctiveness and "inferiority" of the black race in correct "scientific" thought, Jefferson justified the practice of slavery in the American South. To him, blacks were "as far inferior to the rest of mankind as the mule is to the horse, and as made to carry burthens."

Despite talk of uplifting the black race through association with whites, Jefferson was weary of the African presence and hoped for their eventual emancipation and removal from America. He had grown up on a plantation surrounded by slaves and as an adult lived in a preponderantly black community. The blacks' involuntary servitude combined with their superior numbers caused Jefferson to reflect that "we have the wolf by the ears; and we can neither hold him, nor safely let him go. Justice is in one scale, and self-preservation in the other." To complicate matters further, Jefferson believed that slavery had a debilitating effect not just on the slave but on his master as well. The ownership of humans, he believed, fostered cruelty, tyranny, and brutality. Alluding to miscegenation, Jefferson contended that "the whole commerce between master and slave is despotism on the [one] part, and degrading submission on the other." Further, slavery discouraged foreign immigration to the South and slowed internal improvements in the region as capital went for land and slaves, not bridges and canals. Finally, slavery created an atmosphere of suspicion and anxiety not conducive to the peace of mind and contented virtue that a republican government was supposed to afford its people.

Nevertheless, Jefferson championed the institution of slavery throughout his life. He did so, however, in a way that allowed him to retain hope that slavery would eventually expire on its own. The solution, he believed, was "diffusion." Jefferson asserted that it was not merely legal for southerners to take their slaves into the western territories, but it would result in the end of slavery. As the institution expanded beyond its southern base, he surmised, the resiliency of the institution would be bled dry. Jefferson also believed that a paucity of slaves in the West would encourage better treatment of blacks and eventually ensure their freedom. Jefferson used this argument in the debate over whether to allow slavery in the Louisiana Territory. He believed that by opening the region to the domestic slave trade, a safety valve would be created to relieve the South of dangerous concentrations of blacks.

That Jefferson sought the ultimate removal of blacks from America by allowing the institution of slavery to progress across the country is symptomatic of his contradictory thinking on the subject. He believed that blacks were inferior yet was troubled by the prospect that their degraded condition was the result of their environment. He feared slave insurrections yet spent his entire life surrounded by large numbers of blacks. Finally, he devoted his life to exploring freedom, democracy, and republican government while three generations of slave labor provided him the leisure time to make such speculations. At the heart of the matter, Jefferson's faith in diffusion reflected both his trust in the nature of man as well as his inability to wean himself from the debilitating practice of slavery.

See also:
Enlightenment
Notes on the State of Virginia

Reference:
Miller, John Chester. 1977. *The Wolf by the Ears: Thomas Jefferson and Slavery.* Charlottesville: University Press of Virginia.

Smith, Adam (1723–1790)

Adam Smith's theories on economics had a profound effect on Thomas Jefferson and the American republic. Smith was a major architect of the Enlightenment, which proposed to shed insight into new areas of the human condition. Smith was born in Kirkcaldy, Fife, Scotland, in 1723 and educated at the University of Glasgow and at Balliol College, Oxford. Apparently he was forced to leave the university because of his unwillingness to enter the church. From 1748 until 1751 he served as public lecturer at Edinburgh and then moved on to the University of Glasgow, where he was appointed professor of logic. He resigned his academic post in 1763 and devoted the remainder of his life to tutoring, lecturing, and study.

Smith's most famous and influential work is *The Wealth of Nations* (1776). This masterful expression of the Enlightenment view of a "free" economy is rightfully understood to be the most complete expression of laissez-faire capitalism, that is, the theory that government should not impose regulations or restrictions on commerce. Smith contended that economies work best by self-regulation. The natural law of supply and demand, he argued, would dictate the true level of prices, wages, and rents. Government interference in this process would be like injecting a virus into a healthy body: excessive regulation would deter natural economic impulses and consumer needs would not be met.

Jefferson read Smith's works and was much influenced by them. The latter's concept of a political economy that operated "naturally" through the rhythm of public consumption without an intrusive central government to prod production dovetailed nicely with the Virginian's states' rights proclivities. At times, Jefferson could sound very much like Smith. In promoting a vision of internationalism predicated upon liberal commercial principles, for example, Jefferson wrote that

Instead of embarrassing commerce under piles of regulating laws, duties, and prohibitions, could it be relieved from all its shackles in all parts of the world, could every country be employed in producing that which nature has best fitted it to produce, and each

be free to exchange with others mutual surpluses for mutual wants, the greatest mass possible would then be produced of these things which contribute to human life and human happiness; the numbers of mankind would be increased, and their condition bettered.

Jefferson believed in Smith's economic vision and largely followed the latter's principles throughout his own public career.

See also:
Enlightenment
Physiocrats

Reference:
Raphael, D. D. 1985. *Adam Smith*. Oxford: Oxford University Press.

Society of the Cincinnati

The Society of the Cincinnati was organized in 1784 by army officers who participated in the American Revolution. Jefferson was troubled about the elitist character of the society and believed the provision for hereditary membership through eldest sons contradicted the new nation's republican values. Several state legislatures shared Jefferson's fears and passed resolutions criticizing the organization. George Washington, who served as the society's president, was caught off guard by the criticism. He asked for Jefferson's opinion on the subject.

Jefferson assured the general that while he believed the Society had no intention to replace pure republican government with monarchy or militarism, its rules for membership did imply a rejection of republicanism. Jefferson also informed Washington that membership would only sully the prestige and character of those who joined. Several days later, Washington stopped at Jefferson's house and conferred on the subject further. Jefferson noted that "it was a little after candlelight, and he sat with me till after midnight, conversing almost exclusively on that subject." After Washington departed, Jefferson extracted an agreement from the general to use his "determination [and] all his influence for its entire suppression." Though not entirely successful, his appeal to Washington resulted in the elimination of hereditary membership.

In later years Jefferson would view the Society of the Cincinnati as an antecedent to the Federalist party. This conclusion was natural, since most society members were indeed Federalists. As Jefferson battled Alexander Hamilton over the course of American social and economic development, he drew ever sharper critiques of society. In one of his final pronouncements on the subject, Jefferson contended that the Cincinnati members were

> lowering over our Constitution eternally, meeting together in all parts of the Union, periodically, with closed doors, accumulating a capital in their separate treasury, corresponding secretly and regularly, and of which society the very persons denouncing the democrats are themselves the fathers, founders, and high officers. Their sight must be perfectly dazzled by the glittering of crowns and coronets not to see the extravagance of the proposition to suppress the friends of general freedom, while whose who wish to confine that freedom to the few are permitted to go on in their principles and practices.

Secret societies were the bane of republican government, Jefferson concluded, and their perpetuation could only weaken the health of the nation. Jefferson did support social and political clubs, but his favor went to the Democratic-Republican Societies, which had open membership and were dedicated to the egalitarian principles of the American Revolution.

See also:
Democratic Societies
Washington, George

Reference:
Mayo, Bernard, ed. 1942. *Jefferson Himself: The Personal Narrative of a Many-Sided American.* Charlottesville: University Press of Virginia.

Standing Army

*L*ike many men of his generation, Jefferson demonstrated a fear of large standing armies. In his experience a standing army was often used to oppress citizens. During the American Revolution, for example, Jefferson saw how British troops in North America enforced the taxation policies of the empire and then fought the colonists when they resisted paying such fees. During the 1790s, Jefferson believed that the Federalist party created a large standing army to inhibit political dissent at home. He called the Federalist-created armed force an "army without an enemy." During the Whiskey Rebellion of 1794, for example, a large federal army swept into western Pennsylvania to arrest farmers who protested the central government's tax policies. Many Republicans believed, however, that the true purpose of the affair was to have the army awe citizens into uncritical and servile obedience to the government.

Explaining his own views on the proper use of military power in a republic, Jefferson proclaimed that "I am for relying for internal defense on our militia solely, till actual invasion, and for such a naval force only as may protect our coasts and harbors from such depredations as we have experienced; and not for a standing army in time of peace which may overawe the public sentiment, nor for a navy which, by its own expenses and the eternal wars in which it will implicate us, will grind us with public burdens and sink us under them." In place of a martial culture, Jefferson proposed republican frugality, and during his presidency he reduced the budget and size of the military. He would allow geography and neutrality to displace a large standing force in America. Yet his dreams came to naught as the Napoleonic wars of the early nineteenth century spilled over from Europe into North America and forced the United States to take up arms. The War of 1812 demonstrated the deficiencies of a military budget that was too frugal. Lucky to escape the war with its sovereignty intact, the United States, led by the Republican party, accepted the reality of a standing army.

See also:
Federalist Party
War of 1812

Reference:
Brown, Roger H. 1964. *The Republic in Peril: 1812.* New York: Columbia University Press.

States' Rights

Jefferson believed that the United States should develop into a larger version of Virginia. To him, the Old Dominion, with its arable land and yeoman farming class, was a perfect model for the country. Thus Jefferson was jealous of the powers and privileges of the central government and upheld the rights of the individual states. For this reason, he is often portrayed as the champion of liberty (local rights) over power (centralized authority). This portrait is not completely accurate, however, for Jefferson's Virginia was a highly stratified society dominated by a planter-aristocrat class. Thus Jefferson's advocacy of states' rights may also be interpreted as an attempt by a ruling citizen of the nation's largest state to keep power in the hands of local elites like himself rather than allow it to be diffused across the nation. Better, Jefferson apparently thought, that slavery remain the province of the states rather than coming under the eye of a federal government that might choose to end it someday.

Nevertheless, many of Jefferson's pronouncements on the rights of states undoubtedly were inspired by a sincere desire to keep power from becoming centralized in one large and potentially corrupt national government. During the 1790s, for example, Alexander Hamilton's financial system, which called for an aggressive central government, appeared to many Americans to threaten state sovereignty. As secretary of state, Jefferson lamented that Hamilton's schemes were nourishing

> in our citizens habits of vice and idleness instead of industry and morality; that it has furnished effectual means of corrupting such a portion of the legislature as turns the balance between the honest voters, whichever way it is directed; that this corrupt squadron, deciding the voice of the legislature, have manifested their dispositions to get rid of the limitations imposed by the Constitution on the general legislature, limitations on the faith of which the states acceded to that instrument; that the ultimate object of all this is to prepare the way for a change from the present republican form of government to that of a monarchy.

When the central government imposed the Alien and Sedition Acts on the American public in 1797, Jefferson took up his pen and wrote the Kentucky Resolve, which argued that states have an obligation to come between their citizens and a federal government that seeks to inhibit the rights of individuals. The final recourse left to states, Jefferson noted, was to nullify federal law, the ultimate weapon for local power.

On a broader level, Jefferson viewed the centralization of power as an ancient concept that was losing advocates in the "enlightened" age of democratic revolutions and natural rights. Jefferson believed that the

Constitution was written to codify the privileges of the people, not to entrench the national government in power. He declared, for example, that

> our country is too large to have all its affairs directed by a single government. Public servants at such distance. . . . , by rendering detection impossible to their constituents, will invite the public agents to corruption, plunder and waste. . . . The true theory of our Constitution is surely the wisest and best, that the states are independent as to everything within themselves, and united as to everything respecting foreign nations.

In sum, Jefferson's vision of a decentralized agrarian nation largely won out in the first half of the nineteenth century. Local privileges were secured, slavery remained beyond the touch of the federal government, and southern plantation oligarchs dominated not only their states but the federal government as well.

See also:
Alien and Sedition Acts
Kentucky Resolutions

Reference:
Malone, Dumas. 1962. *Jefferson and the Ordeal of Liberty*. Boston: Little, Brown.

A Summary View of the Rights of British America

*I*n July 1774, Jefferson drafted lengthy instructions for the Virginia delegation to the Continental Congress as it pondered the weighty question of whether to remain a colony within the British Empire. The manuscript, entitled *A Summary View of the Rights of British America. Set Forth in Some Resolutions Intended for the Inspection of the Present Delegates of the People of Virginia*, was simply ascribed to "A Native, and Member of the House of Burgesses." Despite its title, the pamphlet was intended for the consumption of the British subjects of North America and the King of England. Jefferson hoped the *Summary View* would appeal to the rational side of the men who governed the empire and induce them to pursue improved relations with their colonies. The piece was published first in Williamsburg but was quickly disseminated throughout the colonies. Though it failed to dispel the main points of contention between Crown and colony, the article did serve as a vehicle for Jefferson's justification of American opposition to British rule. Moreover, the *Summary View* provided an excellent model for the case against arbitrary government, which Jefferson later revisited in the Declaration of Independence.

The *Summary View* intended to demonstrate in a variety of ways that British intrusions in American affairs were unjust. Jefferson appealed, for example, to Enlightenment thought when he wrote that the "natural rights" of the colonials should prevail over the "usurpation" of the British state. The intrinsically just cause of the Americans was therefore morally stronger than the ruling pretensions of the mother country. Jefferson also resorted to a distorted view of the past, arguing incorrectly that the colonials' English ancestors, the Saxons, had themselves been invaded by Norman conquerors who took away their independence. In Jefferson's reading of history, the Normans were the ancestors of the existing aristocracy of England, and they imposed feudalism on the previously "free inhabitants" of the island. Jefferson proposed, in other words, that America's troubles with England did not begin with the Stamp Act in 1765 but rather with the Norman conquest of 1066. Subsequent history, the Virginian offered, was but the playing out of a never-ending struggle between liberty and tyranny, and by now the contest had crossed the Atlantic.

More accurate was Jefferson's contention that the English colonies played a vital role in expanding the British Empire across the American frontier in the face of stiff opposition from both native and European competitors. "For themselves they conquered," he argued, "and for themselves alone they have right to hold." While acknowledging that Britain expended large sums to protect its colonies, Jefferson believed that English support was forthcoming only because of the tremendous natural resources and commercial potential of the continent. "Such assistance, and in such circumstances, they had often before given to Portugal and other allied states," Jefferson noted, "yet these states never supposed that, by calling in her aid, they thereby submitted themselves to her sovereignty." Further, Jefferson contended that it was not simply local rule that was threatened by regulations placed upon colonial trade. Rather, he believed that the limitations imposed on American commerce by the Stamp Act, Declaratory Act, and Townshend Duties clearly impeded the development of the colonial economy, dooming it to backwater status for perpetuity. Finally, Britain's refusal to allow the colonies to industrialize retarded the cause of material as well as community progress. Such actions on the part of the empire, Jefferson contended, violated the natural rights of the individual colonies and brought him to the core of his message: "The true ground on which we declare these acts void is that the British Parliament has no right to exercise authority over us."

The *Summary View* does not seek a break with the British Empire. Rather it called for a return to an Arcadia-like past that Jefferson presumed existed in Old England. In fact, the Virginia delegation was instructed to petition the King for his services as mediator in what most colonials presumed was a confrontation between a liberty-loving constituency in British North America and a corrupted Parliament in England. It was hoped that George III might serve, as Jefferson put it, as a "mediatory power between the several states of the British Empire." Failing a peaceful settlement, Jefferson concluded, Americans were "willing on our part to sacrifice every thing which reason can ask to the restoration of that tranquility for which all must wish."

See also:
American Revolution
Declaration of Independence

Reference:
Ellis, Joseph. 1997. *American Sphinx: The Character of Thomas Jefferson*. New York: Alfred A. Knopf.

T

Taylor, John (1753–1824)

Known as John Taylor of Caroline for the Virginia county where his plantation was located, this American statesman was one of Jefferson's most consistent and able supporters. Taylor was born in 1753 and orphaned at an early age. Like Jefferson, Taylor attended William and Mary College, though he did not take a degree. Instead, he read law and received a license to practice in 1774. Taylor served in the Continental army during the American Revolution as a lieutenant colonel in the Virginia militia. His political career consisted of membership in the Virginia House of Delegates as well as the United States Senate (1792 to 1794, 1803, and 1822 to 1824).

Taylor was a more consistent Jeffersonian-Republican than Jefferson himself. Unlike Jefferson, who demonstrated on several occasions that he was a shrewd statesman capable of compromise, Taylor had no such instincts. He remained firmly attached to the vision of a small, decentralized federal government promoted by the Republican party. He attacked Alexander Hamilton's fiscal program as unconstitutional, even though there were parts of it, such as the "assumption" of state debts, that Jefferson helped to shepherd into law.

What modest fame remains for Taylor today is due not to his legislative efforts but rather to his political writings. In *The Arator* (1813) he argued that agricultural reform in the Old Dominion was necessary to replenish the soil and rejuvenate the traditional customs of a land-based economy. In particular, he advocated that tobacco be replaced as the major staple crop by a rotation system using grains. In *An Inquiry into the Principles and Policy of the Government of the United States* (1814) and *Construction Construed and Constitutions Vindicated* (1820), Taylor advanced an agrarian theory of political economy, arguing that republican citizens could only be free if they were self-sufficient, that is, independent landowners. This was the natural course of life in America, he argued, but business interests were using the federal government to advance their own economic and social agenda. To preserve traditional customs and folkways, he concluded, the states must serve as a bulwark against centralization.

See also:
Hamilton, Alexander

Reference:
Beard, Charles. 1915. *Economic Origins of Jeffersonian Democracy*. Reprint 1943. New York: Free Press.

Tecumseh (1768?–1813)

Though Jefferson retired from public office in 1809, a "Jeffersonian" version of national policy remained intact. At the cornerstone of this agenda was the right of

Americans to expand their social, political, and economic institutions in the West. Opposing this expansion were various Native American tribes who understood that their way of life was threatened by the encroachment of an Anglo-American agricultural society. The British often aided the native peoples in their resistance to U.S. expansion, because they wanted to weaken their former colonies, keeping them dependent upon English credit and markets.

In the first decade of the nineteenth century, the major brake to U.S. expansion was the Shawnee nation, led by the warrior Tecumseh. The Shawnees were in the midst of a revitalization movement in which they rejected Anglo-European clothing, alcohol, weapons, and customs. Tecumseh traveled throughout the Ohio and Mississippi Valleys conducting a sophisticated foreign policy designed to bring outlying tribes into the movement to resist further U.S. demands upon native lands. President James Madison sent an American army into the territory of Indiana to put the movement down. Led by General William Henry Harrison, U.S. forces defeated the Native Americans at the Battle of Tippecanoe and thus ended both the Shawnee revitalization movement and any serious resistance to further expansion into the Ohio Valley.

See also:
Empire of Liberty
Foreign Policy
War of 1812

Reference:
Edmunds, R. David. 1984. *Tecumseh and the Quest for Indian Leadership.* Boston, MA: Little, Brown.

Tertium Quid

The Tertium Quid, or "third something," was a divisive faction in the Republican party that emerged during Jefferson's second term as president. The leader of the Quid was John Randolph of Roanoke, a brilliant but erratic Republican who broke with the Jeffersonians, who he believed had become corrupted by power. Specifically, Randolph was aggrieved that a foreign post, which he coveted, was not forthcoming. He also was angry at Jeffersonian's failure to vigorously pursue the impeachment of Federalist judges and the Republicans' complicity in a fraudulent land speculation deal in Georgia that compromised their integrity. Referring to his former colleagues in the Republican party, Randolph concluded, "I might co-operate or be an honest man—I have therefore opposed and will oppose them."

In many ways, the Quids' adherence to the concept of an agriculturally based republic made them more consistent Jeffersonians than Jefferson. John Taylor of Caroline, the leading Quid theorist, wrote treatises on the virtues of an agricultural society that the Master of Monticello could hardly disagree with. The true animus between the Quids and the Republican party stemmed from Jefferson's willingness to stray from agrarian orthodoxy once he became president. After assuming power in the election of 1800, Jefferson became the head of a nation, not merely the ideologue of an opposition but a pragmatic leader who knew how to adjust his style and actions to circumstances. The Quids expected Jefferson and his party to run the country along simple agrarian lines, but the complexity of the country, its domestic and foreign relations, made this impossible. Instead, the Republicans made deals with various interests around the country to keep harmony within the Union. By daring to oppose the grand Jeffersonian coalition, the Quids rattled the confidence of an administration that had seemed invincible. It gave the Federalists hope for a positive turn in their political fortunes and challenged Jefferson's handpicked successor for president, James Madison, by championing the candidacy of James Monroe. The Quids never became a major political party, but their ideology of states' rights agrarianism continued to inform southern leadership up to the Civil War.

See also:
Randolph, John
Second Administration
Taylor, John

Reference:
Risjord, Norman. 1965. *The Old Republicans: Southern Agrarianism in the Age of Jefferson.* New York: Columbia University Press.

Tobacco

Throughout Jefferson's lifetime, tobacco was the single most important staple crop in Virginia. It dominated the economy, shaped social relationships, and laid the foundations for fortunes of the great Tidewater planter-aristocrats in the Chesapeake Bay area. In Virginia, tobacco was more than an economic system; it defined a culture. But Jef-

William Newman etching of a common tobacco house in the 1800s showing tobacco hanging on a scaffold, the operation of prizing, and an inside view of the public warehouse during an inspection.

ferson became soured on tobacco production in the 1760s and 1770s as the American colonies moved toward rebellion against Great Britain. Jefferson never distinguished himself as a successful plantation manager, and like many other planters of his generation, he found himself slipping into debt to the British merchant class to whom he sold his crop.

At the heart of the problem for the planters was the "factoring" system. Much of the capital to finance and market southern tobacco came from outside the South. The key figure in this process was the factor, or commissioned merchant. Tobacco-importing firms in London sent their agents to Virginia to buy and ship the crop. The factor habitually advanced credit to the planter using future crops as collateral. Moreover, the factor would also function as the planter's purchasing agent to obtain consumer goods from the empire or elsewhere. The factor would take charge of the planter's crop when it reached market, provide storage facilities, and arrange for transportation and sale to the ultimate purchaser. For each of these services he charged a commission. The total amount of the commissions might be as much as 20–25 percent of the value of the crop.

To men like Jefferson, factoring represented a drain of wealth and independence to the British. Moreover, Jefferson subscribed to the theory that British merchants manipulated prices and credit in order to keep the planters in permanent debt and thus permanent subservience. "A powerful engine for this purpose," Jefferson remarked, "was the giving of good prices and credit to the planter till they got him more and more immersed in debt than he could pay without selling his lands or slaves. They then reduced the prices given for his tobacco so that let his shipments be ever so great, and his demand of necessaries ever so economical, that they never permitted him to clear off his debt."

To Jefferson, debt meant a loss of independence, a condition that would be particularly hard for slave owners to endure, since they were intimately knowledgeable about the absence of freedom. Referring to members of the planter class as though they were in danger of becoming slaves, Jefferson remarked that "these debts had become hereditary from father to son for many generations, so that the planters were a species of property annexed to certain mercantile houses in London." Moreover, he concluded, "no [burden] can be more oppressive to the mind or fortune, and long experience has proved to us that there never was an instance of a man's getting out of debt who was once in the hands of a tobacco merchant."

Viewed from the perspective of Jefferson's anxieties over debt and loss of independence, his future public actions become logical. Jefferson welcomed the American Revolution as the utter destruction of the old order, which represented a culture of dependency and debt. The society that Jefferson envisioned would have small, independent wheat farmers spread west, away from the clutches of the tobacco mentality and its corresponding vices of luxury and indebtedness. As secretary of state, Jefferson battled Alexander Hamilton's financial bills precisely because they reminded him of the speculative system that had once mired the Virginia planter class in debt. By promoting a distinctive brand of agrarian republicanism, Jefferson exemplified southern fears that could be traced back to the earlier crisis of the tobacco culture.

See also:
American Revolution
Hamilton, Alexander

Reference:
Breen, T. H. 1985. *Tobacco Culture: The Mentality of the Great Tidewater Planters on the Eve of Revolution*. Princeton, NJ: Princeton University Press.

Transportation Revolution

While Jefferson is generally viewed by historians as an opponent of federally funded internal improvements, he in fact championed such public expenditures throughout his presidency. Thus, far from shying away from the acceleration of American trade and commerce brought about in the period 1815–1850 by the "transportation revolution," Jefferson actively promoted the connection of the nation's roads and canals.

As president, Jefferson was dismayed that Great Britain and France disregarded American neutrality during the Napoleonic wars and confiscated U.S. merchant shipping. Historians generally record that Jefferson's response to European violations of American neutrality was the Embargo Act, an effort of "peaceable coercion" that stopped all export of American goods and prohibited American ships from clearing for foreign ports. Yet this tells only part of the story. Much more significantly, the conflict in Europe and America's inability to adequately assert its rights as a neutral prompted Jefferson to back a comprehensive national system of internal improvements, first brought to the attention of the Senate by the Virginian's secretary of the treasury, Albert Gallatin.

In conjunction with Jefferson's wishes, Gallatin proposed a series of canals to provide internal navigation from Massachusetts to North Carolina and a great turnpike from Maine to Georgia, the single most expensive item in the program. For communication from east to west, Gallatin proposed the improvement of four Atlantic rivers (Susquehanna, Potomac, James, and Savannah) by canals around their falls; the building of roads from four western rivers (Allegheny, Monongahela, Kanawaha, and Tennessee); a canal around the falls of the Ohio at Louisville; and improvement of the roads to Detroit, St. Louis, and New Orleans. For inland navigation between the seacoast and the Great Lakes and the St. Lawrence, he recommended a series of canals. Finally, Gallatin proposed an allowance for local aid to districts that would otherwise not benefit from the improvements. The estimated cost of this vast internal improvements project was $20 million. Gallatin summed up the issue to Jefferson in the spring of 1807: "I think the Act should be accepted [due to] the immense importance of that road, as part of a great Western traveling road, and principally as the main communication for the transportation of all foreign or Atlantic articles which the Western states consume."

Jefferson was in full agreement with Gallatin's proposal. Further, his support for internal improvements in the final years of his presidency was not unprecedented. In 1802 he had signed a bill authorizing the creation of the National Road and, in the wake of the Burr-Wilkinson affair, he proposed a constitutional amendment that would have empowered Congress to set aside funds for public education and internal improvements. When the transportation revolution swept through the country in the antebellum period, altering traditional social, economic, and cultural relationships through the effects of roads, canals, and railroads, Jefferson was nearing the end of his life and could not anticipate the ramifications of such alterations. Nevertheless, he was an eternal optimist, and Jefferson's support for internal improvements during his own presidency speaks of a man who respected the past but believed in a progressive future.

See also:
Burr, Aaron
Embargo of 1807
Gallatin, Albert

Reference:
McCoy, Drew. 1982. *The Elusive Republic: Political Economy in Jeffersonian America*. Chapel Hill: University of North Carolina Press.

Treaty of Ghent

The Treaty of Ghent formally ended the War of 1812 and allowed the United States to resume its experiment in republican government. The Anglo-American peace was signed on Christmas Eve 1814, as the warring nations agreed to end the fighting, return prisoners, and restore previous boundaries. Though the United States did not defeat Great Britain and the peace treaty merely reflected a cessation of conflict, Andrew Jackson's victory over British troops at New Orleans in the war's final battle filled Americans with pride and made it appear that the country had gotten the better of the British lion. On the subject of peace, Jefferson noted that

the successes of New Orleans have established truths too important not to be valued: that . . . the militia are brave; that their deadly aim countervails the maneuvering skill of their enemy; that we have officers of natural genius now starting forward from the mass; and that, putting together all our conflicts, we can beat the British by sea and by land with equal numbers. All this being now proved, I am glad of the pacification of Ghent.

To Jefferson, the peace, coupled with a dramatic American victory, redeemed not only the republican experiment in governing but seemed to single out the United States as a special nation, perhaps even favored by Providence. When Jefferson referred to the skill of the militia, for example, he contended that virtuous citizen armies were superior to professional or paid armies. Jefferson's allusion to the "natural genius" of the American officer corps can be interpreted as a general championing of American institutions and the salutary effect of the American environment. For unlike European nations, the United States had no professional training ground for its officers; thus their superior skills were not the product of a military culture but rather of a democratic perspective. Finally, the Treaty of Ghent ended a generation of antagonism between Britain, France, and the United States. Jefferson's attempts to coerce the European nations into recognizing American neutrality during his own presidency had failed and made his second term a disappointment. With peace now in hand, however, Jefferson could believe that the foreign policy he initiated was the correct one. The war's result, as far as Jefferson was concerned, represented a vindication of republican ideology and Republican party policies.

See also:
Election of 1812
War of 1812
Warhawks

Reference:
Spivak, Burton. 1979. *Jefferson's English Crisis: Commerce, the Embargo, and the Republican Revolution.* Charlottesville: University Press of Virginia.

Twelfth Amendment

The Twelfth Amendment to the United States Constitution was crafted in order that future presidential candidates would not be equaled in vote or outpolled by vice-presidential nominees. This amendment, enacted into law in 1804, was a reaction to the 1800 presidential election, when the Republican party inadvertently gave an equal number of electoral votes to Thomas Jefferson, the party's presidential pick, and to Aaron Burr, its vice-presidential nominee. Because the Constitution did not anticipate the emergence of political parties, electors were allowed to cast two ballots for two separate individuals. The tie in 1800 nearly provoked a national crisis, as the outgoing Federalist majority in the House, which had to decide between Jefferson and Burr, did not make its decision for Jefferson until just weeks before the inauguration date.

To make sure that such events never occurred again, Republicans in Congress pushed for, and the states ratified, an amendment to the Constitution that required separate ballots for president and vice president. The Federalist party, recognizing that its only hope to control presidential elections in the future would be to have them go to the House in case of future ties or irregularities, fought the amendment aggressively. In part, the amendment stipulated that

> The Electors shall meet in their respective states, and vote by ballot for President and Vice-President, one of whome, at least, shall not be an inhabitant of the same state with themselves; they shall name in their ballots the person voted for as President, and in distinct ballots the person voted for as Vice-President. . . . The President of the Senate shall, in the presence of the Senate and House of Representatives, open all the certificates and the votes shall then be counted; —The person having the greatest number of votes for President, shall be the President, if such number be a majority of the whole number of Electors appointed; and if no person have such majority, then from the persons having the highest numbers not exceeding three on the list of those voted for as President, the House of Representatives shall choose immediately, by ballot, the President. But in choosing the President, the votes shall be taken by states, the representation from each state having one vote; a quorum for this purpose shall consist of a member or members from two-thirds of the states, and a majority of all the states shall be necessary to a choice.

See also:
Election of 1800
Election of 1804

Reference:
Peterson, Merrill. 1970. *Thomas Jefferson and the New Nation.* New York: Oxford University Press.

University of Virginia

Jefferson was interested in the establishment of a state system of education from elementary school to college. He believed that education was the key to advancement in a large republic. After his presidency, Jefferson spent the remaining years of his life envisioning and creating the University of Virginia.

At first Jefferson sought to induce the Virginia legislature to create a comprehensive, statewide education system. When this effort failed, he narrowed his focus and worked to establish a state university, believing that attention to lower schools would naturally follow. As early as 1800, Jefferson was collecting ideas on how his proposed institution should operate. He wanted a university, he wrote, "on a plan so broad and liberal and modern, as to be worth patronizing with the public support, and be a temptation to the youth of other states to come and drink of the cup of knowledge and fraternize with us."

Jefferson wanted a university that would be centrally located in the state, and Charlottesville was deemed an ideal site. Regarding tradition-oriented universities like Oxford, Cambridge, and the Sorbonne as "behind the science of the age," Jefferson studied plans from universities that were based on Enlightenment ideals. He found Edinburgh and the National Institute of France to be beneficial models. In deciding upon architectural style and the selection of professors, Jefferson concluded that

> the plan of building is not to erect one single magnificent building to contain everybody and everything, but to make of it an academic village in which every professor should have his separate house [or "pavilion"], containing his lecturing room with two, three, or four rooms for his own accommodation according as he may have a family or no family, with kitchen, garden, etc.; distinct dormitories for the students, not more than two in a room; and separate boarding houses for dieting them by private housekeepers. We concluded to employ no professor who is not of the first order of the science he professes, that when we can find such in our own country we shall prefer them and when we cannot we will procure them wherever else to be found.

Jefferson's proposal first went before the Virginia Assembly in 1806 and failed, largely due to financial considerations. Following the conclusion of his presidency, however, Jefferson was able to devote more time to the project, and in January 1816, the legislature passed a bill, drafted by Jefferson, creating "Central College."

A 1905 photograph of the colonnades of the University of Virginia. "The whole of the pavilion and dormitories to be united by a colonnade in front. . . ." stated Jefferson in a letter requesting sketches from architect William Thornton. The culminating design of Jefferson's career was that of the University of Virginia.

The first regular meeting of the Board of Visitors of the college, who were authorized to purchase land and finance the construction of the institute, convened on May 5, 1817. To give his project added weight, Jefferson ensured that President James Monroe and former president James Madison joined him in attending this meeting. Jefferson continued his fund-raising efforts throughout the year, and that autumn the cornerstone of the first building was laid. In January of the following year, the General Assembly of the state changed the college's name to reflect a more ambitious effort; thus it created the "University of Virginia," and named Jefferson to the Board of Visitors, which elected him rector.

By December of that same year, the walls of seven pavilions and 37 dormitory rooms had been erected. However, the financial depression of that year, known as the "Panic of 1819," bled money out of the economy and inhibited the state's ability to fund the university in the manner that Jefferson wanted. He appealed to the Virginia Assembly to consider the problems of sending its sons out of state to be educated. The recent Missouri controversy over the right to take slaves into western territories demonstrated that sectionalism was increasing rather than decreasing. Playing upon popular fears, Jefferson contended that to have Virginians study in the North would allow them to be "confronted with opinions and principles in discord with those of their own country [Virginia]."

By 1824, Jefferson was able to recruit faculty, the majority of whom came from Europe, with the posts for law and moral philosophy reserved for Americans. In his final years, Jefferson drafted class schedules, rules of student conduct, and exam and degree requirements. On March 7, 1825, the University of Virginia opened its doors to some 30 young men for instruction. Jefferson's "academic village" was a reality and, according to one Harvard professor visiting the campus, could only be described

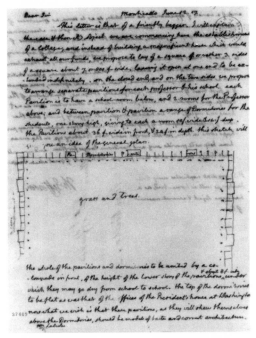

Note written by Thomas Jefferson to architect Benjamin Latrobe in 1817 with Jefferson's earliest sketch of plan for the University of Virginia.

as "more beautiful than anything architectural in New England, and more appropriate to an university than can be found, perhaps, in the world."

See also:
Enlightenment

Reference:
O'Neal, William B. 1976. *A Fine Arts Library: Jefferson's Selections for the University of Virginia Together with His Architectural Books at Monticello.* Charlottesville: University of Virginia Press.

Urban Vices

Jefferson believed that civic virtue, the choice by common citizens to put national concerns over individual desires, was a necessary ingredient in a republic where the people rule themselves. Toward this goal, Jefferson promoted a rural, agrarian lifestyle and deprecated life in urban settings. In his opinion, large cities represented the loss of independence and thus public virtue. A large, ill-educated, propertyless class massed together in small tenements could not, Jefferson concluded, be entrusted with the sacred duty of maintaining republican values. In Jefferson's estimation, this class lacked the requisite "stake" in society that would make it trustworthy in the care of the community. Such care, Jefferson presumed, could only be nurtured in an environment where farmers owned their land, grew their food, and controlled their labor. From such conditions, Jefferson offered, came the more "natural" republican sentiments of honesty, effort, and independence, requirements not merely for a farmer but for a civic leader. The dependence created in large cities where citizens did not own their homes, produce their food, or regulate their working conditions allowed corruption and vice to seep into the foundations of republican life and endanger the experiment of public self-rule.

In a 1785 letter to John Jay, Jefferson demonstrated his regard for the farmers of the country, declaring that "cultivators of the earth are the most valuable citizens. They are the most vigorous, the most independent, the most virtuous, and they are tied to their country, and wedded to its liberty and interests, by the more lasting bonds." In the classic *Notes on the State of Virginia*, Jefferson was even more specific, proclaiming that "those who labour in the earth are the chosen people of God, if ever he had a chosen people, whose breasts he has made his peculiar deposit for substantial and genuine virtue." Taking a swipe at the commercial interests of the country, Jefferson declared that "those, who not looking up to heaven, to their own soil and industry, as does the husbandman, for their subsistence, depend for it on the casualties and caprice of customers. Dependence begets subservience and venality, suffocates the germ of virtue, and prepares fit tools for the designs of ambition."

Jefferson's critique of dependence in *Notes* focused on life in America's urban settings. To calls for a more industrial America, Jefferson answered:

While we have land to labour . . . let us never wish to see our citizens occupied at a work-bench, or twirling a distaff. Carpenters, masons, smiths, are wanting in husbandry: but, for the general operations of manufacture, let our work-shops remain in Europe. It is better to carry provisions and materials to workmen there than bring them to the provision and materials, and with them their manners and principles. The loss by the transportation of commodities across the Atlantic will be made up in happiness and permanence of government. The mobs of great cities add just so much to the support of pure government, as sores do to the strength of the human body. It is the manners and spirit of a people which preserve a republic in vigour. A degeneracy in these is a canker which soon eats to the heart of its laws and constitution.

Jefferson certainly carried on this spirit of antagonism toward cities throughout the 1780s and 1790s. A letter to James Madison written the same year as the Constitution proclaimed in graphic terms Jefferson's fear that urbanization would destroy democracy. While the Master of Monticello optimistically proclaimed his faith that there would always "remain vacant lands in any part of America," he also issued a warning that "when we get piled upon one another in large cities, as in Europe, we shall become corrupt as in Europe, and go to eating one another as they do there."

But to portray Jefferson as merely an unabashed enemy of cities would not do justice to the complexity of his vision for the United States. Jefferson's greatest opposition to cities came while he was battling those who would increase the powers of the central government. In Jefferson's mind, a vigorous federal system included government aid to manufacturers, which would increase the size of urban settings. While Jefferson and his Virginia successors served as presidents, however, he became more nationalistic and thus more willing to accept growth in both federal powers and in the urban environment. Moreover, the War of 1812 demonstrated to Jefferson the ineffectiveness of an agrarian republic in waging war against a major industrial power. Thus, by the 1810s, Jefferson recanted much of his antiurban bias in the hope that the development of cities would be accompanied by a strengthening in the power and independence of the United States on the world stage. In 1816, Jefferson complained to a colleague that

> I am quoted by those who wish to continue our dependence on England for manufactures. There was a time when I might have been so quoted with more candor, but within the thirty years which have since elapsed, how are circumstances changed! We were then in peace. Our independent place among nations was acknowledged . . . we must now place the manufacturer by the side of the agriculturist.

Jefferson's acknowledgment of the importance of cities late in his public career was never complete, however. To the end of his life he retained the unshakeable suspicion that an agricultural America would produce a more healthy and long-lasting republic than an urban America would.

See also:
Empire of Liberty
Notes on the State of Virginia
Virginia Dynasty

Reference:
Jefferson, Thomas. 1787. *Notes on the State of Virginia*. New York: W. W. Norton.

Van Buren, Martin
(1782–1862)

Martin Van Buren believed that he was the ideological heir to Jefferson and the Virginian's brand of democracy. Though he served as the nation's eighth president, Van Buren is perhaps best remembered for his revival of the Jeffersonian political coalition in the 1820s.

Van Buren was born in Kinderhook, New York, in 1782. The son of a tavern keeper, he could lay no claim to privileged background and thus found his path to political relevancy blocked by the Clinton faction, a group of older Jeffersonians who ran New York as though it were a private family fiefdom. Van Buren's efforts to crack the Clinton hold on New York are instructive, for he represented the type of personality that would come to dominate the second generation of American leadership. Whereas the founding generation of Washington, Jefferson, and Adams was characterized by its devotion to patrician values, men like Van Buren represented the aspirations of a rising middle class. Unable to enter politics through the traditional route of family connections, Van Buren created a new political organization in New York in the 1810s that was more democratic than its opponent. Success followed. The demise of the Clinton faction brought Van Buren's Albany Regency to power and made him a

U.S. senator in one of the most powerful states in the Union.

Though from the North, Van Buren was sympathetic to southern interests. He prided himself on his Jeffersonian principles of strict construction of the Constitution, state sovereignty over a centralized federal government, and an agrarian-based economy. Van Buren believed, along with Jefferson, that an excessively capital-driven economy would do more harm than good to the country by ushering in the spirit of greed and corruption. In Van Buren's opinion, the best example of how a republic should operate was the American South. There the pace of life was slow, agriculture dominated, and the moneyed culture, which characterized the North, had not sunk its talons into the tradition-oriented states below the Mason-Dixon Line.

From 1800 to 1824, the Virginia Dynasty of Jefferson, James Madison, and James Monroe ruled the nation. Van Buren approved of this Republican leadership but was dismayed when there was no suitable Virginia candidate to replace Monroe in the presidential contest of 1824. In May of that year, Van Buren made a pilgrimage to Monticello to confer with Jefferson and sip from the fount of pure republicanism. "It may well be imagined with how much satisfaction I listened to Mr. Jefferson's conversation," Van Buren later recalled. "His imposing appearance as he sat uncovered—never wearing his hat except when he left the carriage and often not then—and the earnest and the impressive manner in which he spoke of men and things, are as yet fresh in my recollections as if they were experiences of yesterday." The two men discussed politics, took early morning carriage drives, and exchanged compliments. Summing up his trip to Monticello, Van Buren recalled that Jefferson was indeed his "beau ideal of thorough patriotism and accomplished statesmanship."

The year did not end well for Van Buren, however, as John Quincy Adams, a National Republican from Massachusetts and an advocate of northern principles, was awarded the presidency by the House of Representatives. In Van Buren's opinion, Quincy Adams represented the second coming of Federalism. His father, John Adams, had occupied the presidency as a Federalist partisan in the 1790s, and it was not difficult to see in the son the pretensions of that party. Van Buren believed that Republicans constituted a natural majority in the nation but had foundered with the demise of Federalism after the War of 1812. With no opposition to keep the party sharp, Republicans had lost their focus and allowed Quincy Adams to slip into the presidency. What was necessary, Van Buren contended, was a revitalization of the first party system where Jeffersonians battled Hamiltonians along clearly drawn party lines. "We must always have party distinctions," he contended, "and the old ones are the best of which the nation of the case admits. Political combinations between the inhabitants of the different states are unavoidable and the most natural and beneficial to the country is that between the planters of the South and the plain Republicans of the North. The country has once flourished under a party thus constituted and may again."

Toward this goal Van Buren championed the presidential candidacy of General Andrew Jackson. Jackson's southern roots along with his suspicions of a credit-driven economy made him an ideal Jeffersonian candidate. Jackson's victory over Quincy Adams in 1828 elevated Van Buren to the new president's cabinet and from there to the vice presidency. In 1836, Van Buren was elected president and proved committed to running the nation along agrarian principles. Historical forces worked against Van Buren, however. Rather than returning to the values of the "Old Republic," the nation was being pulled forward by the forces of industry and commerce. Van Buren was a consistent Jeffersonian, but he found it impossible to carry the Jeffersonian dream into the reality of the emerging industrial age.

See also:
Adams, John Quincy
Jackson, Andrew

Reference:
Niven, John. 1983. *Martin Van Buren: The Romantic Age of American Politics*. New York: Oxford University Press.

Virginia Dynasty

The Virginia Dynasty refers to the presidencies of George Washington, Thomas Jefferson, James Madison, and James Monroe. In addition to the fact that each of these men was a Virginian, other similarities stand out as well. Every member of this dynasty owned slaves, served two terms in office, and aside from Washington, promoted the interests of the South while operating as chief executives of the nation. Moreover, Jefferson, Madison, and Monroe all served as secretaries of state and thus helped to make that office, by virtue of its becoming a stepping-stone to the White House, the most powerful and prized cabinet position.

A hallmark of the Virginia Dynasty was its agrarian vision, which tended to work in favor of southerners and against the interests of the urban-industrial North. Under Jefferson and his successors, the Louisiana Territory, the Floridas, and the Oregon Territory were brought into the republic. During the presidencies of Massachusetts's favorite statesman, John Adams, and his son, John Quincy

Adams, no land was acquired by the United States. While Jeffersonians championed the accumulation of millions of acres of western lands as a necessary component in agrarian-republicanism, in reality they were opening up territory not merely for independent small farmers, but for plantation slavery as well. Thus, national expansion under the Virginia Dynasty in the period 1800–1820 played a significant role in the breakdown of the federal system along sectional lines in the 1850s, which ultimately led to the Civil War.

Jefferson's role as the leader of the Virginia Dynasty was unquestioned. On the strength of his personality he successfully tabbed Madison to succeed him and therefore prolonged the control of the federal government by agrarians. Following the Monroe presidency, Jeffersonians everywhere hoped to re-create, in some form, the old alliance that had ushered the Jeffersonians to power in 1800. One year after Jefferson's death, Martin Van Buren began to form a revised Jeffersonian party based, as he put it, on a "substantial reorganization of the old Republican Party . . . between the planters of the South and the plain Republicans of the North." To this end, Van Buren became the champion of Andrew Jackson, a Tennessee frontier aristocrat who would proclaim throughout his own presidency that his actions were motivated solely by Jeffersonian principles. The domination of the Democratic party in national politics up to the Civil War demonstrated continuity in the Virginia Dynasty and its successors. Like the Virginians, future southern presidents like James Polk acquired millions of acres in western lands below the Mason-Dixon Line. Moreover, the Democrats who followed Jefferson adhered to his sympathies for states' rights over the powers of an encroaching national government. In sum, Jefferson's role as the critical personality in the Virginia Dynasty shaped the political culture of national politics for a period of 60 years, commenced an era of southern domination of the Union, and helped precipitate the Civil War.

See also:
Jackson, Andrew
Van Buren, Martin

Reference:
Hunt, Michael. 1987. *Ideology and U.S. Foreign Policy.* New Haven, CT: Yale University Press.

Virginia House of Burgesses

*I*n the spring of 1769, Jefferson rode his horse Jupiter to Williamsburg to take the oath as a new member in the House of Burgesses in the council chamber at the capital. This event marked the beginning of a period of service to Virginia and the other North America colonies that would continue throughout his life.

In formal sessions of the legislature, Jefferson proved a silent member, even after maturing as a legislator. Always at his best in small groups, the Virginian rarely drew attention to himself in public debate. At this point, the Burgesses was quite large. The colony's 57 counties were each entitled to two members, while three boroughs and the College of William and Mary each had one. Jefferson filled one of Albemarle County's seats. In his first session Jefferson served only ten days, as the stance the Burgesses took against the British Crown concerning the privilege of the colony to tax itself prompted the royal governor to dissolve it. Rather than merely go home, the Burgesses formed what was known as the "Association" and drafted a nonimportation and nonconsumption agreement aimed at British manufactures. Jefferson affixed his name to this first significant public paper of his career and was rewarded that autumn by reelection.

For the next several months Jefferson's legislative career was largely concerned with routine affairs over questions of entail and land. Imperial relations were more serene as the British removed nearly every act that attempted to get revenues from the colonies. Though somewhat placated, Jefferson continued to protest that the empire's tax on tea remained and, keeping principles clearly in mind, he signed another Association agreement in June 1770 that called upon England to discontinue its current tax policies. As a public man Jefferson now entered a lull. With the British making no further injurious actions against the colonists and the Virginians having no immediate grievances, relations between Crown and colony were quieted.

Nevertheless, during his early legislative career, Jefferson acquired valuable experience in the art of politics. He made an effort to provide for the emancipation of slaves in Virginia, for example, but when it was defeated he showed himself a practical statesman by not injuring his reputation through further antagonism on the issue. On the broader stage of colonial affairs, he associated with the more radical elements of the Burgesses who attempted to circumvent the powers of the Crown in the colony. Though reelected in the fall of 1771, Jefferson declined to serve, and when the Burgesses met in February of the next year, he was not among them. Personal concerns took over Jefferson's energies at this time, as his impending marriage to Martha Wayles Skelton and the building of his home at Monticello diverted his attention from the issue of colonial rights.

Jefferson returned to the Burgesses in the spring of 1773 for what proved to be a relatively quiet session. In the following months, however, the destruction of British tea in the colonial port of Boston in response to the hated tea tax prompted the empire to crack down on the patriot cause in Massachusetts. The Burgesses immediately threw its support behind the beleaguered northern colony and was promptly dissolved by the governor. Though officially suspended, the Burgesses convened in Richmond in early 1775 to protest British violations of colonial rights. Jefferson was a member of the committee of 12 that was set up to make preparations for the militia.

Like most Americans, Jefferson resisted breaking away from the mother country and still sought some means of reconciliation. That summer he wrote a proposal to the Crown that suggested that any colony that contributed to the defense of the empire and made provisions to finance its own civil government should be exempt from imperial taxation for purposes of revenue. Attached to this proposal was a warning that Virginia would not desist from its activities to promote increased colonial autonomy. "We consider ourselves as bound in honor," Jefferson reminded the British, "as well as interest, to share one general fate with our sister Colonies; and would hold ourselves base deserters of that union to which we have acceded, were we to agree on any measures distinct and apart from them." The proposal proved to be one of Jefferson's last efforts as a member of the House of Burgesses. Within a few months, he became a national delegate in the Continental Congress and soon authored the Declaration of Independence, championing the rights of Americans in every colony.

See also:
Declaration of Independence

Reference:
Malone, Dumas. 1948. *Jefferson the Virginian.* Boston: Little, Brown.

Virginia Statute of Religious Freedoms

Jefferson's role in amending the Virginia Declaration of Rights to address issues that arose over continued state support of the Anglican Church resulted from his growing interest in the revolutionary cause as well as his faith in reason over organized religion. The Declaration of 1776 affirmed religious freedom but stopped short of disestablishing Anglicanism in Virginia, which meant that taxpayers would continue to support the church whether they practiced its faith or not. It was soon apparent that the leaders had not gone far enough in their revision of church policy, since dissenters petitioned the legislature for equality in the exercise of religious beliefs and the disestablishment of the Church of England in Virginia.

Jefferson was named to a 19-member committee on religion that was to address the concerns of the states' citizens. It was while working on this committee that Jefferson began a long friendship with a delegate from Orange County, James Madison. But Jefferson's views, while respected, were deemed too radical at the time. He favored the disestablishment of the Anglican Church and complete freedom of religion. Without this, he argued, there tended to be a corruption of "the principles of that very religion it is meant to encourage, by bribing, with a monopoly of worldly honours and imoluments, those who will externally profess and conform to it." Jefferson criticized both organized religion and the intrusiveness of civil governments by claiming that "the opinions of men are not the object of civil government, nor under its jurisdiction." But after drawing up resolutions to this effect, he was disappointed to learn that the committee would not pass a bill exempting dissenters from contributing to the support of the Church of England. Thus, while the act that made it through the committee solved some of the more general questions facing congregations in Virginia, it left unresolved the issue of support to clergy. Jefferson put the blame solidly on the prejudices of the committee, noting that "although the majority of our citizens were dissenters . . . a majority of the legislature were churchmen."

As the Revolution progressed and tolerance for things British, including Anglicanism, waned sharply, various components of Jefferson's original bill for establishing religious freedom were enacted. In 1779 the law providing salaries for the Anglican clergy was repealed, and seven years later Virginia established laws protecting complete religious freedom. Ten years in the making, Jefferson's statute for religious freedom championed the primacy of reason in society by declaring that

> no man shall be compelled to frequent or support any religious worship, place, or ministry whatsoever, nor shall be enforced, restrained, molested, or burthened in his body or goods, nor shall otherwise suffer, on account of his religious opinions or belief; but that all men shall be free to profess, and by argument to maintain, their opinions in matters of religion, and that the same shall in no wise diminish, enlarge, or affect their civil capacities.

Finally, the bill emphasized the "natural" rights of a liberal society to govern itself, concluding that "we are free to declare, and do declare, that the rights hereby asserted are of the natural rights of mankind, and that if any act shall be hereafter passed to repeal the present or to narrow its operation, such act will be an infringement of natural right."

See also:
Deism
Enlightenment

Reference:
Healey, Robert M. 1962. *Jefferson on Religion in Public Education.* New Haven, CT: Yale University Press.

W

War of 1812

Jefferson entertained great hopes for the United States as it entered the War of 1812. In particular he relished the opportunity to destroy the residue of British influence in American government and culture. To Jefferson the war became "the second weaning from British principles, British attachments, British manners and manufactures." The effect of this second war for independence would be "salutary," he contended, "and will form an epoch of the spirit of nationalism and of consequent prosperity, which would never have resulted from a continued subordination to the interests and influence of England." On a more practical level, the war provided the United States with the opportunity to occupy coveted British possessions to the north. Enthusiastically but, as things turned out, unrealistically, Jefferson proclaimed that "the acquisition of Canada this year, as far as the neighborhood of Quebec, will be a mere matter of marching." With the Floridas also presenting an opportunity for territorial conquest, Jefferson envisioned the advancement of the American flag as the precursor of his beloved "Empire of Liberty," an agrarian paradise where yeoman farmers would practice simple republicanism for generations.

Broad-minded thinkers like Jefferson interpreted the coming war as a dramatic struggle between New World liberalism and Old World autocracy. Victory on the part of the United States would validate republicanism and natural rights as viable and preferable alternatives to rule by aristocracy and divine right. Jefferson saw this struggle between competing political ideologies clearly, noting that "the whole system of Europe towards America" is

> an atrocious and insulting tyranny. One hemisphere of the earth, separated from the other by wide seas on both sides, having a different system of interests flowing from different climates, different soils, different productions, different modes of existence, and its own local relations and duties, is made subservient to all the petty interests of the other, to their laws, their regulations, their passions and wars, and interdicted from social intercourse, from the interchange of mutual duties and comforts with their neighbors, enjoined on all men by the laws of nature.

To Jefferson, a victorious war promised a renegotiation of America's relations with Europe. The new relationship would acknowledge U.S. liberty, dignity, and above all, republican independence in a world dominated by monarchies.

The reality of war brought a different message to Jefferson. Military defeats in 1812, beginning with the surrender of Detroit, destroyed Jefferson's early faith in a quick and easy victory. To a colleague he bitterly complained that a "wretched . . . succession of generals never before destroyed the fairest expectations of a nation." Some historians have attributed America's poor showing early in the conflict to Jefferson himself. By concentrating on paying off the national debt, Jeffersonians had gutted the army, neglected the navy, and left the nation ill-equipped to fight a major war. American ministers had been recalled from nearly every foreign outpost, and the National Bank, the enemy of Republicans since its inception in 1791, was allowed to expire once its charter ran out in 1811. Jeffersonians quickly learned that Republican frugality was unable to sustain the nation's interests in the face of European aggression. Following the war, they quickly chartered the Second Bank of the United States and made provisions for a protective tariff against European goods.

Nevertheless, Jefferson took pleasure in Andrew Jackson's victory at New Orleans, which coincided with an honorable peace treaty signed by American representatives in the Belgian city of Ghent. Moreover, the optimistic Virginian believed the war had benefited the country immensely by demonstrating American strength and destroying the Federalist party, which had opposed the conflict. "The British war has left us in debt," Jefferson concluded,

> but that is a cheap price for the good it has done us. The establishment of the necessary manufactures among ourselves, the proof that our government is solid, can stand the shock of war, and is superior even to civil schism, are precious facts for us; and of these the strongest proofs were furnished. . . . But its best effect has been the complete suppression of party. . . . Even Connecticut, as a state, and the last one expected to yield its

> steady habits . . . has chosen a Republican governor and Republican legislature. . . . The war then has done us all this good, and the further one of assuring the world that although attached to peace from a sense of its blessings, we will meet war when it is made necessary.

See also:
Election of 1812
Empire of Liberty
Warhawks

Reference:
Hickey, Donald. 1989. *The War of 1812: A Forgotten Conflict*. Urbana: University of Illinois Press.

Warhawks

During the second term of Jefferson's presidency, the Anglo-French wars spilled over to America. The United States was the nation with the largest neutral carrying fleet, and American shippers transported goods to Europe and Europe's empires. Gradually both Great Britain and France attempted to dissuade American trade to their respective enemies by confiscating American ships headed toward enemy ports. Jefferson responded with an embargo on American goods sold abroad that injured the British and French economies but did not discourage their continued violations of America's neutral rights on the seas.

With Jefferson in retirement, James Madison attempted to coerce the European powers to respect American neutrality without going to war. His policy was a continuation of Jefferson's, and like his predecessor's, was ineffective. The election of the twelfth Congress in 1810, however, produced a shake-up in American foreign policy. Although the elections were victorious for the Republican party, political change was in the air. With the constant westward movement of pioneers, new states with different agendas were brought into the Union. Thus, when Republicans like Henry Clay from Kentucky and Felix Grundy from Tennessee joined Congress in the autumn of 1810, they were at odds with the older leaders of the party, more traditional Jeffersonians.

The new western Republicans, referred to as "Warhawks," were younger, had less legislative experience, and were more willing than their Tidewater colleagues to take decisive, even belligerent action against Britain and France. Moreover, the new western congressmen represented constituencies that were hurt by America's inability to safely sell its farm produce across the Atlantic. Without access to European markets, these men argued, the western agricultural economy was being damaged. Further, westerners were more willing to go to war than were their eastern counterparts.

Unlike those residing along the Atlantic coast, residents living in the nation's interior did not fear British attack. In fact, war would allow the West to take up arms against Britain's Native American allies and would provide an opportunity to take British territory in Canada and Spanish possessions in Florida. Finally, the Warhawks represented a repudiation of Jeffersonian/Madisonian foreign policy. Where these two statesmen relied on "peaceable coercion" to dictate their relations with a European continent at war, the new western representatives pushed aggressively for a showdown with America's enemies, and they played a decisive role in bringing about a declaration of war against the British in 1812.

See also:
Anglo-French Wars
Election of 1812
Foreign Policy

Reference:
Brown, Roger. 1964. *The Republic in Peril: 1812.* New York: Columbia University Press.

Washington, George (1731–1799)

*J*efferson once offered as proof of the intrinsic worthiness of America the fact that "we have produced a Washington, whose memory will be adored while liberty shall have votaries, whose name shall triumph over time, and will in future ages assume its just station among the most celebrated worthies of the world." He was correct. Over time and indeed within the course of his own life, Washington's name did "triumph" over all others, even Jefferson's. Today, as then, Washington is remembered as the preeminent figure in the struggle for independence and the formation of a workable republican government.

Washington lived what could be termed an "honorable" life. He felt the burden of responsibility persistently throughout his life as a planter-aristocrat, military leader, and president, and carried himself accordingly. Like Jefferson, Washington had a sense of who he was, and he lived up to the awesome responsibilities of his name and reputation with consummate care and professionalism. Though mythmakers would exemplify the Washington mystique with fables and parables of the great man's honesty and integrity, they need not have bothered. Perhaps more than any other member of the founding generation, Washington secured his legacy through his own efforts. At the time of his death in 1799, his station in the pantheon of national heroes was secure.

Washington was born in Virginia in 1731 to an affluent family of English descent. Trained as a surveyor, he traveled throughout the wilderness areas of the Old Dominion and developed an abiding affection for the "West" that remained throughout his life. In youth his desire was to be an officer in the British army. A brief trip to the West Indies had introduced Washington to the cultivated lifestyle among the British officer corps that he wished to emulate. Though unable to secure a commission, he nevertheless forged a military career. In the 1750s he participated in the French and Indian War and later commanded the military phase of the American Revolution. Though not a brilliant general from the perspective of wins and losses on the battlefield, Washington proved to be the perfect type of general for the war against Britain. Nearly always outnumbered in the field, Washington managed to avoid a catastrophic defeat while continually maintaining a viable army. If he won no smashing victories, neither did he suffer the kind of crippling loss that would have killed the American war effort.

Washington was called out of retirement in 1787 to be both delegate to and president of the Constitutional Convention in Philadelphia. Though he had little to do with the drafting of the Constitution, he played a key role in persuading the Virginia legislature to ratify the document. Moreover, many influential men indicated that their support for the Constitution was based upon the assumption that the nation's first president would be Washington. This assumption proved correct, as Washington became the nation's first executive officer and formed what is probably the most competent presidential cabinet in the history of the republic. Seeking balance, Washington chose two agrarian liberals, Jefferson and Edmund Randolph, who came from the South, and two urban conservatives, Alexander Hamilton and Henry Knox, who resided in the North. Washington's administration quickly came under attack from southerners who believed that Hamilton, operating as a kind of power behind the throne, was attempting to enhance the powers of the central government at the expense of states' rights. In a series of bills, including the Funding Act, Assumption Act, and National Banking Bill, Washington supported programs that secured powers for the federal government. Men like Jefferson argued that these programs went beyond the limits of the Constitution.

Though always respectful to Washington, Jefferson believed the great man had fallen under the spell of Hamilton. What Jefferson did not understand, however, was that Washington's nationalism was greater than his own. Washington's career was based on military service. He traveled throughout the states during the Revolution, spending the bulk of his time in the North. He also used his own resources to finance his army when the states were slow to adequately fund the patriot cause. More than Jefferson, in other words, Washington had experienced the weaknesses of a limited central government firsthand. He worked as president to shore up such weaknesses, which he believed endangered the health of the nation. By the end of Washington's presidency, communication between the two men slowed to a trickle. To complicate the estrangement further, a letter critical of Washington, written by Jefferson to a European friend, found its way into American newspapers. Though no reconciliation occurred prior to Washington's death, Jefferson nevertheless felt a keen sense of respect for the statesman. In what is undoubtedly the most perceptive existing summary of Washington's character, Jefferson concluded that

> perhaps the strongest feature in his character was prudence, never acting until every circumstance, every consideration, was maturely weighed; refraining if he saw a doubt, but, when once decided, going through with this purpose whatever obstacles opposed. His integrity was most pure, his justice the most inflexible I have ever known, no motives of interest or consanguinity, of friendship or hatred, being able to bias his decision. He was, indeed, in every sense of the words, a wise, a good, and a great man. His temper was naturally irritable and high-toned, but reflection and resolution had obtained a firm and habitual ascendancy over it. If ever, however, it broke

Shown left to right are Patrick Henry, George Washington, and Edmund Pendleton traveling to the first Congress. Engraving by H. B. Hall after a drawing by Durley, 1850.

its bonds, he was most tremendous in his wrath. In his expenses he was honorable but exact, liberal in contributions to whatever promised utility but frowning and unyielding on all visionary projects and all unworthy calls on his charity. His heart was not warm in its affections, but he exactly calculated every man's value and gave him a solid esteem proportioned to it.

His person . . . was fine, his stature exactly what one would wish, his deportment easy, erect and noble; the best horseman of his age, and the most graceful figure that could be seen on horseback. Although in the circle of his friends, where he might be unreserved with safety, he took a free share in conversation, his colloquial talents were not above mediocrity, possessing neither copiousness of ideas nor fluency of words. In public, when called on for a sudden opinion, he was

unready, short, and embarrassed. Yet he wrote readily, rather diffusely, in an easy and correct style. This he had acquired by conversation with the world, for his education was merely reading, writing, and common arithmetic, to which he added surveying at a later day. His time was employed in action chiefly, reading little, and that only in agriculture and English history. . . .

On the whole, his character was, in its mass, perfect, in nothing bad, in few points indifferent; and it may truly be said that never did nature and fortune combine more perfectly to make a man great, and to place in him the same constellation with whatever worthies have merited from man an everlasting remembrance. For his was the singular destiny and merit of leading the armies of his country successfully through an arduous war for the establishment of its independence; of conducting its councils through the birth of a government, new in its forms and principles, until it had settled down into a quiet and orderly train; and of scrupulously obeying the laws through the whole of his career, civil and military, of which the history of the world furnishes no other example. . . .

I am satisfied that great body of Republicans think of him as I do. . . . We knew his honesty, the wiles with which he was encompassed, and that age had already begun to relax the firmness of his purposes; and I am convinced he is more deeply seated in the love gratitude of the Republicans than in the Pharisaical homage of the Federal monarchists. For he was no monarchist from preference of his judgment. The soundness of that gave him correct views of the rights of man, and his severe justice devoted him to them.

See also:
American Revolution
Constitution
Federalist Party

Reference:
Flexner, James Thomas. 1969. *Washington: The Indispensable Man.* Boston, MA: Little, Brown.

Webster, Noah (1758–1843)

Noah Webster and Thomas Jefferson were neither friends nor political allies. Webster's support for the Federalist party marked him, in Jefferson's opinion, as "a mere pedagogue of very limited understanding." Yet despite their political differences, the two men shared a deep love for education and believed in the promise of the American Revolution. Jefferson's concerns for the development of a uniquely American or republican culture thrust him into politics. Webster, on the other hand, studied philology, the development and evolution of languages. It was his hope to create a new "Americanized" form of English that would emphasize the differences between the Old and New Worlds.

Born in New England, Webster was educated at Yale College, where he took a bachelor of arts degree in 1778. He studied law and was admitted to the bar but pursued a career in education. In the 1780s, Webster began to produce elementary textbooks for children. His most famous work, *A Grammatical Institute of the English Language*, attempted to simplify the spelling of English words to accommodate the economy of nature that seemed to be represented in the new nation. More commonly known as the "Blue-backed Speller" due to the color of its binding, the work sold remarkably well. In the late nineteenth century, after nearly 100 years in use, it still sold in excess of one million copies a year. To financially safeguard his efforts Webster became a proponent of copyright laws in America and was instrumental in securing a federal code in 1790.

Webster's lasting achievement is the dictionary that bears his name. In 1800, Webster announced his intention to produce three dictionaries. In 1806 he published *A Compendious Dictionary of the English Language* and in 1807 *A Dictionary for the Use of Common Schools*. His magnum opus, an American interpretation of the English language, took much longer to complete. Research in England necessarily prolonged the project, but Webster was able to complete the dictionary at Cambridge in 1825. Unable to find an English publisher, Webster finally had the manuscript printed in New Haven in 1828. *An American Dictionary of the English Language* was the crowning achievement of Webster's life and was recognized as the best dictionary of its time. It contained 70,000 words, some 12,000 more than Samuel Johnson's latest edition.

It seems likely that had politics not separated Webster and Jefferson, the two men might have enjoyed a friendship built on a mutual appreciation knowledge. Jefferson's interest in the natural world and the archeology of the past was emulated in Webster's intent to get to the root of English linguistics.

See also:
American Philosophical Society
American Revolution

Reference:
Ellis, Joseph. 1979. *After the Revolution: Profiles in Early American Culture.* New York: W. W. Norton.

West Indies

*T*he British and French West Indies figured prominently in Jefferson's economic vision for America. With their large slave populations the European-controlled Indies were an ideal market for American grains and other foodstuffs. During the American Revolution, however, the British shut America out of its Caribbean trade, and the French allowed only limited access. As secretary of state, Jefferson proposed a pro-French trading policy designed to isolate the British and open French West Indies markets to America. In the process, he hoped that trade "discrimination" would prod Great Britain into opening its empire to the United States. As president, Jefferson continued to promote American access to Caribbean markets. His efforts were unsuccessful, however, and British violations of American rights on the seas pushed Jefferson to a general embargo aimed against Europe. Although the embargo was ultimately ineffective, America's inability to tap into the West Indies trade stimulated agriculturists at home to adapt their commercial relationships and sell to internal rather than merely external markets.

See also:
Atlantic Economy
Embargo of 1807

Reference:
Appleby, Joyce O. 1984. *Capitalism and a New Social Order: The Republican Vision of the 1790s.* New York: New York University Press.

Whiskey Rebellion

*I*n Jefferson's opinion, liberty and power were in a perpetual struggle for dominance. Jefferson interpreted the Republican coalition as representing the more democratic and thus more liberty-minded men of the nation. Consequently he viewed Federalists as men who wished to impose the rigid control of the federal government on every aspect of American life. The Whiskey Rebellion served to confirm in Jefferson's mind that Federalism was hostile to basic civil rights and needed to be vigorously countered by a credible political opposition.

In response to Alexander Hamilton's financial plans, Congress authorized an excise tax on distilled whiskey. Though Hamilton had proposed the tax primarily as a method for collecting revenue, he was aware that the duty would be very unpopular in the West, where the bulk of the nation's alcohol was produced. Not only was the tax intrusive by the very nature of its collection provisions, but its revenues were to be used in part to fund federal programs beneficial to the East but hostile to the West. Moreover, the duties on the merchandise were oppressively high in a region where bank notes and hard money were scarce and only limited currency was available. Whiskey served as a form of revenue in the West, and the tax was in fact a direct duty on incomes.

Taking the high road, Hamilton claimed that if westerners did not wish to pay the tax, they could simply stop drinking whiskey. In response, one critic protested in Congress that his brethren had the right to drink as much as they pleased, "that they have been long in the habit of getting drunk and that they will get drunk in defiance of a dozen . . . excise duties which Congress might be weak or wicked enough to impose." By the summer of 1794, rebels in the western counties of Pennsylvania were terrorizing excise officers who attempted to collect the tax. Further, federal judicial proceedings were interrupted, and a group of insurgents threatened to attack Pittsburgh.

President George Washington issued a proclamation calling upon the "whisky rebels" to disperse and offered amnesty for those who did. When this effort failed to obtain a satisfactory response, Washington called upon the states to provide nearly 13,000 militiamen to take the field in the service of the federal government against the rebels. Washington feared that if the government could not enforce its laws, it would fall. Following Hamilton's lead, the president contended that "the crisis was arrived when it must be determined whether the Government can maintain itself." Jefferson's view was quite different than Washington's, as he watched the events in Pennsylvania unfold from the security of his home at Monticello. In Jefferson's estimation, the government was in the wrong and had antagonized its western constituents to a dangerous degree. The Virginian concluded that "their detestation of the Excise Law is universal, and has now associated to it a detestation of the government and that a separation [of the western people], which was perhaps a very distant and problematical event, is now near and certain, and determined in the mind of every man."

Raising Jefferson's ire further, Hamilton joined Washington at the head of the federal army that marched into western Pennsylvania searching for rebels. With word out that a massive army opposed them, the Whiskey rebels gave up their opposition and returned to their homes. The Federalists could claim that they had successfully put down an internal insurrection that threatened the sovereignty of the federal government, but Jeffersonians could just as accurately claim that the Federalists had weakened their legitimacy as rulers by overreacting to a minor tax revolt on the part of Pennsylvania farmers. The ill will engendered by the government's reaction to the Whiskey Rebellion solidified Republican opposition to Federalism and more firmly entrenched westerners in the Republican fold. Jefferson owed more than a small part of his presidential election victory in 1800 to the after-effects of this event.

See also:
Assumption
Hamilton, Alexander

Reference:
Slaughter, Thomas. 1986. *The Whiskey Rebellion: Frontier Epilogue to the American Revolution*. New York: Oxford University Press.

Wilkinson, James (1757–1825)

General James Wilkinson was Jefferson's highest-ranking military and civil officer in the American West. He was also a Spanish agent engaged at various times in attempts to sever the western territories from the United States.

Wilkinson's military career began in 1776 when he was commissioned as a captain in the Continental army. He served with Benedict Arnold's heroic expedition to Montreal and later became an aide-de-camp to Horatio Gates. Through the guiding hand of the latter, Wilkinson became a brigadier general but lost his rank when he participated in the Conway cabal, an ineffectual attempt to have George Washington removed as the Continental army's commanding officer. Wilkinson was dismissed from his next post as Continental clothier general when irregularities were discovered in his accounts.

Following the Revolution, Wilkinson moved to the Kentucky Territory where, in 1784, he became involved in a Spanish plot to gain control of the region. He made several trips to New Orleans and even took an oath of allegiance to the Spanish crown, promising that he would work for the separation of the infant United States from its western territories, which the Spanish coveted. For his services, Wilkinson, known to the Spanish as Agent #13, was granted a pension as well as a private trade monopoly on goods heading to the port of New Orleans. In the 1790s, Wilkinson returned to active duty in the United States army, where he participated in a series of attacks against Native American villages on the Ohio frontier. The American "hero" in the conflict was General "Mad" Anthony Wayne, who in 1794 forced upon the natives the Treaty of Greenville, which opened most of Ohio to white settlement. Following Wayne's death two years later, Wilkinson became the ranking American officer in the West.

Following Jefferson's purchase of the Louisiana Territory in 1803, Wilkinson occupied New Orleans. The president anticipated that the region would serve as the backbone for an agriculturally based way of life for generations of Americans. Wilkinson, however, was willing to pawn the territory off on any person or nation that could promise him glory and wealth. This opportunity came in 1805–1806, when Aaron Burr, Jefferson's first vice president and chief rival in the Republican party, formulated a plan to sever the western territories from Spain and the United States. As head of the American military presence in the West, Wilkinson would undoubtedly play a major role in Burr's scheme. Though details are sketchy, it seems likely that Wilkinson was never convinced of the certainty of Burr's plans and secured for himself plausible ways to extricate himself from the scheme if it began to fall apart.

In the spring of 1806, Wilkinson was the ranking American officer in the West, a Spanish agent and a partner to Burr's secession efforts. Despite his many positions and interests, however, it is most accurate to conclude of Wilkinson that he worked for himself. When the Burr conspiracy fell apart, Wilkinson denounced the plot and arrested his former compatriot, delivering him to Richmond to stand trial for treason. Oblivious of Wilkinson's role in the affair, Jefferson praised his service in a letter to Congress. The general served in the War of 1812 until relieved of command in 1814. Honorably discharged, Wilkinson died in Mexico City in 1825.

See also:
Burr, Aaron
Louisiana Purchase

Reference:
Malone, Dumas. 1974. *Jefferson the President: Second Term, 1805–1809*. Boston, MA: Little, Brown.

Wythe, George (1726–1806)

*I*n many ways, George Wythe (pronounced "with") was the closest thing to a mentor that Jefferson had. Patriot, educator, lawyer, and signer of the Declaration of Independence, in terms of importance Wythe belongs to the second tier of the founding generation, under George Washington, John Adams, and Jefferson, but sitting comfortably with Samuel Adams and Patrick Henry.

Wythe was born in what is now the city of Hampton, Virginia. His mother taught him the rudiments of a classical education, and he briefly attended school. Because he was not the eldest son and would not be entailed his father's property, Wythe was marked for a profession and read law. He traveled the legal circuit for two years and, following the death of his wife, moved to the capital at Williamsburg. There he served as attorney general and member of the House of Burgesses.

In 1755, Wythe remarried and inherited the family estate from his deceased brother. A reputation for clear and logical thought brought several students to Wythe's practice each year, including Jefferson. The latter had nothing but good things to say of his mentor. At the advanced age of 77, Jefferson recalled that Wythe "acquired by his own reading a good knowledge of mathematics and of natural and moral philosophy. He engaged in the study of the law . . . and . . . became . . . the first at the bar, taking into consideration his superior learning, correct elocution, and logical style of reasoning, for in pleading he never indulged himself with a useless or declamatory thought or word."

With an astute legal mind, Wythe could not help but become involved in the colonial protestations that led to the American Revolution. He wrote Virginia's resolution protesting the Stamp Act's unconstitutionality in 1765 and was an early advocate for colonial autonomy within the broader limits of the British Empire. When a break with England appeared imminent, Wythe championed the cause of separation from the mother country, was a delegate at the Second Continental Congress, and signed the Declaration of Independence.

Wythe spent the Revolution in Virginia, beginning a distinguished career as a judge. One of his most important offices at this time, along with Jefferson, George Mason, and Edmund Pendleton, was his appointment to draw up a new legal code for the state. These men performed yeoman service for the Old Dominion, putting into motion the forces that would separate church and state and end the practice of primogeniture and entail. Though he briefly attended the Constitutional Convention of 1787, Wythe's real claim to fame in his latter years was as a professor of law at the College of William and Mary. From 1779 to 1790, he trained the state's leading lawyers and jurists. His most famous students were John Marshall, James Monroe, and Henry Clay. Wythe died in 1806, poisoned by a grandnephew seeking an inheritance. In Jefferson's words, "No man ever left behind him a character more venerated. . . . His virtue was of the purest tint, his integrity inflexible, and his justice exact; of warm patriotism and, devoted as he was to liberty and the natural and equal rights of man . . . for a more disinterested person never lived."

See also:
Declaration of Independence
Virginia House of Burgesses

Reference:
Blackburn, Joyce. 1975. *George Wythe of Williamsburg*. New York: Harper & Row.

X

XYZ Affair

While serving as vice president and leader of the Republican party, Jefferson attempted to undercut the influence of the Federalist party. His efforts were nearly destroyed by the XYZ Affair.

By 1798, Republicans constituted a majority in the House of Representatives, and a Jefferson presidential victory in 1800 seemed likely. With the Jeffersonian coalition on the rise, the hitherto unpopular Federalist party was suddenly rehabilitated by a rapid deterioration in Franco-American relations. In the wake of America's pro-British foreign policy, codified in 1795 with the Jay Treaty, the French began to confiscate U.S. shipping heading toward Britain or parts of its empire. President Adams resisted a call to go to war with the French and instead sent American ministers to Paris to negotiate.

For several weeks, however, the three American plenipotentiaries in Paris experienced only rebuffs from the representatives of the French Directory, the ruling body of France. Finally, when they prepared to cancel their mission and return to America, they were approached by agents of France's foreign minister, Talleyrand. For purposes of discretion, these agents were later given the pseudonyms X, Y, and Z. These men suggested that the American ministers could commence negotiations with the French if they agreed to pay a $250,000 bribe to Talleyrand and advanced the government a $12 million loan that would go toward combating the British. The agents further stipulated that negotiations could not begin until apologies were offered for disparaging remarks made by Adams toward the French Republic in a message to Congress. Only after these conditions were met, the agents insisted, could a Franco-American rapprochement be made. In disgust, Jefferson referred to the conditions as the "base propositions . . . of Talleyrand" and "very unworthy of a great nation."

Though bribes were considered a part of foreign diplomacy, they were usually paid after successful negotiations, not as a condition to opening discussions. The American ministers ceased to have further communications with the French agents, and most of them left the country. After the ministers returned to the United States, the envoys' correspondence was printed and brought before the American people. The publication of the XYZ dispatches united American opinion against the French and seemed to confirm the pro-British, anti-French policy of the Federalist party. Further, it discredited the Jeffersonians' attempts to bring together republican America and republican France against autocratic Great Britain.

Jefferson's response to the XYZ Affair was mixed. He showed contempt for the French who, he claimed, "calculated to excite disgust and indignation in Americans generally, and alienation in the Republicans particularly, whom they so far mistake as to presume an attachment to France and hatred to the Federalist party, and not the love of their country, to be their first passion." Of the Federalists, who used the affair to stir up anti-French war hysteria, he was equally critical, considering it "evident . . . in reflection, that these papers do not offer one motive the more for our going to war." In sum, Jefferson interpreted the XYZ Affair as an unfortunate incident that came dangerously close to fatally weakening the Republican party.

See also:
Anglo-French Wars
Francophilia
French Revolution

Reference:
Stinchcombe, William C. 1980. *The XYZ Affair.* Westport, CT: Greenwood Press.

Yazoo Lands

*I*n 1795 a corrupt Georgia legislature sold over 30 million acres of land at less than two cents per acre to four "Yazoo Companies" in return for lucrative concessions. This fraud did not go unchallenged, however, and some members in the legislature repudiated the contract. By this time, however, speculators had sold much of the land at market price to New Englanders, who moved quickly to protect their purchases. With the state of Georgia now threatening to nullify the original acquisition by the Yazoo Companies, which would in turn strip the New Englanders of their legitimate purchases, the latter group lobbied Congress to recognize their claims in Georgia.

A committee composed of Republican party members James Madison, Albert Gallatin, and Levi Lincoln advised Congress to set aside 5 million acres to provide relief to the New Englanders. At this point, "Old Republicans" like John Randolph alleged that Republicans were perpetuating land fraud in Georgia in order to win political votes in New England. Their efforts blocked congressional relief measures for years, and not until the Supreme Court held that Georgia could not undo the original sale to the corrupt Yazoo Companies were the New Englanders compensated. Randolph and others attacked Jefferson for heading a government that encouraged land fraud in order to win personal popularity. Though the conflict over the Yazoo lands did not irreparably harm Republicans, it did weaken Jefferson's and Madison's reputations as champions of agrarianism and the sworn enemies of speculation.

See also:
Randolph, John
Tertium Quid

Reference:
Risjord, Norman. 1965. *The Old Republicans: Southern Conservatism in the Age of Jefferson.* New York: Columbia University Press.

PRIMARY SOURCE DOCUMENTS

THE DECLARATION OF INDEPENDENCE
JULY 4, 1776

The following text is Jefferson's draft of the Declaration and is slightly different from that which was adopted. The parts stricken by Congress are in italics.

WHEN, IN THE COURSE OF HUMAN EVENTS, it becomes necessary for one people to dissolve the political bands which have connected them with another, and to assume among the powers of the earth the separate and equal state to which the laws of nature and of nature's God entitle them, a decent respect to the opinions of mankind requires that they should declare the causes which impel them to the separation.

We hold these truths to be self evident: that all men are created equal; that they are endowed by their Creator with *inherent and* inalienable rights; that among these are life, liberty, and the pursuit of happiness; that to secure these rights, governments are instituted among men, deriving their just powers from the consent of the governed; that whenever any form of government becomes destructive of these ends, it is the right of the people to alter or to abolish it, and to institute new government, laying its foundation on such principles, and organizing its powers in such form, as to them shall seem most likely to effect their safety and happiness. Prudence, indeed, will dictate that governments long established should not be changed for light and transient causes; and accordingly all experience hath shown that mankind are more disposed to suffer while evils are sufferable, than to right themselves by abolishing the forms to which they are accustomed. But when a long train of abuses and usurpation, *begun at a distinguished period and* pursuing invariably the same object, evinces a design to reduce them under absolute despotism, it is their right, it is their duty to throw off such government, and to provide new guards for their future security. Such has been the patient sufferance of these colonies; and such is now the necessity which constrains them to *expunge* their former systems of government. The history of the present King of Great Britian is a history of *unremiting* injuries and usurpations, *among which appears no solitary fact to contradict the uniform tenor of the rest, but all have* in direct object the establishment of an absolute tyranny over these states. To prove this, let facts be submitted to a candid world *which we pledge a faith yet unsullied by falsehood.*

He has refused his assent to laws the most wholesome and necessary for the public good.

He has forbidden his governors to pass laws of immediate and pressing importance, unless suspended in their operation till his assent should be obtained; and, when so suspended, he has utterly neglected to attend to them.

He has refused to pass other laws for the accommodation of large districts of people, unless those people would relinquish the right of representation in the legislature, a right inestimable to them, and formidable to tyrants only.

He has called legislative bodies at places unusual, uncomfortable, and distant from the depository of their public records, for the sole purpose of fatiguing them into compliance with his measures.

He has dissolved representative houses repeatedly *and continually* for opposing with manly firmness his invasions on the rights of the people.

He has refused for a long time after such dissolutions to cause others to be elected, whereby the legislative powers, incapable of annihilation, have returned to the people at large for their exercise, the state remaining, in the meantime, exposed to all the dangers of invasion from without and convulsions within.

He has endeavored to prevent the population of these states; for that purpose obstructing the laws for naturalization of foreigners, refusing to pass others to encourage their migrations hither, and raising the conditions of new appropriations of lands.

He has *suffered* the administration of justice *totally to cease in some of these states,* refusing his assent to laws for establishing judiciary powers.

He has made *our* judges dependent on his will alone for the tenure of their offices, and the amount and payment of their salaries.

He has erected a multitude of new offices *by a self-assumed power* and sent hither swarms of new officers to harass our people and eat out their substance.

He has kept among us in times of peace standing armies *and ships of war* without the consent of our legislatures.

He has affected to render the military independent of, and superior to, the civil power.

He has combined with others to subject us to a jurisdiction foreign to our constitutions and unacknowledged by our laws, giving his assent to their acts of pretended legislation for quartering large bodies of armed troops among us; for protecting them by a mock trial from punishment for any murders which they could commit on the inhabitants of these states; for cutting off our trade with all parts of the world; for imposing taxes on us without our consent; for depriving us of the benefits of trial by jury; for transporting us beyond seas to be tried for pretended offenses; for abolishing the free system of English laws in a neighboring province, establishing therein an arbitrary government, and enlarging its boundaries, so as to render it at once an example and fit instrument for introducing the same absolute rule into these *states*; for taking away our charters, abolishing our most valuable laws, and altering fundamentally the forms of our governments; for suspending our own legislatures, and declaring themselves invested with power to legislate for us in all cases whatsoever.

He has abdicated government here *withdrawing his governors, and declaring us out of his allegiance and protection.*

He has plundered our seas, ravaged our coasts, burnt our towns, and destroyed the lives of our people.

He is at this time transporting large armies of foreign mercenaries to complete the works of death, desolation and tyranny already begun with circumstances of cruelty and perfidy unworthy the head of a civilized nation.

He has constrained our fellow citizens taken captive on the high seas, to bear arms against their country, to become the executioners of their friends and brethren, or to fall themselves by their hands.

He has endeavored to bring on the inhabitants of our frontiers, the merciless

Indian savages, whose known rule of warfare is an undistinguished destruction of all ages sexes and conditions *of existence.*

He has incited treasonable insurrections of our fellow citizens, with the allurements of forfeiture and confiscation of our property.

He has waged cruel war against human nature itself, violating its most sacred rights of life and liberty in the persons of a distant people who never offended him, captivating and carrying them into slavery in another hemisphere, or to incur miserable death in their transportation hither. This piratical warfare, the opprobrium of INFIDEL powers, is the warfare of the CHRISTIAN king of Great Britain. Determined to keep open a market where MEN should be bought and sold, he has prostituted his negative for suppressing every legislative attempt to prohibit or to restrain this execrable commerce. And that this assemblage of horrors might want no fact of distinguished die, he is now exciting those very people to rise in arms among us, and to purchase that liberty of which he has deprived them by murdering the people on whome he also obtruded them: thus paying off former crimes committed against the LIBERTIES of one people with crimes which he urges them to commit against the LIVES of another.

In every stage of these oppressions we have petitioned for redress in the most humble terms: our repeated petitions have been answered only by repeated injuries.

A prince whose character is thus marked by every act which may define a tyrant is unfit to be the ruler of a people *who mean to be free. Future ages will scarcely believe that the hardiness of one man adventured, within the short compass of twelve years only, to lay a foundation so broad and so indisguised for tyranny over a people fostered and fixed in principles of freedom.*

Nor have we been wanting in attentions to our British brethren. We have warned them from time to time of attempts by their legislature to extend *a* jurisdiction over us. We have reminded them of the circumstances of our emigration and settlement here, *no one of which could warrant so strange a pretension: that these were effected at the expense of our own blood and treasure, unassisted by the wealth or the strength of Great Britain: that in constituting indeed our several forms of government, we had adopted one common king, thereby laying a foundation for perpetual league and amity with them: but that submission to their parliament was no part of our constitution, nor ever in idea, if history may be credited: and,* appealed to their native justice and magnanimity *as well as to* the ties of our common kindred to disavow these usurpations which *were likely to* interrupt our connection and correspondence. They too have been deaf to the voice of justice and of consanguinity. *And when occasions have been given them, by the regular course of their laws, of removing from their councils the disturbers of our harmony, they have, by their free election, re-established them in power. At this very time too, they are permitting their chief magistrate to send over not only soldiers of our common blood, but Scotch and foreign mercenaries to invade and destroy us. These facts have given the last stab to agonizing affection, and manly spirit bids us to renounce forever these unfeeling brethren. We must endeavor to forget our former love for them, and hold them as we hold the rest of mankind, enemies in war, in peace friends. We might have a free and a great people together; but a communication of grandeur and of freedom, it seems, is below their dignity. Be it so, since they will have it. The road to happiness and to glory is open to us, too. We will tread it apart from them, and* acquiesce in the necessity which denounces our *eternal* separation.

We, therefore, the representatives of the United States of America in General Congress assembled, appealing to the supreme judge of the world for the rectitude of our intentions, do in the name, and by the authority of the good people of these *states reject and renounce all allegiance and subjection of the kings of Great Britain and all others who may hereafter claim by, through or under them; we utterly dissolve all political connection which may heretofore have subsisted* between us and the people or parliament of *Great Britain: and finally we do assert and declare these colonies to be free and independent states*, and that as free and independent states, they have full power to levy war, conclude peace, contract alliances, establish commerce, and to do all other acts and things which independent states may of right do.

And for the support of this declaration, with a firm reliance on the protection of divine providence, we mutually pledge to each other our lives, our fortunes, and our sacred honor.

To Giovanni Fabbroni
June 8, 1778

Jefferson's letter illuminates his great interest in science and music.

. . .Tho' much of my time is employed in the councils of America I have yet a little leisure to indulge my fondness for philosophical studies. I could wish to correspond with you on subjects of that kind. It might not be unacceptable to you to be informed for instance of the true power of our climate as discoverable from the Thermometer, from the force and direction of the winds, the quantity of rain, the plants which grow without shelter in the winter &c. On the other hand we should be much pleased with contemporary observations on the same particulars in your country, which will give us a comparative view of the two climates. Farenheit's thermometer is the only one in use with us. I make my daily observation as early as possible in the morning and again about 4 o'clock in the afternoon, these generally showing the maxim of cold and heat in the course of 24 hours. I wish I could gratify your Botanical taste; but I am acquainted with nothing more than the first principles of that science, yet myself and my friends may furnish you with any

Botanical subjects which this country affords, and are not to be had with you: and I shall take pleasure in procuring them when pointed out by you. The greatest difficulty will be the means of conveyance during the continuance of the war.

If there is a gratification which I envy any people in this world it is to your country [Italy] its music. This is the favorite passion of my soul, and fortune has cast my lot in a country where it is in a state of deplorable barbarism.

"Histories, Memorial, and State-Papers"
1781

This extract, taken from *Notes on the State of Virginia*, was written in 1781 and enlarged the following year. Taken from the only book Jefferson wrote, it discusses the early history and historiography of Virginia from the age of colonization to the movement for independence.

CAPTAIN SMITH, who next to Sir Walter Raleigh may be considered as the founder of our colony, has written its history, from the first adventures to it till the year 1624. He was a member of the council, and afterwards president of the colony; and to his efforts principally may be ascribed its support against the opposition of the natives. He was honest, sensible, and well informed; but his style is barbarous and uncouth. His history, however, is almost the only source from which we derive any knowledge of the infancy of our state.

The reverend William Stith, a native of Virginia, and president of its college, has also written the history of the same period, in a large octavo volume of small print. He was a man of classical learning, and very exact, but of no taste in style. He is inelegant, therefore, and his details often too minute to be tolerable, even to a native of the country, whose history he writes.

Beverley, a native also, has run into the other extreme; he has comprised our history, from the first propositions of Sir Walter Raleigh to the year 1700, in the hundredth part of the space which Stith employs for the fourth part of the period.

Sir William Keith has taken it up at is earliest period, and continued it to the year 1725. He is agreeable enough in style, and passes over events of little importance. Of course he is short, and would be preferred by a foreigner.

During the regal government, some contest arose of the exaction of an illegal fee by governor Dinwiddie, and doubtless there were others on other occasions not at present recollected. It is supposed, that these are not sufficiently interesting to a foreigner to merit a detail.

The petition of the council and burgesses of Virginia to the king, their memorial to the lords, and remonstrance to the commons in the year 1764, began the present contest: and these having proved ineffectual to prevent the passage of the stamp-act, the resolutions of the house of burgesses of 1765 were passed, declaring the independence of the people of Virginia on the parliament of Great-Britain, in matters of taxation. From that time till the declaration of independence by Congress in 1776, their journals are filled with assertions of the public rights.

The pamphlets published in this state on the controverted question were, 1766, An Inquiry into the Rights of the British Colonies, by Richard Bland. 1769, The Monitor's Letters, by Dr. Arthur Lee. 1774, A Summary View of the Rights of British America [written by Jefferson].

To Martha Jefferson
November 28, 1783

Jefferson's letter to his 11-year-old daughter indicates his expectation that she receive a typically "female" kind of education. The business-like tone of the correspondence may also reveal an emotional detachment that Jefferson felt following the death of his wife.

After four days journey I arrived here without any accident and in as good health as when I left Philadelphia. The conviction that you would be more improved in the situation I have placed you than if still with me, has solaced me on my parting with you, which my love for you has rendered a difficult thing. The acquirements which I hope you will make under the tutors I have provided for you will render you more worthy of my love, and if they cannot increase it they will prevent its diminution. Consider the good lady who has taken you under her roof, who has undertaken to see that you perform all your exercises, and to admonish you in all those wanderings from what is right or what is clever to which your inexperience would expose you, consider her I say as your mother, as the only person to whom, since the loss with which heaven has been pleased to afflict you, you can now look up; and that her displeasure or disapprobation on any occasion will be an immense misfortune which should you be so unhappy as to incur by any unguarded act, think no concession too much to regain her good will. With respect to the distribution of your time the following is what I should approve.

from 8. to 10 o'clock practice music.
from 10. to 1. dance one day and draw another
from 1. to 2. draw on the day you dance, and write a letter the next day.
from 3. to 4. read French.
from 4 to 5. exercise yourself in music.
from 5. till bedtime read English, write &c.

. . . I have placed my happiness on seeing you good and accomplished, and no distress which this world can now bring on me could equal that of your disappointing my hopes. If you love men then, strive to be good under every situation and to all living creatures, and to acquire those accomplishments which I have put in your power, and which will go far towards ensuring you the warmest love of your affectionate father.

P.S. keep my letters and read them at times that you may always have present in your mind those things which will endear you to me.

REPORT OF A PLAN OF GOVERNMENT FOR THE WESTERN TERRITORY
MARCH 1, 1784

Although turned down by Congress when proposed in 1784, Jefferson's plans for the development of the West were adopted in essence in the Northwest Ordinance of 1787.

The Committee appointed to prepare a plan for the temporary government of the Western territory have agreed to the following resolutions.

Resolved, that the territory ceded or to be ceded by Individual states to the United states shall be formed into distinct states, bounded in the following manner as nearly as such cessions will admit, that is to say; Northwardly and Southwardly by parallels of latitude so that each state shall comprehend from South to North two degrees of latitude beginning to count from the completion of thirty one degrees North of the Equator: but any territory Northwardly of the 47th. degree shall make part of the state next below. And Eastwardly and Westwardly they shall be bounded, those on the Mississippi by that river on one side and the meridian of the lowest point of the rapids of Ohio on the other; and those adjoining on the East by the same meridian on their Western side, and on their Eastern by the meridian of the Western cape of the mouth of the Great Kanhaway.

And the territory Eastward of this last meridian between the Ohio, Lake Erie, and Pennsylvania shall be one state.

That the settlers within any of the said states shall, either on their own petition, or on the order of Congress, receive authority from them, with appointments of time and place for their free males of full age to meet together for the purpose of establishing a temporary government, to adopt the constitution and laws of any one of these states, so that such laws nevertheless shall be subject to alteration by their ordinary legislature, and to erect subject to a like alteration, counties or townships for the elections of members for their legislature.

That such temporary government shall only continue in force in any state until it shall have acquired 20,000. free inhabitants; when giving due proof thereof to Congress, they shall receive from them authority with appointments of time and place to call a Convention of representatives to establish a permanent constitution and government for themselves.

Provided that both the temporary and permanent governments be established on these principles as their basis. 1. That they shall for ever remain a part of the United states of America. 2. That in their persons, property and territory they shall be subject to the government of the United states in Congress assembled, and to the Articles of confederation in all those cases in which the original states shall be so subject. 3. That they shall be subject to pay a part of the federal debts contracted or to be contracted to be apportioned on them by Congress according to the same common rule and measure by which the apportionments thereof shall be made on the other states. 4. That their respective governments shall be in republican forms, and shall admit no person to be a citizen who holds any hereditary title. 5. That after the year 1800 of the Christian era, there shall be neither slavery nor involuntary servitude in any of the said states, otherwise than in punishment of crimes, whereof the party shall have been duly convicted to have been personally guilty.

That whensoever any of the states shall have, of free inhabitants, as many as shall than be in any one the least numerous of the thirteen original states, such state shall be admitted by its delegates into the Congress of the United states, on an equal footing with the said original states: after which the assent of two thirds of the United states in Congress assembled shall be requisite in all those cases, wherein by the Confederation, the assent of nine states is now required. Provided the consent of nine states to such admission may be obtained according to the eleventh of the articles of Confederation. Until such admission by their delegates into Congress, any of the said states, after the establishment of their temporary government, shall have authority to keep a sitting member in Congress, with a right of debating, but not of voting.

TO JAMES MADISON
OCTOBER 12, 1785

In this letter, Jefferson develops the argument that the frontier of the North American continent contributes to a nation of independent landholders.

The property of this country [France] is absolutely concentered in a very few hands, having revenues of from half a million of guineas a year downwards. These employ the flower of the country as servants, some of them having as many as 200 domestics, not labouring. They employ also a great number of manufacturers, and tradesmen, and lastly the class of labouring husbandmen. But after all these comes the most numerous of all the classes, that is, the poor who cannot find work. I asked myself what could be the reason that so many should be permitted to beg who are willing to work,

in a country where there is a very considerable proportion of uncultivated lands? These lands are kept idle mostly for the sake of game. It should seem that it must be because of the enormous wealth of the proprietors which places them above attention to the increase of their revenues by permitting these lands to be laboured. I am conscious that an equal division of property is impracticable. But the consequences of this enormous inequality producing so much misery to the bulk of mankind, legislators cannot invent too many devices for subdividing property, only taking care to let their subdivisions go hand in hand with the natural affections of the human mind. . . . It is clear that the laws of property have been so far extended as to violate natural right. The earth is given as a common stock for man to labour and live on. If, for the encouragement of industry we allow it to be appropriated, we must take care that other employment be furnished to those excluded from the appropriation. If we do not the fundamental right to labour the earth returns to the unemployed. It is too soon yet in our country to say that every man who cannot find employment but who can find uncultivated land, shall be at liberty to cultivate it, paying a moderate rent. But it is not too soon to provide by every possible means that as few as possible shall be without a little portion of land.

TO JOHN BANISTER, JR.
OCTOBER 15, 1785

Jefferson's letter makes it clear that he views a European education as decadent and decidedly inferior to the kind of education, suitable "for public life," one could acquire at his alma mater, William and Mary College.

But why send an American youth to Europe for education? What are the objects of an useful American education? Classical knowledge, modern languages and chiefly French, Spanish, and Italian; Mathematics; Natural philosophy; Natural History; Civil History; Ethics. In Natural philosophy I mean to include Chemistry and Agriculture, and in Natural history to include Botany as well as the other branches of those departments. It is true that the habit of speaking the modern languages cannot be so well acquired in America, but every other article can be as well acquired at William and Mary College as at any place in Europe. When College education is done with and a young man is to prepare himself for public life, he must cast his eyes (for America) either on Law or Physic. For the former where can he apply so advantageously as to Mr. Wythe? For the latter he must come to Europe; the medical class of students therefore is the only one which need come to Europe. Let us view the disadvantages of sending a youth to Europe. To enumerate them all would require a volume. I will select a few. If he goes to England he learns drinking, horse-racing and boxing. These are the peculiarities of English education. The following circumstances are common to education in that and the other countries of Europe. He acquires a fondness for European luxury and dissipation and a contempt for the simplicity of his own country; he is fascinated with the privileges of the European aristocrats, and sees with abhorrence the lovely equality which the poor enjoys with the rich in his own country: he contracts a partiality for aristocracy or monarchy; he forms foreign friendships which will never be useful to him, and loses the season of life for forming in his own country those friendships which of all others are the most faithful and permanent: he is led by the strongest of all the human passions into a spirit for female intrigue destructive of his own and others happiness, or a passion for whores destructive of his health, and in

both cases learns to consider fidelity to the marriage bed as an ungentlemanly practice and inconsistent with happiness: he recollects the voluptuary dress and arts of the European women and pities and despises the chaste affections and simplicity of those of his own country; he retains thro' life a fond recollection and a hankering after those places which were the scenes of his first pleasures and of his first connections; he returns to his own country, a foreigner, unacquainted with the practices of domestic economy necessary to preserve him from ruin. . . . It appears to me then that an American coming to Europe for education loses in his knowledge, in his morals, in his health, in his habits, and in his happiness. . . . Cast your eye over America: who are the men of most learning, of most eloquence, most beloved by their country and most trusted and promoted by them? They are those who have been educated among them, and whose manners, morals and habits are perfectly homogeneous with those of the country.

TO JAMES MADISON
JANUARY 20, 1787

Jefferson's faith in liberty is evident in this communication in which he applauds the spirit of Shays' Rebellion, a tax revolt in western Massachusetts.

I am impatient to learn your sentiments of the late troubles in the Eastern states [Shays' Rebellion]. So far as I have yet seen, they do not appear to threaten serious consequences. Those states have suffered by the stoppage of the channels of their commerce, which have not yet found other issues. This must render money scarce, and make the people uneasy. This uneasiness has produced acts absolutely unjustifiable: but I hope they will provoke no severities from their governments. A consciousness of those in power that their administration of the public affairs has been honest, may apprehend too much from these instances of irregularity. They may conclude too hastily that nature has formed man insusceptible of any other government but that of force, a conclusion not founded in truth, nor experience. Societies exist under three forms sufficiently distinguishable. 1. Without government, as among our Indians. 2. Under governments wherein the will of every one has a just influence, as is the case in England in a slight degree, and in our states in a great one. 3. Under governments of force: as is the case in all other monarchies and in most of the other republics. To have an idea of the curse of existence under these last, they must be seen. It is a government of wolves over sheep. It is a problem, not clear in my mind, that the 1st condition is not the best. But I believe it to be inconsistent with any great degree of population. The second state has a great deal of good in it. The mass of mankind under that enjoys a precious degree of liberty and happiness. It has it's evils too: the principal of which is the turbulence to which it is subject. But weigh this against the oppressions of monarchy, and it becomes nothing. *Malo Periculosam, libertatem quam quietam servitutem.* Even this evil is productive of good. It prevents the degeneracy of government, and nourishes a general attention to the public affairs. I hold it that a little rebellion now and then is a good thing, and as necessary in the political world as storms in the physical. Unsuccessful rebellions indeed generally establish the encroachments on the rights of the people which have produced them. An observation of this truth should render honest republican governors so mild in their punishment of rebellions, as not to discourage them too much. It is a medicine necessary for the sound health of government.

TO FRANCIS HOPKINSON
MARCH 13, 1789

In this letter, Jefferson makes clear both his support as well as criticism of the Constitution. He also declines to affiliate himself with a political party, but within two years would be the titular leader of the Republican faction.

You say that I have been dished up to you as an anti-federalist, and ask me if it be just. My opinion was never worthy enough of notice to merit citing: but since you ask it I will tell it you. I am not a Federalist, because I never submitted the whole system of my opinions to the creed of any party of men whatever in religion, in philosophy, in politics, or in any thing else where I was capable of thinking for myself. Such an addiction is the last degradation of a free and moral agent. If I could not go to heaven but with a party, I would not go there at all. Therefore I protest to you I am not of the party of federalists. But I am much farther from that of the Anti-federalists. I approved from the first moment, of the great mass of what is in the new constitution, the consolidation of the government, the organization into Executive, legislative and judiciary, the subdivision of the legislative, the happy compromise of interests between the great and little states by the different manner of voting in the different houses, the voting by persons instead of states, the qualified negative on laws given to the Executive which however I should have liked better if associated with the judiciary also as in New York, and the power of taxation. I thought at first that the latter might have been limited. A little reflection soon convinced me it ought not to be. What I disapproved from the first moment also was the want of a bill of rights to guard liberty against the legislative as well as executive branches of the government, that is to say secure freedom in religion, freedom of the press, freedom from monopolies, freedom from unlawful imprisonment, freedom from a permanent military, and a trial by jury in all cases determinable by the laws of the land. I disapproved also the perpetual reeligibility of the President. To these points of disapprobation I adhere. My first wish was that the 9. first conventions might accept the constitution, as the means of securing to us the great mass of good it contained, and that the 4. last might reject it, as the means of obtaining amendments. But I was corrected in this wish the moment I saw the much better plan of Massachusetts and which had never occurred to me. With respect of the declaration of rights I suppose the majority of the United states are of my opinion: for I apprehend all the antifederalists, and a very respectable proportion of the federalists think that such a declaration should now be annexed. The enlightened part of Europe have given us the greatest credit for inventing this instrument of security for the rights of the people, and have been not a little surprised to see us so soon give it up. With respect to the re-eligibility of the president, I find myself differing from the majority of my countrymen, for I think there are but three states of the 11. which have desired an alteration of this. And indeed, since the thing is established, I would wish it not to be altered during the life of our great leader, whose executive talents are superior to those I believe of any man in the world, and who alone by the authority of his name and the confidence reposed in his perfect integrity, is fully qualified to put the new government so under way as to secure it against the efforts of opposition. But having derived from our error all the good there was in it I hope we shall correct it the moment we can no longer have the same person at the helm. These, my dear friend, are my sentiments, by which you will see I was right in saying I am neither federalist nor antifederalist; that I am of neither party, nor yet a trimmer between parties.

TO JAMES MADISON
SEPTEMBER 6, 1789

In this famous letter, Jefferson developed the theory that "the earth belongs to the living" and thus future generations were not bound by their predecessors.

The question Whether one generation of men has a right to bind another, seems never to have been started either on this or our side of the water. Yet it is a question of such consequences as not only to merit decision, but place also, among the fundamental principles of every government. The course of reflection in which we are immersed here on the elementary principles of society has presented this question to my mind; and that no such obligation can be so transmitted I think very capable of proof.—I set out on this ground, which I suppose to be self evident, "that the earth belongs in usufruct to the living": that the dead have neither powers nor rights over it. The portion occupied by any individual ceases to be his when himself ceases to be, and reverts to the society. . . . I say the earth belongs to each of these generations, during this course, fully, and in their own right. The 2d. generation receives it clear of the debts and incumberances of the 1st. the 3d of the 2d. and so on. For if the 1st. could charge it with a debt, then the earth would belong to the dead and not the living generation. Then no generation can contract debts greater than may be paid during the course of its own existence. . . . On similar ground it may be proved that no society can make a perpetual constitution or even a perpetual law. The earth belongs always to the living generation. They may manage it then, and what proceeds from it, as they please, during their usufruct. They are masters too of their own persons, and consequently may govern them as they please. . . . Every constitution then, and every law, naturally expires at the end of 19 years [one generation]. If it be enforced longer, it is an act of force, and not of right.

RESPONSE TO THE CITIZENS OF ALBEMARLE
FEBRUARY 12, 1790

Jefferson delivered this address at Monticello, informing a group of local citizens of his decision to accept President Washington's invitation to serve as the nation's first secretary of state.

My feeble and obscure exertions in their service, and in the holy cause of freedom, have had no other merit than that they were my best. We have all the same. We have been fellow-labourers and fellow-sufferers, and heaven has rewarded us with a happy issue from our struggles. It rests now with ourselves alone to enjoy in peace and concord the blessings of self-government, so long denied to mankind: to shew by example the sufficiency of human reason for the care of human affairs and that the will of the majority, the Natural law of every society, is the only sure guardian of the rights of man. Perhaps even this may sometimes err. But its errors are honest, solitary and short-lived.—Let us then, my dear friends, for ever bow down to the general reason of the society. We are safe with that, even in its deviation, for it soon returns again to the right way. These are lessons we have learnt together. We have prospered in their practice, and the liberality with which you are pleased to approve my attachment to the general rights of mankind assures me we are still together in these its kindred sentiments.

Wherever I may be stationed, by the will of my country, it will be my delight to see, in the general tide of happiness, that yours too flows on in just place and measure. That it may flow thro' all times, gathering strength as it goes, and spreading the happy influence of reason and liberty over the face of the earth, is my fervent prayer to heaven.

TO THE PRESIDENT OF THE UNITED STATES (GEORGE WASHINGTON)
SEPTEMBER 9, 1792

In this powerful letter, Jefferson describes his conflict with Hamilton and his fear that corruption is stalking the newly formed republican government.

I now take the liberty of proceeding to that part of your letter wherein you notice the internal dissentions which have taken place within our government, & their disagreeable effect on its movements. That such dissentions have taken place is certain, & even among those who are nearest to you in the administration. To no one have they given deeper concern than myself: to no one equal mortification at being myself a part of them. . . . If it has been supposed that I have ever intrigued among the members of the legislatures to defeat the plans of the Secretary of the Treasury, it is contrary to all truth. As I never had the desire to influence the members, so neither had I any other means than my friendships, which I valued too highly to risk by usurpations on their freedom of judgment, & the conscientious pursuit of their own sense of duty. That I have utterly, in my private conversations, disapproved of the system of the Secretary of the treasury, I acknolege & avow: and this was not merely a speculative difference. His system flowed from principles adverse to liberty, & was calculated to undermine and demolish the republic, by creating an influence of his department over the members of the legislature. I saw this influence actually produced, & its first fruits to be the establishment of the great outlines of his project by the votes of the very persons who, having swallowed his bait were laying themselves out to profit by his plans: & that had these persons withdrawn, as those interested in a question ever should, the vote of the disinterested majority was clearly the reverse of what they made it. . . . In a Report on the subject of manufactures (still to be acted on) it was expressly assumed that the general government has a right to exercise all powers which may be for the *general welfare*, that is to say, all the legitimate powers of government: since no government has a legitimate right to do what is not the welfare of the governed. There was indeed a sham-limitation of the universality of this power *to cases where money is to be employed*. But about what is it that money cannot be employed? Thus the object of these plans taken together is to draw all the powers of government into the hands of the general legislature, to establish means for corrupting a sufficient corps in that legislature to divide the honest votes & to have that corps under the command of the Secretary of the Treasury for the purpose of subverting step by step the principles of the constitution, which he has so often declared to be a thing of nothing which must be changed.

To Phillip Mazzei
April 24, 1796

This letter, censorious of President George Washington and the administration he led, damaged Jefferson's reputation and caused him much embarrassment. Intended as a private correspondence, Jefferson's cogent critique of the Federalist party was published in European and American newspapers.

The aspect of our politics has wonderfully changed since you left us. In place of that noble love of liberty and republican government which carried us triumphantly through the war, an Anglican monarchical aristocratical party has sprung up, whose avowed object is to draw over us the substance, as they have already done the forms, of the British government. The main body of our citizens, however, remain true to their republican principles; the whole landed interest is republican, and so is a great mass of talents. Against us are the Executive, the Judiciary, two out of three branches of the Legislature, all the officers of the government, all who want to be officers, all timid men who prefer the calm of despotism to the boisterous sea of liberty, British merchants and Americans trading on British capital, speculators and holders in the banks and public funds, a contrivance invented for the purposes of corruption, and for assimilating us in all things to the rotten as well as the sound parts of the English model. It would give you a fever were I to name to you the apostates who have gone over to these heresies, men who were Samsons in the field and Solomons in the council, but who have had their heads shorn by the harlot England. In short, we are likely to preserve the liberty we have obtained only by unremiting labors and perils. But we shall preserve it; and our mass of weight and wealth on the good side is so great, as to leave no danger that force will ever be attempted against us. We have only to awake and snap the Lilliputian cords with which they have been entangling us during the first sleep which succeeded our labors.

The Kentucky Resolutions
October 1798

Jefferson composed the Kentucky Resolutions to protest the passage of the Alien and Sedition Acts, which infringed upon basic civil rights.

Resolved, that the several States composing the United States of America; are not united on the principle of unlimited submission of their General Government; but that, by a compact under the style and title of a Constitution for the United States, and of amendments thereto, they constituted a General Government for special purposes,—delegated to that government certain definite powers, reserving, each State to itself, the residuary mass of right to their own self-government; and that whensoever the General Government assumes undelegated powers, its acts are unauthoritative, void, and of no force: that to this compact each State acceded as a State, and is an integral party, its co-States forming, as to itself, the other party: that the government created by this compact was not made the exclusive or final judge of the extent of the powers delegated to itself; since that would have made its discretion, and not the Constitution, the measure of its powers; but that, as in all other cases of compact among powers having no common judge, each party has an equal right to judge for itself, as well of infractions as of the mode and measure of redress.

. . . . Resolved, that it is true as a general principle, and is also expressly declared by one of the amendments to the Constitution, that "the powers not delegated to the United States by the Constitution, nor prohibited by it to the States, are reserved to the States respectively, or to the people"; and that no power over the freedom of religion, freedom of speech, or freedom of the press being delegated to the United States by the Constitution, nor prohibited by it to the States, all lawful powers respecting the same did of right remain, and were reserved to the States or the people: that thus was manifested their determination to retain to themselves the right of judging how far the licentiousness of speech and of the press may be abridged without lessening thier useful freedom, and how far those abuses which cannot be separated from their use should be toler-

ated, rather than the use be destroyed. And thus also they guarded against all abridgment by the United States of the freedom of religious opinions and exercises, and retained to themselves the right of protecting the same, as this State, by a law passed on the general demand of its citizens, had already protected them from all human restraint or interference.

To Elbridge Gerry
January 26, 1799

Written in the form of a personal letter, Jefferson's communication with Gerry is actually a party platform, enunciating the principles that the soon-to-be presidential candidate held.

I shall make to you a profession of my political faith; in confidence that you will consider every future imputation on me of a contrary complexion, as bearing on its front the mark of falsehood & calumny.

I do then, with sincere zeal, wish an inviolable preservation of our present federal constitution, according to the true sense in which it was adopted by the States, that in which it was advocated by its friends, & not that which its enemies apprehended, who therefore became its enemies; and I am opposed to the monarchising its features by the formes of its administration, with a view to conciliate a first transition to a President & Senate for life, & from that to a hereditary tenure of these offices, & thus to worm out the elective principle. I am for preserving to the States the powers not yielded by them to the Union, & to the legislature of the Union it's constitutional share in the division of powers; and I am not for transferring all the powers of the States to the general government, & all those of that government to the Executive branch. I am for a government rigorously frugal & simple, applying all the possible savings of the public revenue to the discharge of the national debt; and not for a multiplication of officers & salaries merely to make partisans, & for increasing, by every device, the public debt, on the principle of it's being a public blessing. I am for relying, for internal defence, on our militia solely, till actual invasion, and for such a naval force only as may protect our coasts and harbors from such depredations as we have experienced; and not for a standing army in time of peace, which may overawe the public sentiment; nor for a navy, which, by its own expenses and the eternal wars in which it will implicate us, will grind us with public burthens, & sink us under them. I am for free commerce with all nations; political connection with none; & little or no diplomatic establishment. And I am not for linking ourselves by new treaties with the quarrels of Europe; entering that field of slaughter to preserve their balance, or joining in the confederacy of kings to war against the principles of liberty. I am for freedom of religion, & against all maneuvres to bring about a legal ascendancy of one sect over another: for freedom of the press & against all violations of the constitution to silence by force & not by reason the complaints or criticisms, just or unjust, of our citizens against the conduct of their agents. And I am for encouraging the progress of science in all its branches; and not for raising a hue and cry against the sacred name of philosophy; for awing the human mind by stories of raw-head & bloody bones to distrust of its own vision, & to repose implicitly on that of others, to go backwards instead of forwards to look for improvement; to believe that government, religion, morality, & every other science were in the highest perfection in ages of the darkest ignorance, and that nothing can ever be devised more perfect than what was established by our forefathers. To these I will add, that I was a sincere well-wisher to the success of the French revolution, and still wish it may end in the establishment of a free & well-ordered republic; but I have not been insensible under the atrocious depredations they have committed on our commerce. The first object of my heart is my own country. In that is embarked my family, my fortune, & my own existence. I have not one farthing of interest, nor one fibre of attachment out of it, nor a single motive of preference of any one nation to another, but in proportion as they are more or less friendly to us. But though deeply feeling the injuries of France, I did not think war the surest means of redressing them. I did believe, that a mission sincerely disposed to preserve peace, would obtain for us a peaceable & honorable settlement & retribution; and I appeal to you to say, whether this might not have been obtained, if either of your colleagues had been of the same sentiment with yourself.

These, my friend, are my principles; they are unquestionably the principles of the great body of our fellow citizens.

FIRST INAUGURAL ADDRESS
MARCH 4, 1801

In Jefferson's first inaugural, he condemned the party spirit that had marked the 1790s and called for unity around the country.

Friends and Fellow Citizens:
Called upon to undertake the duties of the first executive office of our country, I avail myself of the presence of that portion of my fellow citizens which is here assembled, to express my grateful thanks for the favor with which they have been pleased to look toward me, to declare a sincere consciousness that the task is above my talents, and that I approach it with those anxious and awful presentiments which the greatness of the charge and the weakness of my powers so justly inspire. . . . During the contest of opinion through which we have passed, the animation of discussion and the exertions

has sometimes worn an aspect which might impose on strangers unused to think freely and to speak and to write what they think; but this being now decided by the voice of the nation, announced according to the rules of the constitution, all will, of course, arrange themselves under the will of the law, and unite in common efforts for the common good. All, too, will bear in mind this sacred principle, that though the will of the majority is in all cases to prevail, that will, to be rightful, must be reasonable; that the minority possess their equal rights, which equal laws must protect and to violate which would be oppression. Let us, then, fellow citizens, unite with one heart and one mind. Let us restore to social intercourse that harmony and affection without which liberty and even life itself are but dreary things. And let us reflect that having banished from our land that religious intolerance under which mankind so long bled and suffered, we have yet gained little if we countenance a political intolerance as despotic, as wicked, and capable of as bitter and bloody persecutions. During the throes and convulsions of the ancient world, during the agonizing spasms of infuriated man, seeking through blood and slaughter his long-lost liberty, it was not wonderful that the agitation of the billows should reach even this distant and peaceful shore; that this should be more felt and feared by some and less by others; that this should divide opinions as to measures of safety. But every difference of opinion is not a difference of principle. We have called by different names brethren of the same principle. We are all republicans—we are all federalists. If there be any among us who would wish to dissolve this Union or to change its republican form, let them stand undisturbed as monuments of the safety with which error of opinion may be tolerated where reason is left free to combat it. I know, indeed, that some honest men fear that a republican government cannot be strong; that this government is not strong enough. But would the honest patriot, in the full tide of successful experiment, abandon a government which has so far kept us free and firm, on the theoretic and visionary fear that this government, the world's best hope, may by possibility want energy to preserve itself? I trust not. I believe this, on the contrary, the strongest government on earth. I believe it is the only one where every man, at the call of the laws, would fly to the standard of the law, and would meet invasions of the public order as his own personal concern. Sometimes it is said that man cannot be trusted with the government of himself. Can he, then, be trusted with the government of others? Or have we found angels in the forms of kings to govern him? Let history answer this question.

TO ROBERT R. LIVINGSTON
APRIL 18, 1802

The cession of the Louisiana Territory from Spain to France caused Jefferson much distress. A vigorous French presence in the West threatened the Virginian's "Empire of Liberty" and seemed to geographically hem in American ambitions on the continent. In this letter of instruction to Robert Livingston, American minister to France, Jefferson stressed the importance of U.S. occupation of Louisiana.

The cession of Louisiana and the Floridas by Spain to France works most sorely on the U.S. On this subject the Secretary of State has written to you fully. Yet I cannot forbear recurring to it personally, so deep is the impression it makes in my mind. It completely reverses all the political relations of the U.S. and will form a new epoch in our political course. Of all nations of any consideration France is the one which hitherto has offered the fewest points on which we could have any conflict of right, and the most points of a communion of interests. From these causes we have ever looked to her as our natural friend, as one with which we never could have an occasion of difference. Her growth therefore we viewed as our own, her misfortunes ours. There is on the globe one single spot, the possessor of which is our natural and habitual enemy. It is New Orleans, through which the produce of three-eighths of our territory must pass to market, and from its fertility it will ere long yield more than half of our whole produce and contain more than half our inhabitants. France placing herself in that door assumes to us the attitude of defiance. Spain might have retained it quietly for years. Her pacific dispositions, her feeble state, would induce her to increase our facilities there, so that her possession of the place would be hardly felt by us, and it might arise which might make the cession of it to us the price of something of more worth to her. Not so can it ever be in the hands of France. The impetuosity of her temper, the energy and restlessness of her character, placed in a point of eternal friction with us, and our character, which though quiet, and loving peace and the pursuit of wealth, is high-minded, despising wealth in competition with insult or injury, enter-prising and energetic as any nation on earth, these circumstances render it impos-sible that France and the U.S. can continue long friends when they meet in so irritable a position. They as well as we must be blind if they do not see this; and we must be very improvident if we do not begin to make arrangements on that hypothesis. The day that France takes possession of N. Orleans fixes that sentence which is to restrain her forever within her low water mark. It seals the union of two nations who in conjunc-tion can maintain exclusive possession of the ocean. From that movement we must marry ourselves to the British fleet and nation. We must turn all our attentions to a maritime force, for which our resources place us on very high grounds: and having

formed and cemented together a power which may render reinforcement of her settlements here impossible to France, make the first cannon, which shall be fired in Europe the signal for tearing up any settlement she may have made, and for holding the two continents of America in sequestration for the common purposes of the united British and American nations. This is not a state of things we seek or desire. It is one which this measure, if adopted by France, forces on us, as necessarily as any other cause, by the laws of nature, brings on its necessary effect. . . . Every eye in the U.S. is now fixed on this affair of Louisiana. Perhaps nothing since the revolutionary war has produced more uneasy sensations through the body of the nation.

TO DOCTOR BENJAMIN RUSH
APRIL 21, 1803

Though often described as an atheist, Jeffer-son had very definite views on Christianity, as this letter to Benjamin Rush attests.

In some of the delightful conversations with you, in the evenings of 1798–99 . . . the Christian religion was sometimes our topic; and I then promised you, that one day or other, I would give you my views of it. They are the result of a life of inquiry and reflection, and very different from that anti-Christian system imputed to me by those who know nothing of my opinions. To the corruptions of Christianity I am, indeed, opposed; but not to the genuine precepts of Jesus himself. I am a Christian, in the only sense in which he wished any one to be; sincerely attached to his doc-trines, in preference to all others; ascribing to himself every human *excellence*; and believing he never claimed any other. . . . I am . . . averse to the communication of my religious tenets to the public; because it would countenance the presumption of those who have endeavored to draw them before that tribunal, and to seduce public opinion to erect itself into that inquisition over the rights of conscience, which the laws have so justly proscribed. It behooves every man who values liberty of conscience for himself, to resist invasion of it in his own case, to give no example of concession, betraying the common right of independent opinion, by answering questions of faith, which the laws have left between God and himself. . . . Jesus appeared. His parentage was obscure; his condition poor; his education null; his natural endowments great; his life correct and innocent: he was meek benevolent, patient, firm disinterested, and of the sublimest eloquence. The disadvantages under which his doctrines appear are remarkable.

1. Like Socrates and Epictetus, he wrote nothing himself.

2. But he had not, like them, a Xenophon or an Arrian to write for him. I name not Plato, who only used the name of Socrates to cover the whimsies of his own brain. On the contrary, all the learned of his country, entrenched in its power and riches, were opposed to him, lest his labors should undermine their advantages; and the committing to writing his life and doctrines fell on unlettered and ignorant men; who wrote, too, from memory, and not till long after the transactions had passed.

3. According to the ordinary fate of those who attempt to enlighten and reform mankind, he fell an early victim to the jealousy and combination of the altar and the throne, at about thirty-three years of age, his reason having not yet attained the maximum of its energy, nor the course of his preaching, which was but of three years at most, presented occasions for developing a complete system of morals.

4. Hence the doctrines which he really delivered were defective as a whole, and fragments only of what he did deliver have come to us mutilated, misstated, and often unintelligible.

5. They have been still more disfigured by the corruptions of schismatizing followers, who have found an interest in sophisticating and perverting the simple doctrines he taught, by engrafting on them the mysticisms of a Grecian sophist, frittering them into subtleties, and obscuring them with jargon, until they have caused good men to reject the whole in disgust, and to view Jesus himself as an impostor.

Notwithstanding these disadvantages, a system of morals is presented to us, which, if filled up in the style and spirit of the rich fragments he left us, would be the most perfect and sublime that has ever been taught by man.

The question of his being a member of the Godhead, or in direct communication with it, claimed for him by some of his followers, and denied by others, is foreign to the present view, which is merely an estimate of the intrinsic merits of his doctrines.

TO JEAN BAPTISTE SAY
FEBRUARY 1, 1804

Jefferson relates to the Frenchman, Say, an argument for American exceptionalism, arguing that a "republican" political economy could flourish in the United States because of the favorable ratio of land to people.

The difference of circumstance between this and the old countries of Europe, furnish differences of fact whereon to reason, in questions of political economy, and will consequently produce sometimes a difference of result. There, for instance, the quantity of food is fixed, or increasing in a slow and only arithmetical ratio, and the proportion is limited by the same ratio. Supernumerary births consequently add only to your mortality. Here the immense extent of uncultivated and fertile lands enables every one who will labor, to marry young, and to raise a family of any size.

Our food, then, may increase geometrically with our laborers, and our births, however multiplied, become effective. Again, there the best distribution of labor is supposed to be that which places the manufacturing hands alongside the agricultural; so that the one part shall feed both, and the other part furnish both with clothes and other comforts. Would that be best here? Egoism and first appearances say yes. Or would it be better that all our laborers should be employed in agriculture? In this case a double or treble portion of fertile lands would be brought into culture; a double or treble creation of food be produced, and its surplus go to nourish the now perishing births of Europe, who in return would manufacture and send us in exchange our clothes and other comforts. Morality listens to this, and so invariably do the laws of nature create our duties and interests, that when they seem to be at variance, we ought to suspect some fallacy in our reasoning. In solving this question, too, we should allow its just weight to the moral and physical preference of the agricultural, over the manufacturing, man.

To Henri Gregoire
February 25, 1809

Jefferson's letter underlines his hope that slaves in the United States might one day reach "the grade of understanding" that will put them "on par" with whites. The letter also indicates, however, Jefferson's doubtfulness of such an outcome.

I have received the favor of your letter of August 17th, and with it the volume you were so kind as to send me on the "Literature of Negroes." Be assured that no person living wishes more sincerely than I do, to see a complete refutation of the doubts I have myself entertained and expressed on the grade of understanding alloted to them by nature, and to find that in this respect they are on a par with ourselves. My doubts were the result of personal observation on the limited sphere of my own State, where the opportunities for the development of their genius were not favorable, and those of exercising it still less so. I expressed them therefore with great hesitation; but whatever be their degree of talent it is no measure of their rights. Because Sir Isaac Newton was superior to others in understanding, he was not therefore lord of the person or property of others. On this subject they are gaining daily in the opinions of nations, and hopeful advances are making towards their re-establishment on an equal footing with the other colors of the human family. I pray you therefore to accept my thanks for the many instances you have enabled me to observe of respectable intelligence in that race of men, which cannot fail to have effect in hastening the day of their relief; and to be assured of the sentiments of high and just esteem and consideration which I tender to yourself with all sincerity.

To the Inhabitants of Albemarle Country, in Virginia
April 3, 1809

Within one month of retiring from the presidency and thus from public life, Jefferson returned home and wrote this address to acknowledge the formal congratulations extended to him by friends and neighbors.

Returning to the scenes of my birth and early life, to the society of those with whom I was raised, and who have been ever dear to me, I receive, fellow citizens and neighbors, with inexpressible pleasure, the cordial welcome you are so good as to give me. Long absent on duties which the history of a wonderful era made incumbent on those called to them, the pomp, the turmoil, the bustle and splendor of office, have drawn but deeper sighs for the tranquil and irresponsible occupations of private life, for the enjoyment of an affectionate intercourse with you, my neighbors and friends, and the endearments of family love, which nature has given us all, as the sweetener of every hour. For these I gladly lay down the distressing burthen of power, and seek, with my fellow citizens, repose and safety under the watchful cares, the labors, and perplexities of younger and abler minds. The anxieties you express to administer to my happiness, do, of themselves, confer that happiness; and the measure will be complete, if my endeavors to fulfill my duties in the several public stations to which I have been called, have obtained for me the approbation of my country. The part which I have acted on the theatre of public life, has been before them; and to their sentence I submit it; but the testimony of my native country, of the individuals who have known me in private life, to my conduct in its various duties and relations, is the more grateful, as proceeding from eye witnesses and observers, from triers of the vicinage. Of you, then, my neighbors, I may ask, in the face of the world, "whose ox have I taken, or whom have I defrauded? Whome have I oppressed, or of whose hand have I received a bribe to blind mine eyes therewith?" On your verdict I rest with conscious security. Your wishes for my happiness are received with just sensibility, and I offer sincere prayers for your own welfare and prosperity.

To Edward Coles
August 25, 1814

In one of his final statements on slavery, Jefferson wrote that he would not lead an anti-slavery crusade in Virginia because it would fail and cost him popularity in the process.

Mine [sentiments] of the subject of slavery of negroes have long since been in posses-

sion of the public, and time has only served to give them stronger root. The love of justice and the love of country plead equally the cause of these people, and it is a moral reproach to us that they should have pleaded it so long in vain, and should have produced not a single effort, nay I fear not much serious willingness to relieve them & ourselves from our present conditions of moral & political reprobation. From those of the former generation who were in the fullness of age when I came into public life, which was while our controversy with England was on paper only, I soon saw that nothing was to be hoped. Nursed and educated in the daily habit of seeing the degradation that was very much the work of themselves & their fathers, few minds have yet doubted but that they were as legitimate subjects of property as their horses and cattle. The quiet and monotonous course of colonial life has been disturbed by no alarm, and little reflection on the value of liberty. And when alarm was taken at an enterprize on their own, it was not easy to carry them to the whole length of the principles which they invoked for themselves. In the first or second session of the Legislature after I became a member, I drew to this subject the attention of Col. Bland, one of the oldest, ablest, & most respected members, and he undertook to move for certain moderate extensions of the protection of the laws to these people. I seconded his motion, and, as a younger member, was more spared in the debate; but he was denounced as an enemy of his country, & was treated with the grossest indecorum. From an early stage of our revolution other & more distant duties were assigned to me, so that from that time till my return from Europe in 1789, and I may say till I returned to reside at home in 1809, I had little opportunity of knowing the progress of public sentiment here on this subject. I had always hoped that the younger generation receiving their early impressions after the flame of liberty had been kindled in every breast, & had become as it were the vital spirit of every American, that the generous temperament of youth, analogous to the motion of their blood, and above the suggestions of avarice, would have sympathized with oppression wherever found, and proved their love of liberty beyond their own share of it. But my intercourse with them, since my return has not been sufficient to ascertain that they had made towards this point the progress I had hoped. Your solitary but welcome voice . . . first . . . brought this sound to my ear; and I have considered the general silence which prevails on this subject as indicating an apathy unfavorable to every hope. Yet the hour of emancipation is advancing, in the march of time it will come; and whether brought on by the generous energy of our own minds; or by the bloody process of St Domingo, excited and conducted by the power of our present enemy, if one stationed permanently within our Country, and offering asylum & arms to the oppressed, is a leaf of our history not yet turned over. . . . My opinion has ever been that, until more can be done for them, we should endeavor, with those whom fortune has thrown on our hands, to feed and clothe them well, protect them from all ill usage, require such reasonable labor only as is performed voluntarily by freemen, & be led by no repugnancies to abdicate them, and our duties to them. The laws do not permit us to turn them loose, if that were for their good: and to commute them for other property is to commit them to those whose usage of them we cannot control. I hope then, my dear sir, you will reconcile yourself to your country and its unfortunate condition.

To Benjamin Austin
January 9, 1816

In this correspondence, Jefferson calls for the development of an industrial base in America

and thus an increase in the powers and prerogatives of the central government. This seeming refutation of Jefferson's states' rights philosophy was spurred by America's weak showing in the War of 1812. At the conclusion of the conflict, Jefferson presumed that only a strong nation could combat European incursions on American liberties.

You tell me I am quoted by those who wish to continue our dependence on England for manufactures. There was a time when I might have been so quoted with more candor, but within the thirty years which Have since elapsed, are circumstances changed! We were then in peace. Our independent place among nations was acknowledged. A commerce which offered the raw material in exchange for the same material after receiving the last touch of industry, was worthy of welcome to all nations. It was expected that those especially to whom manufacturing industry was important, would cherish the friendship of such customers by every favor, by every inducement, and particularly cultivate their peace by every act of justice and friendship. Under this prospect the question seemed legitimate, whether, with such an immensity of unimproved land, courting the hand of husbandry, the industry of agriculture, or that of manufactures, would add most to the national wealth? And the doubt was entertained on this consideration chiefly, that to the labor of the husbandman a vast addition is made by the spontaneous energies of the earth on which it is employed: for one grain of wheat committed to the earth, she renders twenty, thirty, and even fifty fold, whereas to the labor of the manufacturer nothing is added. Pounds of flax, in his hands, yield, on the contrary, but pennyweights of lace. This exchange, too, laborious as it might seem, what a field did it promise for the occupations of the ocean; what a nursery for that class of citizens who were to exercise and maintain our equal rights on that element? This was the state of things in 1785, when the "Notes on Virginia" were first printed; when, the ocean being open to all nations, and their common right in it acknowledged and exercised under regulations sanctioned by the assent and usage of all, it was thought that the doubt might claim some consideration. But who in 1785 could forsee the rapid depravity which was to render the close of that century the disgrace of the history of man? Who could have imagined that the two most distinguished in the rank of nations, for science and civilization, would have suddenly descended from that honorable eminence, and setting at defiance all those moral laws established by the Author of nature between nation and nation, as between man and man, would cover earth and sea with robberies and piracies, merely because strong enough to do it with temporal impunity; and that under this disbandment of nations from social order, we should have been despoiled of a thousand ships, and have thousands of our citizens reduced to Algerine slavery. Yet all this has taken place. . . . We have experienced what we did not then believe, that there exist both profligacy and power enough to exclude us from the field of interchange with other nations: that to be independent for the comforts of life we must fabricate them ourselves. We must now place the manufacturer by the side of the agriculturist. The former question is suppressed, or rather assumes a new form. Shall we make our own comforts, or go without them, at the will of a foreign nation? He, therefore, who is now against domestic manufacture, must be for reducing us either to dependence on that foreign nation, or to be clothed in skins, and to live like wild beasts in dens and caverns. I am not one of these; experience has taught me that manufactures are now as necessary to

our independence as to our comfort; and if those who quote me as of a different opinion, will keep pace with me in purchasing nothing foreign where an equivalent of domestic fabric can be obtained, without regard to difference of price, it will not be our fault if we do not soon have a supply at home equal to our demand, and wrest that weapon of distress from the hand which has wielded it.

To Roger C. Weightman
June 24, 1826

This is Jefferson's final letter and a fitting testimony to his lifelong belief in human progress.

Our fellow citizens, after half a century of experience and prosperity, continue to approve the choice we made [independence from Britain]. May it be to the world, what I believe it will be, (to some parts sooner, to others later, but finally to all,) the signal of arousing men to burst the chains under which monkish ignorance and superstition had persuaded them to bind themselves, and to assume the blessings and security of self-government. That form which we have substituted, restores the free right to the unbounded exercise of reason and freedom of opinion. All eyes are opened, or opening, to the rights of man. The general spread of the light of science has already lain open to every view the palpable truth, that the mass of mankind has not been born with saddles on their backs, nor a favored few booted and spurred, ready to ride them legitimately, by the grace of God. These are grounds of hope for others. For ourselves, let the annual return of this day forever refresh our recollections of these rights, and an undiminished devotion to them. . . .

CHRONOLOGY

1743   TJ born at Shadwell, Virginia.

1757   Peter Jefferson, TJ's father, dies.

1760–   TJ attends the College of William
1762   and Mary.

1767   TJ admitted to the Virginia bar.

1769   TJ elected to the House of Burgesses.

1772   TJ marries Martha Wayles Skelton.

       Birth of daughter Martha.

1774   TJ writes "A Summary View of the
Rights of British America."

       Birth of daughter Jane.

1775   Member of Continental Congress.

       Death of daughter Jane.

1776   TJ writes the Declaration of Independence.

       Death of Jane Randolph Jefferson, TJ's mother.

       TJ elected to the Virginia legislature.

1777   Birth and death of son (no name given).

1778   Birth of daughter Mary.

1779–   TJ serves as governor of
1781   Virginia.

1780   Birth of daughter Lucy.

1781   The former colonies' victory at Yorktown concludes the American Revolution.

       Death of daughter Lucy.

1782   Birth of daughter Lucy (named for the child that died the previous year).

       Death of TJ's wife, Martha Wayles Skelton Jefferson.

1783–   TJ serves in the Continental
1784   Congress.

1784   TJ arrives in Paris with daughter Martha.

       Death of daughter Lucy.

1785   TJ succeeds Benjamin Franklin as minister to the French court.

1786   TJ arrives in London to discuss American foreign policy with John Adams.

       TJ draws designs for the Virginia capitol building based on the Maison Carrée at Nîmes.

       TJ sprains wrist while courting Maria Cosway.

       TJ writes his "My Head and My Heart" letter to Maria Cosway.

1787   Shays' Rebellion occurs in Massachusetts.

       TJ tours southern France.

       TJ is elected minister to France for three more years.

       TJ writes to James Madison supporting the newly written Constitution.

1788   TJ arrives in the Netherlands to join John Adams in negotiating a financial agreement.

TJ tours the Rhine region.

The first elections under the new American Constitution are held.

1789 George Washington inaugurated as the nation's first president.

TJ present at the opening of the Estates General.

TJ sends Lafayette a proposed charter for France.

The storming of the Bastille.

The French Declaration of Rights is adopted. Leaders of the patriot party dine frequently with Jefferson.

TJ receives permission to return home on leave.

TJ is appointed to serve as the nation's first secretary of state.

Alexander Hamilton is appointed to serve as the nation's first secretary of the treasury.

1790 Hamilton presents Congress his first "Report on the Public Credit."

James Madison opposes Hamilton's funding proposals.

Martha Jefferson weds Thomas Mann Randolph, Jr.

Hamilton's assumption bill is defeated in the House.

TJ, Madison, and Hamilton reach a bargain on the assumption bill.

TJ drafts a war policy in case of conflict with Great Britain and Spain over the Nootka Sound affair.

TJ submits his "Report on Coinage, Weights, and Measures."

Hamilton presents his second "Report on the Public Credit" to Congress.

1791 TJ submitts a report on the cod and whale fisheries to Congress.

TJ writes a report to Washington rendering his opinion that Hamilton's national banking bill is unconstitutional.

Washington signs the national banking bill into law.

The Jeffersonian–Madisonian movement for commercial discrimination against the British is checked in Congress.

TJ and James Madison go on a "botanizing" trip to Albany in order to form a political axis with Republicans in New York.

TJ appoints Philip Freneau as a translator in the State Department. Freneau, a noted poet, uses his position to start up a pro-Jeffersonian newspaper, the *National Gazette,* which attacks the Hamiltonians.

General St. Clair's army is defeated by Native Americans in the Northwest.

Hamilton presents his "Report on Manufactures" to the House.

1792 TJ decides to retire from office at the end of Washington's first term.

Attack on Hamilton's financial dealings is narrowly defeated.

Washington consults Madison about a farewell address. Jefferson urges Washington to continue in office for another term.

Washington communicates to Jefferson and Hamilton that their newspaper war must end.

The powers of the French king are suspended and the French republic created.

Washington is unanimously reelected president.

1793 TJ is reelected vice president of the American Philosophical Society.

French declaration of war against England and Holland.

Citizen Genet arrives in the United States and attempts to ally America with revolutionary France.

Washington issues a neutrality proclamation concerning the war in Europe.

The Democratic Society of Pennsylvania is founded.

Genet threatens to appeal to the American people if the Washington administration will not aid France's war effort.

Genet recalled to France. Because he fears for his life, the former minister is allowed to stay in the United States.

TJ resigns as secretary of state.

1794   TJ's nailery at Monticello begins production.

John Jay sails on his mission to England.

TJ declines the offer to head a special mission to Spain.

The Whiskey Rebellion is put down in western Pennsylvania.

Washington criticizes the Democratic societies in an address to Congress.

1795   Jay's Treaty is approved by the Senate.

Edmund Randolph resigns as secretary of state.

The Virginia General Assembly condemns Jay's Treaty.

1796   Pinckney's Treaty with Spain is approved by the Senate.

TJ writes a private letter to Philip Mazzei in which he is critical of Washington.

Washington writes to Jefferson; it is the last communication between the two men.

A threshing machine built at Monticello begins to work.

Washington's farewell address is published.

TJ's first grandchild, Ellen Wayles Randolph, is born at Monticello.

TJ finishes second to John Adams in the presidential contest. He is thus elected to the vice presidency.

1797   TJ is made president of the American Philosophical Society.

TJ inagurated as the nation's second vice president.

TJ assumes leadership of the Democratic-Republican party.

Adams sends an American mission to negotiate with France.

TJ purchases James Callender's *History of the United States for 1796.*

1798   Adams reports on the failure of the American mission to France and asks for defense measures. Jefferson is highly critical of Adams.

The Alien and Sedition Acts are approved in Congress.

Several Virginia counties protest the Alien and Sedition Acts.

TJ writes the Kentucky Resolutions, which, after modification, are adopted by the Kentucky Legislature.

1799   Fries' rebellion in Pennsylvania protests Federalist tax policies.

Adams breaks with members of his own party by ordering the departure of American commissioners to seek peace with France.

Washington dies at Mount Vernon.

1800   The Federalist caucus agrees to support Adams for the presidency and C. C. Pinckney for the office of vice president.

The Republican caucus agrees to support Jefferson for the presidency and Aaron Burr for the office of vice president.

TJ defends himself from clerical attacks that accuse him of being an atheist.

TJ and Burr receive the same number of electoral votes in the presidential contest.

1801   TJ is elected to the presidency over Burr on the thirty-sixth House ballot.

TJ delivers his farewell address to the Senate.

John Marshall is appointed chief justice of the Supreme Court by outgoing president Adams.

1801
cont.
Lame-duck Federalist Congress passes the Judiciary Act of 1801.

TJ is inaugurated as the nation's third president.

Albert Gallatin is appointed secretary of the treasury.

TJ learns of the cession of Louisiana to France by Spain.

Tripoli declares war on the United States. An American naval squadron is dispatched to the Mediterranean.

A peace agreement is signed by Britain and France.

TJ sends his first annual message to Congress.

1802   Convention with Great Britain is signed.

Judiciary Act of 1801 is repealed.

Internal taxes are repealed.

A convention to form a constitution for the new state of Ohio is authorized by Congress.

James Callender accuses Jefferson of carrying on a sexual liaison with his slave, Sally Hemings.

Morocco declares war on the United States.

The Deposit of New Orleans is closed to American commerce.

1803   TJ sends James Monroe to France to purchase the point of deposit at New Orleans.

Ohio is admitted to the Union.

TJ writes a syllabus concerning the doctrines of Jesus.

Treaty with France for the cession of Louisiana to the United States is signed in Paris.

Resumption of the European war.

The United States takes possession of Louisiana.

1804   Jefferson announces that he will stand for reelection.

Judge John Pickering impeached.

TJ's daughter, Mary Jefferson Eppes, dies at Monticello.

Essex Junto discusses separation of New England from the Union.

Burr is defeated in gubernatorial campaign in New York.

Burr-Hamilton duel takes place in New Jersey.

Twelfth Amendment is ratified.

TJ is reelected president.

1805   Debate on Yazoo land claims in the House.

Justice Samuel Chase, on trial under articles of impeachment drawn up in the House, is acquitted by the Senate.

Vice President Burr leaves office.

TJ is inaugurated president.

TJ appoints James Wilkinson governor of the Territory of Louisiana.

Aaron Burr tours the West.

TJ receives reports from Lewis and Clark on their journey through the West.

A peace treaty with Tripoli is concluded.

Under the *Essex* decision, American ships are seized by the British.

The British defeat the French at the battle of Trafalgar.

Napoleon defeats a Russo-Austrian army at Austerlitz.

1806   The $2 million bill to provide a financial settlement to France in return for aiding America's attempt to purchase Florida from Spain passes the House and Senate.

John Randolph breaks with the Jefferson administration.

An act authorizing the Cumberland Road is approved.

TJ approves the non-importation bill.

Captain Zebulon M. Pike commences an expedition to the Southwest.

Napoleon issues the Berlin decree, inaugurating his Continental System.

TJ orders Burr arrested for attempting to sever the West from the United States. Burr is captured and taken to Richmond to stand trial for treason.

Lewis and Clark return from their western expedition.

The Monroe-Pinckney treaty is signed in England.

1807 British Orders in Council forbid neutral ships to trade in ports closed to the British.

An act prohibiting the importation of slaves after January 1, 1808, is approved.

TJ is served a subpoena to testify in the trial of Burr. Jefferson refuses to comply with the order.

The British warship *Leopard* fires on the frigate *Chesapeake*.

Burr is acquitted of treason.

Britain declares that a policy of vigorous impressment will be employed in its war against France.

British Orders in Council declare a blockade of the European continent.

TJ declares he will not serve a third term as president.

TJ's Non-Importation Act takes effect.

Napoleon issues his Milan decree.

Congress authorizes 188 gunboats for the American navy.

1808 A Republican congressional caucus nominates Madison for president and George Clinton for vice president.

TJ issues a proclamation calling for enforcement of the embargo at Lake Champlain, an area notorious for its smuggling.

TJ replies to petitions from New England towns that oppose the embargo.

Madison is elected president.

1809 TJ signs the embargo enforcement bill.

TJ signs an act to end the embargo.

Madison is inaugurated as the nation's fourth president.

TJ leaves Washington for Monticello.

TJ visits Richmond.

1811 TJ becomes a great-grandfather.

TJ begins the manufacturing of cloth at Monticello.

1812 TJ and John Adams renew correspondence after a 12-year break.

War with Great Britain is declared.

1814 TJ is named a trustee of Albemarle Academy.

TJ writes Edward Coles that the emancipation of slaves is inevitable but refuses to take a leadership role in the abolitionist movement.

After the Library of Congress is burned by the British, Jefferson offers to sell his library to Congress to replace the old collection.

1815 The Treaty of Ghent ends the War of 1812.

TJ sells his library to Congress.

TJ gives up the daily management of his Albemarle farms.

1816 TJ is named a Visitor of Central College.

1817 James Monroe is inaugurated as the nation's fifth president.

TJ travels to the Natural Bridge in Virginia with his granddaughters.

The cornerstone of the first pavilion at Central College is laid.

1818 TJ completes his weather records.

The Virginia legislature passes a bill for the establishment of a university.

TJ cancels newspaper subscriptions to all but the *Richmond Enquirer.*

1819   TJ is elected rector at the first meeting of the University of Virginia Board of Visitors.

A financial panic causes a massive economic downturn around the country.

The Missouri crisis threatens the Union.

1821   TJ gives up management of his farms at Poplar Forest.

1822   TJ breaks his left arm.

1823   TJ makes his last trip to Poplar Forest.

The Monroe Doctrine is presented.

1824   TJ sees Lafayette for the final time.

John Quincy Adams is elected president.

1825   The University of Virginia opens.

1826   TJ promotes a lottery to alleviate his personal indebtedness.

TJ executes his will.

TJ and John Adams die on July 4, the fiftieth anniversary of the Declaration of Independence.

BIBLIOGRAPHY

Abernathy, Thomas. 1954. *The Burr Conspiracy*. New York: Oxford University Press.

Adams, Henry. 1882. *John Randolph by Henry Adams*. New York: Houghton, Mifflin.

Adams, Herbert B. 1887. *The College of William and Mary*. Washington, DC: Government Print Office.

Ahlstrom, Sydney. 1972. *A Religious History of the American People*. New Haven, CT: Yale University Press.

Ambler, Charles. 1913. *Thomas Ritchie: A Study in Virginia Politics*. Richmond, VA: Bell Hook and Stationary.

Ambrose, Stephen. 1996. *Undaunted Courage: Meriwether Lewis, Thomas Jefferson, and the Opening of the American West*. New York: Simon & Schuster.

Ammon, Harry. 1971. *James Monroe: The Quest for National Identity*. New York: McGraw-Hill.

———. 1973. *The Genet Mission*. W.W. Norton.

Appleby, Joyce O. 1978. *Economic Thought and Ideology in Seventeenth Century England*. Princeton, NJ: Princeton University Press.

———. 1984. *Capitalism and a New Social Order: The Republican Vision of the 1790s*. New York: New York University Press.

———. 1992. *Liberalism and Republicanism in the Historical Imagination*. Cambridge, MA: Harvard University Press.

Banner, James. 1969. *To the Hartford Convention: The Federalists and the Origins of Party Politics in Massachusetts, 1789–1815*. New York: Alfred A. Knopf.

Banning, Lance. 1978. *The Jeffersonian Persuasion: Evolution of a Party Ideology*. Ithaca, NY: Cornell University Press.

Bear, James. 1967. *Jefferson at Monticello: Recollections of a Monticello Slave and a Monticello Overseer*. Charlottesville: University Press of Virginia.

Beard, Charles. 1915. *Economic Origins of Jeffersonian Democracy*. New York: Macmillan.

Becker, Carl L. 1958. *The Declaration of Independence: A Study in the History of Political Ideas*. New York: Random House.

Beitzinger, Alfons J. 1972. *A History of American Political Thought*. New York: Dodd, Mead.

Bemis, Samuel Flagg. 1923. *Jay's Treaty, a Study in Commerce and Diplomacy*. New York: Macmillan.

———. 1926. *Pinckney's Treaty: A Study of America's Advantage from Europe's Distress, 1783–1800*. Baltimore, MD: Johns Hopkins Press.

————. 1949. *John Quincy Adams and the Foundations of American Foreign Policy*. New York: Alfred A. Knopf.

Blackburn, Joyce. 1975. *George Wythe of Williamsburg*. New York: Harper & Row.

Boorstin, Daniel. 1948. *The Lost World of Thomas Jefferson*. Chicago, IL: University of Chicago Press.

Bowen, Catherine Drinker. 1966. *Miracle at Philadelphia: The Story of the Constitutional Convention, May to September 1787*. Boston, MA: Little, Brown.

Boyd, Julian P., ed. 1945. *The Declaration of Independence: The Evolution of the Text*. Princeton, NJ: Princeton University Press.

————. 1964. *Number 7: Alexander Hamilton's Secret Attempts to Control American Foreign Policy, with Supporting Documents*. Princeton, NJ: Princeton University Press.

Brant, Irving. 1970. *The Fourth President: A Life of James Madison*. Indianapolis, IN: Bobbs-Merrill.

Breen, T. H. 1985. *Tobacco Culture: The Mentality of the Great Tidewater Planters on the Eve of Revolution*. Princeton, NJ: Princeton University Press.

Brewer, John. 1988. *The Sinews of Power: War, Money, and the English State, 1688–1783*. New York: Alfred A. Knopf.

Brookhiser, Richard. 1997. *Founding Father: Rediscovering George Washington*. New York: Free Press Paperbacks.

Brown, Ralph. 1975. *The Presidency of John Adams*. Lawrence: University Press of Kansas.

Brown, Richard. 1966. "The Missouri Crisis, Slavery, and the Politics of Jacksonianism." *South Atlantic Quarterly* 65 (Winter): 55–72.

Brown, Roger. 1964. *The Republic in Peril: 1812*. New York: Columbia University Press.

Buel, Richard, Jr. 1972. *Securing the Revolution: Ideology in American Politics, 1789–1815*. Ithaca, NY: Cornell University Press.

Bullock, Helen Claire Duprey. 1945. *My Head and My Heart: A Little History of Thomas Jefferson and Maria Cosway*. New York: G.P. Putnam's Sons.

Burstein, Andrew. 1995. *The Inner Jefferson: Portrait of a Grieving Optimist*. Charlottesville: University Press of Virginia.

Carpenter, William. 1930. *The Development of American Political Thought*. Princeton, NJ: Princeton University Press.

Chambers, William, and Walter Burnham, eds. 1967. *The American Party Systems: Stages of Development*. New York: Oxford University Press.

Chaudhuri, Joyotpaul, ed. 1977. *The Non-Lockean Roots of American Democratic Thought*. Tucson: University of Arizona Press.

Chinard, Gilbert. 1929. *Thomas Jefferson: The Apostle of Americanism*. Boston, MA: Little, Brown.

————, ed. 1926. *The Commonplace Book of Thomas Jefferson: A Repertory of His Ideas on Government*. Baltimore, MD: Johns Hopkins Press.

Clarfield, Gerard. 1980. *Timothy Pickering and the American Republic*. Pittsburgh, PA: University of Pittsburgh Press.

Conlin, Paul K. 1974. *Self-Evident Truths: Being a Discourse on the Origins and Development of the First Principles of American Government*. Bloomington: Indiana University Press.

Countryman, Edward. 1985. *The American Revolution*. New York: Hill and Wang.

Cousins, Norman, ed. 1958. *In God We Trust: The Religious Beliefs and Ideas of the American Founding Fathers*. New York: Harper & Row.

Cripe, Helen. 1974. *Thomas Jefferson and Music*. Charlottesville: University Press of Virginia.

Cruise, Conor. 1996. *The Long Affair: Thomas Jefferson and the French Revolution*. Chicago, IL: University of Chicago Press.

Cunningham, Noble. 1963. *The Jeffersonian Republicans in Power: Party Operations, 1801–1809*. Chapel Hill: University of North Carolina Press.

———. 1996. *The Presidency of James Monroe*. Lawrence: University Press of Kansas.

———, ed. 1968. *The Early Republic, 1789–1828*. Columbia: University of South Carolina Press.

Dabney, Virginius. 1981. *The Jefferson Scandals*. New York: Madison Books.

Dangerfield, George. 1952. *The Era of Good Feelings*. New York: Harcourt, Brace & World.

———. 1965. *The Awakening of American Nationalism, 1815–1828*. New York: Harper & Row.

Dargo, George. 1975. *Jefferson's Louisiana: Politics and the Clash of Legal Traditions*. Cambridge, MA: Harvard University Press.

Davis, David Brion. 1975. *The Problem of Slavery in the Age of Revolution*. Ithaca, NY: Cornell University Press.

Davis, Richard Beale. 1964. *Intellectual Life in Jefferson's Virginia, 1790–1830*. Chapel Hill: University of North Carolina Press.

De Conde, Alexander. 1966. *The Quasi-War: The Politics and Diplomacy of the Undeclared War with France, 1797–1801*. New York: Scribner.

———. 1976. *This Affair of Louisiana*. New York: Scribner.

D'Elia, Donald. 1974. *Benjamin Rush: Philosopher of the American Revolution*. Philadelphia, PA: Transactions of the American Philosophical Society.

Du Bois, W. E. B. 1904. *The Suppression of the African Slave Trade*. New York: Longmans, Green.

Dumbauld, Edward. 1978. *Thomas Jefferson and the Law*. Norman: University of Oklahoma Press.

Edmunds, R David. 1984. *Tecumseh and the Quest for Indian Leadership*. Boston, MA: Little, Brown.

Egerton, Douglas. 1993. *Gabriel's Rebellion: The Virginia Slave Conspiracies of 1800 and 1802*. Chapel Hill: University of North Carolina Press.

Eidelberg, Paul. 1976. *On the Silence of the Declaration of Independence*. Amherst: University of Masachusetts Press.

Elkins, Stanley, and Eric McKitrick. 1993. *The Age of Federalism: The Early American Republic, 1788–1800*. New York: Oxford University Press.

Ellis, Joseph. 1979. *After the Revolution: Profiles in Early American Culture*. New York: W. W. Norton.

———. 1997. *American Sphinx: The Character of Thomas Jefferson*. New York: Oxford University Press.

Ellis, Richard. 1971. *The Jeffersonian Crisis: Courts and Politics in the Young Republic*. New York: Oxford University Press.

Ferguson, Adam. 1966. *An Essay on the History of Civil Society, 1767*. Edinburgh: Edinburgh University Press.

Field, James. 1969. *America and the Mediterranean World: 1776–1882*. Princeton, NJ: Princeton University Press.

Fischer, David Hackett. 1965. *The Revolution of American Conservatism*. New York: Harper & Row.

Flexner, James Thomas. 1969. *Washington: The Indispensable Man*. Boston, MA: Little, Brown.

Foner, Eric. 1977. *Thomas Paine and Revolutionary America*. New York: Oxford University Press.

Fredrickson, George M. 1971. *The Black Image in the White Mind: The Debate on Afro-American Character and Destiny, 1817–1914*. New York: Harper & Row.

Frisch, Morton, ed. 1985. *Selected Writings and Speeches of Alexander Hamilton.* Washington, DC: American Enterprise Institute for Public Policy Research.

Garlick, Richard. 1933. *Philip Mazzei, Friend of Jefferson: His Life and Letters.* Baltimore, MD: Johns Hopkins University Press.

Gay, Peter. 1966–1969. *The Enlightenment, an Interpretation.* 2 vols. New York: Alfred A. Knopf.

Gordon-Reed, Annette. 1997. *Thomas Jefferson and Sally Hemings: An American Controversy.* Charlottesville: University Press of Virginia.

Hammond, Bray. 1957. *Banks and Politics in America from the Revolution to the Civil War.* Princeton, NJ: Princeton University Press.

Hart, Michael. 1992. *The 100: A Ranking of the Most Influential Persons in History.* Secaucus, NJ: Carol.

Hartz, Louis. 1955. *The Liberal Tradition in America: An Interpretation of American Political Thought since the Revolution.* New York: Harcourt, Brace.

Healy, Robert M. 1962. *Jefferson on Religion in Public Education.* New Haven, CT: Yale University Press.

Hickey, Donald. 1989. *The War of 1812: A Forgotten Conflict.* Urbana: University of Illinois Press.

Hofstadter, Richard. 1948. *The American Political Tradition and the Men Who Made It.* New York: Alfred A. Knopf.

———. 1969. *The Idea of a Party System: The Rise of Legitimate Opposition in the United States, 1780–1840.* Berkeley: University of California Press.

Honeywell, Roy J. 1931. *The Educational Work of Thomas Jefferson.* Cambridge, MA: Harvard University Press.

Horsman, Reginald. 1962. *The Causes of the War of 1812.* Philadelphia: University of Pennsylvania Press.

———. 1985. *The Diplomacy of the New Republic, 1776–1815.* Arlington Heights, IL: Harlan Davidson.

Hunt, Michael. 1987. *Ideology and U.S. Foreign Policy.* New Haven, CT: Yale University Press.

Jefferson, Thomas. 1903–1904. *The Writings of Thomas Jefferson.* Washington, DC: Thomas Jefferson Memorial Association.

———. 1904. *The Works of Thomas Jefferson.* New York: Knickerbocker Press.

———. 1950. *The Papers of Thomas Jefferson.* Princeton, NJ: Princeton University Press.

———. 1972. *Notes on the State of Virginia.* New York: W. W. Norton.

Jordan, Winthrop. 1968. *White over Black: American Attitudes toward the Negro, 1550–1812.* Chapel Hill: University of North Carolina Press.

Kaplan, Lawrence S. 1967. *Jefferson and France: An Essay on Politics and Political Ideas.* New Haven, CT: Yale University Press.

Ketcham, Ralph, ed. 1986. *The Anti-Federalist Papers and the Constitutional Convention Debates.* New York: Mentor.

Koch, Adrian. 1950. *Jefferson and Madison: The Great Collaboration.* New York: Alfred A. Knopf.

———. 1964. *The Philosophy of Thomas Jefferson.* Chicago, IL: Quadrangle Books.

Kramnick, Isaac. 1968. *Bolingbroke and His Circle: The Politics of Nostalgia in the Age of Walpole.* Cambridge, MA: Harvard University Press.

———. 1990. *Republicanism and Bourgeois Radicalism: Political Ideology in Late Eighteenth-Century England and America.* Ithaca, NY: Cornell University Press.

Leary, Lewis. 1941. *That Rascal Freneau: A Study in Literary Failure.* New Brunswick, NJ: Rutgers University Press.

Levy, Leonard. 1963. *Jefferson and Civil Liberties: The Darker Side.* Cambridge, MA: Harvard University Press.

Lewis, David. 1976. *District of Columbia: A Bicentennial History*. New York: W.W. Norton.

Lewis, R.W.B. 1955. *The American Adam: Innocence, Tragedy, and Tradition in the Nineteenth Century*. Chicago, IL: University of Chicago Press.

Link, Eugene P. 1942. *Democratic-Republican Societies, 1790–1800*. New York: Columbia University Press.

Locke, John. 1993. *Two Treatises of Government*. London: Everyman.

Lovejoy, Arthur O. 1891. *Reflections on Human Nature*. Baltimore, MD: Johns Hopkins Press.

Mace, George. 1979. *Locke, Hobbes, and the Federalist Papers: An Essay on the Genesis of the American Political Heritage*. Carbondale: Southern Illinois University Press.

Magrath, Peter. 1966. *Yazoo, Law and Politics in the New Republic, the Case of Fletcher vs Peck*. Providence, RI: Brown University Press.

Malone, Dumas. 1948–1981. *Jefferson and His Time*. 6 vols. Boston, MA: Little, Brown.

Martin, Edwin T. 1952. *Thomas Jefferson: Scientist*. New York: Henry Schuman.

Marx, Leo. 1964. *The Machine in the Garden: Technology and the Pastoral Ideal in America*. New York: Oxford University Press.

May, Henry. 1976. *The Enlightenment in America*. New York: Oxford University Press.

Mayo, Bernard, ed. 1968. *Jefferson Himself: The Personal Narrative of a Many-Sided American*. Charlottesville: University Press of Virginia.

McCants, David. 1990. *Patrick Henry: The Orator*. New York: Greenwood Press.

McCloskey, Robert. 1960. *The American Supreme Court*. Chicago, IL: University of Chicago Press.

McColley, Robert. 1973. *Slavery and Jeffersonian Virginia*. Urbana: University of Illinois Press.

McCormick, Richard P. 1982. *The Presidential Game: The Origins of Amerian Presidential Politics*. New York: Oxford University Press.

McCoy, Drew. 1980. *The Elusive Republic: Political Economy in Jeffersonian America*. Chapel Hill: University of North Carolina Press.

McDonald, Forrest. 1976. *The Presidency of Thomas Jefferson*. Lawrence: University Press of Kansas.

———. 1979. *Alexander Hamilton: A Biography*. New York: W.W. Norton.

Meek, Ronald. 1963. *The Economics of Physiocracy: Essays and Translations*. London: Allen & Unwin.

Meyer, Donald H. 1976. *The Democratic Enlightenment*. New York: G.P. Putnam's Sons.

Miller, John Chester. 1960. *The Federalist Era*. New York: Harper & Row.

———. 1977. *The Wolf by the Ears: Thomas Jefferson and Slavery*. Charlottesville: University Press of Virginia.

Moore, Glover. 1953. *The Missouri Controversy, 1819–1821*. Lexington: University of Kentucky Press.

Morgan, Edmund S. 1956. *The Birth of the Republic, 1763–1789*. Chicago, IL: University of Chicago Press.

———. 1976. *The Challenge of the American Revolution*: New York: W.W. Norton.

Morgan, Kenneth, ed. 1984. *The Oxford History of Britain*. Oxford: Oxford University Press.

Morris, Richard. 1987. *The Forging of the Union: 1781–1789*. New York: Harper & Row.

Niven, John. 1983. *Martin Van Buren: The Romantic Age of American Politics*. New York: Oxford University Press.

North, Douglass. 1961. *The Economic Growth of the United States, 1790–1860*. New York: Prentice Hall.

Olson, Alison. 1973. *Anglo-American Politics, 1600–1775*. London: Oxford University Press.

Onuf, Peter, ed. 1993. *Jeffersonian Legacies*. Charlottesville: University of Virginia Press.

Paine, Thomas. 1925. *The Life and Works of Thomas Paine*. 10 vols. New Rochelle, NY: Thomas Paine National Historical Association.

Pangle, Thomas. 1974. *Montesquieu's Philosophy of Liberalism*. Chicago, IL: University of Chicago Press.

Pargellis, Stanley, and D. J. Medley, ed. 1951. *Bibliography of British History: The Eighteenth Century, 1714–1789*. Oxford: Oxford University Press.

Parrington, Vernon Louis. 1927–1930. *Main Currents in American Thought: An Interpretation of American Literature from the Beginning to 1920*. 3 vols. New York: Harcourt, Brace.

Perkins, Bradford. 1962. *The Causes of the War of 1812*. New York: Holt, Rinehart & Winston.

Peterson, Merrill. 1960. *The Jefferson Image in the American Mind*. New York: Oxford University Press.

———. 1970. *Thomas Jefferson and the New Nation*. New York: Oxford University Press.

———. 1976. *Adams and Jefferson: A Revolutionary Dialogue*. Athens: University of Georgia Press.

———, ed. 1975. *The Portable Thomas Jefferson*. New York: Penguin Books.

Plate, Robert. 1967. *Charles Wilson Peale: Son of Liberty, Father of Art and Science*. New York: McKay.

Pocock, J. G. A. 1975. *The Machiavellian Moment: Florentine Political Thoughat and the Atlantic Republican Tradition*. Princeton, NJ: Princeton University Press.

Prucha, Francis Paul. 1962. *American Indian Policy in the Formative Years: The Indian Trade and Intercourse Acts, 1790–1834*. Cambridge, MA: Harvard University Press.

Rakove, Jack N. 1990. *James Madison and the Creation of the American Republic*. New York: HarperCollins.

Randolph, Sarah N. 1958. *The Domestic Life of Thomas Jefferson*. New York: Frederick Ungar.

Raphael, D. D. 1985. *Adam Smith*. Oxford: Oxford University Press.

Rearden, John. 1974. *Edmund Randolph: A Biography*. New York: Macmillan.

Remini, Robert. 1966. *Andrew Jackson*. New York: Harper & Row.

———. 1977. *Andrew Jackson and the Course of American Empire, 1767–1821*. New York: Harper & Row.

Risjord, Norman. 1965. *The Old Republicans: Southern Agrarianism in the Age of Jefferson*. New York: Columbia University Press.

Robinson, William A. 1916. *Jeffersonian Democracy in New England*. New Haven, CT: Yale University Press.

Roelofs, H. Mark. 1976. *Ideology and Myth in American Politics: A Critique of a National Political Mind*. Boston, MA: Little, Brown.

Rousseau, Jean-Jacques. 1974. *The Social Contract, Or, Principles of Political Right*. New York: New American Library.

Russell, Francis. 1962. *The French and Indian Wars*. New York: American Heritage.

Rutland, Robert. 1990. *The Presidency of James Madison*. Lawrence: University Press of Kansas.

Sanford, Charles. 1977. *Thomas Jefferson and His Library: A Study of His Literary Interests and of the Religious Attitudes Revealed by Relevant Titles in His Library*. Hamden, CT: Archon Books.

Scott, William B. 1977. *In Pursuit of Happiness: American Conceptions of Property from the*

Seventeenth to the Twentieth Century. Bloomington: Indiana University Press.

Sellers, Charles. 1991. *The Market Revolution: Jacksonian America, 1815–1846.* New York: Oxford University Press.

Shaw, Ronald. 1966. *Erie Water West.* Lexington: University Press of Kentucky.

Sheehan, Bernard. 1973. *Seeds of Extinction: Jeffersonian Philanthropy and the American Indian.* Chapel Hill: University of North Carolina Press.

Sisson, Daniel. 1974. *The Revolution of 1800.* New York: Alfred A. Knopf.

Slaughter, Thomas. 1986. *The Whiskey Rebellion: Frontier Epilogue to the American Revolution.* New York: Oxford University Press.

Smelser, Marshall. 1968. *The Democratic Republic, 1801–1815.* New York: Harper & Row.

Smith, Henry Nash. 1950. *Virgin Land: The American West as Symbol and Myth.* Cambridge, MA: Harvard University Press.

Smith, James Morton. 1956. *Freedom's Fetters: The Alien and Sedition Laws and American Civil Liberties.* Ithaca, NY: Cornell University Press.

Sofaer, Abraham D. 1976. *War, Foreign Affairs, and Constitutional Power.* Cambridge, MA: Ballinger.

Spivak, Burton. 1979. *Jefferson's English Crisis: Commerce, the Embargo, and the Republican Revolution.* Charlottesville: University Press of Virginia.

Stinchcombe, William C. 1980. *The XYZ Affair.* Westport, CT: Greenwood Press.

Stites, Francis. 1981. *John Marshall: Defender of the Constitution.* Boston, MA: Little, Brown.

Szatmary, David P. 1980. *Shays' Rebellion: The Making of an Agrarian Insurrection.* Amherst: University of Massachusetts Press.

Taylor, George. 1951. *The Transportation Revolution, 1815–1860.* New York: Holt, Rinehart & Winston.

Tucker, Robert, and David Hendrickson. 1990. *Empire of Liberty: The Statecraft of Thomas Jefferson.* New York: Oxford University Press.

Watson, Harry. 1990. *Liberty and Power: The Politics of Jacksonian America.* New York: Noonday Press.

White, Morton. 1978. *The Philosophy of the American Revolution.* New York: Oxford University Press.

Wills, Gary. 1982. *Cincinnatus: George Washington and the Enlightenment.* Garden City, NY: Doubleday.

Wilstach, Paul. 1925. *Jefferson and Monticello.* Garden City, NY: Doubleday, Page.

Wood, Gordon S. 1969. *The Creation of the American Republic, 1776–1787.* Chapel Hill: University of North Carolina Press.

———. 1992. *The Radicalism of the American Revolution.* New York: Alfred A. Knopf.

Young, Alfred. 1967. *The Democratic Republicans of New York: The Origins, 1763–1797.* Chapel Hill: University of North Carolina Press.

ILLUSTRATION CREDITS

ii	Library of Congress
xii	Library of Congress
xiv	Jefferson Memorial Foundation
4	Library of Congress
8	Library of Congress
10	Library of Congress
23	Library of Congress
35	Library of Congress
40	Library of Congress
41	Library of Congress
42	Library of Congress
46	(top) Massachusetts Historical Society
46	(bottom) Library of Congress
51	Library of Congress
53	Library of Congress
54	Library of Congress
55	Library of Congress
59	Library of Congress
69	Library of Congress
82	Library of Congress
92	Library of Congress
95	Library of Congress
96	Library of Congress
101	Library of Congress

103   Library of Congress

104   Library of Congress

106   Library of Congress

108   Library of Congress

113   Library of Congress

117   Library of Congress

122   Library of Congress

123   Library of Congress

127   Library of Congress

128   (top) The Massachusetts Historical Society, Boston

128   (bottom) Jefferson Memorial Foundation

137   Library of Congress

145   Library of Congress

152   Library of Congress

153   Library of Congress

171   University of Virginia Library

181   Virginia Historical Society

191   Library of Congress

196   Library of Congress

197   Library of Congress

211   Library of Congress

INDEX

Note: Page numbers in **bold** indicate articles specifically dedicated to a given index topic.

Adams, Abigail, 5
Adams, John, xv, **3–5,** 202
  on aristocracy, 136
  Callender's newspaper attack, 29
  death of, 39
  Declaration of Independence and, 41
  1800 election and, 53
  French Revolution and, 73
  Hamilton's calls for war against France and, 83
  Jefferson's correspondence and reconciliation, xvii, 7–9, 170
  judicial appointments after 1800 defeat, xvi, 7, 19, 98, 115, 119–120, 167
  Pickering and, 155
  Quasi War with France, xv, 5, 161
  reconciliation policy for Anglo-French War, 155
  on religion, 43–44
  1792 election and, 51
  1796 election and, 5, 52
Adams, John Quincy, **5–7**
  1820 election and, 56, 122–123, 202
  1824 election, 57, 91, 94, 122–123
  Secretary of State under Monroe, 124, 126
Adams, Samuel, 3
Adams-Onis Treaty, 6, **9,** 50
Agrarianism, xi, xii
  Jefferson's antiurban biases, 197–199
  plantation system, 157–158
  Tertium Quid and, 190
  tobacco, 191–192
  Van Buren and, 201
  See also Notes on the State of Virginia; Republican party; Slavery; States' rights
Alien and Sedition Acts, xv, 5, **9–11,** 19, 161
  Jefferson's Kentucky Resolutions, xv, 11, 99–100, 185
  Madison's criticism of, 100, 113

Allen, Ethan, 44
American Philosophical Society, **11,** 70, 136, 137
American Revolution, xiii–xiv, **11–13,** 39–43
  French-British animosity and, 13
  Virginia House of Burgesses and, 204
  Wythe and, 216
  See also Declaration of Independence
Anglican Church, xiv, 12, 204, 205
Anglo-French wars, xvi, **13,** 67, 95, 140–141, 208
  Adams's reconciliation policy, 155
  British impressment policy, 14, 87–88
  Milan Decree allowing French seizure of American ships, 120
  Peace of Paris, 150–151
  Washington's neutrality policy, 76
  See also France; French and Indian War; Great Britain; Neutrality violations
Anti-Federalists, **15–16.** *See also* Republican party
Architecture, xii, 46–47, 128
Aristocracy
  abolished in the Old Dominion, xiv, 12
  natural, 135–136
  Paine on, 147
Arnold, Benedict, 25, 77, 214
Articles of Confederation, **16,** 33, 71, 81
Artists, 152–153
Assumption, **16–18**

Bacon, Francis, 60
Banking system, 49–50, 82, 114, 131–132, 173, 208
  Panic of 1819, 62, 248–249
Barbary War, xvi, **21–22,** 67, 139
Barlow, Joel, 44
Battle of New Orleans, **22,** 84, 91, 193, 208
Battle of Tippecanoe, **23–24,** 190
Bill of Rights, 34

Bolingbroke, Viscount, 61
Bonaparte, Napoleon. *See* Napoleon
Boston Tea Party, xiii, 3, 12, 40, 204
Botanizing tour, **24**
Breckinridge, John, 167
British West Indies. *See* West Indies
Buffon, Count de, 60, 61
Burr, Aaron, **24–26**, 27
    duel with Hamilton, xvi, 24, 25, 26, 83
    1800 election, xv, 53, 194
    secessionist plot, xvi, 63, 175, 215
Burr conspiracy, **26–27**

Calhoun, John C., 100
Callender, James T., **29**
Canada
    Jefferson's hope of acquiring, 60, 207
    Nootka Sound controversy, 142–143
    Peace of Paris and, 150
Canal building, 192
Capital economy, 116–117, 201
Caribbean expansion plans, 37
Caribbean trade, 18, 95, 213
Chase, Samuel, xvi, 199
Cherokee, 23
Chickasaw, 23
Children of Thomas Jefferson, xiii, 85, 97
Choctaw, 23
Cicero, 30
Cities, Jefferson's antiurban biases, 197–199
Clark, William, 102
Classical republicanism, **30–31**
Clay, Henry, 57, 165, 209, 216
Clinton, DeWitt, **31**, 55
Clinton, George, 25, **31–32**, 51, 53, 77
College of William and Mary, xiii, **32–32**, 60, 189,
    216
    House of Burgesses seat, 203
Confederation period, 16, **33**, 81
Congress of the Confederation, 16
Constitution, **34–35**, 177
    Adams and, 4
    Clinton's opposition to, 31
    Hamilton and, xv, 81
    Jefferson and, xv, 15
    Madison and, 113
    Monroe and, 124
    Pinckney and, 156
    Randolph and, 163
    Twelfth Amendment, 194
    Washington and, 210
Continental army, 33
Continental System, 120
Conway cabal, 214
Correspondence
    with Adams, xvii, **7–9**, 170

    with Maria Cosway, 36
    Mazzei letter, 118–119
    preferred to public speaking, 154
Cosway, Maria, **35–36**, 121
Cosway, Richard, 35
Cotton gin, **36–37**
Crawford, William, 57
Creek Indians, 23
Cuba, **37**
Cumberland Road, 133–134
Currency system, 149

Death of Jefferson, xvii, **39**
Declaration of Independence, xi, xiii–xiv, 12,
    39–43
    Franklin and, 71
    Jefferson's classical republican beliefs, 30–31
    Lockean liberalism, 107
    slave trade criticized in original draft, 179–180
    Wythe and, 216
Deism, **43–44**, 137–138
Democracy
    Federalist mistrust of, 65–66
    foreign policy and, 68–69
    Jacksonian, 92–94
Democratic-Republicans, xv, 31. *See* Republican
    party
Democratic Societies, **44–45**, 52
Descartes, René, 60
Diffusion (theory of slavery), **45–46**, 181
District of Columbia, 18, **46–47**
Dunglison, Robley, 39

Economic nationalism, **49–50**, 114
Economy
    Atlantic Ocean trade, **18**
    banking system, 49–50, 62, 82, 114, 131–132,
        173, 208, 248–249
    Confederation period, 33
    Hamilton's policies, 16, 65, 82, 95
    Jefferson's austerity policies, 27, 76, 132–133
    Jefferson's vision of, 18
    Madison's policies, 49, 50, 114
    manufacturing, 115, 167–169
    market revolution, 116–117
    national debt, xvi, 33, 76, 82, 132–133
    Panic of 1819, 62, 197, 248–249
    physiocrats, 66, 154
    Smith's theories, 182
    tobacco and, 191–192
    Van Buren's views, 201
    See also Trade
Education, xiii, 32, 97
    Native Americans and, 135
    See also College of William and Mary;
        University of Virginia

Edwards, Jonathan, 25
Elections
    1792, **50–51**
    1796, 5, **52**
    1800, xv, xvi, 5, 25, 26, **53,** 68, 83, 150, 172, 194
    1804, 26, **53–54,** 156, 175
    1808, **54–55**
    1812, **55**
    1816, **55–56,** 100, 124
    1820, 56
    1824, 6, **56–57,** 91, 94, 122–123, 202–203
    1828, 7, 92, 94, 123, 202
    Twelfth Amendment provisions, 194
Embargo of 1807, xvi, 6, 54, **58–59,** 87, 111, 139, 140, 141, 175, 192, 208
Empire of Liberty, **59–60,** 72, 91, 207
    Cuba and, 37
    Native Americans and, 23, 109
    See also Louisiana Purchase
Enemies Alien Act, 10
Enforcement Act, 58
Enlightenment, **60–61,** 104, 112, 165, 182, 186
Environmentalism, 135, 136–137
Era of Good Feelings, 56, **62–63,** 124
Essex Junto, 25, 26, **63,** 142

Father of Thomas Jefferson. *See* Jefferson, Peter
The Federalist, 113
Federalist party, **65–66,** 68, 149–150
    Adams and, 4–5, 7
    Alien and Sedition Acts and, xv, 9–10
    Anti-Federalists, 15–16
    British sympathies, 68, 169
    Burr and, 25
    consequences of Jay's Treaty with Britain, xv, 96
    Democratic Societies and, 44, 52
    end of, 56, 66, 68
    Essex Junto, 25, 26, 63, 142
    Hartford Convention, 83–84
    Jefferson's embargo and, 58–59
    Jefferson's first inaugural address and, 88–89
    judiciary appointments at end of Adams's presidency, xvi, 7, 19, 98, 115, 119–120, 167
    mistrust of democracy, 65–66
    newspapers, 29, 70, 149, 176
    Quasi War with France and, 161
    secessionist plot, 63
    Society of the Cincinnati, 183
Ferguson, Adam, **66,** 157
Fletcher v. Peck, 118
Florida, 9, 50, 60, 122, 124, 156
Foreign policy, xvi, **68–69**
    Monroe Doctrine, 6, 124–126
    See also Anglo-French wars; Embargo; France; Great Britain; Trade; Treaties; War of 1812

France
    Adams as minister to, 4
    Franklin as commissioner in, 71
    Genet's mission to the U.S., 76–77
    Jay's Treaty with Britain and, xv, 95–96
    Jefferson as minister, xiv, 4, 33, 35–36, 70, 71, 73, 120–121
    Jefferson's affinity for, 69–70, 178
    Louisiana Territory and, 107–109
    Madison's trade policy, 111–112
    Monroe's sympathies toward, 124
    Quasi War with America, xv, 5, 9, 13, 161
    Republican sympathies, 68, 169
    XYZ Affair, 217–218
    See also Anglo-French wars; French and Indian War; French Revolution
Franklin, Benjamin, 4, 11, **70–71,** 136
    on American "environmental degeneracy," 61–62
    Declaration of Independence and, 41
    Priestley and, 159
Free trade, 18
French and Indian War, **72,** 107, 121
    Peace of Paris, 150–151
French Revolution, 13, 69, **72–73,** 78, 79, 121, 176
    American Democratic Societies and, 44
    conservative European reaction, 125
    Paine and, 147–148
    Republican support, 169
    Santo Domingo slave rebellion and, 183
Freneau, Philip, **73,** 176

Gabriel's conspiracy, **75,** 179
Gallatin, Albert, **76,** 192–193, 219
Gates, Horatio, 214
Gazette of the United States, 74
Genet, Edmond Charles, **76–77,** 176
George III, 187
Georgia "Yazoo Companies" land fraud, 219
Ghent, Treaty of, 6, 22, 193–194, 208
Gibbons v. Ogden, 50
Gibbs, James, 128
Giles, William B., 111
Governor of Virginia, 12, **77–78,** 143–144
Graham, John, 27
Great Britain, **78–79**
    A Summary View of the Rights of British America, xiii, 12, 186–187
    Adams as minister to, 4
    American trade policy vs., 18
    exclusion of U.S. trade, 33
    Federalist (especially Hamilton's) sympathies, 68, 71, 78, 83, 85, 95, 113, 143, 149–150, 169

Great Britain, *continued*
    Franklin in, 71
    impressment of Americans, 14, 87–88
    Jay's Treaty with, 65, 95–96, 161
    Jefferson's attitude toward, 14–15
    Madison's trade policy, 111–112
    mercantilist policy, 157
    Monroe as minister to, 124
    Spain in Pacific Northwest and, 142–143
    supports Monroe's foreign policy, 125–126
    taxation of colonies, 12, 40, 151
    Treaty of Ghent, 6, 22, 193–194, 208
Great Britain, American conflicts with. *See* Anglo-French wars; American Revolution; French and Indian War; Neutrality violations; War of 1812
Greene, Nathanael, 77
Grundy, Felix, 209

Hamilton, Alexander, xv, **81–83**
    Adams and, 4
    British affinities, 71, 78, 83, 85, 95, 113, 143, 149–150
    Callender's allegations against, 29
    calls for war against France, 83, 108
    duel with Burr, xvi, 24, 25, 26, 83
    economic policies, 15, 16–18, 82, 131–132, 176, 213
    The Federalist and, 113
    Federalist party and, 65, 149–150
    newspaper attacks, 74, 176, 149
    Pickering and, 155
    Randolph and, 163
    "Report on Manufactures," 115, 167–169
    1792 election and, 50
    Washington and, 81, 210
Hamiltonian Federalism. *See* Federalist party
Harrington, James, 30
Harrison, William Henry, 23, 190
Hartford Convention, **83–84**
Hemings, Elizabeth, 85
Hemings, Sally, 29, 85
Henry, Patrick, 77, **85,** 112
Hesselius, John, 152
Holy Alliance, 125
Hopkins, Francis, 34
House of Burgesses, xiii, 12, 97, 203–204, 215
House of Representatives, 111
Hume, David, 112
Hutchinson, Thomas, 71

Impressment, 14, **87–88,** 124
Inaugural address (first), **88–89**
Industrial economy, 115, 167–169, 198–199
Infrastructure development, 133–134, 192–193

Jackson, Andrew, 6, **91–93**
    Battle of New Orleans, 22, 84, 91, 193, 208
    Burr's conspiracy and, 26
    1824 election and, 6, 57, 91, 123
    election of 1828, 92, 94, 123
    Native Americans and, 135
    Van Buren's support for, 202, 203
Jacksonian democracy, **92–94**
Jacobin Clubs, 44
Jay, John, 4, 95, 113, 156, 164
Jay's Treaty, 65, **95–96,** 161
Jefferson, Jane Randolph (Jefferson's mother), xiii, 97
Jefferson, Martha Wayles (Jefferson's wife), xiii, xiv, 85, **97,** 204
Jefferson, Peter (Jefferson's father), xiii, **97,** 101, 127
Jefferson, Polly (Jefferson's daughter), 85
Jefferson, Thomas, family and life
    Anglophobia, **14–15**
    antiurban biases, 197–199
    birth and early life, xii–xiii
    children, xiii, 85, 97
    death, xvii, **39**
    father, xiii, 97, 101, 127
    Francophilia, **69–70**
    health, 153, 173
    mother, xiii, 97
    personality, **153–154**
    popularity, **153**
    relationship with Maria Cosway, 35–36, 121
    relationship with Sally Hemings, 29, 85
    retirement, xvi, **170–172**
    slaves, xiii, 157–158
    wife, xiii, xiv, 85, 97, 204
    See also Correspondence; Monticello
Jefferson, Thomas, political positions
    governor of Virginia, 12, 77–78, 143–144
    House of Burgesses, xiii, 12, 97, 203–204
    minister to France, xiv, 4, 33, 35–36, 70, 71, 73, 120–121
    "political boss," 67, 149
    vice-presidency, xv, 52
    Virginia Dynasty, 201, 202–203
    See also Governor of Virginia; Presidency; Republican party; Secretary of State
Jeffersonian Republicans. *See* Republican party
Jesus, Jefferson's views on, 165–166
Judicial review, 116
Judiciary
    economic nationalism and, 49–50
    Federalist appointments at end of Adams's presidency, xvi, 7, 19, 98, 115, 119–120, 167
    Marbury v. Madison, 115–116, 118
    Republican attempt to replace Federalist judges, xvi, 19, 67, 118

Judiciary Act of 1801, 19, **98,** 115, 119, 166–167
    repeal of, **166–167**
Kames, Lord, 157
Kentucky Resolutions, xv, 11, **99–100,** 185
King, Rufus, 56, **100,** 124
Knox, Henry, 119, 163, 210

Lee, Richard Henry, 41, 77
L'Enfant, Pierre Charles, 46–47
Lewis, Meriwether, 102
Lewis and Clark expedition, 9, **101–102**
Library of Congress, xvii, **102–104,** 171
Lincoln, Abraham, 117
Lincoln, Levi, 219
Linnaeus, Carl, 60, **104–105**
Livingston, Robert, 41, 107–109, 124
Local rights. *See* States' rights
Locke, John, 43, 60, 61, 104, **105–107,** 112, 134
Louisiana Purchase, xvi, 63, 67, 69, **107–109**
    consequences of L'Ouverture's slave rebellion,
      184
    Native Americans and, 109, 135
    slavery and, 36–37, 45, 60, 109, 121, 122, 181
L'Ouverture, Toussaint, 184

Macon, Nathaniel, **111**
Macon's Bill Number Two, **111–112**
Madison, James, 68, **112–114**
    communication with Jefferson in France, 34
    Constitution and, 113
    1808 election, 54–55
    1812 election, 55
    foreign trade policy, 111–112, 141–142, 208
    Georgia "Yazoo Companies" land fraud and, 219
    Hamilton's economic plans and, xv, 17, 82, 131
    Henry's criticism of, 85
    Jefferson's *Notes on the State of Virginia* and, 144
    John Quincy Adams and, 6
    Marbury v. Madison, 115–116, 118
    national debt and, 133
    National Road project, 133
    nationalistic economic policy, 49, 50, 114
    New York trip with Jefferson, 24
    Republican party and, 149, 169
    Shawnee revitalization movement and, 190
    University of Virginia project and, 197
    Virginia committee on religion, 205
    Virginia Dynasty, 201, 202, 203
    Virginia resolutions condemning Federalist
      curbing of civil liberties, 100, 113
    Virginia state council membership, 77
    War of 1812 and, 113–114
    Washington and, 50
Malthus, Thomas, **114–115**
Manufacturers, 93, **115,** 167–169
Marbois, François de, 144

Marbury, William, 115
Marbury v. Madison, **115–116**
Market revolution, **116–117**
Marshall, John C., 27, 88, 115, **117–118,** 175,
    216
Mason, George, 216
Mazzei, Philip, 118–119
    Mazzei letter, **118–119**
McCulloch v. Maryland, 50, 118
Mercantilism, 157
Midnight appointments, **119–120.** *See also*
    Judiciary
Milan Decree, **120**
Millar, John, 157
Minister to France, xiv, 4, 33, 35–36, 70, 71, 73,
    120–121
Mississippi River access (Pinckney's Treaty with
    Spain), 156–157
Missouri compromise, 62, 63, **121–123**
Money system, 149
Monroe, James, 9, 49, 62, 68, **123–125**
    Constitution and, 124
    1816 election, 55–56, 124
    1820 election, 56
    Era of Good Feelings, 62
    French sympathies, 124
    Gabriel's conspiracy and, 75
    Jefferson's Empire of Liberty and, 60
    Louisiana Purchase negotiations, 108, 109
    minister to Britain, 124
    national debt and, 133
    National Road project, 133
    Republican party and, 124
    territorial expansion, 69
    Tertium Quid and, 190
    University of Virginia project and, 197
    Virginia Dynasty, 201, 202
    Wythe and, 216
Monroe Doctrine, 6, **124–126**
Montesquieu, Baron de, 61, **126–127**
Monticello, **127–129**
    French items, 70
    Jefferson's burial, 39
    slaves at, 157–158
Morris, Gouverneur, 167
Mother of Thomas Jefferson. *See* Jefferson, Jane
    Randolph

Napoleon, 74, 79
    consequences of L'Ouverture's slave rebellion,
      184
    European defeat and end of War of 1812, 13,
      14, 55
    Louisiana Purchase and, 107, 109
    Madison's trade policy and, 112
    Milan Decree, **120**

National bank, 49–50, 82, 93, 114, **131–132,** 173, 208
   Panic of 1819, 248–249
National debt, xvi, 33, 76, 82, **132–133**
National Gazette, 74
National Road, **133–134,** 193
Native Americans, **134–135,** 190
   Battle of Tippecanoe, 23–24, 190
   Florida raids, 156
   Louis and Clark expedition, 102
   Louisiana Territory and, 109, 135
   Tecumseh and Shawnee revitalization, 190
   Treaty of Greenville, 215
Natural aristocracy, **135–136**
Natural philosophy, 104–105, 136–137
Naturalization Act, 10
Navigation Acts, **138–139**
Navy (American), 133, **139,** 184
Neutrality policy, 76
Neutrality violations, xvi, 13, 14, 22, 58, 59, 140–141, 175, 176, 192, 208
   Adams's reconciliation policy, 155
   Adams and the Quasi War with France, 5
   Britain's Navigation Acts and, 138–139
   1808 elections and, 54
   Hamilton and, 83
   impressment, 14, 87–88, 124
   Napoleon's Milan Decree, 120
   See also Anglo-French wars; Embargo; Great Britain; Quasi War with France; War of 1812
New England Courant, 70
New France, 107
New Orleans. *See* Battle of New Orleans; Louisiana Purchase
New York, Jefferson's trip to as Secretary of State, 24
Newspapers, 29, 74, 149, 171, 172, 173, 176
Newton, Isaac, 60, 112, 104, **141**
Nicholas, George, 78
Non-Intercourse Act, **141–142**
Nootka Sound controversy, **142–143**
Northern Confederacy, 63, 155
Northwest Ordinance, **143–144**
Notes on the State of Virginia, xii, **144–146,** 180, 198

Ohio Valley, 72, 143–144
   Treaty of Greenville with natives, 215
Old Dominion. *See* Aristocracy; Virginia
Ordinance of 1784, 143–144

Pacific Northwest
   British-Spanish conflict, 142–143
   Louis and Clark expedition, 9, 102
   Treaty with Spain, 9, 50, 122, 124
Page, John, 77

Paine, Thomas, 44, **147–148**
Pallid, Andrea, 128
Panic of 1819, 62, 197, **148–149**
Peace of Paris (1763), **150–151**
Peace of Paris (1783), **151–152**
Peale, Charles Wilson, **152–153**
Pendleton, Edmund, 216
Pennsylvania Gazette, 70
Personality of Thomas Jefferson, **153–154**
Philadelphia Gazette, 29
Physiocrats, 66, **154**
Pickering, John, 19
Pickering, Timothy, 63, **154–155**
Pinckney, Charles Cotesworth, 54, **155–156**
Pinckney's Treaty, **156–157**
Plantation system, **157–158**
Political parties, 67–68, 149–150
   newspaper wars, 149
   sectional disparities, 177
   See also Federalist party; Republican party
Polk, James, 203
Popularity of Thomas Jefferson, 153
Presidency, 53–54
   first administration, xvi, 66–67
   first inaugural address, 88–89
   Jefferson's relief at end of, 54–55, 175
   second administration, xvi, 175
   Tertium Quid and, 190
Presidential elections. *See* Elections
Priestley, Joseph, **159–160**
Privateers, 76, 176
Prosser, Gabriel, 75
Protective tariffs, 49, 114, 116, 173, 208

Quasi War with France, xv, 5, 9, 13, **161**
Quesnay, François, 157

Randolph, Edmund, 157, **163–164,** 210
Randolph, Jane, 97
Randolph, John, 111, **164–165,** 190, 219
Raynal, Abbe, 61
Rebellions
   Jefferson's philosophy, 178
   Shays' Rebellion, 33, 177–178
   slave insurrections, 75, 178–179, 183–184
   Whiskey Rebellion, 44, 184, 213–214
Religion, xiii, **165–166**
   deism, 43–44, 137–138
   Jefferson's naturalism, 137–138
   Virginia Declaration of Religious Freedom, xiv, 12, 112, 204–205
"Report on Manufactures," 115, **167–169**
Republican party, xv, 4, 7, 68, 83, 121–122, 149–150, **169–170**
   Alien and Sedition Acts and, xv, 10–11, 19
   Anti-Federalists, 15

attempt to remove Federalist judges, xvi, 19, 67
Democratic Societies, 44–45, 52
economic nationalism policy, 49
French affinity, 68, 169
John Randolph and, 164–165, 190
Macon as Speaker of the House of Representatives, 111
Madison and, 112, 113, 169
Monroe and, 124
newspapers, 29, 74, 149, 172, 173, 176
reflection of sectional disparities, 177
Taylor and, 189, 190
Tertium Quid faction, 164, 175, 190
Van Buren and, 201–202, 203
vindicated by War of 1812 victory, 22, 207
Virginia Dynasty, 201, 202–203
western "Warhawks," 209
Retirement, xvi, **170–172**
Revolution of 1800, xvi, 53, **172.** *See also*
    Elections, 1800
Revolutionary War. *See* American Revolution
Richmond Enquirer, 171, 172–173
Richmond Examiner, 29
Ritchie, Thomas, 172–173
Road building, 192–193
Rush, Benjamin, 7–8, 75, **173–174**

Sacajawea, 102
Santo Domingo slave rebellion, **183–184**
Schuyler, Elizabeth, 81
Schuyler, Philip, 25
Second National Bank, 49, 248
Secretary of State, xiv–xv, 15, 121, **176**
    Nootka Sound controversy, 142–143
    states' rights philosophy, 185
    trip to New York, 24
Sectionalism, **176–177**
Sedition Act, xv, 10, 19, 29
Shaftesbury, Lord, 105
Shawnee Nation, 23–24, 190
Shays, Daniel, 33, 177
Shays' Rebellion, 33, **177–178**
Sherman, Roger, 41
Sidney, Algernon, 30
Sierra Leone, 179
Skelton, Martha Wayles. *See* Jefferson, Martha
    Wayles
Slave insurrections, 75, **178–179,** 183–184
Slave trade, **179–180**
Slavery, xii, 170, 177, **180–181**
    cotton gin and, 36–37
    criticism in original draft of Declaration of
        Independence, 179–180
    Cuba and, 37
    diffusion theory, 45–46, 181
    Jefferson's Empire of Liberty, 60

Jefferson's slaves at Monticello, 157–158
John Quincy Adams and, 7
Louisiana Territory and, 36–37, 45, 60, 109,
    121, 122, 181
Missouri crisis and compromise, 62, 63, 121–123
Monroe and, 56
Notes on the State of Virginia, 180
Ordinance of 1784, 144
plantation system, 157–158
three-fifths compromise, 53, 84
Virginia House of Burgesses and, 204
Washington on, 158
Small, William, 32
Smith, Adam, 157, **182**
Smuggling, 58
Society of the Cincinnati, **182–183**
Sons of Liberty, 44
Spain
    Adams-Onis Treaty, 6, 9, 50
    conflict with Britain in Pacific Northwest,
        142–143
    Jay's mission, 156
    Pinckney's Treaty with U.S. (Treaty of San
        Lorenzo), 156–157
    Wilkinson as agent for, 214–215
Stamp Act, 12, 40, 216
Standing army, **184–185**
State debts, Hamilton's assumption plan, 16–18, 82
Statehood requirements, 143–144
States' rights, xv, 56, **184–185**
    Jacksonian democracy, 92–94
    John Taylor and, 189
    Kentucky resolutions, xv, 11, 99–100, 185
    Madison and, 113
    nationalistic federal economic policies vs., 49–
        50
    Old Dominion model, 185
    party system sectional disparities, 177
    taxation power vs. the national debt, 33
    Tertium Quid and, 190
Statute of Virginia, 39
Stuart, Gilbert, 152
A Summary View of the Rights of British America,
    xiii, 12, **186–187**
Supreme Court
    impeachment attempt, 19, 67
    Marbury v. Madison, 115–116
    Marshall and, 115, 117–118
    Repeal of Judiciary Act of 1801, 167
    See also Judiciary

Talleyrand, 109, 217
Tariffs, 49, 114, 116, 173, 208
Taxation
    federal vs. state power, 33
    repealed under Jefferson, xvi

Taxation, *continued*
    origins of American Revolution, 12, 40, 151, 204
    Shays' Rebellion, 177–178
    Virginia House of Burgesses and, 204
    Whiskey Rebellion and, 44, 184, 213–214
Taylor, John, **189**, 190
Tecumseh, 23–24, **189–190**
Tenskwatawa, 23
Tertium Quid, 164, 175, **190**
Texas, 7, 122
Thomson, Charles, 144
Three-fifths compromise, 53, 84
Tippecanoe, 23–24, 190
Tobacco, **191–192**
Tory party, 59
Townshend Duties, 40
Trade
    Barbary War and, xvi, 21–22
    Britain's Navigation Acts, 138–139
    British exclusion of U.S., 33
    embargo, xvi, 6, 54, 58–59, 87, 111, 139, 140, 141, 175, 192, 208
    Jay's Treaty with Britain, 65, 95–96, 161
    Jefferson's view of Atlantic economy, 18
    Madison's policy for Britain and France, 111–112, 141–142, 208
    physiocrat conception, 157
    slave, 179–180
    West Indies, 95, 213
    See also Economy
Transportation revolution, **192–193**
Treaties
    Adams-Onis (with Spain), 6, 9, 50
    Ghent (ending War of 1812), 6, 22, **193–194,** 208
    Greenville with Ohio Valley Indians, 215
    Jay's Treaty with Britain, 65, 95–96, 161
    Peace of Paris, 150–151
    Pinckney's (San Lorenzo) Treaty with Spain, 156–157
Trumbull, John, 152
Twelfth Amendment, **194**

U. S. Navy, 21–22, 139, 184
University of Virginia, xvii, 39, 62, 171, **195–197**
Urban vices, **197–199**

Van Buren, Martin, 94, **201–202,** 203
Vice-presidency, xv, 52
Vice-presidential election, Twelfth Amendment provisions, 194
Virginia
    House of Burgesses, xiii, 12, 97, 203–204, 216
    Jefferson as governor of, 12, 77–78, 143–144
    Jefferson's nationalism, 177

    Jefferson's states' rights philosophy, 184
    nonimportation agreement, xiii
    Notes on the State of Virginia, 144–146, 180, 198
Virginia Declaration of Religious Freedom, xiv, 12, 112, 204–205
Virginia Declaration of Rights, 204
Virginia Dynasty, 201, **202–203.** *See also* Madison, James; Monroe, James; Presidency
Virginia Junto, 172

War of 1812, 13, 14, 113–114, 133, 185, **207–208**
    Battle of New Orleans, 22, 84, 91, 193, 208
    destruction of Library of Congress, xvii, 102, 171
    Randolph's opposition, 164
    Treaty of Ghent, 6, 22, 193–194, 208
    western Republican "Warhawks" and, 209
Warhawks, **208–209**
Washington, George, xiv, **209–212**
    Burr and, 25
    Democratic Societies and, 44–46
    French Revolution and, 73
    Hamilton and, 81, 210
    Jefferson's critique in letter to Mazzei, 119
    John Adams and, 4
    national bank proposal and, 131, 132
    neutrality policy in Anglo-French conflict, 76
    portraits, 152
    Randolph and, 163, 164
    1792 election and, 50–51
    1796 election and, 52
    slavery and, 158
    Society of the Cincinnati, 182–183
    Whiskey Rebellion and, 214
Wayles, John, 85
Wayles, Martha. *See* Jefferson, Martha Wayles
Wayne, "Mad" Anthony, 215
Webster, Noah, **212–213**
West, Benjamin, 152
West Indies, 18, 95, **213**
Whig party, 93
Whiskey Rebellion, 44, 184, **213–214**
Whitney, Eli, 36
Wife of Thomas Jefferson. *See* Jefferson, Martha Wayles
Wilkinson, James, 26, 27, **214–215**
Writings
    A Summary View of the Rights of British America, xiii, 12, 186–187
    Notes on the State of Virginia, xii, 144–146, 180, 198
    See also Declaration of Independence
Wythe, George, xiii, 144, **215–216**

XYZ Affair, **217–218**

Yazoo lands, **219**